Your Reading

Committee on the Junior High and Middle School Booklist

James E. Davis, Cochair, Ohio University, Athens, Ohio
Hazel K. Davis, Cochair, Federal Hocking High School, Stewart, Ohio
J. Christopher Davis, Troy High School, Troy, Ohio
Luanne Dunham, North Union High School, Richwood, Ohio
Phyllis Fischer, Lakewood Middle School, Lakewood, Ohio
Thomas Flynn, Ohio University-Belmont, St. Clairsville, Ohio
Mary-Sue Gardetto, Ankeney Junior High School, Dayton, Ohio
Sally Hale, Putnam Elementary School, Marietta, Ohio
Judith Keck, Licking County Schools, Newark, Ohio
Bonnie Lackey, Federal Hocking High School, Stewart, Ohio
Sue Ellen McFerren, Grover Cleveland Junior High School, Zanesville, Ohio
Peggy Papritan, Glenford Elementary School, Glenford, Ohio
Lois Spencer, Fort Frye High School, Fort Frye, Ohio
F. Helena Sturkey, Copley-Fairlawn Schools, Copley, Ohio
Ted Hipple, *ex officio*
Paul O'Dea, NCTE Staff Liaison
John Lansingh Bennett, NCTE Staff Liaison

Your Reading

A Booklist for Junior High
and Middle School Students

Seventh Edition

James E. Davis and Hazel K. Davis, Editors,
and the Committee on the Junior High
and Middle School Booklist
of the National Council of Teachers of English

National Council of Teachers of English
1111 Kenyon Road, Urbana, Illinois 61801

Staff Editor: Jane M. Curran

Book Design: Tom Kovacs for TGK Design

NCTE Stock Number 59397

It is the policy of NCTE in its journals and other publications to provide a forum for the open discussion of ideas concerning the content and the teaching of English and the language arts. Publicity accorded to any particular point of view does not imply endorsement by the Executive Committee, the Board of Directors, or the membership at large, except in announcements of policy, where such endorsement is clearly specified.

Library of Congress Cataloging in Publication Data

Your reading : a booklist for junior high and middle school students / James E. Davis and Hazel K. Davis, editors, and the Committee on the Junior High and Middle School Booklist of the National Council of Teachers of English. — 7th ed.

p. cm.

Includes indexes.

Summary: An annotated listing of nearly 2,000 books of fiction, nonfiction, poetry, and drama; arranged topically under categories ranging from Abuse to Trivia; and recommended for junior high and middle school students.

ISBN 0-8141-5939-7

1. Children's literature — Bibliography. 2. Bibliography — Best books — Children's literature. 3. Junior high school students — Books and reading. 4. Junior high school libraries — Book lists. 5. School children — Books and reading. 6. Elementary school libraries — Book lists. [1. Bibliography — Best books.] I. Davis, James E., 1934- . II. Davis, Hazel K., 1941- . III. National Council of Teachers of English. Committee on the Junior High and Middle School Booklist.

Z1037.Y68 1988
[PN1009.A1]
011'.62 — dc19

88-25148
CIP
AC

Contents

Acknowledgments

How do editors adequately express their appreciation to committee members who devoted hundreds of hours over a three-year period, for no pay, to reading and writing about books? The answer is we can't adequately express our thanks, but we can at least acknowledge that Chris, Mary-Sue, Luanne, Phyllis, Sally, Judy, Tom, Bonnie, Sue Ellen, Peggy, Lois, and Helena did it! As one of them said, "So what else is new? That's what English teachers do all the time." And that is true, but these teachers and librarians were doing what they do all the time plus the work on *Your Reading*. Admittedly, one committee member did take an unpaid leave during the last year of our work, largely to help finish up the project. At least our committee is very well read and has had frequent intensive experiences with writing for deadlines. Thanks from the bottom of our hearts for your professional dedication and service!

Thanks also are due to the publishers who supplied copies of books for review and to the NCTE editorial staff. Paul O'Dea, former Director of Publications, was unbelievably helpful during the start-up and the first year and a half of the committee's work.

Introduction to Readers

While parents, teachers, and librarians may use this book (and are enthusiastically invited to do so), this book is primarily intended for students. We selected and wrote about books for you, and we believe that you should have a large part in selecting your own reading much of the time. You can use this book as you would use tips from people. We looked at approximately 6,000 books published in the last five years (a few earlier) and selected nearly 2,000 that we believed might interest people like you — for pleasure, for school assignments, or merely to satisfy curiosity. We have also included a section of reissued classics done in extraordinarily high quality editions. All books included have, according to committee judgment, some degree of literary merit, or they would not have been included at all, but we have singled out a select few for special literary merit. The words *(Literary merit)* signify a book of outstanding literary quality.

The book is divided into sixty-one categories ranging from Abuse to Trivia. Within each category, books are arranged alphabetically by the author's last name. After the author's name are the title of the book, the illustrator's name where appropriate, the name of the publishing company, the publication date, and the number of pages. Last comes the International Standard Book Number (ISBN), which will aid your teacher or librarian in ordering a book from the publisher. A brief description is included for each book to introduce you to the main theme or main character. A typical entry reads this way:

> Highwater, Jamake. **Eyes of Darkness.** Lothrop, Lee and Shepard Books, 1985. 189 p. ISBN 0-688-41993-3.
>
> Yesa, a Santee Sioux, is raised by his grandmother during the 1800s after his father and two brothers are killed by whites. To avoid further exploitation, Yesa's tribe leaves Minnesota for Canada. There Yesa is educated as a doctor by whites, but the slaughter of his people at Wounded Knee causes him to reconsider his life's purpose. (Literary merit)

At the end of this book are a list of publishers and their order-department addresses and two indexes — one arranged by author and the other by book title. One way you could use this book would be to start with a title or author that interests you. Forgive us if it is not there — we had limited space and a four-year time period (1983–87) to cover. Also, some publishers did not submit all their books to us. Finally, literary merit and appropriateness to young adults in grades 5–9 had to be considered.

You could also scan the Contents to see how we have selected main topics and theme groupings. Find topics that interest you there. We had to choose the one category most appropriate for each book, so we suggest that you read through book descriptions in several related categories. For example, see Coming of Age, Growing Up Female, and Growing Up Male for books about the difficulties of being a teenager. When you have found a book that interests you, copy down the information and check your school library. If the book is not there, ask the librarian to locate the book for you. Librarians love persistent readers.

If you have enjoyed a particular book, sit down and write to the author. Be bold. Write your letter to the author in care of the publisher at the address listed in the list of publishers at the end of this book. Many publishers and authors consider such a letter an honor, and many authors respond personally. Be sure to include your return address. If you enclose a stamped, self-addressed envelope, you may be more likely to receive a response.

Remember that reading is an active process. You as a reader are not just taking in meaning, you are making meaning as you dance with the text. You are the one who can make the book come alive, but only if you pick it up, open it, and get involved. Make reading a lifelong habit. It's not only entertaining, it's the most important part of your education.

Abuse

Borich, Michael. **A Different Kind of Love.** Holt, Rinehart and Winston, 1985. 165 p. ISBN 0-03-003249-0.

Fourteen-year-old Elizabeth, nicknamed Weeble, lives with her mother on the West Coast, far away from the rest of their family in Indiana. When her mother's twenty-five-year-old brother, Nicky, comes to visit, Weeble turns to him for the love and support that seem to be missing from her life. When Nicky becomes overly affectionate, Weeble must deal with her feelings of guilt and enjoyment.

Branscum, Robbie. **The Girl.** Harper and Row, 1986. 113 p. ISBN 0-06-020702-7 (0-06-020703-5, library binding).

The girl, eleven years old, and her four brothers and sisters are abandoned by their mother after their father dies. Their sharecropper grandparents take the children in, but these relatives are more interested in the welfare payments than in the well-being of the children. An abusive grandmother and uncle make life almost unbearable for the girl as she struggles to survive in a poor Arkansas hill community.

Byars, Betsy. **Cracker Jackson.** Viking Penguin/Viking Kestrel, 1985. 146 p. ISBN 0-670-80546-7.

Eleven-year-old Jackson Hunter faces a dangerous problem. His favorite babysitter, Alma, who calls him Cracker, has bruises and cuts that Cracker is certain are caused by her husband. Cracker tries to persuade Alma to admit the problem and to take herself and her baby to safety, but it takes a tragedy to lead them to a final solution.

Howard, Ellen. **Gillyflower.** Atheneum, 1986. 106 p. ISBN 0-689-31274-1.

Gilly is a victim of sexual abuse and is concerned that her father might also molest her younger sister, Honey. When Gilly's mother is at work in the afternoon and evening, Gilly's dad makes her feel bad, and she wishes she were someone else.

Irwin, Hadley. **Abby, My Love.** Atheneum/Margaret K. McElderry Books, 1985. 146 p. ISBN 0-689-50323-7.

Chip fell in love with Abby when he was thirteen and she was twelve. Even then there were times when she would seem to leave her body behind while her mind and spirit traveled elsewhere. But now Chip and Abby are in high school, and she at last reveals to him that she's been a victim of incest for years. Chip urges her to make her secret public.

Nathanson, Laura. **The Trouble with Wednesdays.** Bantam Books, 1987. 176 p. ISBN 0-553-26337-4.

Becky is in sixth grade and desperately wants braces for her fang-like teeth. At first she's happy when her father's cousin, a dentist, agrees to fit her with braces and make the frequent adjustments. But when he begins to touch her in inappropriate ways, Becky's hopes for improving her appearance become an increasingly alarming nightmare.

Piowaty, Kim Kennelly. **Don't Look in Her Eyes.** Atheneum/Margaret K. McElderry Books, 1983. 186 p. ISBN 0-689-50273-7.

Jason has missed most of his sixth-grade year staying home to take care of his baby brother and to protect him from their abusive mother. He is glad when their mother runs away. But finding food and a place to live are serious problems, and Jason is afraid to ask for help because he fears he will be separated from his brother and sent to an institution. What should he do?

Woolverton, Linda. **Running before the Wind.** Houghton Mifflin, 1987. 152 p. ISBN 0-395-42116-0.

Running is the most important thing in thirteen-year-old Kelly's life, just as it had been for her father before he came down with polio. Now he hurls his anger and abuse on her when the word *running* is even mentioned. Suddenly Kelly is released from his anger, but a new trap awaits her.

Adventure

Adams, Barbara. **On the Air and off the Wall.** Dell/Yearling Books, 1986. 119 p. ISBN 0-440-46771-3.

The first TV show prepared by kids for KID-TV is such a disaster that the producer is threatening to cancel it. The kids need a big story to stay on the air. They get their story, but their reporters are taken hostage. Minnie O'Reilly knows a secret about the producer that could free the hostages and save the show. Can she pull it off?

Adams, Barbara. **Rock Video Strikes Again.** Dell/Yearling Books, 1986. 136 p. ISBN 0-440-47170-2.

When super rock star Simon Gear schedules a visit to his hometown of Wellsburg, "Rock Video" Wigglesworth plans to do a video. But when Simon arrives at Wellsburg, the equipment, costumes, and promoters are missing. Simon says the KID-TV video is out. Can Minnie O'Reilly, staff assistant, get the exclusive interview for KID-TV, find the missing instruments, and convince Simon that the show must go on?

Alexander, Lloyd. **The Illyrian Adventure.** E. P. Dutton, 1986. 132 p. ISBN 0-525-44250-2.

Sixteen-year-old Vesper Holly sets out to clear her father's name in the nineteenth-century world of scholars by taking her guardian, Brinnie, on a trip to a remote European land called Illyria. While searching for proof of the "magical army" of Illyrian legend, Vesper and Brinnie become involved in rebellions and plots to assassinate the king.

Beatty, Patricia. **The Coach That Never Came.** William Morrow, 1985. 164 p. ISBN 0-688-05477-3.

When Paul Braun visits his grandmother in Colorado, she gives him a jeweled belt buckle once owned by a distant relative. As the thirteen-year-old boy tries to discover more about this relative, he learns of the still-unsolved disappearance of a stagecoach and its cargo of gold. Then the belt buckle is stolen. Can it be the key to the mystery of the stagecoach?

Byars, Betsy. **The Blossoms Meet the Vulture Lady.** Illustrated by Jacqueline Rogers. Delacorte Press, 1986. 134 p. ISBN 0-385-29485-9.

Junior Blossom tries to fly with his homemade wings but ends up with two broken legs. Now he hopes to startle the world by inventing the best coyote trap ever. As Junior wanders deep in the forest to try out the trap, he is kidnapped by Mad Mary, who eats varmint stew and lives in a cave. The Blossom family sets out to find Junior. They find the trap — but where's Junior?

Calvert, Patricia. **The Hour of the Wolf.** New American Library/Signet Vista Books, 1985. 159 p. ISBN 0-451-13493-1.

As he spends his senior year in Alaska, Jake Mathiessen enjoys some breathing room away from his demanding father and has time to think about his own problems. He hears about the 1049-mile Iditarod dogsled race across Alaska and decides to face the challenge. Jake learns to train, feed, and care for the sled dogs and then starts out in the grueling race. (Literary merit)

Christopher, John. **Dragon Dance.** E. P. Dutton, 1986. 139 p. ISBN 0-525-44227-8.

When Simon and Brad discover a pagoda in the California of the magical fireball's If World, they are captured by slavers who take them to ancient China, where their future seems hazardous indeed. The boys are banished to a remote mountain retreat of the mysteriously powerful Bei-Kum. There they come face-to-face with the secret of the fireball at last. Volume 3 in the Fireball Trilogy.

Clark, Joan. **Wild Man of the Woods.** Illustrated by David Craig. Viking Penguin/Viking Kestrel, 1985. 171 p. ISBN 0-670-80015-5.

When city-raised Stephen visits his cousin Louie in the Rockies, he hopes to escape bullies. Instead, he meets Williard and Sludge, who prove worse than anyone he's encountered in his city surroundings. Fascinated by primitive masks, Stephen and Louie explore a cave haunted by the Wild Man of the Woods. Stephen's probing of a legend ends in frightening self-discovery.

Dunlop, Eileen. **Clementina.** Holiday House, 1987. 156 p. ISBN 0-8234-0642-3.

Fourteen-year-old Daisy is excited about spending her vacation on the shores of a Scottish lake with her best friend. But problems begin as soon as they arrive, and range from a spooky castle to a strange visitor — Clementina. You, too, will get excited as you learn what's in store for the girls.

Dygard, Thomas J. **Wilderness Peril.** William Morrow, 1985. 194 p. ISBN 0-688-04146-9.

Todd Barkley and Mike Roper carefully planned this last backpacking excursion before leaving for college. As they trek deeper and deeper into the northeastern Minnesota wilderness, they make an incredible discovery — three-quarters of a million dollars hidden in the undergrowth. Can there be a connection between the stash and a recent airline hijacking? And what is to be done about all that money?

Hammer, Charles. **Me, the Beef, and the Bum.** Farrar, Strauss and Giroux, 1984. 215 p. ISBN 0-374-34903-7.

When she learns that her father is going to sell her prize steer, Rosie Mattock knows only one thing to do — run away. But instead of going alone, she takes her steer with her. Rosie finds it difficult to hide a steer in Kansas City, even with the help of a newfound friend, a bum called Mett.

Haseley, Dennis. **The Counterfeiter.** Macmillan, 1987. 231 p. ISBN 0-02-743120-7.

Sixteen-year-old James lives in a suburb of Cleveland. He wants to become an artist right after high school, but his parents want him to attend college. James is obsessed with Heather Nichols, who plays the harpsichord and speaks French, and with his latest art project — painting a perfect $500 bill. Achieving success with this painting leads to further difficulties as he sets out to win Heather.

Holland, Isabelle. **The Island.** Little, Brown, 1984. 182 p. ISBN 0-316-36993-4.

Seventeen-year-old Hilda Tashoff should be thrilled about her visit to the tropical island of Maenad and the attentions of the mysterious Mr. Gomez, but she isn't. To complicate matters, can her Uncle Brace really be holding his wife a prisoner? Befriended only by Wolf, a gentle German shepherd, and Steve Barrington, a young pilot, Hilda discovers the threat to her own freedom. (Literary merit)

Hostetler, Marian. **African Adventure.** Illustrated by Esther Rose Graber. Herald Press, 1982. 124 p. ISBN 0-8361-1329-2 (0-8361-1331-4, paperback).

What can one sixth grader do to solve world hunger? Nothing, insists Denny, as her father uproots the family to move to Africa, where he will head a team of missionary farmers. They experience a plane crash, sickness, and raids by local rebels. Then Denny is captured by government troops, and she realizes she may not live to see her new home.

Kerr, M. E. **Fell.** Harper and Row/Charlotte Zolotow Books, 1987. 165 p. ISBN 0-06-023267-6 (0-06-02368-4, library binding).

Seventeen-year-old John Fell has been asked by Walter Pingree, a rich man, to assume his son's identity and to enroll at the exclusive Gardner School. A cash bonus convinces Fell and his mom that it's a good idea. But little does he know that he'll be entering the world of secret societies and political intrigue.

Levin, Betty. **Put On My Crown.** E. P. Dutton/Lodestar Books, 1985. 182 p. ISBN 0-525-67163-3.

On a ship carrying homeless children from workhouses in England to North America, Vinnie is working as a nursemaid to Grace and Joel, whose mother helped sponsor the trip. They are shipwrecked, and Vinnie regains consciousness to find herself on a desolate island with inhabitants intent on kidnapping the children rescued from the shipwreck.

Lisle, Janet Taylor. **The Great Dimpole Oak.** Illustrated by Stephen Gammell. Orchard Books, 1987. 135 p. ISBN 0-531-05716-X (0-531-08316-0, library binding).

Dark limbed and gnarled, the great oak stands just outside the town of Dimpole. For the casual passerby, it's just a tree. For Dexter Drake and Howlie Howlenburg, it's a treasure trove. For Mrs. George Trawley, Harvey Glover, and Shirley Hand, it's a monument. For the swami, it's a holy center. For the farmer, it's a living history. For all the people of Dimpole, the tree demonstrates the frailty of human nature and shows how the townspeople are prone to astonishing pitfalls and entanglements.

Lutz, Norma Jean. **Oklahoma Summer.** David C. Cook/Chariot Books, 1987. 140 p. ISBN 1-55513-028-3.

Marcia spends her summer trying to help her grandparents sell the ranch and preparing for the big horse show in Oklahoma City. As she does so, Marcia learns a lot about her personal relations.

Lutz, Norma Jean. **Once Over Lightly.** David C. Cook/Chariot Books, 1986. 143 p. ISBN 1-55512-025-9.

Marcia enjoys teaching beginning riders and practicing for her first championship competition until she discovers a stranger watching her. The stranger, Marcia learns, is jealous that she is riding one of the stable's best horses, and he plans to cause trouble for her with the owner. Will he cost Marcia her chance to compete in the championship?

Martin, Guenn. **Forty Miles from Nowhere.** Herald Press, 1986. 147 p. ISBN 0-8361-3417-6.

Melanie LaRue, her parents, and their pets spend the winter in a house they built on Gresham Island, Alaska. Melanie learns to cope with living forty miles from other people. But when she is unexpectedly left alone on the island in a severe storm, she has full responsibility for the animals and the equipment. Melanie begins to wonder if some interaction with other people would add to her life.

Murray, Marguerite. **A Peaceable Warrior.** Atheneum, 1986. 152 p. ISBN 0-689-31186-9.

Four young people, Rod and Julie Patterson and Ann and Mert Kendricks, spend their summer in the mountains. Rod meets a man named Homer, who is out to seek revenge on the man who burned his home and killed his cousin. Rod helps Homer with his feelings, and at the same time Rod discovers many things about himself.

Myers, Walter Dean. **Adventure in Granada.** Viking Penguin/Puffin Books, 1985. 87 p. ISBN 0-14-032011-3.

Teenage brothers Chris and Ken are enjoying their stay in Spain until their friend Pedro is accused of stealing a valuable Spanish cross. Trying to prove Pedro's innocence won't be easy. The boys find themselves caught between the police, who are after Pedro, and art smugglers, who are after them.

Myers, Walter Dean. **Ambush in the Amazon.** Viking Penguin/Puffin Books, 1986. 85 p. ISBN 0-14-032102-0.

Chris Arrow, seventeen, and his brother, fourteen-year-old Ken, are camping along the lush Amazon River when the sudden reappearance of the *Monstruo,* a swamp creature, has the natives ready to flee. As the boys try to discover whether or not the monster is for real, they find themselves in danger.

Myers, Walter Dean. **The Hidden Shrine.** Viking Penguin/Puffin Books, 1985. 85 p. ISBN 0-14-032010-5.

Chris and Ken Arrow are in Hong Kong with their mother, anthropologist Carla Arrow. Someone is stealing artifacts from the temples, and Chris and Ken, with their friend Won Li, are right on the trail. They start to close in on the thieves, but then Ken is taken prisoner by the thieves. Can Chris and Won Li rescue him?

Myers, Walter Dean. **The Nicholas Factor.** Viking Press, 1983. 173 p. ISBN 0-670-51055-6.

Seventeen-year-old Gerald receives an invitation to join the Crusade Society at his college. He dismisses the group as a bunch of do-gooders. But then Gerald is asked by a man named John to join the organization and to keep an eye on what goes on. Before long, Gerald finds himself involved in a Crusader project in the jungle of Peru, and it isn't for do-gooders.

O'Dell, Scott. **Alexandra.** Houghton Mifflin, 1984. 146 p. ISBN 0-395-35571-0.

Alexandra Papadimitrios's family have always been sponge fishers in the Florida village of Tarpon Springs. Tragedy strikes, and the seventeen-year-old Greek daughter takes over as the sponge diver. With help from her grandfather, Stephanos, Alexandra learns the craft. But danger lurks both underwater and on land. Who are Spyros Stavaronas and George Kanarsis? What do they want? (Literary merit)

Oleksy, Walter. **The Pirates of Deadman's Cay.** Westminster Press/Hiway Books, 1982. 109 p. ISBN 0-664-32693-5.

Randy and his father always enjoyed their vacations on their boat. On one sailing venture in the Caribbean, a storm forces them to land on an island inhabited by pirates, who capture

Randy's father. Randy manages to rescue another captive, a young girl, and together they devise a plan to rescue Randy's father.

Pantell, Dora. **Miss Pickerell and the Lost World.** Illustrated by Charles Geer. Franklin Watts, 1986. 154 p. ISBN 0-531-10229-7.

Miss Pickerell discovers Ellie, an endearing creature from a lost world. The little animal begins to refuse food and lose weight, and Miss Pickerell is told that Ellie must be taken home in order to survive. But where is her home? Join Miss Pickerell and others from the town as they sail upstream against the current of a raging river, searching for Ellie's home.

Randall, Florence Engel. **All the Sky Together.** Scholastic, 1983. 279 p. ISBN 0-590-33256-2.

When Cassie moves from Boston to Long Island, she finds it difficult to make friends. Then she meets Ellen and Peter, a very rich and very spoiled brother and sister. Cassie's parents try to discourage her from seeing Ellen and Peter, but this makes them seem more enticing. Cassie continues her friendship with the two, but what she hoped would be a perfect time turns into a nightmare.

Rardin, Susan Lowry. **Captives in a Foreign Land.** Houghton Mifflin, 1984. 218 p. ISBN 0-395-36216-4.

Tawbah, an Islamic anti-nuclear terrorist group, kidnaps six young Americans while their parents are visiting Rome. Taken captive are fifteen-year-old Matthew and his seventeen-year-old brother, Gib. Against the background of life and death dealings for their freedom, Matt tries to resolve his anger and resentment toward his brother and to free his fellow captives.

Roberts, Thom. **The Atlantic Free Balloon Race.** Illustrated by Megan Lloyd. Avon Books/Camelot Books, 1986. 78 p. ISBN 0-380-89868-3.

Ned's eccentric uncle has a top-secret plan to build a helium balloon and to fly from New York to London. His surprise copilot will be Agnes — a baby kangaroo. Eleven-year-old Ned's job is to keep Agnes hidden and happy until the big day. Dangerous adventures await them before they land in London.

Robertson, Keith. **Henry Reed's Think Tank.** Viking Penguin/Viking Kestrel, 1986. 182 p. ISBN 0-670-80968-3.

Summer in Grover's Corners can really drag on. Twelve-year-old Henry Reed and his friend Midge Glass decide to combine money-making and adventure by creating a problem-solving agency. Gum-chewing Deirdre and Agony the beagle help Henry's agency through a series of misadventures.

Rodgers, Raboo. **The Rainbow Factor.** Houghton Mifflin, 1985. 178 p. ISBN 0-395-35643-1.

Van Wulf, one of the richest men in Stockholm, Sweden, has everything in life except the thing he really wants — information about the death of his father. Adventure abounds as college freshmen from another continent unlock the secrets of a Nazi smuggling operation and find the information Van Wulf needs.

Salassi, Otto R. **And Nobody Knew They Were There.** Greenwillow Books, 1984. 179 p. ISBN 0-688-00940-9.

Thirteen-year-old Hogan McGhee isn't looking forward to the summer visit of his city cousin, Jakey Darby. But a quick fistfight takes care of that. When a squad of marines disappears from Houston, Jakey and Hogan accidentally stumble onto their assignment. The boys pursue the marines in secret as they make their way to Vicksburg, Mississippi.

Sharmat, Marjorie Weinman. **Get Rich Mitch!** Illustrated by Loretta Lustig. William Morrow, 1985. 152 p. ISBN 0-688-05790-X.

Sweepstakes winner Rich Mitch, eleven years old, has it all — money, a best-selling new doll created in his image, and talk-show fame. He's also the ideal target for kidnapping by an eccentric toy magnate. Sequel to *Rich Mitch.*

Skurzynski, Gloria. **Swept in the Wave of Terror.** Lothrop, Lee and Shepard Books, 1985. 159 p. ISBN 0-688-05820-5.

Being born to talented parents can be a real problem as "chubby" Tonia and her brother, "no-rhythm" Tiger, find out. They are given small roles in "The Way the West Began," a big Las Vegas production. Much of their time is spent backstage, where they are drawn into a scary adventure.

Skurzynski, Gloria. **Trapped in the Slickrock Canyon.** Illustrated by Daniel San Souci. Lothrop, Lee and Shepard Books, 1984. 123 p. ISBN 0-688-02688-5.

Twelve-year-old cousins Gina, with her city slicker ways, and Justin, with his country customs, are practically worst enemies.

Then the two are placed in a life-threatening situation, and they discover new strengths in themselves as well as in each other.

Snyder, Zilpha Keatley. **Blair's Nightmare.** Dell/Yearling Books, 1984. 192 p. ISBN 0-440-40915-2.

Little Blair Stanley has a wild imagination, so when he starts talking about a huge dog that visits him at night, no one pays much attention. His older brother, David, has the school bully and some escaped convicts to trouble his mind. But then David finds out that the dog is very real. One night the dog disappears, and six-year-old Blair wanders off to find him. Now David's fears become even more intense.

Sutton, Larry. **Taildraggers High.** Farrar, Straus and Giroux, 1985. 151 p. ISBN 0-374-37372-8.

What twelve-year-old Jessie Oates wants most in life are a pilot's license and an airplane. But her grandfather, with whom she lives in Florida, has been against flying ever since her father was killed in a plane crash in Vietnam. An early freeze that threatens to destroy their orange crops provides an opportunity to resolve some of these conflicts.

Wallace, Bill. **Shadow on the Snow.** Holiday House, 1985. 155 p. ISBN 0-8234-0557-5.

City kid Tom moves to his grandfather's farm and meets a new friend, Justin. Together they explore the nearby mountains, canyons, and gullies. Some oldtimers warn them to stay away from Panther's Peak. It seems that a panther appears there every ten years — especially during bad winters like this one.

York, Carol Beach. **On That Dark Night.** Bantam Books, 1985. 100 p. ISBN 0-553-25207-0.

How many lives have you lived before this one? Julie knows that she has lived at least one, but only as a child. Join Julie and her best friend, Allison, as they return to the town of Julie's former life and discover why she did not finish it. Be prepared for a surprise ending.

Animals and Pets

Aiken, Joan. **Mortimer Says Nothing.** Illustrated by Quentin Blake. Harper and Row, 1987. 185 p. ISBN 0-06-020038-3 (0-06-020039-1, library binding).

Arabel Jones and her pet raven, Mortimer (whose diet includes egg beaters, tape recorders, and gold bricks), are involved in adventures with a cat who eats up the food for a special party, a visit from a spoiled cousin whose talking doll is burned by Mortimer, a family vacation at Sleepy Sheep Hotel while Mortimer captures burglars at home, and the family's reaction to crank phone calls.

Aiken, Joan. **Mortimer's Cross.** Illustrated by Quentin Blake. Harper and Row/Charlotte Zolotow Books, 1984. 154 p. ISBN 0-06-020032-4 (0-06-020033-2, library binding).

This collection contains three more adventures of Arabel and her pet raven, Mortimer. Together the two crack the case of the missing library books, rescue a kidnapped rock star, discover who's been borrowing Arabel's father's taxi late at night, and save a town from an iceberg with a dinosaur frozen inside it.

Branscum, Robbie. **Cheater and Flitter Dick.** Viking Press, 1983. 106 p. ISBN 0-670-21350-0.

Fourteen-year-old Cheater lives with her adopted, hard-drinking father, her beloved rooster, Flitter Dick, and an odd assortment of animals on an Arkansas farm. When a tornado forces her to take in the farm owner's family, Cheater must struggle to support the enlarged household and to cope with the owner's difficult wife.

Brenner, Barbara. **The Gorilla Signs Love.** Lothrop, Lee and Shepard Books, 1984. 205 p. ISBN 0-688-00995-6.

Do animals have rights? Eighteen-year-old Maggie hopes to prove they do. She has established communication with Naomi, an African gorilla, and through a series of bizarre events, she has had Naomi brought to her father's zoo in the States. But zoo officials refuse to keep the gorilla for more than a year, and Maggie must either find her friend a new home or see Naomi shipped away to a breeding farm.

Carris, Joan. **Pets, Vets, and Marty Howard.** Illustrated by Carol Newsom. Dell/Yearling Books, 1987. 186 p. ISBN 0-440-46855-8.

Seventh-grader Marty Howard is absolutely, positively sure he wants to be a veterinarian. Well, at least he was sure until he becomes Doc Cameron's assistant and discovers the other side of the profession — dealing with abandoned pets and euthanasia. The novel provides a frank, informative look at veterinary medicine.

Cavanna, Betty. **Banner Year.** William Morrow, 1987. 217 p. ISBN 0-688-05779-9.

It is love at first sight for Cindy Foster when she sees Banner, a glossy black pony with intelligent eyes. Then she meets Tad Wainwright, a newcomer to Martha's Vineyard, and enjoys the times they spend together. Suddenly Banner is seriously injured. Cindy devotes herself to him full-time, ignoring everything and everyone else — even Tad. By the time she realizes that Tad also needs her, it may be too late to recapture his interest.

Cavanna, Betty. **Wanted: A Girl for the Horses.** William Morrow, 1984. 216 p. ISBN 0-688-02757-1.

When sixteen-year-old Charlotte Randolph takes a job grooming horses on the estate of Lord and Lady Holbrooke, she welcomes the chance for a fresh start in new surroundings. While learning all about riding and horse management, Charlotte also learns a lot about other people and their problems. Does winning an important horse race mean she must lose a love?

Chambers, John W. **The Colonel and Me.** Atheneum, 1985. 190 p. ISBN 0-689-31087-0.

Gussie hates the Colonel — but no more than she hates the idea of his teaching her to ride a horse. However, given the nature of her mother, Gussie knows that there is no way to get out of the whole thing. Some amazing developments during the hated lessons begin to change Gussie's views about horses.

Corbin, William. **A Dog Worth Stealing.** Orchard Books, 1987. 163 p. ISBN 0-531-05712-7 (0-531-08312-8, library binding).

Jud knows that Bo is a wonderful dog who needs to be rescued from his owner, a rough marijuana rancher who plans to turn Bo into a killer. Jud also has his own family problems. He has built an angry wall around himself since his mother left and his father remarried. Jud learns a lot about life as he deals with his problems and Bo's.

Diggs, Lucy. **Everyday Friends.** Atheneum, 1986. 256 p. ISBN 0-689-31197-4.

Thirteen-year-old Marcy is constantly being overshadowed by her older sister. She begins to feel insecure because she is not interested in the same things and therefore has a tendency to give up before she completes a project. However, Marcy's life begins to improve when by chance she meets Natasha, an accomplished young horsewoman. Marcy soon develops a deep interest in horses and becomes determined to have her own horse and to learn to ride.

Doty, Jean Slaughter. **Yesterday's Horses.** Macmillan, 1985. 114 p. ISBN 0-02-733040-0.

Kelly Caldwell rescues a funny-looking filly from the mountains and names her Zipper. The filly looks exactly like horses in prehistoric cave paintings, horses that have been extinct in America for thousands of years. Kelly's veterinarian mother is busy fighting a mysterious and deadly horse disease affecting horses in their valley. But Zipper seems immune to the disease. Can Zipper help save the other horses?

Farley, Walter. **The Black Stallion Legend.** Random House, 1983. 177 p. ISBN 0-394-87500-1 (0-394-96026-2, library binding).

Alec Ramsey and the Black Stallion leave Hopeful Ranch when Alec learns of the death of his girlfriend. As they wander in the desert, they hear an amazing story from an Indian. The end of the world is coming, but an ancient legend promises help from a rider on a black horse. Suddenly the fate of a whole tribe of Indians is in Alec's hands.

Gates, Doris. **A Filly for Melinda.** Viking Press, 1984. 170 p. ISBN 0-670-31328-9.

Twelve-year-old Melinda Ross helps deliver a beautiful red-brown filly, Little Missy. The horse blossoms into a classic Morgan. Little

Missy's high-spirited nature is matched only by Melinda's — a quality she must rely on when she finds herself torn between love for her horse and devotion to her family. Sequel to *A Morgan for Melinda.*

Griffith, Helen V. **Foxy.** Greenwillow Books, 1984. 135 p. ISBN 0-688-02567-6.

Jeff doesn't like camping with his parents in the Florida Keys. There are too many insects, too many dangers lurking in the waters. He meets Amber, who has always lived there and who seems to enjoy Jeff's nervousness. Jeff nearly forgets his own fears when he finds Foxy, a homeless dog. But Amber is determined that Foxy will be her dog.

Hall, Lynn. **Danger Dog.** Charles Scribner's Sons, 1986. 108 p. ISBN 0-684-18680-2.

Thirteen-year-old David Purdy meets Max, a Doberman pinscher, in the Johnson County courthouse. Max is not a pet. He has been trained as an attack dog, and now he is on trial for his life. His owner, defended by David's father, is being sued for injuries to a deliveryman attacked by Max. The judge orders payment of damages only, but Max's owner is determined to do away with Max — until David persuades his father to let him try to "de-program" Max.

Hoppe, Joanne. **Pretty Penny Farm.** William Morrow, 1987. 218 p. ISBN 0-688-07201-1.

Fifteen-year-old Beth Bridgewater rebels when her parents take her to New Hampshire for the summer, but her spirits lift when she sees Charmin', a chestnut stallion, and his owner, Dave Fuller. Beth gets a chance to ride Charmin' in a race, but sinister men appear at the racetrack. Beth is swept up in a game of deadly deception that could destroy the horse of her dreams.

Howard, Jean G. **Half a Cage.** Illustrated by the author. Tidal Press, 1978. 319 p. ISBN 0-930954-07-6.

Diana, a spider monkey, comes to live with the family of twelve-year-old Ann Carpenter and turns their lives upside down. Ann learns that a monkey in the house can lead her on exploits that are loving, challenging, funny, and terrifying.

Howe, James. **Morgan's Zoo.** Illustrated by Leslie Morrill. Avon Books/Camelot Books, 1984. 179 p. ISBN 0-380-69994-X.

Morgan has been the animal keeper at the Chelsea Park Zoo for so long that everyone calls it Morgan's Zoo. The animals are his only family. Morgan and the animals are heartbroken to learn that the zoo is to be closed. Together with Allison and Andrew, twins who visit the zoo daily, they lay plans to save Morgan's Zoo.

Katz, Harriet. **Harvey's Last Chance.** Avon Books/Camelot Books, 1985. 110 p. ISBN 0-380-89791-1.

Harvey, the funniest-looking dog imaginable, has been kicked out of six homes after ripping them to pieces. Randal Harris and Scott Fraser want to make a movie for their seventh-grade social studies project. They create such havoc at the animal shelter that they are asked to leave and never come back. They need a dog right away, and Harvey is all they have!

Little, Jean. **Lost and Found.** Illustrated by Leoung O'Young. Viking Penguin/Viking Kestrel, 1985. 82 p. ISBN 0-670-80835-0.

The worst part about moving to a new town, Lucy Bell discovers, is leaving her friends behind. But when Trouble, a vivacious terrier, "adopts" Lucy, she decides her new home isn't all bad. The problem is, can Trouble really become Lucy's pet, or does someone else have prior claim?

McCaig, Donald. **Nop's Trials.** Warner Books, 1985. 337 p. ISBN 0-446-32641-0.

Lewis Burkholder, a Virginia farmer, is very dedicated to his Border collie, Nop. On Christmas Day, Nop disappears. Lewis devotes much of his time to looking for his lost dog, which causes problems in his family. But Lewis is determined to find Nop.

McInerney, Judith Whitelock. **Judge Benjamin: The Superdog Gift.** Illustrated by Leslie Morrill. Holiday House, 1986. 128 p. ISBN 0-8234-0602-4.

Judge Benjamin, a two-hundred-pound Saint Bernard, teams up with a new mate, Agatha. Their human family, the O'Rileys, has befriended Loretta, an elderly woman in a nearby boardinghouse. When Loretta wanders off, Agatha and Judge Benjamin make rescue attempts. Judge Benjamin's sense of humor and heroism shine through once more. Volume 5 in the Judge Benjamin series.

McInerney, Judith Whitelock. **Judge Benjamin: The Superdog Surprise.** Illustrated by Leslie Morrill. Holiday House, 1985. 234 p. ISBN 0-8234-0561-3.

Imagine a two-hundred-pound Saint Bernard in the cockpit of a Cessna 150. Going airborne is only one of Judge Benjamin's adventures as he protects Marge and Tom O'Riley and their four children. Told from the dog's point of view, this hilarious novel will take you through a blizzard, a forced stay in a "haunted" house, and a rescue mission.

MacKellar, William. **A Dog Called Porridge.** Dodd, Mead, 1985. 151 p. ISBN 0-396-0826-8.

In the Scottish Highlands, the sound of Davie's bagpipes is interrupted by an unusual cry. Upon investigation, Davie rescues a dog from the ocean. It is a strange-looking creature, and appearance is not the only peculiarity. Unexplainable events begin to happen to Davie, his uncle, and the town of Kilcardie after the dog's arrival.

Manley, Seon. **A Present for Charles Dickens.** Westminster Press, 1983. 111 p. ISBN 0664-32706-0.

When Grip, a raven, is left on the doorstep for Charles Dickens, he becomes a good companion to the author of *A Christmas Carol.* Grip's mischievous deeds also lead to friendship with the cook, stablehand, and children of Devonshire Terrace.

Menino, H. M. **Pandora: A Raccoon's Journey.** Bradbury Press, 1985. 101 p. ISBN 0-02-766850-9.

Maggie, a twelve-year-old farm girl, brings home a young raccoon that she names Pandora. Pandora and Maggie's year together marks a journey for them both — circling never too far from Pandora's woods, but far enough.

Morrison, Dorothy Nafus. **Whisper Goodbye.** Atheneum, 1985. 183 p. ISBN 0-689-31109-5.

Thirteen-year-old Katie lives in Rollins, Oregon, with Gram and Grandad. She is just beginning to barrel race with her three-year-old horse, Whisper Please. When construction begins on a new dam on the Columbia River, the whole town of Rollins must be moved. But Katie's new home will have no place to keep Whisper.

Pevsner, Stella. **Me, My Goat, and My Sister's Wedding.** Clarion Books, 1985. 180 p. ISBN 0-89919-305-6.

To earn some money, Doug, Woody, and Frank secretly decide to take care of Rudy, a goat, for two weeks while its owner goes on a camping trip. Rudy escapes from the boys' clubhouse, terrorizes the neighborhood, and eats the fabric that Doug's sister was going to use for her wedding gown. The planned garden wedding further complicates things for the boys and the goat.

Riskind, Mary. **Wildcat Summer.** Houghton Mifflin, 1985. 174 p. ISBN 0-395-36217-2.

Lynn Davis, a high school girl, is spending the summer helping her "Grammer" in New Hampshire when two young neighbors, Vicky and Skip Seymour, find some abandoned kittens. The children hope to take the kittens back to the city, but then the whole group discovers these aren't ordinary kittens — they are bobcats.

Roberts, Willo Davis. **Eddie and the Fairy Godpuppy.** Illustrated by Leslie Morrill. Atheneum, 1984. 125 p. ISBN 0-689-31021-8.

Eddie hates living in an orphanage. No one wants him, he is always in trouble, and he feels he is ugly. One day a stray puppy wanders into the orphanage. Eddie hopes the dog is a fairy godpuppy who will help him find a home. Great adventures happen as Eddie tries to keep the puppy a secret. Finally, a miracle does happen.

Rogers, Jean. **The Secret Moose.** Illustrated by Jim Fowler. Greenwillow Books, 1985. 64 p. ISBN 0-688-04248-1 (0-688-04249-X, library binding).

Gerald, a young boy living in Alaska, sees a moose from the kitchen window one morning. Soon he is out following the tracks. He finds the moose lying dead, or so he thinks until it opens an eye. The moose is alive, but it has a bloody gash on its flank. What should Gerald do?

Saunders, Susan. **Mystery Cat and the Monkey Business.** Illustrated by Eileen Christelow. Bantam Books/Skylark Books, 1986. 94 p. ISBN 0-553-15452-4.

Mystery Cat is a scruffy gray tomcat with dual owners. By day he belongs to Kelly Ann McCoy, and by night he's the pet of Hilary Barnett. M.C. likes to come and go wherever he pleases.

One day the circus comes to town — and so does a sneaky thief. Everyone blames Mystery Cat. When his picture appears in the newspaper with a bold headline, his owners set out to save M.C. by finding the real thief.

Savitt, Sam. **A Horse to Remember.** Illustrated by the author. Viking Penguin/Puffin Books, 1984. 113 p. ISBN 0-14-032029-6.

Seventeen-year-old Mike Benson buys a big gray horse that at first glance appears to be down and out. Training the horse seems almost impossible. When Mike's brother hires a hand to help out on the farm, Mike discovers he has been training Viking for the wrong event and in the wrong manner. The Maryland Hunt Cup Race is described, and there is a glossary of horse terms.

Spinelli, Jerry. **Night of the Whale.** Little, Brown, 1985. 147 p. ISBN 0-316-80718-4.

When Moose and his high school friends head to the beach for Senior Week, they hardly expect to become heroes. They anticipate endless hours of basking in the sun and lounging around the local night spots. Stranded whales change their plans, however, and Moose and his pals struggle to save these mammoth creatures.

Springer, Nancy. **A Horse to Love.** Harper and Row, 1987. 181 p. ISBN 0-06-025824-1 (0-06-025825-X, library binding).

Seventh-grader Erin doesn't have any friends and doesn't need any. All she needs is a horse of her own. But when she gets one, she finds that there is a lot of boring work to do and millions of rules. Besides, Spindrift, the horse, is cranky and stubborn and doesn't seem to like Erin very much. Erin has trouble at school and trouble at home when she neglects her chores. Spindrift helps Erin come out of her shell and face the world.

Thompson, Jean. **Ghost Horse of the Palisades.** Illustrated by Stephen Marchesi. William Morrow, 1986. 102 p. ISBN 0-688-06145-1.

While trying to encourage her widowed father to take notice of the pretty, young schoolteacher, eleven-year-old Molly deals with some conflicting emotions caused by the reappearance and capture of the "ghost horse" she once saw before her mother's death. Life on the ranch is hard and lonely, but such a life teaches a respect for living beings, whether they are rattlesnakes or white stallions.

Waddell, Martin. **Harriet and the Haunted School.** Illustrated by Mark Burgess. Atlantic Monthly Press, 1984. 84 p. ISBN 0-87113-000-9.

Eleven-year-old Harriet's best friend, Anthea, wants a horse. When troublemaker Harriet helps Anthea steal one from a circus, the immediate problem is where to keep it. And just how long can you keep a horse, even a "phantom" one, a secret?

Wallace, Bill. **Red Dog.** Holiday House, 1987. 185 p. ISBN 0-8234-0650-4.

Twelve-year-old Adam is living in the rugged mountains of the Wyoming territory in the 1860s, a long way from his native Tennessee. Adam finds that mountain lions aren't the only danger that surrounds him — human dangers lurk in the form of greedy gold seekers. Adam is left in charge one week to defend his family and land.

Wood, Phyllis Anderson. **Pass Me a Pine Cone.** Westminster Press/ Hiway Books, 1982. 160 p. ISBN 0-664-32692-7.

Sam Overton's family is moving to the Sierras, where his father will become a high school principal. Lars Rudeen asks the Overtons to take along a box of pine cones for his niece Sara. Disgusted, sixteen-year-old Sam agrees to deliver the pine cones. He and his cat, Monster, soon make friends with Sara and her dog, Shashi, but he also makes some enemies in their mountain home. It's not easy being the new principal's son.

The Arts

Brooks, Bruce. **Midnight Hour Encores.** Harper and Row, 1986. 263 p. ISBN 0-06-020709-4 (0-06-020710-8, library binding).

Sixteen-year-old Sibilance T. Spooner, a cellist and musical prodigy, lives with her father, Taxi. Sib asks him to take her to see her mother, who gave her up at birth. Sib and Taxi travel cross-country to San Francisco to visit her 1960s-style mother. The trip lets Taxi relive the sixties culture as he explains it to his daughter.

Cross, Gillian. **Chartbreaker.** Holiday House, 1987. 181 p. ISBN 0-8234-0647-4.

Janis can no longer tolerate the cruelty of her mother and her mother's boyfriend, so she runs away to join the rock band Kelp. But will things be as great as she hopes? Will she become famous, or will she wish she could go back home?

Dean, Karen Strickler. **Stay on Your Toes, Maggie Adams!** Avon Books/Flare Books, 1986. 153 p. ISBN 0-380-89711-3.

At nineteen, Maggie Adams finally has a chance to show everybody — including Blikk Erikson, the famous Norwegian choreographer working with Maggie's ballet company — just what she is made of. Torn alliances and complications involving her closest friends demand that Maggie "stay on her toes" and prove her mettle.

Dean, Karen Strickler. **A Time to Dance.** Scholastic/Point Paperbacks, 1985. 216 p. ISBN 0-590-33199-X.

Fifteen-year-old Lara Havas and her friend Summer put their best efforts into winning scholarships to study ballet in New York. Their deepening feelings for the young men in their lives complicate matters. And as Lara's first-generation Hungarian-American parents and Stephanie Martin, the girls' mentor, tighten restrictions, life as a ballerina looks more like sacrifice and less like fun.

Gioffre, Marisa. **Starstruck.** Scholastic/Apple Paperbacks, 1985. 185 p. ISBN 0-590-33797-1.

Alicia, a senior in high school, has a dream to be a singer. Yet her mother has other plans for her — good grades and a good job as a bookkeeper. Alicia has to follow the dream burning inside her. Nothing can make her give it up, no matter how much it hurts.

Godden, Rumer. **Thursday's Children.** Viking Press, 1984. 249 p. ISBN 0-670-71196-9.

It was only by accident that young Doone went to ballet classes with his older sister, Crystal. But it became apparent very soon that the talent for dance was not with Crystal but with her brother instead. This is Doone's story of his life from five until thirteen years and how he earns award after award despite his sister's jealousy and his mother's lack of encouragement. Doone's ability is even kept secret from his father and brothers for several years. (Literary merit)

Harris, Mark Jonathan. **Confessions of a Prime Time Kid.** Lothrop, Lee and Shepard Books, 1985. 208 p. ISBN 0-688-03979-0.

At age thirteen, Meg writes an autobiography about her life as a child actor. She describes her feelings and life with her fifteen-year-old brother, Kelly, a has-been actor; her mother, who lets them make their own decisions; her agent, with whom she can talk; and her fickle public. Meg feels pressured, so she runs away.

Hayes, Sheila. **No Autographs, Please.** E. P. Dutton/Lodestar Books, 1984. 135 p. ISBN 0-525-67157-9.

Cynthia knows she was born to be an actress. When a famous movie star comes to her small New York town to make a movie, Cynthia is sure that her own talent will be recognized and that she, too, will become a star.

Newton, Suzanne. **I Will Call It Georgie's Blues.** Viking Press, 1983. 197 p. ISBN 0-670-39131-X.

Neal Sloan, age fifteen, is the son of a minister who thinks his wife and children should only display perfect behavior in their small Southern community. His unrealistic expectations and harsh discipline are causing Neal's seven-year-old brother, Georgie, to lose touch with reality, and Neal is afraid to reveal to his father his increasing interest and abilities in playing jazz piano.

Oneal, Zibby. **In Summer Light.** Viking Penguin/Viking Kestrel, 1985. 149 p. ISBN 0-670-80784-2.

Seventeen-year-old Kate is home from boarding school for the summer to recover from mononucleosis. Her father, well-known painter Marcus Brewer, dominates the household, and his presence reminds Kate of her decision not to paint again. Then graduate student Ian Jackson joins the household to catalog Marcus Brewer's paintings. With his help, Kate reexamines her decision to give up painting.

Ure, Jean. **Hi There, Supermouse!** Illustrated by Martin White. Viking Penguin/Puffin Books, 1985. 124 p. ISBN 0-14-031716-3.

Two sisters, Rose and Nicola, are as different as night and day. Rose, who appears to be the talented one, is coached and groomed for stardom. Nicola, the other sister, feels that her mischievous behavior makes her a thorn in her parents' side. But it is actually one of her pranks that leads Nicola and those around her to view her differently.

Ure, Jean. **The Most Important Thing.** Illustrated by Ellen Eagle. William Morrow, 1985. 181 p. ISBN 0-688-05859-0.

Fourteen-year-old Nicola begins to work hard to become a ballet dancer after her talented but spoiled sister is gone. However, she is not sure that she wants to commit herself to the long hours of practice needed to reach her goal. Sequel to *Hi There, Supermouse!*

Ure, Jean. **Supermouse.** Illustrated by Ellen Eagle. William Morrow, 1984. 153 p. ISBN 0-688-02742-3.

Can't she ever win? Eleven-year-old Nicola has gone through life coming in second to her beautiful, pampered younger sister, Rose. Now, when the local theater has chosen Nicola for a role, her mother persuades the producers that Nicola has no talent and that Rose is really the one they want. A surprise ending shocks the whole family and brings new hope to Nicola's life.

Black Experiences

Brooks, Bruce. **The Moves Make the Man.** Harper and Row, 1984. 290 p. ISBN 0-06-020679-9 (0-06-020698-5, library binding).

Jerome Foxworthy is not only good at basketball but is an ace student as well. He becomes the first and only black student to integrate the largest white school in Wilmington, North Carolina. There he meets Bix Rivers, who can't stand anything fake, including learning the "moves" in basketball. To Jerome, moves mean self-expression and survival. To Bix, they mean falsehood. Bix swears he will have no lies in his life, but then he pulls the biggest move of all. (Literary merit — 1985 Newbery Honor Book)

Collier, James Lincoln, and Christopher Collier. **War Comes to Willy Freeman.** Dell/Yearling Books, 1987. 178 p. ISBN 0-440-49504-0.

Meet the Arabus family in this first volume in a saga about the life of a black family and their friends during the American Revolution. Most of the characters you'll meet are enslaved, but they have the strength, combined with the help and love of family and friends, to approach the misfortunes and danger in their lives with bravado.

Collier, James Lincoln, and Christopher Collier. **Who Is Carrie?** Dell/Yearling Books, 1987. 158 p. ISBN 0-440-49536-9.

The Arabus family saga continues in this third volume with Dan Arabus's adventures in New York. He joins forces with Carrie, a slave who can help him reach his goal and locate her roots. Sequel to *War Comes to Willy Freeman* and *Jump Ship to Freedom.*

Gordon, Sheila. **Waiting for the Rain.** Orchard Books, 1987. 214 p. ISBN 0-531-05726-7 (0-531-08326-8, library binding).

Two South African boys — Tengo, a black, and Frikkie, an Afrikaaner — grow up together as friends on the farm. This is their story from the time they are ten through their teen years, when the separation of blacks and whites called for by the policy of apartheid causes the boys to grow further and further apart. Finally, violence seems the only solution to bring about necessary change in an unjust system.

Hamilton, Virginia. **Junius Over Far.** Harper and Row/Charlotte Zolotow Books, 1985. 274 p. ISBN 0-06-022194-1 (0-06-022195-X, library binding).

Fourteen-year-old Junius, close to his grandfather since birth, is worried when his grandfather returns to his homeland, Snake Island in the Caribbean. In his letters, Grandfather indicates that there are pirates and that he is in danger. Junius and his father go to Snake Island to help solve the mystery.

Hamilton, Virginia. **A White Romance.** Philomel Books, 1987. 191 p. ISBN 0-399-21213-2.

The all-black high school Talley attends has recently been integrated. Talley, a runner, makes friends with Didi, a white girl who also loves to run. Through Didi, Talley is exposed to drugs, heavy metal music, and romance with the high school's white drug dealer.

Kincaid, Jamaica. **Annie John.** New American Library/Plume Books, 1986. 148 p. ISBN 0-452-25817-0.

Why does Annie argue and disagree so much with her mother, the woman who means the most to her? Annie begins to seek her independence and desires to grow into a young educated woman when she discovers that secret emotions and finally a crisis might tear her away from her beautiful mother and her island home of Antigua.

Linfield, Esther. **The Secret of the Mountain.** Greenwillow Books, 1986. 132 p. ISBN 0-688-05992-9.

The rites of passage of a fifteen-year-old Xhosa boy take the reader on a special adventure through the cattle lands of southeastern Africa. Anta feels and acts the same as all other young boys in his tribe until his father, who is the tribal chief, takes him on a mysterious journey into the mountains. There he learns a secret that will change the rest of his life.

MacKinnon, Bernie. **The Meantime.** Houghton Mifflin, 1984. 181 p. ISBN 0-395-35387-4.

Luke Parrish and his family move out of the ghetto and into suburban Flower Heights, but Luke, seventeen, and his younger sister, Rhonda, quickly learn that racial lines have been clearly drawn in the neighborhood and at school. Luke tries not to get involved in the black-white conflict, but his friendship with a white girl and his respect for an exceptional teacher pull him into the fray.

Miles, Betty. **Sink or Swim.** Alfred A. Knopf/Borzoi Books, 1986. 200 p. ISBN 0-394-85515-9 (0-394-95515-3, library binding).

B. J. Johnson, an eleven-year-old black boy from New York City, goes to New Hampshire for two weeks as part of the Fresh Air Program. There he learns to swim, does daily chores, and experiences life in the country. After his first jitters, the two weeks go by quickly.

Naidoo, Beverley. **Journey to Jo'burg: A South African Story.** Illustrated by Eric Velasquez. J. B. Lippincott, 1985. 80 p. ISBN 0-397-32168-6 (0-397-32169-4, library binding).

Thirteen-year-old Naledi and her nine-year-old brother, Tiro, live with relatives while their mother lives and works in Johannesburg, South Africa. When their baby sister becomes desperately ill, the children know that only their mother can save her. Naledi and Tiro go to Johannesburg to find their mother but encounter difficulties with the police when they enter the white city without the proper credentials. Finding their mother is simple compared to the struggle the black South Africans face in their search for freedom.

Nichols, Joan Kane. **All but the Right Folks.** Stemmer House/Barbara Holdridge Books, 1985. 100 p. ISBN 0-88045-065-7.

When young Marv refuses to spend another summer at camp, his father, who has always expressed disdain for white people, springs a surprise on him — a white grandmother! During his visit with Helga in New York, Marv comes to appreciate the outdoorsy, artistic, sensitive woman and unravels the mystery of his "flower child" mother.

Porte, Barbara Ann. **I Only Made Up the Roses.** Greenwillow Books, 1987. 114 p. ISBN 0-688-05216-9.

As an adult, Cydra reflects upon growing up as part of an interracial family. She realizes how events in her early childhood influenced her life, and reviews the lives of her family members.

Tate, Eleanora E. **The Secret of Gumbo Grove.** Franklin Watts, 1987. 266 p. ISBN 0-531-10298-X.

Mrs. Gore, the school history teacher, justifies the absence of black history in her classes by claiming that no black person in Calvary County has ever accomplished anything. Eleven-year-old Raisin meets Mrs. Effie Pfluggins, who knows more about the skeletons in Calvary than anyone else. Raisin and Effie unearth a mystery that most people in town would rather forget.

Taylor, Mildred D. **The Gold Cadillac.** Illustrated by Michael Hays. Dial Books for Young Readers, 1987. 43 p. ISBN 0-8037-0342-2 (0-8037-0343-0, library binding).

Lois and her sister were little girls thirty years ago when their father brought home the new gold Cadillac. Their mother was upset that he'd spent some of their savings earmarked for another house, but everyone else thought it was wonderful. Then Daddy insisted on driving the car to the South to visit relatives. The girls came to know that the South was no place to be for a black man in a new Cadillac with license plates from a northern state.

Thomas, Joyce Carol. **The Golden Pasture.** Scholastic, 1986. 136 p. ISBN 0-590-33681-9.

The ties binding a boy, his father, and his grandfather have been dissolved by a generation of anger. Twelve-year-old Carl Lee finds a horse on his grandfather's farm one summer, and the animal helps him to understand his difficult father better.

Thomas, Joyce Carol. **Water Girl.** Avon Books/Flare Books, 1986. 119 p. ISBN 0-380-89532-3.

Teenage Amber is a girl of many talents; she plays the flute, swims, and hunts with her younger twin brothers. She's also a compulsive reader who delves into the history of many minority peoples. But one day, as she's searching through the attic, she discovers an unknown piece of her own history.

Voigt, Cynthia. **Come a Stranger.** Atheneum, 1986. 190 p. ISBN 0-689-31289-X.

This is Mina Smith's story from fifth grade to tenth grade. As a child, Mina is selected to go to a ballet dance camp. While her body outgrows her ambition, Mina suspects that she is asked to leave only because she is black. As Mina grows older, she becomes good friends with her minister and thinks she's in love with him. But new friends, including Dicey Tillerman, help her grow up.

Walter, Mildred Pitts. **Justin and the Best Biscuits in the World.** Illustrated by Catherine Stock. Lothrop, Lee and Shepard Books, 1986. 122 p. ISBN 0-688-06645-3.

Ten-year-old Justin has a tough life with his mother and two sisters, who expect him to do "women's work." During a visit to Grandpa's ranch, Justin acquires not only housekeeping and culinary skills, but also an appreciation for his black heritage.

Walter, Mildred Pitts. **Trouble's Child.** Lothrop, Lee and Shepard Books, 1985. 157 p. ISBN 0-688-04214-7.

Martha, born during a storm and thus destined to a life of trouble, has finished eighth grade and is now expected to choose a quilt pattern, letting everyone know she is ready for marriage. But Martha doesn't want to marry. She wants to leave Blue Isle to go to school on the Louisiana mainland, something few young girls from the island have ever done. Martha must struggle against her family, tradition, and her own misgivings to reach a solution right for her.

Wilkinson, Brenda. **Not Separate, Not Equal.** Harper and Row, 1987. 152 p. ISBN 0-06-026479-9.

Malene is one of six blacks to integrate a Georgia public high school in the mid-sixties. There she experiences hatred and racism, as well as the beginnings of the civil rights movement.

Classics

Bagnold, Enid. **National Velvet.** Illustrated by Ted Lewin. William Morrow, 1985. 258 p. ISBN 0-688-05788-8.

Fifty years after its first publication comes the golden anniversary edition of *National Velvet.* This is the story of fourteen-year-old Velvet, who wins the Pie, an untamed race horse, in a lottery. She dreams of the horse becoming good enough to win the Grand National steeplechase. With the help of Mi Taylor, the hired hand, the horse just might be able to win.

Baum, L. Frank. **The Marvelous Land of Oz.** Illustrated by John R. Neill. William Morrow, 1985. 292 p. ISBN 0-688-05439-0.

The land of Oz is inhabited by many fun characters, like the Scarecrow, the Tin Woodman, and the Highly Magnified Woggle-Bug. A boy named Tip and his own creation, Jack Pumpkinhead, meet these and other less friendly people as they travel through Oz. Their adventures of outsmarting the evil witch Mombi and General Jinjur and her army of girls are as exciting today as when they were first published over eighty years ago.

Cooper, James Fenimore. **The Last of the Mohicans.** Illustrated by N. C. Wyeth. Charles Scribner's Sons, 1986. 372 p. ISBN 0-684-18711-6.

The second volume in Cooper's famed saga, *The Leatherstocking Tales,* this book is a tale of adventure, treachery, and friendship in the battle-torn wilderness of eighteenth-century upstate New York. The story is filled with Indian lore and the further adventures of frontiersman Natty Bumppo and his loyal Indian friend, Chingachgook. Reissue of the 1919 edition with Wyeth's original illustrations newly photographed and reproduced.

Creswick, Paul. **Robin Hood.** Illustrated by N. C. Wyeth. Charles Scribner's Sons, 1984. 362 p. ISBN 0-684-18162-2.

This book tells the legendary story of Robin Hood, who becomes an outlaw in twelfth-century England to fight against Sir Guy of

Gisborne and the Sheriff of Nottingham because they are oppressing the common people. Robin Hood and his band of merry men rob the rich and give to the poor. Loved by the people he helps, he is also eventually loved by Maid Marian, whom he captures and then releases. When King Richard at last comes back to England, Robin Hood helps him regain his throne. Reissued with Wyeth's color illustrations.

Davies, Valentine. **Miracle on 34th Street.** Illustrated by Tomie de Paola. Harcourt Brace Jovanovich, 1984. 118 p. ISBN 0-15-254526-3.

You may be familiar with the 1946 Twentieth Century-Fox film version of this classic. It is the story of a man who actually believes he is Santa Claus. Many people's lives are changed, and they too begin to believe that the old man is Santa. Tomie de Paola uses the New York setting to create nineteen paintings that are a treat to the eye and an enhancement to the story.

Defoe, Daniel. **Robinson Crusoe.** Illustrated by N. C. Wyeth. Charles Scribner's Sons, 1983. 368 p. ISBN 0-684-17946-6.

Robinson Crusoe was first published in 1719 in England. This book is a reissue of the 1920 edition with Wyeth's illustrations. Robinson Crusoe's story begins when he is a young man. He recounts his first adventures at sea, his capture in Brazil, and his becoming a planter in Brazil. He then tells about the fateful voyage when he becomes shipwrecked on a desert island. He spends nearly thirty years on the island, makes friends with Friday, and eventually is rescued.

Dickens, Charles. **A Christmas Carol.** Illustrated by Michael Foreman. E. P. Dutton/Dial Books for Young Readers, 1983. 128 p. ISBN 0-8037-0032-6.

Scrooge, a miserly old man, is visited by four ghosts: the ghost of Christmas Past, the ghost of Christmas Present, the ghost of Christmas Yet to Come, and the ghost of his old partner, Marley. In an attempt to convince Scrooge to change his miserly ways, the ghosts show Scrooge his true character and the distress he brings to others. A new edition of the 1843 classic.

Haviland, Virginia. **Favorite Fairy Tales Told around the World.** Illustrated by S. D. Schindler. Little, Brown, 1985. 327 p. ISBN 0-316-35044-3.

This is a collection of fairy tales from such countries as Ireland, India, Denmark, and Japan. Such well-known stories as "Hansel and Gretel" from Germany, "Puss in Boots" from France, "The Three Billy Goats Gruff" from Norway are featured here. Also included are the less well known stories of "Billy Beg and the Bull" from Ireland, "The Flying Ship" from Russia, and "The Old Woman and the Tramp" from Sweden.

Hoffmann, E.T.A. (translated by Andrea Clark Madden). **Nutcracker.** Illustrated by Carter Goodrich. Alfred A. Knopf/Ariel Books, 1987. 77 p. ISBN 0-394-55384-5.

The *Nutcracker* ballet is based on only one of the many adventures in this original story. Madam Mouserinks, for example, is banished from the palace and her family is executed after they eat all the fat for the king's favorite meal. Her seven-headed son gets revenge by turning the King's once-lovely daughter, Pirlipat, into an ugly, shrunken girl with a huge head and bulging eyes. What becomes of Pirlipat, as well as the more well known Clara and the Nutcracker prince, still makes for engaging reading after nearly two hundred years.

Kipling, Rudyard. **Just So Stories.** Illustrated by Safaya Salter. Henry Holt, 1987. 96 p. ISBN 0-8050-0439-4.

Kipling's stories range from how the leopard got its spots to tales of Elephant's Child's "satiable curiosity" and to the tale of the cat who walked by himself — and still does. Each story is accompanied by a poem by Kipling. Kipling's stories go back to a time when animals were different than they are now — elephants had big, fat noses instead of trunks, leopards had no spots, and camels did not have humps. The stories describe how these and other animals got their trunks, spots, humps, and skins.

McCaughrean, Geraldine. **The Canterbury Tales.** Illustrated by Victor G. Ambrus. Rand McNally, 1985. 117 p. ISBN 0-528-82673-5.

This is a retelling of Geoffrey Chaucer's *Canterbury Tales,* originally written in the 1300s. A group of pilgrims is traveling to Canterbury to visit the shrine of St. Thomas. To pass the time on the way, each tells a story. Topics include magic and trickery, animals with blazing eyes, people with their trousers on fire, and stories of love and death and the devil.

MacDonald, George. **The Princess and the Goblin.** Illustrated by Jessie Willcox Smith. William Morrow, 1986. 208 p. ISBN 0-688-06604-6.

This classic fantasy novel tells the story of a little princess who is threatened by the goblin miners living beneath the castle. She is saved by a young miner who makes it his business to protect her. A facsimile of the rare 1920 edition.

Pyle, Howard. **The Story of Sir Launcelot and His Companions.** Illustrated by the author. Charles Scribner's Sons, 1985. 340 p. ISBN 0-684-18313-7.

This book tells the full story of the most famous of the Arthurian heroes — Sir Launcelot of the Lake, who is the father of Sir Galahad. Reissue of the 1907 edition with Pyle's illustrations and decorations.

Pyle, Howard. **The Story of the Champions of the Round Table.** Illustrated by the author. Charles Scribner's Sons, 1985. 328 p. ISBN 0-684-18171-1.

Here is the recounting of the adventures of three of King Arthur's famous knights: Percival, Tristram, and Launcelot of the Lake. Reissue of the 1905 edition with Pyle's illustrations and decorations.

Pyle, Howard. **The Story of the Grail and the Passing of Arthur.** Illustrated by the author. Charles Scribner's Sons, 1985. 258 p. ISBN 0-684-18483-4.

The adventures of Sir Geraint, Galahad's quest for the Holy Grail, the battle between Launcelot and Gawaine, and the slaying of Mordred are retold in this book. Last volume in the retelling of the legend of King Arthur and the Knights of the Round Table. Reissue of the 1910 edition with Pyle's illustrations and decorations.

Rawlings, Marjorie Kinnan. **The Yearling.** Illustrated by N. C. Wyeth. Charles Scribner's Sons, 1985. 400 p. ISBN 0-684-18461-3.

Twelve-year-old Jody, growing up in central Florida in the 1930s, finds a young fawn that he names Flag. The deer becomes Jody's pet and follows him like a dog. But as Flag becomes older, he causes problems for Jody's family. There are tough decisions for Jody to make. Reissue of the original edition with Wyeth's original illustrations newly photographed and reproduced. (Literary merit — winner of the Pulitzer Prize in 1938)

Riordan, James. **Tales from the Arabian Nights.** Illustrated by Victor G. Ambrus. Rand McNally, 1985. 125 p. ISBN 0-528-82672-7.

In ancient times, Scheherezade saves her life by telling the Shah of Tartary one tale a night for 1,001 nights. The ten stories retold here include Aladdin and his lamp, Sinbad the sailor, and Ali Baba and the forty thieves. Ambrus's illustrations help weave the magical spell as monsters are vanquished and good finally triumphs over evil.

Thomas, Dylan. **A Child's Christmas in Wales.** Illustrated by Trina Schart Hyman. Holiday House, 1985. 47 p. ISBN 0-8234-0565-6.

Welsh poet Dylan Thomas recalls the celebration of Christmas in Wales when it snowed unlike the snow today — "it came shawling out of the ground and swam and drifted out of the arms and hands and bodies of the trees. . . ." Those were the days when Christmas really was *Christmas.* Hyman's illustrations reflect the joy and magic of a special day in the youth of Dylan Thomas.

Tolkien, J.R.R. **The Hobbit; or, There and Back Again.** Illustrated by Michael Hague. Houghton Mifflin, 1984. ISBN 0-395-36290-3.

Bilbo Baggins, a Hobbit living in enchanted Middle Earth, joins a group of dwarfs who are trying to reclaim their inheritance from Smaug, a dragon. They are aided on their journey by the wizard Gandalf as they encounter trolls, goblins, giant spiders, and elves on their way to the treasure. Bilbo and his companions must struggle against all odds to survive and to keep their inheritance.

Coming of Age

Abels, Harriette S., and Joyce Schenk. **Seaside Heights.** New American Library/Signet Vista Books, 1985. 192 p. ISBN 0-451-13671-3.

Almost seventeen, Alix Ross has one dream — to find a summer gig for herself and her backup band, the Cutting Edge. Smooth-talking Tony Mangini convinces Alix that singing nightly at the dumpy-looking Seaspray Club with him as her manager is the beginning of a promising career. For a while things seem fine. But are Tony's "connections" legit? And, most important, is Alix headed for serious trouble on the rough ocean front?

Bennett, Paul. **Follow the River.** Orchard Books, 1987. 190 p. ISBN 0-531-05714-3 (0-531-08314-4, library binding).

Lighthorse Harry Lee is a ten-year-old boy growing up in the small Appalachian Ohio town of Gnadenhutten during the 1930s. His family, like many others in this time period, must struggle to make ends meet. During the seven years covered in this novel, Lighthorse mows grass at the graveyard, learns the legend of the lost Indian maiden, falls in love with Nancy Lee Sutton, and delivers fresh laundry for his mother.

Bond, Nancy. **A Place to Come Back To.** Atheneum/Margaret K. McElderry Books, 1984. 187 p. ISBN 0-689-50302-4.

Charlotte Paige is upset to discover that her relationship with Kath, Andy, and Oliver — so stable a few months ago — is suddenly shifting. When Oliver's great-uncle and guardian, Commodore Shattuck, dies suddenly in his sleep, Oliver knows his life will be changing. He puts demands for commitment on fifteen-year-old Charlotte that she is not ready to meet.

Corcoran, Barbara. **The Woman in Your Life.** Atheneum, 1984. 159 p. ISBN 0-689-31044-7.

Eighteen-year-old Monty Montgomery has been rejected by her mother, and her father is dead. Searching for love, Monty meets Aaron Helding. She is caught transporting mescaline across the

Mexican border for Aaron and is sent to a federal prison. This book alternates between her diary entries and a prose description of her time in prison. For Monty, it is the hard way to learn, but she learns a lot.

Curry, Jane Louise. **The Lotus Cup.** Atheneum/Margaret K. McElderry Books, 1986. 230 p. ISBN 0-689-50384-9.

Corry Tipson is painfully shy. She realizes that if she wants to try her hand at pottery, she must be willing to overcome her shyness and ask for help. Becoming less shy might also help Corry respond to the attention she's receiving from two boys.

Ferris, Jean. **The Stainless Steel Rule.** Farrar, Straus and Giroux, 1986. 170 p. ISBN 0-374-37212-8.

Kitty, Fran, and Mary have always been best friends. Together they drive to and from school, swim on the swimteam, and discuss everything. They even have their own "coming of age" ceremony. Everything is fine until Nick comes to Las Piedras High and wants complete control over everything and everyone. Things begin to change and not always for the best.

Fox, Paula. **Lily and the Lost Boy.** Orchard Books, 1987. 149 p. ISBN 0-531-05720-8 (0-531-08320-9, library binding).

Lily, eleven, her thirteen-year-old brother, Paul, and their parents are living on a Greek island for a few months. Lily and Paul adapt to village life and to depending on each other for companionship, until the appearance of another American boy causes all that to change. Lily finds herself watching helplessly as Paul is caught up in Jack's escapades, which do not all have happy endings. (Literary merit)

Fox, Paula. **One-Eyed Cat.** Bradbury Press, 1984. 216 p. ISBN 0-02-735540-3.

When Uncle Hilary gives Ned an air rifle for his eleventh birthday, Ned's father takes it away and hides it until Ned is older. But Ned gets the gun from its hiding place in the attic that night and shoots it into the darkness. A one-eyed cat turns up, and Ned fears that he may have hit it with that shot in the darkness. How he works out his guilt is suspensefully and sensitively told. (Literary merit — Newbery Honor Book)

Hunter, Mollie. **Cat, Herself.** Harper and Row/Charlotte Zolotow Books, 1985. 278 p. ISBN 0-06-022634-X (0-06-022635-8, library binding).

Catriona McPhie, daughter of traveling Scottish tinkers, is proud of her family's ways. They roam free throughout the countryside, live by their own wits, and cling to an antiquated way of life in a swiftly changing modern world. Still, Cat resents the confining roles demanded of all the traveler women.

Klass, Sheila Solomon. **Alive and Starting Over.** Charles Scribner's Sons, 1983. 137 p. ISBN 0-684-17987-3.

At fifteen, Jessica Van Norden feels she is suddenly surrounded by people with problems. Her seemingly durable grandmother suffers a heart attack; her friend Sylvia is denied association with her group by an insensitive stepmother; and the new boy in town, Peter, is hiding something from everybody. Jessica discovers she has to find more than compassion for those in trouble.

Klein, Norma. **Snapshots.** E. P. Dutton/Dial Books for Young Readers, 1984. 167 p. ISBN 0-8037-0129-2.

Thirteen-year-old Sean and his friend Marc find themselves in serious trouble when some photographs they take of Marc's eight-year-old sister are interpreted by the district attorney's office to be pornographic. Sean is already confused by his upcoming bar mitzvah and by his conflicting feelings about girls, so the uproar over the pictures just adds to his confusion.

Littke, Lael. **Shanny on Her Own.** Harcourt Brace Jovanovich, 1985. 179 p. ISBN 0-15-273531-3.

Fifteen-year-old Shannon is sent to the country to help an elderly aunt pack up to move to a retirement home. But her aunt realizes that she doesn't want to leave her own home, and Shanny learns a great deal about life and herself while helping some newfound friends put on a musical.

Malmgren, Dallin. **The Whole Nine Yards.** Delacorte Press, 1986. 137 p. ISBN 0-385-29452-2.

Storm Russell is obsessed with girl chasing and spends his high school years seeking romance. With the help of Paula, he slowly begins to mature.

Mango, Karin N. **Somewhere Green.** Four Winds Press, 1987. 202 p. ISBN 0-02-762270-3.

To Bryony Hicks, sixteen, moving from the country to Brooklyn is disastrous. When the family housekeeper quits while the parents are on an anthropological dig, Bryony, her teenage sister, and her ten-year-old brother are left to their own resources. Bryony's one bright spot is Angel, the Puerto Rican boy next door.

Peck, Robert Newton. **Spanish Hoof.** Alfred A. Knopf/Borzoi Books, 1985. 181 p. ISBN 0-394-87261-4 (0-394-97261-9, library binding).

Harriet Beecher is twelve and saying farewell to childhood as the circumstances of her life on Spanish Hoof, her family's Florida cattle ranch, change. Her sixteen-year-old brother, Dab, is becoming a man, her capable mother is aging, and the family's claim to its ranch is threatened when an epidemic spreads throughout the herd's calves. (Literary merit)

Schwandt, Stephen. **A Risky Game.** Henry Holt, 1986. 115 p. ISBN 0-8050-0091-7.

Juliet has a unique English teacher for her senior year. He often presents his lessons through role-playing. Drawn to him because she misses her own father's active presence, Juliet agrees to participate in a bizarre plan for a classroom psychodrama that only she and her teacher know about. But Juliet doesn't know the whole plan either.

Sebestyen, Ouida. **On Fire.** Atlantic Monthly Press, 1985. 207 p. ISBN 0-87133-010-6.

What can Tator, Sammy's older brother, be reliving in those horrible nightmares? And to what dangerous lengths will loyalty to Tator take the twelve-year-old Sammy? Set in a 1911 frontier mining town, this is a story of responsibility and coming of age.

Terris, Susan. **Baby-Snatcher.** Farrar, Straus and Giroux, 1985. 170 p. ISBN 0-374-30473-4.

Thirteen-year-old Laurel is spending the summer at Hoop Lake with her brother and sister. She finds that her favorite private place, an abandoned trapper's cabin, is occupied by a handsome young man and his baby daughter. Laurel babysits, cleans, and cooks for Ivan, and she soon becomes romantically attached to him. But where is the baby's mother? This turns out to be a summer full of discoveries about Ivan and about herself.

Thompson, Julian F. **Simon Pure.** Scholastic, 1987. 329 p. ISBN 0-590-40507-1.

Simon Storm, only fifteen years old, is enrolled as a freshman at Riddle University. He would like to catch up socially and emotionally with the other college freshmen, so he agrees to be part of an experiment in which he records what he's doing and feeling whenever the beeper he carries goes off. By chance, he uncovers a plot to overthrow his university.

Tilly, Nancy. **Golden Girl.** Farrar, Straus and Giroux, 1985. 216 p. ISBN 0-374-32694-0.

Penny Askew is struggling with the social and emotional changes of being thirteen. She longs to write her first novel with her best friend, Tracey, but Tracey has been too busy getting in and out of trouble to be bothered with writing. To complicate matters, the new girl next door has all the refinement and style that Penny longs for. Penny learns that, close up, nothing is as golden as it appears from a distance.

Computers

Bach, Alice. **Double Bucky Shanghai.** Dell/Yearling Books, 1987. 143 p. ISBN 0-440-41996-4.

Jess and Stanwyck, known as Stan, are as different as two friends can be. Stan's "other friend" is her computer. When mysterious robberies hit the homes of school friends, Stan bets that she can solve the crimes faster than the police — with the help of her computer. Together Stan and Jess set out to crack the police access code, to stage a setup for the robbers, and to catch the crooks.

Byars, Betsy. **The Computer Nut.** Illustrated by Guy Byars. Viking Penguin/Viking Kestrel, 1984. 153 p. ISBN 0-670-23548-2.

Ten-year-old Kate receives a message on her computer from a mysterious admirer and hopes it was sent by her secret crush, Willie Lomax. No one wants to help her solve the mystery — her parents don't want her involved with computer weirdos, her sister is busy planning a dog's birthday party, and her friend Linda can only suggest sure-to-backfire schemes. Willie proves he's innocent and helps Kate with a close encounter with an alien comedian.

Harris, Lavinia. **Cover Up.** Scholastic/Point Paperbacks, 1985. 170 p. ISBN 0-590-33056-X.

Sidney and her boyfriend, Josh, are sophomores who own a computer consulting company in which they act as detectives. When Sidney is falsely accused of shoplifting, the store hires Sidney and Josh to find the real shoplifters and to write a better security computer program. But the real criminals find out and set a trap for Josh. Will Sidney get to Josh in time?

Harris, Lavinia. **A Touch of Madness.** Scholastic/Point Paperbacks, 1985. 167 p. ISBN 0-590-33057-8.

Computer espionage sends teenage detectives Joshua Rivington III and Sidney Scott Webster on a trail of murder, romance, gambling, and a congressional investigation. With the help of their computer, named Samantha, Josh and Sidney undertake clearing the name of a billion-dollar computer game company and saving it from bankruptcy.

Kidd, Ronald. **The Glitch.** E. P. Dutton/Lodestar Books, 1985. 117 p. ISBN 0-525-67160-09.

Eleven-year-old Benjy, who doesn't even like computers, is trapped inside one. There he meets a strange gathering of characters, including Charles Babbage, the King of ROM, the Queen of RAM, Delete (the woman in black), and the Computer Police. He can only escape when he successfully arrives at CPU City.

Landsman, Sandy. **The Gadget Factor.** New American Library/ Signet Books, 1984. 158 p. ISBN 0-451-13536-9.

Michael, a thirteen-year-old college freshman, and his roommate, Worm, have created their own computer universe. Mike's job is to ensure the survival of their new world while Worm attempts to destroy it. Both boys panic when they realize how closely their game resembles real life and when another scientist steals their secret formula for time travel. Can they recover the formula in time to save both worlds?

Leroe, Ellen W. **Robot Romance.** Harper and Row, 1985. 179 p. ISBN 0-06-023745-7 (0-06-023746-5, library binding).

Sixteen-year-old Bixby Wyler transfers to SilCo Valley High, the no-nonsense robot-run school. Unlike his fellow students who live and breathe computerese, Bixby has his own ideas of fun. It's not long before Bixby's scheme for constructing the first girl humanoid to win the Computer Science Fair prize has the entire school overloading its circuits.

McMahan, Ian. **Lake Fear.** Macmillan, 1985. 120 p. ISBN 0-02-765580-6.

A mysterious rash has the kids of Cascade, Washington, scratching. Doctors are stumped, but Ricky Foster, the Microkid, and his secret electronic sidekick, ALEC, set out to find the cause. As the sick kids are interviewed, ALEC does behind-the-scenes research in the computer complex. Clues point to the city reservoir called Lake Fear. Part of the Microkid Mystery series.

McMahan, Ian. **The Lost Forest.** Macmillan, 1985. 113 p. ISBN 0-02-765570-9.

Ricky Foster, the Microkid, and his secret sidekick, ALEC, are in the middle of their most important case when the Schlieman

Institute — home to ALEC's electronic personality — decides to shut its computer system down. Ricky's mother has disappeared during a field trip. His father is away, and no one else will believe that his mom might be in trouble. Part of the Microkid Mystery series.

Simon, Seymour. **Chip Rogers, Computer Whiz.** Illustrated by Steve Miller. William Morrow, 1984. 84 p. ISBN 0-688-03855-7.

Chip Rogers uses his computer for everything, but even Chip never dreams his computer can track down a robber. Chip's best friend, Katie, notices something wrong in the rare gem collection in the city museum. This discovery puts them on the trail of a jewel thief. Chip prepares a computer program that readers with computers can use to track down the thief, but you don't have to own a computer to solve this whodunit.

Dating and Love

Beckman, Delores. **Who Loves Sam Grant?** E. P. Dutton, 1983. 167 p. ISBN 0-525-44055-0.

Samantha wishes that her ex-boyfriend still liked her, but he has thrown her over for a new girl. Sam finds herself in quite a predicament when the mascot of her school's arch rival is stolen and she is suspected. Then Sam discovers that love can be right in your own backyard.

Brown, Irene Bennett. **Just Another Gorgeous Guy.** Atheneum, 1984. 223 p. ISBN 0-689-31011-0.

Hillary Germaine doesn't look forward to spending her seventeenth summer playing nursemaid to elderly Aunt Fay, owner of Rainsong Inn in Reesville, Oregon. She is pleasantly surprised to discover hordes of gorgeous construction workers in Reesville preparing for an electronics plant and figures she might have some fun after all. Hillary's involvement with new friends almost overcomes her worries over the *real* reason her parents insisted she stay with Aunt Fay.

Cavanna, Betty. **Romance on Trial.** Westminster Press, 1984. 96 p. ISBN 0-664-32715-X.

Valerie Kelton, seventeen, finds life at home impossible. With the permission of the mother of her boyfriend, Ben Steele, Valerie goes to the Steeles' house for the night — and that one night soon becomes two weeks. Life isn't quite so easy at the Steeles', but Valerie manages to adjust and even lands two jobs so she can begin to support herself. Her attraction for Ben just may present problems, however.

Cohen, Barbara. **Lovers' Games.** Atheneum, 1984. 239 p. ISBN 0-689-30981-3.

Sixteen-year-old Mandy feels that she gets enough excitement in her life from the Victorian novels she reads. Then she decides to do some romantic matching between her cousin Lissa and Lissa's recently acquired stepbrother, Rory. Mandy's attempts lead her to see that real-life romance can be even more confusing than the romance in books.

Cooney, Caroline B. **I'm Not Your Other Half.** Berkley Books/Pacer Books, 1987. 157 p. ISBN 0-425-09780-3.

Fraser, a high school junior, enjoys dating Michael, but she doesn't feel she needs to give up her best girlfriend or do everything with Michael. Does growing up mean choosing between old friends and new love?

Daly, Maureen. **Acts of Love.** Scholastic, 1986. 164 p. ISBN 0-590-33873-0.

Sixteen-year-old Retta Caldwell's world is changing. A new highway will cut right through her family's property, destroying the trees and pond where she spent much of her childhood. And Dallas Dobson appears; he's older than the other boys in her high school and seems more world-wise. Retta wonders why her parents seem especially anxious about him. (Literary merit)

Ellis, Carol. **Summer to Summer.** Ballantine Books, 1985. 166 p. ISBN 0-345-31631-2.

At fourteen, Jamie Watson feels sentenced to another boring summer at Sunrise Lake with her family and with Todd Mitchell and his parents. Todd still insists that Jamie take part in ghost hunts, while Jamie would rather daydream about the gorgeous lifeguard, Jim. Three years later, Jamie returns to the lake to find her feelings and Todd's have changed. Volume two in the Heart to Heart series.

Enderle, Judith. **Meet Super Duper Rick Martin.** New American Library/ Signet Vista Books, 1985. 156 p. ISBN 0-451-13868-6.

Meeting Rick Martin shouldn't be too difficult for Annie O'Malley. Her best friend, Nora, is eager to pitch in and help plan a party designed to make Rick aware of Annie. Rick even appears to be cooperating, until Nora pulls one too many stunts and confuses matters. Is Rick out of Annie's life forever?

Filichia, Peter. **Everything but Tuesdays and Sundays.** Ballantine Books/ Fawcett Juniper Books, 1984. 132 p. ISBN 0-449-70047-X.

Amy Dunning has to decide if she can continue to balance two relationships that are getting more and more difficult to keep straight. David, who is her *boyfriend,* is a straight, safe guy. Scott, who is a *boy friend,* is exciting — and introduces Amy to his faster lifestyle. Will Scott bring changes in sixteen-year-old Amy's lifestyle and her relationship with David?

Girion, Barbara. **In the Middle of a Rainbow.** Charles Scribner's Sons, 1983. 197 p. ISBN 0-684-17885-0.

Every day Corrie's mother reminds her how hard she needs to work and save for college next year. Because she got married so young and couldn't go on to school, Mrs. Dickerson is determined that her daughter will get a college degree. But Corrie would rather spend her time thinking about her new boyfriend. Can mother and daughter reach a decision about what is most important?

Goudge, Eileen. **Hands Off, He's Mine.** Dell/ Laurel-Leaf Books, 1985. 150 p. ISBN 0-440-93359-5.

Alex Enomoto is eager to meet her new foster sister, but she quickly learns that Stephanie is in no hurry to become friends. In fact, Stephanie has little interest in her new home and school, except for Alex's near-perfect boyfriend, Danny. Sixteen-year-old Alex begins to realize that her relationship with Danny isn't as stable as she had thought. Part of the Seniors series.

Greene, Constance C. **The Love Letters of J. Timothy Owen.** Harper and Row, 1986. 181 p. ISBN 0-06-022156-9 (0-06-022157-7, library binding).

Sixteen-year-old Tim thinks he has found the ultimate romantic courtship when he starts sending his secret love anonymous copies of the world's greatest love letters. But Tim gets unexpected results.

Holland, Suellen. **Mountain Whippoorwill.** New American Library/ Signet Vista Books, 1985. 159 p. ISBN 0-451-12580-6.

Tara Foster keeps house, cooks, and manages the money for a father who doesn't appreciate her. When a neighbor, old Mr. Beggs, introduces her to "fiddlin'" and bluegrass, a new world opens to Tara, a world "on stage" with talented, aloof Dusty.

Hopper, Nancy J. **Lies.** E. P. Dutton/Lodestar Books, 1984. 119 p. ISBN 0-525-67148-X.

Allison sees herself as a no-personality, colorless type who will never be able to interest anyone like Jerry. She thinks maybe one or two lies about herself and her family will help attract Jerry's interest. But before long Allison is so deep in lies that there seems to be no way out.

Jones, McClure. **Fix-Up Service.** Pacer Books, 1985. 152 p. ISBN 0-448-47756-4.

What's one little favor when it's for a good friend? With this thought in mind, Nicky Russell begins her matchmaking service. Soon her talents are in demand by everyone in the ninth grade — or are they?

Kaplow, Robert. **Alex Icicle: A Romance in Ten Torrid Chapters.** Houghton Mifflin, 1984. 117 p. ISBN 0-395-36230-X.

Eighth-grader Alexander Swinburne is in love with his beautiful classmate Amy Hart, but she'll soon be moving to California. In a journal inspired by the writing style of Edgar Allan Poe, Alexander describes his attempts to declare his love to Amy before she leaves his life forever.

Killien, Christi. **All of the Above.** Houghton Mifflin, 1987. 153 p. ISBN 0-395-43023-2.

MacBeth Langley is using the book *The Thirty-Six Dramatic Situations* as a guide to make her own life more exciting. When she meets the dashing son of a famous actor, she thinks she has found both excitement and romance. MacBeth finds there is a difference between being loved and being used.

Knudson, R. R. **Just Another Love Story.** Farrar, Straus and Giroux, 1983. 201 p. ISBN 0-374-33967-8.

Unhappy because the girl he loves has rejected him, Dusty drives his car into the Atlantic Ocean. A bodybuilder saves Dusty from drowning and urges him to get involved in bodybuilding. Dusty spends the summer getting ready for the Mr. Xanadu contest and trying to get Mariana to love him.

Levy, Elizabeth. **The Dani Trap.** William Morrow, 1984. 136 p. ISBN 0-688-03867-0.

Dani's first boyfriend, Michael, seems to bring her nothing but trouble. He drinks too much and drives too fast. When they are in an accident, Dani meets the cutest cop she's ever seen and agrees to become an undercover agent for a special squad cracking down on liquor stores selling to minors. She soon discovers that there is more to the assignment than she anticipated.

MacLachlan, Patricia. **Unclaimed Treasures.** Harper and Row/Charlotte Zolotow Books, 1984. 118 p. ISBN 0-06-024093-8 (0-06-024094-6, library binding).

Twelve-year-old Willa wants to feel extraordinary and to discover her true love, who she is sure will be tall and solemn. She spends hours with her twin brother, Nicholas, and the boy next door, Horace Morris, pondering what is ordinary (Willa and Nicholas's mother having a baby) and what is not (Horace's maiden aunts, the Unclaimed Treasures, playing Beethoven in the garden). But what Willa feels for Horace's tall and solemn father and what she and Nicholas accomplish by the end of the summer are perhaps the most extraordinary of all.

Martin, Ann M. **Just a Summer Romance.** Holiday House, 1987. 163 p. ISBN 0-8234-0649-0.

Just a summer romance? This question troubles fourteen-year-old Melanie as Labor Day draws near and she realizes she and Justin will have to separate for the school year. Can she keep their relationship going?

Paulsen, Gary. **Dancing Carl.** Viking Penguin/Puffin Books, 1987. 105 p. ISBN 0-14-032241-8.

Twelve-year-old Marsh and Willy think only of ice hockey until Carl's arrival at the skating rinks during the winter of 1958. Carl, a veteran of World War II, has a drinking problem, but he is put in charge of the ice rinks. The boys watch as Carl, through dancing on the ice, begins to regain his self-esteem.

Posner, Richard. **Sweet Pain.** M. Evans, 1987. 248 p. ISBN 0-87131-501-7.

Seventeen-year-old Casey has a habit of picking bad boyfriends. Paul Van Horn is no exception. He dislikes her friends, her family, her good grades, and her participation in track. But even though he's moody and negative, Casey likes to be with Paul — even when he starts to abuse her physically.

Regan, Dian Curtis. **I've Got Your Number.** Avon Books/Flare Books, 1986. 138 p. ISBN 0-380-75082-1.

Fifteen-year-old Emily Crocker desperately wants to be beautiful and in love. A make-over helps her looks, but meeting the wrong boy over the telephone just makes her love life worse. Is there help for Emily?

Reit, Ann. **Love at First Sight.** Scholastic/Point Books, 1987. 171 p. ISBN 0-590-40051-7.

What can happen at a high school dance? Love at first sight? For Elizabeth and Johnny, it happens just that way, and the two become inseparable. But then Elizabeth wonders if there should also be time for her friends, family, and school activities.

Sachs, Marilyn. **The Fat Girl.** E. P. Dutton, 1984. 168 p. ISBN 0-525-44076-3.

Appearances have always been important to seventeen-year-old Jeff. Why, then, is he drawn to Ellen, the clumsy, grossly fat girl in his ceramics class? Working against a backdrop of domestic manipulation in his family, Jeff determines to transform Ellen into "Lady Bountiful." But when Jeff's obsession with her begins to hinder her chances for personal growth, Ellen faces a difficult decision about their friendship.

Shannon, Jacqueline. **Too Much T.J.** Delacorte Press, 1986. 159 p. ISBN 0-385-29482-4.

Sixteen-year-old Razz has fallen in love with the fickle T.J. of the piercing turquoise eyes. Imagine her surprise when her divorced mother makes plans to marry T.J.'s divorced father. Razz is really confused about living in the same house with a boy she loves, while he only wants to treat her like a sister.

Sharmat, Marjorie. **He Noticed I'm Alive . . . and Other Hopeful Signs.** Dell/Laurel-Leaf Books, 1984. 146 p. ISBN 0-440-93809-0.

Jody has had a difficult time ever since her mother left home to find herself. Jody watches over her father, keeps house, and does the cooking. Now her father is dating a woman whose son, Matt, is the most gorgeous hunk Jody has ever seen. The trouble is that every time she is around Matt, she acts like a klutz.

Sharmat, Marjorie. **How to Have a Gorgeous Wedding.** Dell/Laurel-Leaf Books, 1985. 137 p. ISBN 0-440-93794-9.

Grandma Seeny's third wedding is certain to be a huge success — seventeen-year-old Shari and Meg will see to that. But who can blame the girls for shifting their attention slightly when the nephew of Grandma's fiancé arrives? Does either girl have a chance with Evan? If so, what will happen to their friendship?

Sierra, Patricia. **One-Way Romance.** Avon Books/Flare Books, 1986. 121 p. ISBN 0-380-75107-0.

What do you do when the man of your dreams wants your help in getting ready for his big date with your best friend? Handling this problem results in a surprise ending for tenth-grade Emily.

Towne, Mary. **Supercouple.** Dell/Laurel-Leaf Books, 1986. 183 p. ISBN 0-440-98378-9.

Thrown together through a series of chance meetings, Binky and Piers become known as the supercouple of Cameron High. But since neither can see beyond the cheerleader and football hero exterior to the shy, sensitive person inside, the supercouple breaks up. Discover how they learn to share surprising mutual interests.

Townsend, John Rowe. **Cloudy-Bright.** New American Library/Signet Vista Books, 1985. 159 p. ISBN 0-451-13817-1.

Sam, a photography student, is determined to win the school's photography contest and hopes it will lead to a newspaper job. Jenny just wants to take some snapshots, but her father insists she use his expensive camera, which is exactly like the one Sam lost. Jenny fears that Sam is interested in her only to use her camera, but she may be wrong.

Wersba, Barbara. **Fat: A Love Story.** Harper and Row/Charlotte Zolotow Books, 1987. 156 p. ISBN 0-06-026400-4 (0-06-026415-2, library binding).

Sixteen-year-old Rita Formica is fat and believes that her looks will never change. Then she meets Robert Swann, a gorgeous athlete, and her appetite fades. Rita determines to become thin for his sake and to change her image forever. The complications that result from this decision have an incredible effect on everyone.

Winslow, Joan. **Romance Is a Riot.** Dell/Laurel-Leaf Books, 1985. 156 p. ISBN 0-440-97479-8.

Sixteen-year-old Ann's life is suddenly turned upside down. Her parents separate, and she decides she must reevaluate her relationship with her boyfriend, the overly emotional Dixon. Things get increasingly complicated for Ann as Dixon refuses to accept the fact that she is no longer his steady and as Brit Bellamy, every girl's dream, begins to pay attention to her.

Wood, Tonya. **The Princess Routine.** New American Library/Signet Vista Books, 1985. 158 p. ISBN 0-451-13926-7.

Chelsea Hyatt spends five whole days shooting rapids on the Colorado River with a raft full of Boy Scouts just so her friend Sandy can impress Chelsea's nerd twin brother, "Ranger Rick." The expedition may prove that Chelsea is more than a sixteen-year-old cream puff. And it may lead to a lasting friendship with the rough-cut Jess Calahan — that is, if Chelsea survives!

Death and Dying

Bacon, Katharine Jay. **Shadow and Light.** Macmillan/Margaret K. McElderry Books, 1987. 197 p. ISBN 0-689-50431-4.

Almost sixteen, Emma expects just another carefree summer in the company of her grandmother and the beloved horses on the Vermont farm. Instead, she learns that Gee is dying and that she is expected to keep the secret as well as manage the farm. During the summer Emma discovers a sense of responsibility, learns about her own sexuality, and experiences the special joy of loving selflessly.

Bauer, Marion Dane. **On My Honor.** Clarion Books, 1986. 90 p. ISBN 0-89919-439-7.

Seventh-graders Tony and Joel ride their bikes out to Starved Rock State Park to climb the bluffs. While there, Tony challenges Joel to swim across the dangerous Vermilion River. It is not until they both jump in that Joel remembers Tony cannot swim. When Tony drowns, Joel is faced with having to admit to both sets of parents what happened and why. (Literary merit — 1987 Newbery Honor Book)

Bennett, Jay. **The Haunted One.** Franklin Watts, 1987. 175 p. ISBN 0-531-15059-3.

Paul Barrett, a championship swimmer and lifeguard at one of the beach resorts in New Jersey, falls in love with Jody Miller, a beautiful young dancer. While swimming, Jody gets a cramp and calls for Paul's help. But Paul has been smoking marijuana while on duty and doesn't hear her call. He must deal with the loss of her life and with his own guilt.

Boyd, Candy Dawson. **Breadsticks and Blessing Places.** Macmillan, 1985. 210 p. ISBN 0-02-709290-9.

Toni has never seen a dead person, and she certainly doesn't want to go to the funeral for her best friend, Susan. But the whole sixth-grade class has been invited to sing. What can she do? This problem makes getting her first period and passing the entrance exam to King Academy seem insignificant.

Carter, Alden R. **Sheila's Dying.** G. P. Putnam's Sons, 1987. 207 p. ISBN 0-399-21405-4.

A junior in high school, Jerry Kinkaid thinks his biggest problem is how to keep Bonnie Harper from dominating a school committee he chairs. Then he learns that his girlfriend, Sheila, is dying of cancer. Bonnie and Jerry share the nightmare of watching Sheila die.

Colman, Hila. **Suddenly.** William Morrow, 1987. 151 p. ISBN 0-688-05865-5.

One minute Emily is a carefree sixteen year old planning a great Halloween getup; the next, she is shattered by the death of her small friend Joey. How can she deal with the guilt she feels since she was riding in the car when her boyfriend, Russ, struck Joey? And what about her mixed emotions concerning Chet, Joey's older brother?

DeClements, Barthe. **I Never Asked You to Understand Me.** Viking Penguin/Viking Kestrel, 1986. 138 p. ISBN 0-670-80768-0.

"I don't belong here!" is Didi's first reaction to Cooperation High. After all, she is on suspension for non-attendance, not hardcore problems like everyone else here. Surprisingly, through association with other students, Didi learns to readjust her attitude and finally accept her mother's death.

Ethridge, Kenneth E. **Toothpick.** Holiday House, 1985. 118 p. ISBN 0-8234-0585-0.

Jamie Almont has spent his three years at Glenwood High hanging out with his friends, who are masters of the put-down, and daydreaming about the unapproachable Ginger. When "Toothpick," a girl who is dying of a terminal illness, comes into Jamie's life, he begins to rethink his old ideals and to reevaluate his own sensitivity and convictions.

Faucher, Elizabeth. **Surviving.** Scholastic, 1985. 169 p. ISBN 0-590-33664-9.

Rick, sixteen, has always been the model son, pushing himself to excel academically in order to meet his physician father's expectations. Lonnie is a "problem teen" who has already made one suicide attempt. When the two are drawn together, their common bond puzzles Rick's parents — until the couple decides life just isn't worth the hassle. Based on the television motion picture by Joyce Eliason.

Holland, Isabelle. **God, Mrs. Muskrat and Aunt Dot.** Illustrated by Beth and Joe Krush. Westminster Press, 1983. 77 p. ISBN 0-664-32703-6.

Being an orphan can be very lonely, but Rebecca has a friend. Soft and furry, Mrs. Muskrat lives in the forest and always is a good listener. In a letter to God, Rebecca explains how lonely she is now that she is living with her aunt and uncle, and how helpful Mrs. Muskrat has been.

Little, Jean. **Mama's Going to Buy You a Mockingbird.** Viking Penguin/Viking Kestrel, 1984. 213 p. ISBN 0-670-80346-4.

When his father becomes seriously ill, twelve-year-old Jeremy is faced with a series of upsets. The family moves from their long-time home, and his mother and younger sister turn to him for support. The awkward Tess and her silent grandfather add an unexpected dimension to Jeremy's life. (Literary merit)

Martin, Ann M. **With You and without You.** Holiday House, 1986. 179 p. ISBN 0-8234-0601-6.

Her father is dying, but with his help, twelve-year-old Liza and her family are determined to make this last Christmas the best one ever. Share in their preparations and in their sorrows as you see how each member of the family learns to accept death.

Martin, Guenn. **Remember the Eagle Day.** Herald Press, 1984. 125 p. ISBN 0-8361-3351-X.

Melanie LaRue, a junior high student, loves her horse Kenai more than anything else. But when her family buys a fishing business and moves to a remote Alaskan island, she must leave Kenai at home. On the island, Melanie befriends a grouchy hermit named Long Jake. Each teaches the other something that changes their lives.

Mazer, Harry. **When the Phone Rang.** Scholastic, 1985. 181 p. ISBN 0-590-32167-6.

When Billy answers the phone, the message he hears changes the three Keller children's lives forever. Their parents have been killed in a plane crash. Kevin, the oldest, drops out of college to try to keep the family together. The three teenagers must struggle against the advice of relatives, financial difficulties, and nearly overwhelming personal problems to stay together.

Mazer, Norma Fox. **After the Rain.** William Morrow, 1987. 290 p. ISBN 0-688-06867-7.

Sixteen-year-old Rachel, the youngest child of older parents, wants to be a writer. She is bored by the writing topics assigned by her English teacher. Initially her time for writing is compromised as she takes over as afternoon "babysitter" for Izzy, her dying grandfather. But as she cares for and writes about her grandfather, Rachel comes to understand the problems of the elderly.

Olsen, Violet. **Never Brought to Mind.** Atheneum, 1985. 176 p. ISBN 0-689-31110-9.

Four months after the death of two friends, Mary Beth and Hollis, seventeen-year-old Joe Conway can't escape from depression and a nagging sense of guilt. He tries to evade the memory of that January night when Hollis smashed his car into a tree. Once Joe realizes forgetting is impossible, he gropes for understanding and acceptance from supporters who have always been there, waiting to help.

Payne, Bernal C., Jr. **The Late, Great Dick Hart.** Houghton Mifflin, 1986. 133 p. ISBN 0-395-41453-9.

Six months ago Tom's best friend, Dick, died. Since then Tom has been desolate. While walking one snowy night, Tom hears Dick's voice and is drawn into Dick's world, a world in which everything seems perfect. But then Dick asks Tom to make a choice.

Peck, Richard. **Remembering the Good Times.** Dell/Laurel-Leaf Books, 1986. 181 p. ISBN 0-440-97339-2.

Sixteen-year-olds Buck, Kate, and Travis have been best friends since eighth grade, but how well do they really know each other? And how well can the two survivors carry on when one of the trio finds life too difficult?

Talbert, Marc. **Dead Birds Singing.** Little, Brown, 1985. 170 p. ISBN 0-316-83125-5.

Matt wins a swim meet, but on the way home his mother is killed in an automobile accident. Suddenly he must make a new life with his best friend's family. Matt cannot shake the feelings of grief, sadness, and anger toward the drunk who hit them. Then more tragedy strikes. Can Matt forgive?

Wood, Phyllis Anderson. **Then I'll Be Home Free.** Dodd, Mead, 1986. 238 p. ISBN 0-396-08766-3.

Rosemary Magnuson, sixteen, has always taken for granted the security of living with her doting grandparents, just as she has come to depend on Kevin Melero's friendship. When Gram dies suddenly, Rosie's cheerful Gramps becomes a lonely, dependent old man. Rosemary must reassess her situation quickly and make decisions, especially about her response to Kevin's new attentions.

Ecology

Collier, James Lincoln. **When the Stars Begin to Fall.** Delacorte Press, 1986. 160 p. ISBN 0-0385-29516-2.

Harry White will finish high school in three years. In the meantime his life is miserable — his dad is known for stealing, his family lives in an unpainted house surrounded by junk cars, and his sister has a reputation for being available whenever high school guys want her. Harry is determined to prove his worth by revealing the truth about the carpet factory's pollution of the river.

George, Jean Craighead. **One Day in the Alpine Tundra.** Illustrated by Walter Gaffney-Kessell. Thomas Y. Crowell, 1984. 44 p. ISBN 0-690-04325-2 (0-690-04326-0, library binding).

A boy spends a mid-August day in the alpine tundra on Rendezvous Mountain in the Teton Mountains of Wyoming. Here, while animals prepare for winter, a slab of rock teeters on a cliff above. It barely holds its place until a late afternoon storm causes the rock to fall, immediately changing the face of the tundra.

George, Jean Craighead. **One Day in the Prairie.** Illustrated by Bob Marstall. Thomas Y. Crowell, 1986. 42 p. ISBN 0-690-04564-6 (0-690-04566-2, library binding).

Young Henry Rush has come to the prairie wildlife refuge determined to take a photo of a prairie dog doing a backflip. The animals sense an approaching tornado and seek protection before it touches down and destroys everything in its path. What will happen to them and to Henry?

Herzig, Alison Cragin. **Shadows on the Pond.** Little, Brown, 1985. 244 p. ISBN 0-316-35895-9.

Ninth-grader Jill has a bad feeling about the summer already. Her best friend, Migan, suddenly seems very childish, her parents are having problems, and what has always been a sanctuary for her beloved beavers is threatened. Is Jill ready for Ryan's interest in her? If so, what about her friendship with Migan?

Howard, Jean G. **Bound by the Sea: A Summer Diary.** Photographs by the author. Tidal Press, 1986. 90 p. ISBN 0-930954-26-2 (0-930954-25-4, hardback).

Sandy will be a senior in the fall, but during the summer she and her family will live on an island off the coast of Maine. Her father gives her a camera and lots of black-and-white film. Her photographs, her journal, and her letters to her friend Bob document the passage of time during a very special summer.

Lasky, Kathryn. **Home Free.** Four Winds Press, 1985. 244 p. ISBN 0-02-751650-4.

This story of personal sacrifice, loss, and recovery began fifty years ago, when four New England towns were destroyed to create the Quabbin Reservoir, now home for the endangered bald eagle. Developers are turning it into a recreational area. However, fifteen-year-old Sam, a dying photographer, and an autistic girl vow to protect the eagles and the land from further exploitation.

Tchudi, Stephen. **The Green Machine and the Frog Crusade.** Delacorte Press, 1987. 221 p. ISBN 0-385-29529-4.

Sixteen-year-old David usually collects pollywogs in the spring from the marsh near his home and releases the young frogs in June. However, this spring the marsh is being filled in and turned into a housing development. With the help of his sister and her friends, the Green Machine, David begins a fight to save the marsh and its wildlife.

Ethnic Experiences

Bethancourt, T. Ernesto. **The Me inside of Me.** Lerner Publications, 1985. 155 p. ISBN 0-8225-0728-5.

Freddie Flores is seventeen, Chicano, rich, and alone. Before his family left on a plane trip, his mother bought a quarter million dollars of insurance. Freddie inherited the money when the plane crashed and his family died. His guardian, Mr. Callen, gets Freddie into an expensive prep school for his senior year, but Freddie discovers that it takes more than money to buy acceptance, not to mention self-respect.

Chaikin, Miriam. **Lower! Higher! You're a Liar!** Illustrated by Richard Egielski. Harper and Row/Charlotte Zolotow Books, 1984. 133 p. ISBN 0-06-021186-5 (0-06-021187-3, library binding).

Ten-year-old Molly organizes a club to boycott Celia, the neighborhood bully, during a summer in Brooklyn at the time of the Second World War. Molly discovers an awful secret about Celia. She must meet her alone and face her own secret fears.

Cohen, Barbara. **People Like Us.** Bantam Books, 1987. 135 p. ISBN 0-533-05441-4.

Dinah Adler, sixteen, never expected to be asked out by quarterback Geoff Ruggles. Her dream come true is shadowed by complications as her rigid Jewish family objects to her friendship with Geoff, a Gentile.

Garrigue, Sheila. **The Eternal Spring of Mr. Ito.** Bradbury Press, 1985. 163 p. ISBN 0-02-737300-2.

Sara cannot leave World War II behind, even when she moves to Canada. Her cousin's fiancé is killed at Pearl Harbor, and her best friend's mother is killed in the bombing of her city. Still, Sara is stunned when her Canadian-born Japanese friends are forced to leave their homes and move into mountain shacks. This punishment of innocent people is too much!

George, Jean Craighead. **Water Sky.** Harper and Row, 1987. 208 p. ISBN 0-06-022198-4 (0-06-022199-2, library binding).

Lincoln travels from Boston to Barrow, Alaska, to join his Uncle Jack, who has come to Alaska to help save the bowhead whale from extinction. A young Eskimo girl and an Eskimo whaling captain help Lincoln learn about the importance of the whale to the Eskimo culture.

Gilson, Jamie. **Hello, My Name Is Scrambled Eggs.** Illustrated by John Wallner. Lothrop, Lee and Shepard Books, 1985. 159 p. ISBN 0-688-04095-0.

Harvey Trumble embarks on a historic mission. His family is hosting a Vietnamese family that has come to settle in their town. Harvey tries to Americanize twelve-year-old Tuan. His results are rather — well, scrambled. Tuan learns a lot about American ways, but it's not always just what Harvey has planned.

Goodwin, Harold. **Cargo.** Illustrated by the author. Bradbury Press, 1984. 127 p. ISBN 0-02-736870-X.

Growing up in the South Pacific can be a peaceful life for a thirteen-year-old boy, but not for Wei. A white man enters his world, takes away his father, and sets the stage for an adventure that will lead Wei to Sydney, Australia, and eventually to the streets of New York City. His world becomes invaded with the twentieth century, and there is no turning back.

Hansen, Joyce. **Yellow Bird and Me.** Clarion Books, 1986. 155 p. ISBN 0-89919-335-8.

Sixth-grader Doris misses her best friend, Amir, who left the Bronx and was placed in a group home in Syracuse, New York, by his foster parents. Yellow Bird, the class clown, asks Doris to help him with his reading, as she did with Amir. Reluctantly Doris finds herself helping him. Sequel to *The Gift Giver.*

Houston, James. **The Falcon Bow: An Arctic Legend.** Illustrated by the author. Macmillan/Margaret K. McElderry Books, 1986. 96 p. ISBN 0-689-50411-X.

Kungo is an Inuit who lives on the far north coast. His people are hungry and suspect that the inland Indians are somehow responsible for the disappearance of the summer fish and caribou. Are they competing for the same food? Kungo goes to investigate. Based on an Arctic legend.

Hull, Eleanor. **The Summer People.** Atheneum, 1984. 217 p. ISBN 0-689-31037-4.

Twenty-year-old Genevieve Rosenthal travels from Denver to Baltimore, facing a decision about her life. Will she marry or work for Pettingill missions? As she remembers various summers at the Glen and the "summer people" and locals who influenced her perception of herself and her world, she is certain that her being Jewish made real friendship impossible. But has she misread her friends' reactions?

Kaufman, Stephen. **Does Anyone Here Know the Way to Thirteen?** Houghton Mifflin, 1985. 157 p. ISBN 0-395-35974-0.

Why are turning thirteen and facing the inevitable ceremony pronouncing his manhood tormenting the class brain? What do baseball and being the team benchwarmer have to do with Myron's bar mitzvah? As Myron's thirteenth birthday nears, the class bully and the stodgy Hebrew teacher provide the answers.

Klass, David. **Breakaway Run.** E. P. Dutton/Lodestar Books, 1987. 169 p. ISBN 0-525-67190-0.

Tony, a sixteen-year-old American, will be spending five months in the home of a Japanese family, the Maedas, as an exchange student. He's hoping to impress the area guys with his soccer ability. But he soon discovers that all aspects of life are different in Japan, even as he falls in love with the Maedas' daughter.

Klein, Norma. **Bizou.** Viking Press, 1983. 140 p. ISBN 0-670-17053-4.

Bizou's first trip to the United States turns into much more than a sight-seeing adventure. Abandoned by her mother, thirteen-year-old Bizou locates an old friend from her French junior high school and continues on a trail of discovery that leads to a surprise ending.

Lasky, Kathryn. **Pageant.** Four Winds Press, 1986. 221 p. ISBN 0-02-751720-9.

Sarah Benjamin is Jewish but attends a private Christian girls' school in Indianapolis in the 1960s. You will meet her family, friends, and teachers, and will see how the events of the 60s affect her life.

Lord, Bette Bao. **In the Year of the Boar and Jackie Robinson.** Illustrated by Marc Simont. Harper and Row, 1984. 169 p. ISBN 0-06-024003-2 (0-06-02404-0, library binding).

Shirley Temple Wong, called Bandit, comes from China in 1947 to live with her father in Brooklyn. Knowing only a few words of English, she struggles to make friends with the other children at her school. The world of baseball comes to the rescue. Playing right field, Bandit feels that she is a part of the American Dream at last.

Mark, Michael. **Toba.** Illustrated by Neil Waldman. Bradbury Press, 1984. 105 p. ISBN 0-02-762300-9.

Life in Poland in 1913 is not easy for Toba, a young Jewish girl, but she goes through her childhood feeling that she is secure and that plentiful opportunities await her. The stark reality that surrounds the marriage of her sister, Anna, plunges Toba into a world of darkness.

Marzollo, Jean. **Do You Love Me, Harvey Burns?** Scholastic/Point Paperbacks, 1983. 202 p. ISBN 0-590-33192-2.

Harvey Burns is Jewish, which in Bar Ferry matters to almost everyone — except Lisa Barnes, who at fifteen finds herself susceptible to Harvey's on-again, off-again attentions. As she and Harvey share an unusual science project and as Harvey's instability becomes evident, Lisa has to make some mature decisions.

Miklowitz, Gloria D. **The War between the Classes.** Dell/Laurel-Leaf Books, 1986. 158 p. ISBN 0-440-99406-3.

Amy, daughter of traditionalist Japanese parents, and Adam, son of a snobby upper-class mother, are determined to make a go of their relationship. As a further challenge, their social studies teacher involves their class in a "color game," an experiment that's designed to make students aware of class and racial prejudices.

Mohr, Nicholasa. **Going Home.** Dial Books for Young Readers, 1986. 192 p. ISBN 0-8037-0338-4.

Eleven-year-old Felita, a Puerto Rican girl who has grown up in New York City, has an opportunity to spend the summer in Puerto Rico. At first she's reluctant to leave her city friends and finds it difficult to make friends with the kids in Puerto Rico.

But finally she becomes part of a major project in a mountain village, which brings some unexpected surprises.

Mooser, Stephen. **Shadows on the Graveyard Trail.** Dell/Yearling Books, 1986. 100 p. ISBN 0-440-40805-9.

Thirteen-year-old Ivan Romanoff and his mother travel the Old West in their gypsy wagon, telling fortunes and reading palms. They acquire their fortune-telling information from local gravestones. When a local sheriff accuses Ivan of being a grave robber, Ivan, his mother, and a befriended orphan try to save themselves from the hanging judge.

Paulsen, Gary. **The Crossing.** Orchard Books, 1987. 114 p. ISBN 0-531-05709-8 (0-531-08309-8, library binding).

Characters cut from contrasting pieces of cloth are thrust together in this adventure about an attempted border crossing from Mexico into the United States. Manuel, an orphaned fourteen-year-old boy who lives in doorways and begs for food and money, and Sergeant Locke, a Vietnam veteran who tries to silence his nightmares about Vietnam with whiskey, become involved in a dramatic struggle. (Literary merit)

Paulsen, Gary. **Dogsong.** Bradbury Press, 1985. 177 p. ISBN 0-02-770180-8.

A boy's search for the traditions of the Eskimos is the focus of this book. Russel embarks on a 1400-mile journey by dogsled across mountains, tundra, ice fields — and across years — to a hunter of a mammoth and to Nancy, a fourteen-year-old girl left to die on the tundra.

Pitt, Nancy. **Beyond the High White Wall.** Charles Scribner's Sons, 1986. 135 p. ISBN 0-684-18663-2.

In her small village in the Russian Ukraine, Libby Kagan witnesses a murder. But in 1903 a Jew in Russia does not report such atrocities to the police. As the villagers turn against the Kagans, hope for survival rests upon their moving to America. For Libby, this too is frightening — for what does she know of America's language, customs, or people?

Price, Susan. **From Where I Stand.** Faber and Faber, 1984. 130 p. ISBN 0-571-13247-2.

Kamla Momen, an eighteen-year-old girl from Bangladesh living in England, emerges from her protective shell in order to aid

Jonathan Ulman, who is obsessed with society's inhumanity. They publish a bulletin to alert others to the prejudicial behavior found in Kamla's school. In return, younger students led by the militaristic Sharon Walker harass Jonathan's younger sister.

Ron-Feder, Galila (translated by Linda Stern Zisquit). **To Myself.** Illustrated by Irwin Rosenhouse. Adama Books, 1987. 133 p. ISBN 1-55774-003-8.

Eleven-year-old Mike keeps a diary describing his experiences living in Israel as a foster child with the well-to-do Singer family.

Ruby, Lois. **This Old Man.** Houghton Mifflin, 1984. 195 p. ISBN 0-395-36563-5.

Her mother's "old man" is the reason sixteen-year-old Greta enters Anza House for wayward girls. Her friend Wing's "old man" plays a major role in turning Greta from a near delinquent into a loving, trusting human being.

Snyder, Carol. **Ike and Mama and the Seven Surprises.** Illustrated by Charles Robinson. Lothrop, Lee and Shepard Books, 1985. 160 p. ISBN 0-688-03732-1.

More than anything, Ike Breenberg wants his father home from the hospital where he is being treated for tuberculosis. Instead, during the five weeks until his bar mitzvah his cousin Jake begins to dominate Ike's life and get in the way. But both Ike's preparation for his bar mitzvah and Jake hold many surprises.

Sommer, Karen. **Satch and the New Kid.** David C. Cook/Chariot Books, 1987. 127 p. ISBN 0-89191-746-2.

There's a new kid in town from Vietnam, and he's the same age as the Fearless Foursome — Satch, Spinner, Pete, and A.J. He fits right into their sixth grade, and best of all, he's a soccer star — just what the team needs. But something's wrong between the new kid and A.J., and Satch feels caught in the middle. He likes both boys. Why can't they get along?

Uchida, Yoshiko. **The Best Bad Thing.** Atheneum/Margaret K. McElderry Books, 1985. 120 p. ISBN 0-689-50290-7.

Rinko is dismayed at having to spend the last month of her summer vacation helping a widowed Japanese woman and her two sons pick cucumbers. But as the month progresses, Rinko discovers that not everything that appears to be bad is bad — perhaps it is worse! Sequel to *A Jar of Dreams.*

Family Situations

General

Arrick, Fran. **Nice Girl from Good Home.** Dell/Laurel-Leaf Books, 1984. 199 p. ISBN 0-440-96358-3.

Sixteen-year-old Dory has a family with problems. Her dad has lost his job and seems to find his only consolation in alcohol. Her mother is a compulsive shopper who can't reconcile herself to a more frugal way of life. Dory's brother Jeremy is being accepted to colleges his family can no longer afford, while Dory is just angry over situations out of her control.

Asher, Sandy. **Everything Is Not Enough.** Delacorte Press, 1987. 155 p. ISBN 0-385-29530-8.

For seventeen-year-old Michael, everything is not enough. He wants to find a life of his own, not follow the pattern handed down by his parents. But his parents have worked all their lives so Michael won't have to. Will he break their hearts and go his own way, or do what his parents want?

Asher, Sandy. **Teddy Teabury's Fabulous Fact.** Illustrated by Bob Jones. Dell/Yearling Books, 1985. 110 p. ISBN 0-440-48576-2.

Teddy Teabury's parents run the Thistledown Inn, but business and traffic into town have been slow since the superhighway was built. Teddy's been collecting facts for years. Now it's time to put them to use. Can he save his town from bankruptcy?

Auch, Mary Jane. **Cry Uncle!** Holiday House, 1987. 212 p. ISBN 0-8234-0660-1.

It's bad enough to be a scrawny eleven-year-old boy recently transplanted from city to farm, subjected to Mom's 101 zucchini dishes, and bedeviled by the nasty Spider Twins. Now Davy has to relinquish his room to loony Great-Uncle Will.

Auch, Mary Jane. **The Witching of Ben Wagner.** Houghton Mifflin, 1987. 132 p. ISBN 0-395-44522-1.

Twelve-year-old Ben Wagner's older sister, Susan, always gets her way, while Ben never gets a break. After his family moves to a new town on the shore of Lake Ontario, Ben meets Regina. Strange things happen whenever Regina is around, and Ben begins to believe the rumors that she comes from a family of witches.

Bograd, Larry. **Bernie Entertaining.** Illustrated by Richard Lauter. Delacorte Press, 1987. 101 p. ISBN 0-385-29543-X.

Meet ten-year-old Bernie, who prefers science to sports and who plans a career as an astronaut. Join Bernie as he destroys the embarrassing heirloom he brings for Family Heritage Day. And share with Bernie the punishment he receives and the other adventures that he experiences in fifth grade.

Byars, Betsy. **The Blossoms and the Green Phantom.** Illustrated by Jacqueline Rogers. Delacorte Press, 1987. 146 p. ISBN 0-385-29533-2.

Junior Blossom has a new invention that he knows is marvelous, but no one has noticed. After he adds the final secret ingredient, everyone gathers to cheer Junior on — except his grandfather, Pap, who's missing, and mom, who's at home worried and waiting. Sequel to *The Not-Just-Anybody Family* and *The Blossoms Meet the Vulture Lady.*

Byars, Betsy. **The Glory Girl.** Viking Penguin/Puffin Books, 1983. 122 p. ISBN 0-14-03-1785-6.

Anna Glory cannot carry a tune, but her family performs as the Glory Gospel Singers. Never in the spotlight, Anna feels like a misfit. But when her robber uncle, Newt, returns from prison, Anna feels she has found a kindred soul. The two outcasts team up to save the Glory family from the worst crisis of its career.

Byars, Betsy. **The Not-Just-Anybody Family.** Illustrated by Jacqueline Rogers. Dell/Yearling Books, 1986. 149 p. ISBN 0-440-45951-6.

When Junior Blossom wakes up in the hospital, his last memory is of crouching on the barn roof with cloth wings tied to his arms and of Maggie and Vern in the yard, urging him to fly. Meanwhile, Pap, their grandfather, sits in disgrace in the city jail after he accidentally dumped 2,147 beer and soda cans on Spring Street, disturbing the peace. With their mother away on the rodeo circuit, it's up to Maggie and Vern to find a way to rescue Pap and Junior.

Cleary, Beverly. **Ramona Forever.** Illustrated by Alan Tiegreen. Dell/Yearling Books, 1984. 182 p. ISBN 0-440-47210-5.

Mr. Quimby worries about getting a teaching job, and Ramona worries about the family having to move if he does. She gets her big chance to be bridesmaid when Aunt Bea announces she's getting married in two weeks. But can they plan a wedding in so short a time? One surprise follows another throughout the book. But the biggest surprise is one that will change Ramona's life forever. What will she say?

Cleaver, Vera. **Sugar Blue.** Lothrop, Lee and Shepard Books, 1984. 155 p. ISBN 0-688-02720-2.

Eleven-year-old Amy's world is shattered when her four-year-old niece, Ella, arrives and needs constant attention. There is no more time for being alone or for talking with her image in the mirror. Then Ella leaves, and Amy experiences a deep need to love and be loved.

Clymer, Eleanor. **The Horse in the Attic.** Illustrated by Ted Lewin. Dell/Yearling Books, 1983. 87 p. ISBN 0-440-43798-9.

The Keating family has a dream come true when they buy a house in the country. Now Mr. Keating can draw and paint, and Caroline can take riding lessons. But the old house requires more work than they ever imagined. Then Caroline makes a surprising discovery in the attic — a forgotten painting.

Collier, James Lincoln. **Outside Looking In.** Macmillan, 1987. 179 p. ISBN 0-02-723100-3.

Fourteen-year-old Fergy is tired of living in a van with his parents and his younger sister, Ooma. After Fergy's father steals a plush recreational vehicle, Fergy becomes even more disgusted and frightened. He is determined to run away with his sister and build a better life. With help from his grandparents, Fergy comes to grips with his relationships and his own expectations.

Corcoran, Barbara. **I Am the Universe.** Atheneum, 1986. 136 p. ISBN 0-689-31208-3.

"Who I Am" is the eighth-grade English assignment, and Kit finds it's not such an easy one. Beyond hating math and having a mouthful of braces, Kit is busy worrying about her eight-year-old brother's problems at school, her older brother's girlfriends, and her mom's headaches. Kit's troubles intensify when her mom has to have surgery to remove a brain tumor. Even Kit's usual writing talent fails her when she doesn't win a story contest. All these troubles, though, ultimately help Kit discover who she really is.

Corcoran, Barbara. **Strike!** Atheneum, 1984. 158 p. ISBN 0-689-30952-X.

Barry, fifteen, wants to teach shop and make fine furniture, but his father wants him to be a carbon copy of himself: a successful executive, a former All-American running back, and a member of the local school board. A teachers' strike widens the generation gap even more. Barry supports the teachers' rights against censorship and outside interference in the curriculum, while his father refuses to negotiate with the teachers. How will they resolve their differences?

Cresswell, Helen. **Bagthorpes Haunted.** Macmillan, 1985. 182 p. ISBN 0-02-725380-5.

Life with the Bagthorpes is never quiet, whether in England or in Wales. The story of the eccentric family's search for Welsh ghosts continues in this volume, which begins where *Bagthorpes Abroad* left off. Daisy's pet goat terrorizes the village, an auction makes the Bagthorpes owners of some awful objects, and flocks of sheep invade their house, while Mr. Bagthorpe's feud with the Welsh escalates. Part six of the Bagthorpe Saga.

Geller, Mark. **What I Heard.** Harper and Row/Charlotte Zolotow Books, 1987. 117 p. ISBN 0-06-022160-7 (0-06-022161-5, library binding).

Given a phone for his twelfth birthday, Michael begins to eavesdrop on his parents' phone calls. When he is discovered, his mother asks him never to do it again. Michael doesn't until one day, home sick from school, he listens to his father talk to a young woman. Michael then must sort out his feelings for his father and how this new knowledge affects the family relationships.

Guest, Elissa Haden. **Over the Moon.** William Morrow, 1986. 201 p. ISBN 0-688-04048-5.

Wanting to find out why her older sister, Mattie, ran away four years ago, sixteen-year-old Kate decides to go visit her. Losing her money, finding a new boyfriend, and coming to terms with her sister are all a part of her journey.

Hamilton, Dorothy. **Joel's Other Mother.** Illustrated by Esther Rose Graber. Herald Press, 1984. 109 p. ISBN 0-8361-3355-2.

Having an alcoholic for a mother is no fun. Joel's mother used to be pretty and fun to be with, but now she sleeps all day, never gets dressed, and staggers around the house. Joel is so ashamed of her that he no longer will let his best friend, Chris, come to his house. But something Joel unknowingly does helps his mother see herself as others see her.

Holl, Kristi D. **Footprints up My Back.** Dell/Yearling Books, 1984. 151 p. ISBN 0-440-42649-9.

Jean Harvey is tired of everyone taking advantage of her because she's so dependable — she can't say no when someone asks a favor. Jean sets up her own business and is on her way to buying Marshmallow, a cuddly cocker spaniel. But then she loans money to her unreliable older sister and fears she may never see it or Marshmallow again.

Hopper, Nancy J. **Rivals.** E. P. Dutton/Lodestar Books, 1985. 119 p. ISBN 0-525-67171-4.

When seventeen-year-old Joni learns that her cousin Kate will spend her senior year with Joni's family, Joni feels sorry for Kate and looks forward to taking care of her. But when Kate turns out to be a self-confident beauty who is quite capable of taking care of herself, Joni is confused about what her role should be. Can they ever be friends?

Hyde, Dayton O. **Thunder down the Track.** Atheneum, 1986. 171 p. ISBN 0-689-31203-2.

When ten-year-old Birch Delger's father retires from the railroad, he and Pork, a fellow railroad engineer, purchase some old train engines and deserted honeymoon cottages. With Birch's help, they start a small railroad for tourists. Then an industrial waste company decides to dump near their dream railroad.

Jarrow, Gail. **If Phyllis Were Here.** Houghton Mifflin, 1987. 132 p. ISBN 0-395-43667-2.

Everybody thinks sixth-grader Libby is old enough to look after herself now that her doting grandmother Phyllis has won the lottery and moved to Florida. Libby, however, views the situation as desertion, but what do her busy and preoccupied parents care?

Johnston, Norma. **Carlisle's Hope.** Bantam Books, 1986. 166 p. ISBN 0-553-25467-7.

Jessamyn Carlisle, fifteen, needs roots and traditions more than most teenagers because she is an "army brat" and has moved from home to home. She depends upon her favorite aunt and the Carlisle homestead to provide this sense of belonging. But Jessamyn's world falls apart with the loss of her aunt. Book one of the Carlisle Chronicles.

Konigsburg, E. L. **Up from Jericho Tel.** Atheneum, 1986. 178 p. ISBN 0-689-31194-X.

Jeanmarie Troxell and Malcolm Soo are latchkey children who feel that they are invisible. The two set out, under the hill Jericho Tel, on a journey of intrigue, adventure, and mystery to find themselves. They are given a goal to reach and must locate the three ingredients of a real star before they can become truly visible.

Landis, J. D. **Daddy's Girl.** William Morrow, 1984. 191 p. ISBN 0-688-02763-6.

Thirteen-year-old Jennie Marcowitz is in the wrong place at the wrong time when she sees her father kissing a woman who isn't his wife. Jennie doesn't know what to do next since she and her parents have always been so close. Should she confront her father? Should she tell her mother? Should she keep this terrible secret to herself?

Lasky, Kathryn. **Prank.** Dell/Laurel-Leaf Books, 1984. 171 p. ISBN 0-440-97144-6.

Sixteen-year-old Birdie Flynn is looking forward to her new job at a department store, hoping that it will take her away from a family that is always fighting. Her brother is guilty of defacing a synagogue, and her sister is frequently beaten by her husband. Birdie is determined to find a better life and future for herself.

Lindbergh, Anne. **The Worry Week.** Illustrated by Kathryn Hewitt. Harcourt Brace Jovanovich, 1985. 131 p. ISBN 0-15-299675-3.

"A whole week when we can do anything we want" is what eleven-year-old Allegra promises her sisters (thirteen-year-old Alice and seven-year-old Edith) if they go along with her plan to stay alone at the family cottage in Maine. For Allegra, the week turns into one of finding food, trying to keep her sisters from accidentally killing themselves, and searching for the treasure that is supposed to be hidden in the cottage.

Lowry, Lois. **Anastasia, Ask Your Analyst.** Houghton Mifflin, 1984. 119 p. ISBN 0-395-36011-0.

Seventh-grader Anastasia thinks her problem is her abnormal family. Then she realizes that she has become seriously disturbed and needs psychiatric help. Her parents, however, don't hold this opinion and refuse to send her to an analyst. So Anastasia spends most of a year secretly undertaking psychiatric therapy with the most famous analyst of them all.

Lowry, Lois. **Anastasia on Her Own.** Houghton Mifflin, 1985. 131 p. ISBN 0-395-38133-9.

Thirteen-year-old Anastasia and her father create the Krupnik Family Nonsexist Housekeeping Schedule to organize her frazzled mother. Soon Anastasia's organizational theories are challenged when Mrs. Krupnik goes to California for ten days and leaves Anastasia in charge of running the house. Little by little, the schedule falls apart as various emergencies occur.

MacLeod, Charlotte. **Maid of Honor.** Atheneum, 1984. 158 p. ISBN 0-689-31019-6.

The Green family is all wrapped up in preparations for their older daughter's wedding. The younger daughter, Persis, is an accomplished pianist who wins a gold medal in a state piano contest and who is awarded a college scholarship. Persis's parents and sister were too busy to attend the contest, and Persis doesn't tell them of her award. Then disaster strikes in the form of a robbery.

Martin, Ann M. **Me and Katie (the Pest).** Illustrated by Blanche Sims. Holiday House, 1985. 152 p. ISBN 0-8234-0580-X.

Wendy's sister, Katie, spies and tattles on Wendy and is successful at everything she tries. Katie has won all kinds of awards. Wendy would like to prove to herself and Katie that she can be a success, too. She decides to take riding lessons, thinking Katie won't be interested. But within a week Katie has enrolled in the same class.

Mazer, Norma Fox. **Three Sisters.** Scholastic, 1986. 231 p. ISBN 0-590-33254-6.

At age fifteen, Karen has many difficulties in her life. Being the youngest sister isn't always easy. She has to meet Grandmother's expectations and tries to impress everyone. Then there are her romantic feelings for her sister's fiancé. Can she resolve these problems?

Miller, Sandy. **Freddie the Thirteenth.** New American Library/Signet Books, 1985. 155 p. ISBN 0-451-13421-4.

Whatever possessed Freddie Oliver, the thirteenth child in a family of sixteen, to tell Bart Cunningham, the neatest boy in the whole school, that she had only *one* sister? Freddie, a new sophomore, suffers agony as her older brother Glen and Bart become friends, and Bart gets to know Glen's big boisterous family — minus Freddie, who bribes eight-year-old Danny to keep her identity secret.

Mills, Claudia. **Boardwalk with Hotel.** Macmillan, 1985. 131 p. ISBN 0-02-767010-4.

Eleven-year-old Jessica has always known she was adopted. But she just learned from a babysitter that her parents adopted her only because they thought they couldn't have children. But Julie and Brian were born soon after Jessica became a Jarrell. Jessica decides if she can't be best loved, she isn't going to be least noticed. She becomes fiercely competitive with Brian and lashes out at Julie.

Newton, Suzanne. **A Place Between.** Viking Penguin/Viking Kestrel, 1986. 201 p. ISBN 0-670-80778-8.

Too many changes, coming too fast, deal Arden Gifford the biggest blow of her thirteen years. Grandpa's death, Dad's loss of a job, and the family's moving to Grandma's house in Grierson combine to test Arden's ability to adapt. Despite efforts of her new friend Tyrone, Arden longs for her old home back in Haverlee. Just how long must her "wilderness wandering" continue?

O'Connor, Jane. **Just Good Friends.** Dell/Laurel-Leaf Books, 1983. 216 p. ISBN 0-440-94329-9.

Whom do you tell when one of your parents is having an affair? This is the question that bothers Joss as she keeps seeing her father and one of his pretty graduate students together. Her best friend, Fletcher, has been acting strangely himself. Should she tell him, or a girlfriend, or maybe even Mom?

Paterson, Katherine. **Come Sing, Jimmy Jo.** E. P. Dutton/Lodestar Books, 1985. 197 p. ISBN 0-525-67167-6.

The Johnson Family has been a singing group for over thirty years, but when the youngest member of the family, eleven-year-old James, joins the group, some major changes take place. Not only is he uprooted from his country home and moved to town, but his name is changed as well as his whole definition of a family. Then a stranger appears, and Jimmy Jo begins to wonder who he really is.

Pfeffer, Susan Beth. **Kid Power Strikes Back.** Illustrated by Leigh Grant. Franklin Watts, 1984. 116 p. ISBN 0-531-04839-X.

Janie Golden created Kid Power to earn money for a bike. After school begins, there isn't much time for working, and the business just about dies. With the arrival of winter and snow, Kid Power comes back to life with snow-shoveling jobs. A rival group also wants the shoveling jobs, and Janie must learn to negotiate and hold onto her jobs. Sequel to *Kid Power.*

Pfeffer, Susan Beth. **The Year without Michael.** Bantam Books, 1987. 164 p. ISBN 0-553-05430-9.

It couldn't happen. Thirteen-year-old Michael Chapman couldn't just disappear without a trace. As Jody, sixteen, and her younger sister, Kay, survive the nightmarish months following their brother's disappearance, they must deal with their mother's irrational behavior and their father's withdrawal. Also, they must learn to handle their own contradictory feelings.

Porte, Barbara Ann. **The Kidnapping of Aunt Elizabeth.** Greenwillow Books, 1985. 141 p. ISBN 0-688-04302-X.

Ashley's parents do not believe in sharing the secrets of their family history. When Ashley is assigned to complete a family history project for her social studies class, she cleverly disguises her probing questions in order to piece together the history of her ancestors. Ashley and her family uncover many tales and tall tales that mesh together to create an unusual and comical family story.

Robinson, Nancy K. **Oh Honestly, Angela!** Scholastic, 1985. 114 p. ISBN 0-590-32983-9.

Most of the time Tina likes having a little sister. But sometimes Angela drives her crazy. Tina wants the family to help those less fortunate by "adopting" an orphan through the Rescue the Children program. Angela doesn't understand, and Tina often explodes with, "Oh honestly, Angela!"

Ruby, Lois. **Pig-Out Inn.** Houghton Mifflin, 1987. 171 p. ISBN 0-395-42714-2.

Fourteen-year-old Dovi Chandler contributes her entire pig collection to decorate her mother's newly acquired truckstop restaurant. Once Johnny learns to cook, they are in business. When a trucker leaves his nine-year-old son, Tag, in their care, the family becomes involved in much more than just the restaurant business.

Sachs, Marilyn. **Almost Fifteen.** E. P. Dutton, 1987. 135 p. ISBN 0-525-44285-5.

Isn't it terrible when your boyfriend breaks up with you before you can break up with him? Thirteen-year-old Imogen thinks so until she starts her new babysitting job. Why does she change her mind?

Smith, Robert Kimmel. **Mostly Michael.** Illustrated by Katherine Coville. Delacorte Press, 1987. 184 p. ISBN 0-385-29545-6.

When Michael Marder receives a diary for his eleventh birthday, he is angry and disappointed, but the diary becomes the one place where he can express his private feelings. As he writes, his feelings begin to change. He even starts to like himself. But most important, Michael discovers a love for his family he never knew he felt, even when big changes occur at home.

Sommer, Sarah. **And I'm Stuck with Joseph.** Illustrated by Ivan Moon. Herald Press, 124 p. ISBN 0-8361-3356-0.

Sheila Shenk, entering sixth grade, wants a baby sister just like her friends have. At first her parents don't respond, even though she promises to help with the extra work. Then Sheila's parents announce plans to adopt — not a baby sister but a three-year-old brother, who turns out to be a difficult child and almost impossible to love. Sheila wonders, "Why did God do this to me?"

Springstubb, Tricia. **Which Way to the Nearest Wilderness?** Dell/Yearling Books, 1984. 166 p. ISBN 0-440-49554-7.

Eleven-year-old Eunice Gottlieb decides to run away because she is tired of solving her family's problems. Then her parents have an argument that is worse than usual. Eunice must decide whether to carry out her plans to leave or whether to stay and help again.

Storr, Catherine. **February Yowler.** Illustrated by Gareth Floyd. Faber and Faber, 1982. 76 p. ISBN 0-571-11854-2.

Freddie Roberts starts out in trouble on his first day at a new school. He can't remember to answer to "Freddie" since his real name is February Yowler. But Freddie makes friends with Rorey and begins to share some information about life with his rich and famous parents.

Tapp, Kathy Kennedy. **Smoke from the Chimney.** Atheneum/Margaret K. McElderry Books, 1986. 169 p. ISBN 0-689-50389-X.

After reading the original Tarzan stories, Erin Callahan and her friend Heather Prescott fantasize their own jungle hideaway. For Erin it becomes an escape from her father's alcoholism. The more her father drinks, the more Erin escapes to the rooftop jungle she has created. A chain of events forces Erin to confront her father and face the realities of his illness.

Tolan, Stephanie S. **The Great Skinner Enterprise.** Four Winds Press, 1986. 175 p. ISBN 0-02-789270-0.

The Skinner family is at it again. This time Dad has lost his job but is determined to establish a family business called At Your Service. All the family members will share in the work and profits as they run errands, walk dogs, shop, and transport kids to and from various appointments. Sequel to *The Great Skinner Strike.*

Tolan, Stephanie S. **The Great Skinner Strike.** New American Library/Signet Vista Books, 1985. 156 p. ISBN 0-451-13345-5.

How embarrassing for Jenny, Ben, Marcia, and Rick Skinner when their mother pitches strike headquarters on the front lawn and walks off her job as mother, wife, and woman of all work. Fourteen-year-old Jenny and her siblings come to realize why their mother feels she has to make her statement regarding a "woman's place." But will Jenny's very traditional father capitulate to the demands?

Weller, Frances Ward. **Boat Song.** Macmillan, 1987. 168 p. ISBN 0-02-792611-7.

Spending summer vacation at the beach is a treat for eleven-year-old Jonno, even if it means hearing continual criticisms from a father who doesn't approve of him. A mysterious visitor and a daring rescue in the fog give Jonno new confidence in himself. But can he win his father's approval?

White, Ellen Emerson. **White House Autumn.** Avon Books/Flare Books, 1985. 209 p. ISBN 0-380-89780-6.

Meghan Powers, seventeen, must deal with the usual problems of dating, family relationships, and making choices for the future. But added to these pressures is the fact that Meghan's mother is president of the United States. An assassination attempt brings Meghan's feelings to the critical point.

Williams, Barbara. **Mitzi and Frederick the Great.** Illustrated by Emily Arnold McCully. Dell/Yearling Books, 1987. 113 p. ISBN 0-440-45867-6.

Mitzi McAllister is spending the summer on an archaeological dig with her mother and stepbrother, Frederick. She feels grown up, but all the adults are so tickled with "Frederick the Great." Why doesn't anybody care about the strange creature she saw? Frederick seems to be a scaredy-cat who'd rather read than anything else, while Mitzi is sure she's the brave one — until the tables are turned.

Wolitzer, Meg. **Caribou.** Greenwillow Books, 1985. 167 p. ISBN 0-688-03991-X.

When Becca Silverman's brother Stevie decides to go to Canada to dodge being drafted and being sent to Vietnam, Becca begins to look at the world in a different way. There is trouble at home — her father thought Stevie should join the army. Becca also must deal with challenges at school, an art contest, and a close friendship with Kate.

Wright, Betty Ren. **The Summer of Mrs. MacGregor.** Holiday House, 1986. 157 p. ISBN 0-8234-0628-8.

Linda is seriously ill with a heart problem, yet her twelve-year-old sister, Caroline, is jealous of all the attention Linda receives, her attractive looks, and her sweet disposition. All seems lost for this ugly duckling until she meets seventeen-year-old Mrs.

MacGregor, who is able to help Caroline improve her self-image. But Caroline begins to doubt that Lillina MacGregor is telling her the truth about her life.

Divorce and Single Parents

Adler, C. S. **Split Sisters.** Macmillan, 1986. 161 p. ISBN 0-02-700380-9.

Eleven-year-old Case is willing to go to extremes to keep her mother and father from separating and her world from changing. Although Case's sister, Jen, may be ready for some changes, Case is determined that the sisters must stay together no matter what.

Ames, Mildred. **Cassandra-Jamie.** Charles Scribner's Sons, 1985. 135 p. ISBN 0-684-18472-9.

Cassandra-Jamie has a new wife picked for her father and tries every way she knows to get the two of them together. Mr. Cole, however, has found someone else and is not really interested in Jamie's junior high English teacher.

Bates, Betty. **Thatcher Payne-in-the-Neck.** Illustrated by Linda Strauss Edwards. Holiday House, 1985. 130 p. ISBN 0-8234-0584-2.

Kib Slocum and Thatcher Payne enjoy hanging out together at Trout Lake every summer. Thatcher's father and Kib's mother were killed in a plane crash, and the two friends come up with the bright idea of matching up their surviving parents. When the parents decide to marry, things begin to go downhill — for Kib, at least.

Beatty, Patricia. **Behave Yourself, Bethany Brant.** William Morrow, 1986. 172 p. ISBN 0-688-05923-6.

Preachers' children have difficult lives. So thinks Bethany Brant, especially after her mother dies. Everyone expects her to be perfect, even though she seems to enjoy getting into trouble. But her most important escapade involves building the new church for her father.

Betancourt, Jeanne. **Turtle Time.** Avon Books/Camelot Books, 1985. 96 p. ISBN 0-380-39675-3.

Aviva's school year begins with a teacher who looks like Mr. T and who runs the classroom like a military camp. Then her mom's boyfriend, George, moves into the house. Aviva's friends think she has a crush on Josh Greene, when all Aviva wants to do is beat him in basketball. And Josh just wants Aviva to take care of his turtle, Myrtle. Sometimes Aviva would like to do what Myrtle does — just crawl into her shell and hide.

Bograd, Larry. **Poor Gertie.** Illustrated by Dirk Zimmer. Delacorte Press, 1986. 103 p. ISBN 0-385-29487-5.

Ten-year-old Gertie can make all the world's problems disappear by creating a world where everything is perfect — and naming it after herself. When she thinks of Mom's dreary job or begins worrying about the rent for the apartment, Gertie can draw pictures of Gertsworld and pretend she's safe there. Gertie is an inventive and sensitive girl who learns that dreams can come true in unexpected ways.

Bridgers, Sue Ellen. **Permanent Connections.** Harper and Row, 1987. 264 p. ISBN 0-06-020711-6 (0-06-020712-4, library binding).

Seventeen-year-old Rob is doing poorly in school and is experimenting with drugs. He is sent to North Carolina to help care for an uncle who has broken his hip. Rob dislikes his new life until he falls in love with Ellery, a beautiful, talented girl who has just moved to the area. Despite his self-destructive behavior involving alcohol and pot, Rob learns that what he does affects others, and they in turn affect him. (Literary merit)

Burch, Robert. **Christmas with Ida Early.** Viking Penguin/Puffin Books, 1985. 157 p. ISBN 0-14-031971-9.

Over six feet tall and wearing overalls, Ida Early keeps house for the motherless Sutton family in rural Georgia during the Depression of the 1930s. The Sutton children attempt to get the new minister interested in Ida during the holiday season. Sequel to *Ida Early Comes over the Mountain.*

Calvert, Patricia. **Yesterday's Daughter.** Charles Scribner's Sons, 1986. 137 p. ISBN 0-684-18746-9.

Sixteen-year-old Lennie O'Brien, tall and gangly, prefers to be a tomboy roaming the swamp rather than to be at all like her mother, who became pregnant at seventeen. Lennie is angry with her mother for leaving her as an infant, and she determines to reject her mother forever. As she guides a young photographer around the swamp, however, Lennie begins to see her life from a new perspective.

Chambers, John W. **Footlight Summer.** Atheneum, 1983. 194 p. ISBN 0-689-30980-5.

Chris Abbot and her friend Sherry Baxter sign up eagerly as junior apprentices at the Lion Rock Playhouse. They work with the technical staff and at the end of the season present a play of their own. They don't understand the dislike Sherry's mother has for the theater until she is overheard talking to one of the actors.

Colman, Hila. **Just the Two of Us.** Scholastic, 1984. 168 p. ISBN 0-590-32512-4.

Fourteen-year-old Samantha and her father, Lenny, get along just fine, so what gives Liz the right to interfere? Since her mother's death, Sammy has traveled the country with Lenny as he opens new restaurants. But now that Lenny has settled down and opened his own place, Sammy faces the problem of making real friends for the first time. Even worse, Lenny is talking about remarrying.

Colman, Hila. **Weekend Sisters.** William Morrow, 1985. 169 p. ISBN 0-688-05785-3.

Fourteen-year-old Mandy loses everything: her family to divorce, her father to a new wife, and her boyfriend to a new stepsister who lies and steals and who causes trouble between Mandy and her father. What is the right way to deal with these problems?

Conrad, Pam. **Holding Me Here.** Harper and Row, 1986. 184 p. ISBN 0-06-021338-8 (0-06-021339-6, library binding).

Fourteen-year-old Robin's parents have gone through an amicable divorce. Her mother rents Robin's old playroom to Mary Walker, a battered wife who has left her husband and children. Robin decides she will help Mary become reunited with her family, but her plan backfires, causing Robin to look at the world of adults with new eyes — a world where parents do become divorced and children suffer from the separation.

Corcoran, Barbara. **Face the Music.** Atheneum, 1985. 178 p. ISBN 0-689-31139-7.

Marcie's love of music and her need to play the guitar with a small performing group cause friction with her mother, who has grown to depend on Marcie since her divorce from Marcie's father. Marcie must somehow break away from her mother without destroying the mother-daughter relationship.

Dana, Barbara. **Necessary Parties.** Harper and Row/Charlotte Zolotow Books, 1986. 341 p. ISBN 0-06-021408-2 (0-06-021409-0, library binding).

Fifteen-year-old Chris Mill's parents are getting a divorce. As his family starts to fall apart, Chris fears all their lives are going down the drain. With the help of an eccentric lawyer/auto mechanic and an irascible grandfather, Chris forces a situation in his family that changes the course of all their lives.

Davis, Jenny. **Good-bye and Keep Cold.** Orchard Books, 1987. 210 p. ISBN 0-531-05715-1 (0-531-08315-2, library binding).

After Edda's father dies in a strip-mine accident, her mother becomes romantically involved with Henry John. But he is the one responsible for her father's death. Edda, on the brink of adulthood, can't figure out how the adult world works.

DeClements, Barthe. **No Place for Me.** Viking Penguin/Viking Kestrel, 1987. 136 p. ISBN 0-670-81908-5.

Due to the alcoholism of her mother, seventh-grader Copper Jones has lived with one relative after another since the death of her father. So far none of the relatives has provided her with the "perfect" family that she longs for. Then Copper is sent to live with Aunt Maggie, who everyone thinks is a witch. Copper discovers that Aunt Maggie has a lot to offer and that maybe her future is not quite as bleak as she feared.

Fleischman, Paul. **Rear-View Mirrors.** Harper and Row/Charlotte Zolotow Books, 1986. 117 p. ISBN 0-06-021866-5 (0-06-021867-3, library binding).

At sixteen, Olivia goes to New Hampshire from her California home to visit the father she has not seen since she was eight months old. Olivia discovers a world of butterflies, the Red Sox, mosquitoes, and Bluebird ale. She and her father slowly develop a bond of kinship. Now, one year later, Olivia is returning to New Hampshire after her father's accidental death to claim her legacy — not only a house but a different way of seeing the world.

Fox, Paula. **The Moonlight Man.** Bradbury Press, 1986. 179 p. ISBN 0-02-735480-6.

Fifteen-year-old Catherine Ames has never spent more than just an occasional day with her father because her parents have been divorced for so long. Now she and her father are to spend weeks together in Nova Scotia. But her father is three weeks late in picking her up at boarding school, and Catherine soon discovers that alcohol is directing his life and entangling their relationship. (Literary merit)

Froehlich, Margaret Walden. **Reasons to Stay.** Houghton Mifflin, 1986. 181 p. ISBN 0-395-41068-1.

When Mama dies, twelve-year-old Babe's life changes — especially when the "secret" is revealed by the town busybody. Suddenly the man whom she'd called Pa is now Mr. Garber, and Babe is drawn to another family, the Petersons.

Hamilton, Dorothy. **Carlie's Pink Room.** Illustrated by Esther Rose Graber. Herald Press, 1984. 83 p. ISBN 0-8361-3354-4.

Carlie moves to a mobile home with her family when her father leaves, but she feels crowded and longs for a room of her own. Then Carlie discovers an abandoned studio, which she thinks of as her own Pink Room. As she spends time alone there, Carlie's feelings about her crowded mobile home become more favorable.

Hamilton, Dorothy. **Winter Caboose.** Illustrated by James Converse. Herald Press, 1983. 107 p. ISBN 0-8361-3341-2.

Jody doesn't know what to say when his father wants to come back. Now that he is eleven, Jody is a big help to his mother, and they are doing just fine living in the Blue Caboose. He is even helping his new friend Carlos and the Mendez family adjust to American life. Were his father's reasons for leaving the family good enough to welcome him back? Jody must decide. Sequel to *The Blue Caboose.*

Hurwitz, Johanna. **DeDe Takes Charge!** Illustrated by Diane de Groat. William Morrow, 1984. 121 p. ISBN 0-688-03853-0.

Fifth-grader DeDe's parents are divorced. She must face the fact that her father has left home for good. DeDe tries to help her mother adjust to the realities of their new life.

Klass, Sheila Solomon. **Page Four.** Charles Scribner's Sons, 1986. 166 p. ISBN 0-684-18745-0.

David Smith, Jr., a high school senior, has it all: the perfect home and parents, good grades and friends, and a position on the varsity basketball team. Then David's world falls apart. His father leaves for Alaska to start a new life with a younger woman. Out of spite and bitterness, David nearly destroys his own life.

Klein, Norma. **Angel Face.** Viking Press, 1984. 208 p. ISBN 0-670-12517-2.

Sixteen-year-old Jason discovers that it's not always easy to keep a delicate balance between the ups and downs in life. His father walks out, leaving Jason with his slightly crazy mother. Then Jason finds out that his classmate Vicki thinks he's terrific.

Luger, Harriett. **The Un-Dudding of Roger Judd.** Viking Press, 1983. 137 p. ISBN 0-670-73886-7.

Sixteen-year-old Roger Judd lives with his father, stepmother, and half-sister, Vanessa, whom he dislikes. Roger has trouble with school and with girls and misses his mother. After an explosive disagreement, Roger is sent to New York to visit his mother, a recovering alcoholic. When his mother imposes rules on his behavior, Roger discovers that acceptance of rules and responsibility is part of growing up.

MacLachlan, Patricia. **Sarah, Plain and Tall.** Harper and Row, 1985. 58 p. ISBN 0-06-024101-2 (0-06-024102-0, library binding).

Caleb and Anna are captivated by the mail-order bride who answers their father's ad and comes to live with the family in their prairie home. But Sarah misses the sea, her brother, and the three old aunts. When Sarah takes the wagon to town alone, Caleb and Anna worry. What happens tells much about happiness and hope and about what it is that makes a family. (Literary merit — Newbery Medal)

Mahoney, Mary Reeves. **The Hurry-up Summer.** G. P. Putnam's Sons, 1987. 191 p. ISBN 0-399-21430-5.

Twelve-year-old Letty is faced with the possibility of boarding school. She no longer has Maria to care for her at home, and now her father seems very serious about a woman companion. Letty must somehow try to convince her father that she is old enough to make her own decisions.

Moore, Ruth Nulton. **Danger in the Pines.** Illustrated by James Converse. Herald Press, 1983. 164 p. ISBN 0-8361-3313-7 (0-8361-33145, paperback).

Fourteen-year-old Jeff's world turns upside down with his father's death. Moving from a ranch in Wyoming to city life in Philadelphia is more than Jeff can handle until he discovers the Pinelands of New Jersey. But what begins as a pleasant hike soon turns into a nightmare of quicksand, wild dogs, and danger for his newfound friends as a forest fire rages.

Morris, Judy K. **The Crazies and Sam.** Viking Penguin/Puffin Books, 1985. 136 p. ISBN 0-14-031833-X.

The crazies hold a special fascination for sixth-grader Sam Siefenback as he follows their antics through the streets of Washington, D.C. The lives of the street people seem carefree, while Sam feels his divorced father places far too many restrictions on him. When a case of the "crazies" prompts Sam to ride home with a stranger, will his own wit and the help of a new friend be sufficient to return Sam to the world he suddenly learns to value?

Mulford, Philippa Greene. **The World Is My Eggshell.** Delacorte Press, 1986. 157 p. ISBN 0-385-29432-8.

Sixteen-year-olds Abbey and Shell Reilly are twins, but they have little in common. When their father dies and the family moves to a different town, Abbey must learn how to adapt to her new life and to develop her own identity.

Naylor, Phyllis Reynolds. **The Agony of Alice.** Atheneum, 1985. 131 p. ISBN 0-689-31143-5.

Alice McKinney is about to become a teenager but doesn't know how. Her mother is dead, and she gets little guidance from her father and her nineteen-year-old brother, who is a slob. When Alice enters a new school, she hopes to be in the class of beautiful Miss Cole, but she draws homely Mrs. Plotkin instead. How can she serve as a role model for Alice?

Naylor, Phyllis Reynolds. **Night Cry.** Atheneum, 1985. 154 p. ISBN 0-689-31017-X.

Ellen is often left alone at the cabin and five-acre plot in Mississippi because her father is a traveling salesman. She is careful to avoid Sleet, the horse that threw and killed her brother. New fears are stirred in Ellen when a stranger and his wife arrive at the cabin, a child is kidnapped, and it looks like Ellen's father and Granny Bo are somehow involved.

Naylor, Phyllis Reynolds. **The Solomon System.** Atheneum, 1983. 210 p. ISBN 0-689-30991-0.

Ted, fourteen, and Nory, sixteen, have always been close. This summer the brothers go to camp as usual, but everything seems different to Ted. Maybe it's because their parents are separating. Both Ted and Nory must reevaluate their relationship and their expectations of each other.

Nelson, Theresa. **The 25¢ Miracle.** Bradbury Press, 1986. 214 p. ISBN 0-02-724370-2.

Eleven-year-old Ellie has more than her share of ups and downs. Her mother is dead, her father is unemployed most of the time, and she fears being shipped off to live with her Aunt Darla, a fat busybody. Ellie hopes to find a wife for her father, but her attempts at matchmaking trigger a chain of mishaps.

Osborne, Mary Pope. **Love Always, Blue.** E. P. Dutton/Dial Books for Young Readers, 1984. 183 p. ISBN 0-8037-0031-8.

Blue does not understand why her parents have separated, and she blames her mother for the breakup of the marriage. Her father goes to New York's Greenwich Village to live, and after much pleading, Blue is permitted to visit him. She is stunned when she sees her father's dingy apartment. Blue begins to realize he has an illness and sadness that even her love cannot penetrate.

Parker, Cam. **Camp Off-the-Wall.** Avon Books/Camelot Books, 1987. 120 p. ISBN 0-380-75196-8.

Twelve-year-old Tiffin's happy home life starts falling apart when her parents separate and she is shipped off to camp. Camp Chucalucup is the wackiest place in the world. Soon Tiffin's mother is renting a place on camp property, and her father is camping out in a nearby tree house. Can they resolve their problems?

Perske, Robert. **Show Me No Mercy.** Abingdon Press, 1984. 144 p. ISBN 0-687-38435-4.

Andy Banks, paralyzed in an accident that kills his wife and teenage daughter, struggles to overcome his disability. Can he also keep his teenage son, who has Down's syndrome, from being institutionalized?

Pryor, Bonnie. **Rats, Spiders, and Love.** Illustrated by J. Winslow Higginbottom. William Morrow, 1986. 116 p. ISBN 0-688-05867-1.

Samantha loves her oceanside home, but if her mother marries Jim, the family will move to Ohio. Sam has found a better "father candidate" — her science teacher. She determines she will have to be very good, very bad, or very sick in science class to arrange a meeting between her mother and the teacher. Sam tries them all! In the process, her feelings change about a lot of things — rats, spiders, love, Jim, and herself.

Rinaldi, Ann. **But in the Fall I'm Leaving.** Holiday House, 1985. 250 p. ISBN 0-8234-0560-5.

Brieanna McQuade decides she can tolerate her father's strictness and her brother's overprotectiveness just until fall. Then she'll leave to live with her mother in California. After all, stories that her mother abandoned Brie when she was four are ridiculous — or are they? (Literary merit)

Rodowsky, Colby. **Fitchett's Folly.** Farrar, Straus and Giroux, 1987. 166 p. ISBN 0-374-32342-9.

Sarey's father is gone, her stepmother is working, and an orphan girl named Faith has moved in with the family, so Sarey is spending her summer working inside while the other children are out playing. When Sarey's plan to find a new home for Faith falls through, she must face the truth on the slippery, haunted rocks of Fitchett's Folly.

Rodowsky, Colby. **Julie's Daughter.** Farrar, Straus and Giroux, 1985. 231 p. ISBN 0-374-33963-5.

Slug has never known the mother who abandoned her seventeen years ago at the bus depot, and she is not at all sure that she wants to go to live with this woman. But after Grandma Gussie dies, that is the only place for Slug to live. She and her mother begin to build a relationship as they care for a dying neighbor.

Sirof, Harriet. **The Real World.** Franklin Watts, 1985. 184 p. ISBN 0-531-10080-4.

Cady, fifteen, has been raised by her mother in an all-female commune. She has grown up accepting the idea that she must change the world to live in it. But when she visits her father, a successful architect, Cady sees that people can adapt to the world as it is and can still be happy. The conflict increases when Cady's mother leads a female carpenter's strike at her father's construction site. Which values will Cady choose?

Smith, Doris Buchanan. **Return to Bitter Creek.** Viking Penguin/Viking Kestrel, 1986. 174 p. ISBN 0-670-80783-4.

Lacey, twelve years old, is returning to Southern Appalachia with her mother, who left the area when Lacey was a baby. There is a large extended family ready to give their love as long as Lacey lives up to their expectations. Lacey discovers a special cousin and has a horse all her own. But there are problems for Lacey, and a tragedy occurs that sets her world spinning. (Literary merit)

Smith, Doris Buchanan. **Tough Chauncey.** Viking Penguin/Puffin Books, 1986. 222 p. ISBN 0-14-031928-X.

Living first with his irresponsible mother and then his cruel grandfather has taught Chauncey one lesson in his thirteen years: if you want to survive, get tough. Can a kitten called Little Orange and a friend named Black Jack change Chauncey's idea of toughness? (Literary merit)

Snyder, Zilpha Keatley. **The Birds of Summer.** Atheneum, 1984. 195 p. ISBN 0-689-30967-8.

Fifteen-year-old Summer lives in a trailer with her mother, Oriole, and a younger sister, Sparrow. Oriole is neither a very predictable nor responsible mother, and Summer fears that she is involved with growing marijuana in the hills of Alameda County, California. Summer goes to work for two different families as housekeeper and plots a change of life for herself and Sparrow. (Literary merit)

Stone, Bruce. **Half Nelson, Full Nelson.** Harper and Row, 1985. 218 p. ISBN 0-06-025921-3 (0-06-025922-1, library binding).

Nelson Gato is called Half Nelson in honor of his dad's imaginary career as a professional wrestler. When his parents separate, Nelson's mother takes Vanessa, his little sister, with her. Nelson and his friend Heidi concoct a plan to kidnap Vanessa and bring his family back together.

Voigt, Cynthia. **A Solitary Blue.** Atheneum, 1983. 189 p. ISBN 0-689-31008-0.

Jeff Green's mother, Melody, left him and his perfectionist father, the Professor, when he was only seven so that she could work for social causes she believed in, like nuclear disarmament and preserving endangered species. Now, four years later, Melody invites Jeff to spend the summer with her in South Carolina. He soon places her in the center of his world, adoring her beauty and quick wit. But Melody unwittingly betrays Jeff, and he understands for the first time how hurt his father was. Crushed, Jeff turns to Dicey Tillerman, from the novels *Dicey's Song* and *Homecoming,* for friendship and support. (Literary merit)

Foster Parents and No Parents

Adler, C. S. **Some Other Summer.** Macmillan, 1982. 126 p. ISBN 0-02-700290-X.

Lynette, twelve, is an orphan living with her uncle and his family on a ranch. Jeremy, her seventeen-year-old best friend, no longer has much time for Lynette, especially when her pretty cousin Debbi is around. Lynette feels that her place in Jeremy's affection is as uncertain as her place in Uncle Josh's family. Sequel to *The Magic of the Glits.*

Branscum, Robbie. **The Adventures of Johnny May.** Illustrated by Deborah Howland. Harper and Row, 1984. 87 p. ISBN 0-06-020614-4 (0-06-020615-2, library binding).

Eleven-year-old Johnny May, who lives in the hills of Arkansas, struggles to provide a good Christmas for her grandpa and grandma by killing a deer. But she is troubled — she witnessed a murder and is uncertain whether she should report it.

Conrad, Pam. **What I Did for Roman.** Harper and Row, 1987. 218 p. ISBN 0-06-021331-0 (0-06-021332-9, library binding).

Fifteen-year-old Darcie is spending the summer with her aunt and uncle while her mother is on a honeymoon with her new husband. Darcie searches for the reason why her own father disappeared before she was born. She also befriends a zoo worker, who leads her to a desperate decision inside the lions' den.

Cresswell, Helen. **Dear Shrink.** Macmillan, 1982. 186 p. ISBN 0-02-725560-3.

A living nightmare! While their parents explore the Amazon River, two English teenage brothers and their little sister are left in the care of an elderly nanny. The woman dies suddenly, and the children's nightmare begins. They have no relatives, and their parents cannot be reached, so the children are sent to different foster homes. Can they cope?

Eige, Lillian. **Cady.** Illustrated by Janet Wentworth. Harper and Row, 1987. 183 p. ISBN 0-06-021792-8 (0-06-021793-6, library binding).

Passed around from relative to relative, twelve-year-old Cady finally comes to live with Thea McVey, a stranger who won't tell him who she is or why he has been sent to live with her. Cady feels like an outcast, as do the two neighborhood children whose mother has sent them to live with an uncle. This odd assortment of people, plus a hermit Cady meets in the woods, begins to become a family for Cady as he learns about his past.

Gibbons, Faye. **Mighty Close to Heaven.** William Morrow, 1985. 183 p. ISBN 0-688-04147-7.

Twelve-year-old Dave Lawson lives with his grandparents on a Georgia farm. He is expected to work like a man, and he resents the demands made on him. Dave decides to leave this life behind and to find his dad, who is rumored to be living in a little town across the mountain. There Dave hopes to find he is wanted and appreciated.

Hamilton, Dorothy. **Ken's Bright Room.** Illustrated by James L. Converse. Herald Press, 1983. 86 p. ISBN 0-8361-3327-7 (0-8361-3328-5, paperback).

After getting in trouble with his mother and the police for running away from home, Ken tries to build up trust and a new life for himself with new friends. He starts a greenhouse business with Frank and tries to steer clear of bad friends and bad times. Sequel to *Ken's Hideout.*

Jones, Adrienne. **Street Family.** Harper and Row/Charlotte Zolotow Books, 1987. 274 p. ISBN 0-06-023049-5 (0-06-023050-9, library binding).

What happens to the homeless in big cities is the subject of this story. A fourteen-year-old boy running away from an abusive stepfather, a fifteen-year-old girl trying to avoid the threat of prostitution, two eighteen-year-old mental misfits, an alcoholic Vietnam vet, and a bag lady join together for survival. Living under a Los Angeles freeway, the group begins to think of itself as a family facing an uncertain future.

Mazer, Norma Fox. **Downtown.** William Morrow, 1984. 216 p. ISBN 0-688-03859-X.

Fifteen-year-old Pete Greenwood tells everyone that his parents are dead, but actually they are fugitives from the law. They went into hiding eight years ago when their peace group accidentally killed two people in an antiwar demonstration. In all that time, Pete received only an occasional letter, phone call, or secretly arranged visit. Now his mother reappears and wants to come back into his life.

Miller, Frances A. **Aren't You the One Who . . .?** Atheneum, 1983. 224 p. ISBN 0-689-30961-9.

The newspaper headlines said that a teenage boy murdered a young girl, but sixteen-year-old Matt McKendrick has been cleared by the police. Now he is living with police officer Ryder and his family. Matt knows for certain that he never killed his younger sister, Katie, but he fears everyone will say, "Aren't you the one who . . .?" Sequel to *The Truth Trap.*

Nixon, Joan Lowery. **Maggie, Too.** Harcourt Brace Jovanovich, 1985. 101 p. ISBN 0-15-250350-1.

Margaret Ledoux is a lonely twelve-year-old whose father, a famous Hollywood director, constantly sends her away to boarding schools. This time she is to spend the summer with her grandmother in Houston, Texas. Bewildered by the hubbub of the large family surrounding her grandmother, Margaret wants to run away — until she realizes that her grandmother needs to get away even more.

Stepparents

Lowry, Lois. **Switcharound.** Dell/Yearling Books, 1987. 118 p. ISBN 0-440-48415-4.

Caroline Tate, age eleven, and her thirteen-year-old brother, J.P., are miserable about leaving New York to spend the summer with their father and his new family in Des Moines, Iowa. Caroline, who hates babies, is expected to babysit the six-month-old twins, and J.P., who hates sports, has to coach six-year-old Poochie's baseball team. The brother and sister decide they must take action.

Lutz, Norma Jean. **Good-bye, Beedee.** David C. Cook/Chariot Books, 1986. 127 p. ISBN 0-89191-738-1.

Marcia, thirteen, leaves her grandparents' farm and moves to the city with her father and his new wife. Life there is terrible, and Marcia devises a scheme to bring her horse, Beedee, to the city, too. But her scheme nearly leads to tragedy.

McGraw, Eloise. **Hideaway.** Atheneum/Margaret K. McElderry Books, 1983. 217 p. ISBN 0-689-50284-2.

Twelve-year-old Jerry's mother has married a stranger with three kids. Jerry's father has "forgotten" that Jerry was to stay with him during the wedding trip. So Jerry goes to his grandparents' house on the Oregon coast — only to find his grandparents gone and sixteen-year-old Hanna watching the house. Now what does he do?

McHugh, Elisabet. **Karen and Vicki.** Greenwillow Books, 1984. 150 p. ISBN 0-688-02543-9.

Karen's special seventh-grade project is to organize her family's activities to save time. Her teacher says the project sounds good enough to win a science fair prize. But can Karen really organize a family of nine people who haven't even adjusted to living together? Sequel to *Raising a Mother Isn't Easy* and *Karen's Sister.*

Nixon, Joan Lowery. **And Maggie Makes Three.** Harcourt Brace Jovanovich, 1986. 112 p. ISBN 0-15-250355-2.

Maggie's famous father was too busy to come see her perform the major role she captured, so why does he have to come see her now? Besides, he is bringing his new wife, and twelve-year-old Maggie definitely does not want to meet her. Sequel to *Maggie, Too.*

Senn, Steve. **In the Castle of the Bear.** Atheneum, 1985. 135 p. ISBN 0-689-31167-2.

Twelve-year-old Jason is unhappy to have a new stepmother, especially one like Lauren. She is determined that Jason follow her rules for responsible behavior. Then Jason and his friend Cleve happen onto some old books about witchcraft, and Jason becomes aware of the signs of magic surrounding Lauren.

Sharmat, Marjorie. **Two Guys Noticed Me . . . and Other Miracles.** Dell/Laurel-Leaf Books, 1986. 149 p. ISBN 0-440-98846-2.

After Jody's mother spends two years finding herself, she returns and expects to be treated as before. But Jody's father has made plans to marry the mother of Jody's boyfriend. Can this mess be untangled?

Williams, Barbara. **Mitzi's Honeymoon with Nana Potts.** Illustrated by Emily Arnold McCully. Dell/Yearling Books, 1983. 104 p. ISBN 0-440-45674-6.

When her mother remarries, Mitzi finds herself stuck with two stepbrothers, bossy Frederick and Darwin, a little genius who thinks he's a *Tyrannosaurus rex.* And then there's Frederick and Darwin's grandmother, Nana Potts. She thinks Darwin is smart and adorable, she fails to see how helpful Mitzi can be, and she doesn't even seem to know Mitzi's name. Can Mitzi turn this disaster into a victory?

Fantasy

Alexander, Lloyd. **The Beggar Queen.** E. P. Dutton, 1984. 237 p. ISBN 0-525-44103-4.

The defenders of Westmark, who have established their government with Mickle as queen, must defend themselves. Their old enemy, Cabbarus, returns with the help of Duke Conrad of Regia. Old and new friends must unite to fight for freedom once more.

Anthony, Piers. **Golem in the Gears.** Ballantine Books/Del Rey Books, 1986. 326 p. ISBN 0-345-31886-2.

Tiny Grundy Golem searches for his friend Ivy's pet dragon. On this quest, he falls in love with Rapunzel, prisoner of the dreaded Sea Hag. Grundy helps Rapunzel escape, but the Sea Hag pursues them to recover Rapunzel, her prize possession. Part of the Xanth series.

Asch, Frank. **Pearl's Pirates.** Illustrated by the author. Delacorte Press, 1987. 167 p. ISBN 0-385-29546-4.

When Jay is injured in a bike accident, his pet mice, Pearl and Wilbur, are left on their own. Trapped in a crate in a warehouse, they soon find themselves in a ship on the way to France. The two mice and their friends launch the captain's model pirate ship and sail to Frog Island in search of pirate treasure.

Belden, Wilanne Schneider. **The Rescue of Ranor.** Atheneum/Argo Books, 1983. 173 p. ISBN 0-689-30951-1.

Sixteen-year-old White Witch Minna is called upon by a Non, Sven Pentalion, to rescue his troublemaker brother, Ranor, from the Black Enchanter. As they travel to the combat with Minna's goblin/demon familiar, Ordure, and Prilla, a cat/witch, Sven and Minna make some startling discoveries about themselves and the separate worlds in which they live.

Bell, Clare. **Clan Ground.** Atheneum/Margaret K. McElderry Books and Argo Books, 1984. 258 p. ISBN 0-689-50304-0.

Ratha is the leader of the Named, a clan of intelligent cats living twenty-five million years ago. Ratha's right to rule is challenged by a stranger, Orange Eyes, after Ratha allows him to join the clan. Orange Eyes realizes both the power and the menace of controlling fire better than Ratha does, and she must face his power before he destroys her clan. Sequel to *Ratha's Creature.*

Bell, Clare. **Ratha's Creature.** Atheneum/Margaret K. McElderry Books and Argo Books, 1985. 259 p. ISBN 0-689-50262-1.

Ratha, who belongs to the clan of cats called the Named, discovers that she cannot live in peace under the rule of Meoran. The clan fears her and chases her away to join the Un-Named, cats who can neither herd nor speak. She again faces bitter disappointment and returns to her home to fight the battle that will decide how both cat clans will live.

Chetwin, Grace. **Gom on Windy Mountain.** Lothrop, Lee and Shepard Books, 1986. 206 p. ISBN 0-688-05767-5.

Stig, a woodcutter, lives alone for years until he marries the small, nut-brown woman he calls Wife. She raises nine children, but once her small, nut-brown son, Gom, is born, she goes to Faraway, leaving Gom with Stig. Gom is unlike the other children — he can talk to animals and the wind and he sees unusual pictures in his head. Gom holds fast to the rune left by his mother. Book one of *Tales of Gom, Legends of Ulm.*

Chetwin, Grace. **The Riddle and the Rune.** Bradbury Press, 1987. 257 p. ISBN 0-02-718312-2.

When Stig the woodcutter dies, Gom decides to leave Windy Mountain so that he can find his wizard mother, Harga the Brown, and return her rune. A sparrow poses a riddle, and Gom knows that only when the riddle is solved will he find Harga. The evil death's-head pursues him and makes several attempts to steal the rune from his neck. Book two of *Tales of Gom, Legends of Ulm.*

Conly, Jane Leslie. **Racso and the Rats of NIMH.** Illustrated by Leonard Lubin. Harper and Row, 1986. 278 p. ISBN 0-06-021361-2 (0-06-021362-0, library binding).

Timothy Frisby, a fieldmouse, and his friend Racso, a rat, investigate some strange happenings in Thorn Valley, such as why the river is rising and what those men are doing with dynamite and bulldozers. The two friends come up with a plan to save Thorn Valley, but will it work? Sequel to Robert C. O'Brien's *Mrs. Frisby and the Rats of NIMH.*

Corbett, W. J. **The Song of Pentecost.** Illustrated by Martin Ursell. E. P. Dutton, 1983. 216 p. ISBN 0-525-44051-8.

A strange animal parade makes the journey to Lickey Top Hills: the snake who plans to reclaim his home at Oily Green Pool, a lying frog, a vole, and a community of harvest mice seeking a new home. All are encouraged in their journey by the young leader called the Pentecost mouse. The group survives the perils of the Great River, Ambush Path, and Weasel Woods to hold the final confrontation with Fox and Owl at Lickey Top.

Cresswell, Helen. **The Secret World of Polly Flint.** Illustrated by Shirley Felts. Viking Penguin/Puffin Books, 1984. 176 p. ISBN 0-14-031542-X.

"Time's nothing," says the boy in the ragged shirt and breeches that look several sizes too big for him. "Time mightn't mean anything to you," says Polly. "Because you're Time Gypsies." Polly knows that there is magic in Wellow; she's an unusual girl who sees things that other people can't. Can Polly discover what the Time Gypsies want?

Eckert, Allan W. **The Wand: The Return to Mesmeria.** Illustrated by David Wiesner. Little, Brown, 1985. 214 p. ISBN 0-316-20882-5.

Twins Lara and Barnaby return to their secret world, Mesmeria, a world that they discovered while on a visit to the Everglades. Hundreds of years have passed in Mesmeria, and the land has fallen under the evil hand of King Krumpp, who keeps it in continual darkness. The twins join with a strange assortment of rescuers, including a dwarf and three hawklike beings, and try to find the magic wand and magic books to help free Mesmeria and its population. Sequel to *The Dark Green Tunnel.*

Fosburgh, Liza. **Bella Arabella.** Illustrated by Catherine Stock. Four Winds Press, 1985. 102 p. ISBN 0-02-735430-X.

Ten-year-old Arabella thinks her companionship with doting servants and her cat, Miranda, is enough. Her stepfather thinks she needs playmates, and persuades her mother to send Arabella away to school at Simon Hall. There seems to be no escape until Arabella learns the secret of Simon Hall: one who begins life there as a child may end it as a cat.

Garden, Nancy. **The Door Between.** Farrar, Straus and Giroux, 1987. 184 p. ISBN 0-374-31833-6.

Eighth-grader Melissa Dunn continues her fight against the evil hermit at Fours Crossing, a small town in New Hampshire. With the help of her friend Jed, Ulfin the dog, and Llyr the hawk, Melissa must somehow convince the hermit that she will join the old ways to the new. Sequel to *Fours Crossing* and *Watersmeet.*

Gloss, Molly. **Outside the Gates.** Atheneum/Argo Books, 1986. 120 p. ISBN 0-689-31275-X.

Vren has been accused of having ESP powers, which has banned him from his ancient village. Afraid of the monsters and giants he has been told live outside the walls, Vren moves into the forest. To his surprise he makes friends, especially with Rusche. Then Rusche disappears, and Vren sets out to rescue him.

Goldman, William. **The Silent Gondoliers: A Fable by S. Morgenstern.** Illustrated by Paul Giovanopoulos. Ballantine Books/Del Rey Books, 1985. 110 p. ISBN 0-345-32583-4.

Luigi wants desperately to be a singing boatman on a gondola in the waterways of Venice. Luigi is a skilled gondolier, but he has no talent as a singer. Only an incident of major proportions could ever convince all the gondoliers to join Luigi and never sing again.

Jones, Diana Wynne. **Archer's Goon.** Greenwillow Books, 1984. 241 p. ISBN 0-688-02582-X.

Howard, thirteen, comes home from school to find in the kitchen a huge man with a tiny head. The goon refuses to leave until two thousand words are written by Howard's father and sent to the wizard Archer. Howard, his sister Awful, and the goon visit Archer and his six brothers and sisters in an attempt to find out which wizard has stolen the words and why the wizards are holding each other captive.

Jones, Diana Wynne. **Howl's Moving Castle.** Greenwillow Books, 1986. 212 p. ISBN 0-688-06233-4.

Sophie, the eldest of three sisters, is resigned to being a hat shop apprentice, but then a witch turns her into an old woman. Sophie becomes the housekeeper for the feared Wizard Howl, and she helps him battle the evil witch.

Kennedy, Richard. **Amy's Eyes.** Illustrated by Richard Egielski. Harper and Row, 1985. 437 p. ISBN 0-06-023219-6 (0-06-023220-X, library binding).

Amy's eyes are as blue as the ocean and as bright as buttons. In fact, they are buttons, for Amy is a doll. Once she was an orphan child. But when her beloved sailor doll turned into a real little man and sailed off as Captain of the frigate *Ariel,* Amy pined away and turned into a doll herself. When the Captain returns, he takes Amy to sail the pirate-ridden seas along with a crew of animals in search of a treasure of gold.

King, Stephen. **The Eyes of the Dragon.** Illustrated by David Palladini. Viking Penguin, 1987. 326 p. ISBN 0-670-81458-X.

Flagg, the evil court magician, has walked the secret passages of the castle for four hundred years. He sees a mouse find a grain of Dragon Sand behind Prince Peter's bookcase and watches it die crying tears of fire and belching gray smoke. King Roland dies at the same time, Prince Peter is imprisoned, and the kingdom is left in the hands of young Prince Thomas, whom Flagg will be able to influence. However, Prince Thomas has a secret that is driving him crazy. Only by rescuing Prince Peter from the royal prison can Prince Thomas save the kingdom.

Klein, Robin. **Halfway across the Galaxy and Turn Left.** Viking Penguin/Viking Kestrel, 1986. 144 p. ISBN 0-670-80636-6.

If you like to imagine living in a time when you can zip among planets and space cities, you'll enjoy this story of Charlotte's space-hopping family and her life in a futuristic world.

Lillington, Kenneth. **Selkie.** Faber and Faber, 1985. 145 p. ISBN 0-571-13421-1.

When Cathy's father loses his job, everything changes for the Gascoyne family. Cathy leaves her friends, home, and boyfriend to move with her family into a shabby cottage in a Cornish village filled with hostility. Cathy soon realizes that Fiona is the reason for the problems with the villagers. Fiona can swim with superhuman powers; but is she human?

Lindbergh, Anne. **Bailey's Window.** Illustrated by Kinuko Craft. Harcourt Brace Jovanovich, 1984. 115 p. ISBN 0-15-205642-4.

Anna and Carl hate the idea of their cousin Bailey coming to visit. Then they discover Bailey's talent for escaping through a magic window to faraway places. The cousins are in for a summer of adventures and close calls during their magic escapades.

Lindgren, Astrid (translated by Patricia Crampton). **Ronia, the Robber's Daughter.** Viking Press, 1983. 176 p. ISBN 0-670-60640-5.

Ronia and Birk are the children of two robber chiefs who are mortal enemies. Born during the same severe thunderstorm, the children eventually find each other in Matt's Wood. Both love the cliffs, waterfalls, and forest creatures and enjoy the adventure of seeing dwarfs and harpies in the forest. But their friendship causes pain for them and their families, forcing Ronia to make a heartbreaking decision.

McKiernan, Dennis L. **The Dark Tide.** New American Library/Signet Books, 1985. 303 p. ISBN 0-451-13668-3.

Tuckerby Underhill, a young buccan from the Boskydells, has trained to defend his home from the dreaded Modru. Tuck and his companions are called on to aid their king, Aurion Redeye, and must face the horrendous Vulgs, Ghuls, Rucks, Ogrus, and Helsteeds. King Aurion's forces are scattered, and Tuck finds himself in the company of Prince Galen on the trail of the kidnapped Princess Laurelin. Book one of the Iron Tower Trilogy.

McKiernan, Dennis L. **The Darkest Day.** New American Library/Signet Books, 1985. 302 p. ISBN 0-451-13865-1.

The concluding work in this trilogy continues to follow the characters as they head toward the final battle with Modru in his Iron Tower. The safety of the world depends upon their defeating Modru before he can summon the evil Gyphon from beyond the stars at the hour of the Sun Death (eclipse). Book three of the Iron Tower Trilogy.

McKiernan, Dennis L. **Shadows of Doom.** New American Library/Signet Books, 1985. 300 p. ISBN 0-451-13815-5.

The saga of the Host against the Horde of Darkness is told in three parallel strands that describe the kidnapped Princess Laurelin as she is held in the Iron Tower, the battle between the people of the land fighting the Ghuls, and the rally when the survivors of the destruction of Challerain Keep fight Modru. Warrow Tuck, Dwarf Brega, King Galen, and Elfin Lord Gildor encounter dreaded monsters on their journey to join the Host. Book two of the Iron Tower Trilogy.

Mahy, Margaret. **Aliens in the Family.** Scholastic, 1985. 174 p. ISBN 0-590-40320-6.

Twelve-year-old Jacqueline Raven feels like an alien when she goes to visit her father and his new wife and children. However, they all join together to rescue a real alien named Bond. In their struggles to help Bond escape his enemies and travel through time to his home, the family learns the meaning of happy endings and beginnings.

Mark, Jan. **Aquarius.** Atheneum/Argo Books, 1984. 224 p. ISBN 0-689-31051-X.

Viner gets his name from being a water diviner — he is able to locate water underground. But his craft is not appreciated in his own land, where he is blamed for the floods. Viner leaves in search of a land where his skills will be appreciated, but he is captured immediately.

Mayhar, Ardath. **Lords of the Triple Moons.** Atheneum/Argo Books, 1983. 141 p. ISBN 0-689-30978-3.

Johab and Ellora, the last of the Old Lords, have been held captive since they were small children. But now that they are in their teens, their power is strengthened, and they are able to escape. Johab and Ellora search for the weapons of destruction left for them by their forefathers so that they can free the plains folk from tyranny.

Mayhar, Ardath. **The Saga of Grittel Sundotha.** Atheneum/Argo Books, 1985. 196 p. ISBN 0-689-31097-8.

Seven-foot tall Grittel is not only strong in body but also in spirit, so she sets out on a series of adventures that includes battling ruffians on the road and defeating a witch by stealing her spell book. Grittel even happens onto a spacecraft and crew who have been caught by a sorcerer out of their time, place, and dimension.

Melling, O. R. **The Singing Stone.** Viking Penguin/Viking Kestrel, 1986. 206 p. ISBN 0-670-80817-2.

Kay Warrick, eighteen, travels from the United States to Ireland in search of her mysterious past. She falls through a stone gate into another world, where she and a younger girl embark on a search for four weapons of power to save that doomed world.

Morris, Winifred. **With Magical Horses to Ride.** Atheneum, 1985. 152 p. ISBN 0-689-31108-7.

Twelve-year-old Elizabeth runs from another fight between her parents to the old cemetery, where she finds some measure of peace and quiet by reading the old tombstones. But on one particular night she meets Delathorn, the Elf Prince, and Zorauk, the Wizard. Could they be real? Could she really be the spiritual self of a person long dead? Elizabeth is both confused and excited when this adventure enters her life.

Murphy, Shirley Rousseau. **The Ivory Lyre.** Harper and Row, 1987. 250 p. ISBN 0-06-024362-7 (0-06-024363-5, library binding).

Dragons live on Tirror. Sixteen-year-old Tebriel, his dragon Seastrider, and three other dragons travel about Tirror singing about the past to wrest humans away from the powers of the Dark. Tebriel's search for the magical ivory lyre takes him inside the castle of the enemy, where he is aided by fourteen-year-old Kiri. Sequel to *Nightpool.*

Murphy, Shirley Rousseau. **Nightpool.** Harper and Row, 1985. 249 p. ISBN 0-06-024360-0 (0-06-024361-9, library binding).

As the Dark Raiders invade the world of Tirror, the singing dragon, who serves as the guardian of Tirror's glorious past by carrying its history in her song, awakens from her long slumber. She is searching for Tebriel, son of the murdered king. After he is injured in battle, sixteen-year-old Tebriel is healed in Nightpool, a colony of talking otters, and then sets out to fight the Dark and its forces of evil in Tirror.

Pierce, Meredith Ann. **Birth of the Firebringer.** Four Winds Press, 1985. 234 p. ISBN 0-02-774610-0.

Aljan and his friend Dagg are young unicorns who will soon be initiated once they complete a coming-of-age pilgrimage. But the journey is difficult, and they encounter antagonistic wyverns, gryphons, and pans. Unicorn legend holds that the band will return to their ancestral home once the Firebringer comes to lead them.

Pratchett, Terry. **The Colour of Magic.** New American Library/Signet Books, 1985. 253 p. ISBN 0-451-13577-6.

As you join Twoflower on his visit to the disc world, you will encounter dragons and dwarves and other mystical creatures. The wizard Rincewind will serve as your guide while you meet giants, a dragonwoman, and a friendly troll. Your walking luggage will accompany you on your trip to this fantasy world.

Price, Susan. **The Ghost Drum: A Cat's Tale.** Farrar, Straus and Giroux, 1987. 167 p. ISBN 0-374-32538-3.

Witchgirl Chingis lives out in the frozen wastes in a magic hut that can run on chicken legs. There she studies the words and runes that will give her the ability to wander in many worlds and to understand the messages of the ghost drum.

Ray, Mary. **The Golden Bees.** Faber and Faber, 1984. 152 p. ISBN 0-571-13201-4.

When Princess Aridela is stung by bees, Kenofer, the master storyteller, soothes her with the legend of the golden bee earrings. His story is one of a simple prank that turns into a quest for the valuable symbol of all wild things that grow and multiply — the Golden Bees of Melos. Kenofer must find the Golden Bees and return them to the princess so that she may lead the maidens in their dancing before the shrine of the mistress at her summer festival.

Reynolds, Alfred. **Kiteman of Karanga.** Alfred A. Knopf/Borzoi Books, 1985. 217 p. ISBN 0-394-86347-X (0-394-96347-4, library binding).

In a world where young men prove their manhood by killing large flying reptiles with sticks and spears, Karl runs away during a hunt. As a result, his teacher is killed. Choosing banishment rather than death, Karl determines to cross the wasteland and begin a new life for himself.

Salsitz, R.A.V. **Where Dragons Lie.** New American Library/Signet Books, 1985. 255 p. ISBN 0-451-14055-9.

When Aarondar first meets Sharlin, he sees her as a peddler's servant. Little does he know that she is a princess who will lead him into a daring adventure to resurrect the fabled gold dragon. The peddler tells them that he knows how to get to the dragon's graveyard where Turiance's corpse rests. And so begins their journey.

Sargent, Sarah. **Lure of the Dark.** Four Winds Press, 1984. 118 p. ISBN 0-590-07894-1.

According to Norse mythology, Fenris, a wolflike monster, was bound and hidden in a cave, but his father, Loki, the god of chaos, feels that the time of his destructive release is near. In a Wisconsin town, fifteen-year-old Ginny feels as if something is repeatedly drawing her back to visit the wolf at the zoo. Sometimes she feels strong and confident, but mostly she feels uncertain, angry, and even destructive. What is the connection between herself, the wolf, and the Norse Myth?

Selden, George. **The Old Meadow.** Illustrated by Garth Williams. Farrar, Straus and Giroux, 1987. 193 p. ISBN 0-374-35616-5.

Mr. Budd and his dog, Dubber, are being evicted from the Old Meadow. All the animals of the Old Meadow realize they must put aside their differences and must join forces if they are to save Mr. Budd's home.

Service, Pamela F. **Winter of Magic's Return.** Atheneum/Argo Books, 1985. 192 p. ISBN 0-689-31130-3.

Welly and Heather attend a boarding school in Wales five hundred years after the nuclear Devastation that came close to destroying the world. There they befriend fourteen-year-old Earl Bedwas, who has remarkable, if somewhat confused, powers. A fall restores his partial memory that he is, in fact, Merlin, the magician at the court of King Arthur. He has been imprisoned in a mountain for hundreds of years. Because science has failed the world, perhaps the magic that was once a prominent feature in Britain might return.

Smith, Stephanie A. **Snow-Eyes.** Atheneum/Argo Books, 1985. 184 p. ISBN 0-689-31129-X.

Creeping out of bed one night, Snow-Eyes sees her father talking to a beautiful woman, possibly the goddess Lake Mother herself. Later Snow-Eyes is asked to make three wishes, but nothing happens. She discovers that the mysterious woman is actually her mother and is a servant of the Lake Mother. Snow-Eyes must also serve the Lake Mother, but first she must discover what her powers can do as she sets out on the road to fulfill her destiny.

Stolz, Mary. **The Scarecrows and Their Child.** Illustrated by Amy Schwartz. Harper and Row, 1987. 67 p. ISBN 0-06-026007-6 (0-06-026008-4, library binding).

Handy, a cornfield scarecrow, and Blossom, a garden scarecrow, fall in love. After the farm is abandoned, they get married and set up housekeeping in a stall in the barn, where their son Bohel, a cat, is born. When the scarecrows are taken away to be Halloween lawn ornaments, Bohel sets out on a journey to find his parents.

Strauss, Victoria. **Worldstone.** Four Winds Press, 1985. 245 p. ISBN 0-02-788380-9.

All of her life, sixteen-year-old Alexina has known that she is different from other people. Sought out by visitors from a parallel world, she is finally able to use her special powers and gain entrance to the superior world of mindpower. But is this world of mindpower really superior?

Westall, Robert. **The Cats of Seroster.** Greenwillow Books, 1984. 306 p. ISBN 0-688-03944-8.

It all begins when the Duke is murdered at his own dinner table in medieval France. Then the cats begin to gather — especially the Miw, cats of unique breed and long history. Eighteen-year-old Cam is also on the move, looking for a place to stay and work where none will call him a wizard.

Wiseman, David. **Adam's Common.** Houghton Mifflin, 1984. 175 p. ISBN 0-395-35976-7.

Fourteen-year-old Peggy finds England drab. The only thing that makes life bearable is Adam's Common, a rambling park in the middle of Traverton. Unfortunately, it is doomed to become a shopping mall. Discovering a house hidden within the common, Peggy enters and travels back through time to meet William. Together they must find the key to preserving their beloved common.

Wrightson, Patricia. **A Little Fear.** Atheneum/Margaret K. McElderry Books, 1985. 111 p. ISBN 0-689-50291-5.

"You're going to run away, aren't you?" young Valerie asks her grandmother, Old Mrs. Tucker. The older woman hates Sunset House, where her daughter has arranged for her to live, and she secretly sets off to live in the cottage that her brother has left her.

But Mrs. Tucker must battle a Njimbin, a small and ancient gnome, for the right to live there.

Yep, Laurence. **Dragon Steel.** Harper and Row, 1985. 275 p. ISBN 0-06-026748-8 (0-06-026751-8, library binding).

Deep in the ocean, in the caverns of an underwater volcano, a clan of dragons forges the fabled dragon steel. Slaves of the High King, they have no hope of ever leaving the steaming depths of the mines. To free her clan from this slavery, the dragon princess Shimmer and her human companion Thorn combat the Dragon King's jealousy and treachery.

Folklore, Myths, and Legends

Bierhorst, John, editor. **The Hungry Woman: Myths and Legends of the Aztecs.** William Morrow, 1984. ISBN 0-688-02766-0.

Interested in mythology? These tales of the Aztecs are entertaining and provide a look into the beliefs and folklore of the advanced Aztec culture before and after the Spanish Conquest. The tales emphasize the Aztecs' desire to understand the beginnings of humankind, their interest in understanding the forces of good and evil, and the important role that women play in their folklore. Miniature paintings by sixteenth-century Aztec artists illustrate the tales.

Bierhorst, John, editor. **The Monkey's Haircut, and Other Stories Told by the Maya.** William Morrow, 1986. 143 p. ISBN 0-688-04269-4.

The classic period for the Maya was from A.D. 200 to 800. Today their descendants live in Mexico and Guatemala. This collection of twenty-two traditional tales reflects the culture of the Maya, especially their interest in riddles.

Bierhorst, John. **The Mythology of North America.** William Morrow, 1985. 259 p. ISBN 0-688-04145-0.

This comprehensive look at the myths of native North Americans includes some that are familiar to modern readers and some that have just come to light. All geographical areas are represented, and myths are explained in the context of the various cultures. Connections are drawn between similar myths.

Crossley-Holland, Kevin. **British Folk Tales: New Versions.** Orchard Books, 1987. 383 p. ISBN 0-531-05733-X.

Fifty-five British stories have been chosen to represent all the major types of folktales, including fairy stories, heroic legends, tales of enchantment, and tales of country people, poor girls and princes, seal-women, boggarts, giants, and ghosts. Also included are a pronunciation guide and a section on sources and notes.

Crossley-Holland, Kevin. **The Fox and the Cat: Animal Tales from Grimm.** Illustrated by Susan Varley. Lothrop, Lee and Shepard Books, 1986. 59 p. ISBN 0-688-04636-3.

Eleven stories from the Brothers Grimm feature animals behaving very much like human beings — showing the same traits of loyalty and disloyalty, and of kindness and cruelty. Included are "The Fox and the Cat," "The Wolf and the Seven Kids," and "The Hare and the Hedgehog."

Day, David. **The Emperor's Panda.** Illustrated by Eric Beddows. Dodd, Mead, 1987. 109 p. ISBN 0-396-09036-2.

The mythical Master Panda, of China's fabled Celestial Empire, was the first panda the world had known. Kung the Fluteplayer, a young shepherd boy, is searching for his uncle, Latzy, who has been kidnapped by wicked wizards. Panda helps Kung rescue Latzy, outwits the wizards, and leads Kung through other wonderous adventures.

Evslin, Bernard. **Hercules.** Illustrated by Jos. A. Smith. William Morrow, 1984. 144 p. ISBN 0-688-02748-2.

Hercules, the mythical Greek hero known for his extraordinary strength and courage, must perform twelve difficult labors, including killing the Nemean lion and the many-headed Hydra and capturing the Cretan bull and the horses of Diomed. This version describes his adventures in modern language while retaining the excitement and spirit of the original versions.

Evslin, Bernard. **Jason and the Argonauts.** Illustrated by Bert Dodson. William Morrow, 1986. 165 p. ISBN 0-688-06245-8.

The Greek hero Jason is promised a kingdom if he can obtain the Golden Fleece. He and the bravest heroes of Greece set sail on the *Argo* in quest of the fleece, and on their journey they encounter unfriendly warriors, fierce storms, and monstrous creatures. Further adventures await them once they reach Colchis, where the fleece is kept.

Garner, Alan. **A Bag of Moonshine.** Illustrated by Patrick James Lynch. Delacorte Press, 1986. 144 p. ISBN 0-385-29517-0.

Boggarts, gowks, fools, and hobgoblins are only some of the strange creatures in this collection of twenty-two folktales from England and Wales. Included are tales of the Welsh boy who hooks a salmon that pulls him back into the river and demands to be his sweetheart, a baby who bounces out of its cradle and dances to the tune of a fiddle, and tales of magic and enchantment and of wizardry and trickery.

Gerstein, Mordicai. **Tales of Pan.** Illustrated by the author. Harper and Row, 1986. 63 p. ISBN 0-06-021996-3 (0-06-021997-1, library binding).

Pan, the Greek god of pastures, flocks, and shepherds, is usually depicted as a merry, ugly man with the horns, ears, and legs of a goat. This collection of tales describes how Pan falls in love with the moon, how he makes his pipes and marries Echo, and how the word *panic* comes from his name.

Hamilton, Virginia, retold by. **The People Could Fly: American Black Folktales.** Illustrated by Leo and Diane Dillon. Alfred A. Knopf/ Borzoi Books, 1985. 173 p. ISBN 0-394-86925-7 (0-394-96925-1, library binding).

The twenty-four American black folktales in this collection are divided into four categories: animal tales ("Bruh Rabbit and Bruh Bear"), realistic and fanciful tales ("Wiley and the Hairy Man"), supernatural tales ("Jack and the Devil"), and slave tales of freedom ("The People Could Fly"). An introduction and conclusion to each story relate some history of the stories and comment on the language. Included are more than forty black-and-white illustrations by the award-winning Dillons. (Literary merit)

Jaffrey, Madhur. **Seasons of Splendour: Tales, Myths and Legends of India.** Illustrated by Michael Foreman. Atheneum, 1985. 124 p. ISBN 0-689-31141-9.

Madhur Jaffrey, who grew up in India, retells both family stories and traditional stories of India that were told to her as a child. More than twenty-five stories are arranged to correspond with the religious festivals in the Hindu calendar year. Also included is a guide to the pronunciation of Indian names.

Lester, Julius, retold by. **The Tales of Uncle Remus: The Adventures of Brer Rabbit.** Illustrated by Jerry Pinkney. Dial Books, 1987. 151 p. ISBN 0-8037-0271-X (0-8037-0272-8, library binding).

This new version of the rich Afro-American folktale set in the fields of the Old South puts Uncle Remus, Brer Rabbit, and Tar Baby in a contemporary setting.

Liyi, He, translator (edited by Neil Philip). **The Spring of Butterflies and Other Folktales of China's Minority Peoples.** Illustrated by Pan Aiquing and Li Zhao. Lothrop, Lee and Shepard, 1986. 144 p. ISBN 0-688-06192-3.

The fourteen folktales in this collection represent the stories of several minority peoples who live in western China. These people have different languages and customs than the Han Chinese, who dominate China. Although the tales have a Chinese setting, you'll find many familiar devices: rewards to be earned, magical animals including flying horses and dragons, seemingly impossible trials, and beautiful maidens. The illustrators won a competition that earned them the opportunity to illustrate these folktales.

Low, Alice. **The Macmillan Book of Greek Gods and Heroes.** Illustrated by Arvis Stewart. Macmillan, 1985. 184 p. ISBN 0-02-761390-9.

The myths of ancient Greece have fascinated and inspired people for years, probably because they bring nature, the world, and the universe to life by making them very human. In this collection, roughly three dozen myths and legends about Greek gods and heroes are retold. Some, like the tales of Zeus and Prometheus, deal with the origins of the world. Others, such as the stories of Hercules and Odysseus, explain nature, personal relationships, and the struggles of gods and heroes.

Martin, Eva. **Tales of the Far North.** Illustrated by László Gál. Dial Books, 1986. 123 p. ISBN 0-8037-0319-8.

Intrigued by beasts and unicorns, by beautiful maidens and princes challenged to impossible feats? These stories reflect the French and English folklore tradition of Canada and maintain the flair and style of fairy tales. Color illustrations enhance each tale.

Monroe, Jean Guard, and Ray A. Williamson. **They Dance in the Sky: Native American Star Myths.** Illustrated by Edgar Stewart. Houghton Mifflin, 1987. 130 p. ISBN 0-395-39970-X.

Every culture has created myths to explain the patterns of the stars. Native American myths reflect motifs that are repeated around the world — curiosity, love, defiance. Included are explanations of the Milky Way and constellations like the Big Dipper.

Philip, Neil. **The Tale of Sir Gawain.** Illustrated by Charles Keeping. Philomel Books, 1987. 102 p. ISBN 0-399-21488-7.

King Arthur's nephew, Sir Gawain, is wounded in the attack on Sir Launcelot's castle. As he lies dying, he tells his young squire about the glories of King Arthur's court and the adventures of his knights. Gawain gives an account of his own adventures, including meeting the Lady of the Fountain, his battle with the Green Knight, and his marriage. In his dying words, he foretells King Arthur's death at the hands of Mordred.

Rhyne, Nancy. **More Tales of the South Carolina Low Country.** John F. Blair, 1984. 121 p. ISBN 0-89587-042-8.

This is an assortment of strangely eerie, but very enchanting, tales. Some stories will cause you to laugh; some will make you cry from fright. Beware!

Riordan, James. **The Woman in the Moon and Other Tales of Forgotten Heroines.** Illustrated by Angela Barrett. Dial Books for Young Readers, 1985. 86 p. ISBN 0-8037-0194-2 (0-8037-0196-9, library binding).

This collection of thirteen stories features girls and women as central characters who are bold, strong, and clever. Stories are included from Sicily, Lapland, Asia, Russia, Ireland, and North America. The preface and reading list are worth a closer look.

Schwartz, Alvin. **Telling Fortunes: Love Magic, Dream Signs, and Other Ways to Learn the Future.** Illustrated by Tracey Cameron. J. B. Lippincott, 1987. 128 p. ISBN 0-397-32132-5 (0-397-32133-3, library binding).

Drawing upon hundreds of examples from folklore, this book describes the many ways that people have tried to predict what is going to happen. These traditional beliefs, popular sayings, and superstitions also can be used as games for predicting the future.

Shannon, George. **Stories to Solve: Folktales from around the World.** Illustrated by Peter Sis. Greenwillow Books, 1985. 55 p. ISBN 0-688-04303-8 (0-688-04304-6, library binding).

If you enjoy puzzles, you'll find these folktale brainteasers intriguing. And if you can't figure them out, you can read "How It Was Done" after each tale. Notes provide background on each puzzle.

Tehranchian, Hassan, translator and adapter. **Kallilah and Dimnah: Fables from the Ancient East.** Illustrated by Anatole Ur. Harmony Books, 1985. 79 p. ISBN 0-517-55566-2.

Seen through the eyes of two jackals, these imaginative tales of a fantastic animal kingdom explore the universal questions of truth and deceit, ambition and loyalty, fear and power. The tales are translated from a twelfth-century Persian text and have been told aloud since the third century.

Thomas, Gwyn, and Kevin Crossley-Holland. **Tales from the Mabinogion.** Illustrated by Margaret Jones. Overlook Press, 1985. 88 p. ISBN 0-87951-978-8.

Many centuries ago, when Britain was still covered with forests, the Celtic people told magical tales around the fireplaces, tales about Pyll, Prince of Dyfed, Branwen, daughter of Llŷr, Manawydan, son of Uŷr, and Math, son of Mathonwy. Seven hundred years ago, these tales were written down as the *Mabinogion,* and now they are translated in this wonderfully illustrated book.

Timpanelli, Gioia, retold by. **Tales from the Roof of the World: Folktales of Tibet.** Illustrated by Elizabeth Kelly Lockwood. Viking Press, 1984. 53 p. ISBN 0-670-71249-3.

Timpanelli retells four traditional tales from Tibet, giving us a glimpse of a little-known culture. The illustrations were inspired by Tibetan art; an explanation of eight symbols used in the drawings is included.

Voigt, Cynthia. **Jackaroo.** Atheneum/Argo Books, 1985. 291 p. ISBN 0-689-31123-0.

The legends about Jackaroo, who comes to the aid of the helpless and gives money to the poor, have been around for years. When her own people are suffering under the rule of the Lords, the Innkeeper's daughter, Gwyn, takes matters into her own hands. Jackaroo reappears, but will he be able to fight against the power of the Lords and make life once again bearable for the common people? The answer is in Gwyn's hands.

Friendship

Adams, Barbara. **Can This Telethon Be Saved?** Dell/Yearling Books, 1987. 117 p. ISBN 0-440-41427-X.

Wellsburg High has a sliding gym floor that covers the swimming pool. It's stuck halfway open, and repairs will cost a fortune. Minnie O'Reilly, production assistant at KID-TV, suggests they raise money by putting on a telethon on Halloween night. It's nearly time for the telethon to end, but the students are less than halfway to their goal. Can even Minnie save the telethon?

Adams, Laurie, and Allison Courdert. **Who Wants a Turnip for President, Anyway?** Bantam Skylark Books, 1986. 89 p. ISBN 0-553-15432-X.

The fifth-grade class at Miss Barton's School for Girls is ready to elect the class president. It's the Peaches and Alice Whipple against the Turnips and Donna Ellington. Each girl can count on ten votes, but there are five girls who can't decide. Alice and Donna fight it out over those five votes with every prank they can think of — until their teacher tells them the election is off unless they play fair. Who will win?

Anderson, Mary. **Tune In Tomorrow.** Avon Books/Flare Books, 1985. 179 p. ISBN 0-380-69870-6.

Fourteen-year-old Josephine Kaputkin lives for the next episode of her favorite soap opera and a glimpse of its leading stars. She imagines her own grossly overweight self to be the beautiful Fern pursued by handsome Travis. A dream appears to come true when Josephine discovers the stars at her very own vacation spot.

Angell, Judie. **First the Good News.** Bradbury Press, 1983. 147 p. ISBN 0-02-705820-4.

Five friends form a group known as Adam's Ribbers in order to land an interview with Hap Rhysbeck, TV's fastest rising young comedian. From the beginning, they never believe they'll be successful, but they won't admit defeat. They try everything they can think of, and finally decide on the direct approach: getting tickets. Then Hap makes a surprise announcement.

Avi. **Romeo and Juliet Together (and Alive!) at Last.** Orchard Books, 1987. 122 p. ISBN 0-531-05721-6 (0-531-08321-7, library binding).

Peter Saltz has fallen for Anabell Stackpoole, but each of them is too shy to look at the other. When the eighth grade casts their version of Shakespeare's *Romeo and Juliet,* the roles of the famous lovers go to Peter and Anabell. Not only will they have to look at each other and talk, they'll have to kiss! Most of the school is basically interested in those kisses.

Bess, Clayton. **Big Man and the Burn-out.** Houghton Mifflin, 1985. 197 p. ISBN 0-395-36173-7.

Seventh-grader Jess lives with his grandparents, and it seems that there's nothing on which he and his grandmother can ever agree. Especially not on his friend Lee Meechum, who's failed several grades. Jess takes on a science fair project to hatch a goose egg and learns responsibility and caring for both Lee and the gosling, The Cid.

Boatright, Lori. **Out of Bounds.** Ballantine Books/Fawcett Juniper Books, 1982. 159 p. ISBN 0-449-70028-3.

Judie makes many enemies when she wins a place on the boys' basketball team at her high school. She also has problems when she discovers that her feelings for one of her teammates are turning into more than just feelings for a best friend.

Bunting, Eve. **Sixth-Grade Sleepover.** Harcourt Brace Jovanovich, 1986. 96 p. ISBN 0-15-275350-8.

The sixth-grade Rabbit Reading Club is going to have a sleep over in the cafeteria. Everyone, except Janey, will be there. She has a horribly embarrassing secret problem. Her friend Claudia tells Janey she'll help her, but Janey knows nothing can help — until she thinks of a plan that will make everything possible. Unfortunately, plans can go wrong.

Burch, Robert. **King Kong and Other Poets.** Viking Penguin/Viking Kestrel, 1986. 121 p. ISBN 0-670-80927-6.

There's a new girl in Andy's sixth-grade class. She's so quiet and mousy that no one really notices her until she wins a poetry contest. Then the kids learn that she comes from the ritzy part of town. Just who is Marilyn and will she "reveal" herself in her poems?

Chambers, Aidan. **The Present Takers.** Harper and Row/Charlotte Zolotow Books, 1983. 156 p. ISBN 0-06-021251-9 (0-06-021252-7, library binding).

Eleven-year-old Lucy is tormented by class bullies who demand that she bring them gifts. She tries to solve her problem alone but discovers that she must turn to the whole class to find a solution.

Clements, Bruce. **Coming About.** Farrar, Straus and Giroux, 1984. 185 p. ISBN 0-374-31457-8.

As he begins his junior year at Burgess High, new kid Bob Royle is almost immediately adopted by a weirdo, Carl Reimer. Carl convinces Bob that he's interesting and not like everybody else. It's only a matter of time until Bob starts to behave in ways new to him. Perhaps Carl's influence has really made a difference.

Cohen, Miriam. **Born to Dance Samba.** Illustrated by Gioia Fiammenghi. Harper and Row, 1984. 149 p. ISBN 0-06-021358-2 (0-06-021359-0, library binding).

It's Carnival time in Brazil, and Maria Antonia is sure that she will be chosen Queen of the Samba and will be "Star of the Kids" in the Procession. But when the new girl turns out to be a good samba dancer, Maria Antonia must learn to cope with her jealousy.

Colman, Hila. **Nobody Told Me What I Need to Know.** William Morrow, 1984. 165 p. ISBN 0-688-03869-7.

Sixteen-year-old Alix is drawn to Nick because he is completely different from her family. He represents the wild and carefree kind of life she wants to live. But is this life so great? Alix discovers that there are flaws in both worlds and that she must devise her own set of values.

Conrad, Pam. **Seven Silly Circles.** Illustrated by Mike Wimmer. Harper and Row, 1987. 55 p. ISBN 0-06-021333-7 (0-06-021334-5, library binding).

Seven times Nicki licks the rubber tip of a toy arrow and presses it on her face to see how long it will hang there. The resulting red circles embarrass her. She decides she will stay in her room until the circles go away, even if it takes weeks. A moth keeps her company and entertains her while she waits. Nicki and her two friends wear masks at a leaf-raking party until the three decide on a way to solve Nicki's problem.

Danziger, Paula. **Remember Me to Harold Square.** Delacorte Press, 1987. 139 p. ISBN 0-385-29610-X.

Frank Lee is spending the summer with eighteen-year-old Kendra Kaye and her parents in their New York City apartment. Frank is from a Wisconsin farm, so Kendra's parents plan a scavenger hunt that will encourage the teenagers to explore the city's museums, restaurants, and other landmarks. As they see the sights, their friendship grows.

Fleischman, Sid. **The Whipping Boy.** Illustrated by Peter Sis. Greenwillow Books, 1986. 90 p. ISBN 0-688-06216-4.

Jemmy, the son of a ratcatcher, has been chosen to live in the castle and to serve as the whipping boy for Prince Brat. No one is permitted to spank, thrash, cuff, smack, or whip the prince, so Jemmy receives the prince's punishment instead. When the prince decides to run away, Jemmy is forced to go along. The two are involved in more adventures than they bargain for, and the prince undergoes important changes. (Literary merit — Newbery Medal)

Garden, Nancy. **Peace, O River.** Farrar, Straus and Giroux, 1986. 246 p. ISBN 0-374-35763-3.

After four years of city living, Kate Kincaid and her family go back to River View, Massachusetts, where she had spent her childhood. She finds a long-standing feud between the wealthy River View residents and the people of Hastings, the working-class town across the river. Kate's efforts to bring the two factions together trigger a dangerous chain of events.

Giff, Patricia Reilly. **Love, from the Fifth-Grade Celebrity.** Illustrated by Leslie Morrill. Delacorte Press, 1986. 118 p. ISBN 0-385-29486-7.

Casey Valentine and Tracy Matson spend time together one summer and then meet again when Tracy's dad gets a job in Casey's town. Casey is sure she'll be elected fifth-grade class president, but to her surprise, it's Tracy who is elected. Also, Tracy steals Casey's friends and embarrasses her by telling everyone about all the stupid things Casey did when she visited Tracy in High Flats. Can the friendship be saved?

Giff, Patricia Reilly. **Purple Climbing Days.** Illustrated by Blanche Sims. Dell/Yearling Books, 1985. 70 p. ISBN 0-440-47309-8.

Richard "Beast" Best, a sixth grader, is afraid to climb the fat brown rope with fat brown knots in the gym. He hopes his friends won't find out, but they do. So does Mrs. Miller, the meanest substitute teacher in the whole school. She tells Richard to meet her in the gym after school. What will Miller the Killer do to him?

Gormley, Beatrice. **Best Friend Insurance.** Illustrated by Emily Arnold McCully. Avon Books/Camelot Books, 1985. 147 p. ISBN 0-380-69854-4.

Maureen Harrity is too miserable to listen to the salesman who has come to tell her fifth-grade class about insurance, until he mentions Best Friend Insurance. Maureen's best friend has just deserted her. Is there really a policy to protect her from such misery?

Greenberg, Jan. **The Pig-out Blues.** Dell/Laurel-Leaf Books, 1985. 121 p. ISBN 0-440-96977-8.

When Jodie, an overweight fifteen year old, decides to try out for the school production of *Romeo and Juliet,* she knows she has to lose pounds fast. But after losing both the lead and the leading man to a newcomer, she falls victim to despair and hunger pangs. Can Jodie deal with these? Or will she revert to marathon feasting?

Greene, Constance C. **Al(exandra) the Great.** Viking Press, 1982. 133 p. ISBN 0-670-11197-X.

Al's ready to get out of hot, sticky New York City and go visit her father and stepfamily in the country. But then Al's mother gets pneumonia, and Al's plans must be changed. She and her best friend get together and comfort each other with a little imagination and lots of sympathy.

Greene, Constance C. **Ask Anybody.** Viking Press, 1983. 150 p. ISBN 0-670-13813-4.

Schuyler and her pals are planning a yard sale for their club. But they aren't prepared for the help they get from a newcomer, the out-of-the-ordinary out-of-stater, Nell. In the Chum Club's subsequent misadventures with Nell and her family, Schuyler quickly learns something about friendship and about herself.

Greenwald, Sheila. **Rosy Cole's Great American Guilt Club.** Altantic Monthly Press, 1985. 87 p. ISBN 0-87113-044-0.

Rosy Cole, who is convinced she has none of the material things she'd like, creates the Great American Guilt Club to help her "rich" friends share their preppie possessions with the less fortunate — including Rosy. Her scheme works flawlessly until she discovers value is measured by more than just money.

Greer, Gery, and Bob Ruddick. **This Island Isn't Big Enough for the Four of Us!** Thomas Y. Crowell, 1987. 151 p. ISBN 0-690-04612-X (0-690-04614-6, library binding).

Pete and Scott excitedly plan a camping trip to a deserted island, but when they arrive they discover that two girls with zany senses of humor are already in residence. The first thing the girls do is take a photograph of the boys as their canoe capsizes. The boys try to get revenge, but the attack of the Vampire Wolverine is only the beginning of a summer-long battle between the boys and the girls.

Hall, Lynn. **Uphill All the Way.** Charles Scribner's Sons, 1984. 121 p. ISBN 0-684-18066-9.

Seventeen-year-old Callie Kiffin knows that she wants to be a farrier — a horseshoer. She has a summer job with veterinarian Doc Fulcher and is trying to save enough money to buy and outfit the truck she will need. Everything is going smoothly until Truman, Doc's stepson, comes home from a state correctional institution. Callie feels that Truman needs her, and she takes him in like a stray kitten.

Hamlin, Gwen. **Beneath the Surface.** New American Library/Signet Vista Books, 1985. 191 p. ISBN 0-451-13672-1.

Spending the Christmas holidays aboard a yacht in the Caribbean sounds like paradise to fifteen-year-old Jackie. Or at least it would be if Jeremy, the son of her parents' best friends, weren't coming along. Jeremy, however, has heavier concerns than Jackie bargained for, and she's not sure she can handle some of his revelations.

Harris, Lavinia. **The Great Rip-off.** Scholastic/Point Paperbacks, 1984. 217 p. ISBN 0-590-33059-4.

When sixteen-year-old Sidney agrees to help her father with top-secret experiments, she doesn't realize how much danger she will be in. Her computer genius leads her to the discovery of student hacking, criminal interference, and suspicions that her new lab partner is linked to the theft of her father's test results. Can she establish computer contact and expose the thief before the test results are used for harmful purposes?

Hayes, Sheila. **You've Been Away All Summer.** E. P. Dutton/Lodestar Books, 1986. 149 p. ISBN 0-525-67182-X.

Twelve-year-old Fran has returned to her home in New York City anxious to share her summer's adventures with her best friend, Sarah. She is unpleasantly surprised to discover that Sarah has found a new friend named Marcie. Fran's life becomes even more unpleasant when Marcie's liberated mother, C.B., has an unsettling influence on Fran's mother. Sequel to *The Carousel Horse.*

Haynes, Betsy. **Taffy Sinclair, Baby Ashley, and Me.** Bantam Skylark Books, 1988. 120 p. ISBN 0-533-15557-1.

Jana and Taffy, sixth graders at Mark Twain Elementary School, find a baby in a basket on the school steps as they are on their way to the office detention room. The girls, enemies before this, now share a special moment. Each wants to take credit and claim the baby. Newspaper articles, an appearance on TV, a haircut by four friends, and a want ad lead to unusual developments.

Hermes, Patricia. **Friends Are Like That.** Harcourt Brace Jovanovich, 1984. 123 p. ISBN 0-15-229722-7.

Did you ever have to choose between friends? This is the problem that eighth-grader Tracy faces. Will she choose Kelly, her friend since first grade, or Angie, the leader of the "in crowd"?

Hermes, Patricia. **Kevin Corbett Eats Flies.** Illustrated by Carol Newsom. Harcourt Brace Jovanovich, 1986. 160 p. ISBN 0-15-242290-0.

Fifth-grader Kevin Corbett faces two problems. First, he is about to lose his class status when a newcomer insists he must chew up the dead goldfish before he swallows it. Second, Kevin's father is ready to move again, and Kevin doesn't want to leave his newfound fame as champion eater of gross dead things. Discover the cunning ways Kevin handles his problem.

Hines, Anna Grossnickle. **Cassie Bowen Takes Witch Lessons.** Illustrated by Gail Owens. E. P. Dutton, 1985. 136 p. ISBN 0-525-44214-6.

When fourth grader Cassie learns she has to do a school project with "Saggy Aggy," she wants to sink through the floor. Everyone knows that Aggy lives in an old, rundown house that is haunted and that her grandmother is a witch. But when Cassie goes to Aggy's house, she finds that it is not at all as she and her friends thought.

Honeycutt, Natalie. **Josie's Beau.** Orchard Books, 1987. 153 p. ISBN 0-531-05718-6 (0-531-08318-7, library binding).

Beau will do anything to pay for his skateboard deck by the end of summer. And Josie will do anything for Beau, especially when it means keeping him away from tattooed, street-mean Matt Ventura. Josie's best friend dreams up a solution to both of Beau's problems.

Hopper, Nancy J. **Hang On, Harvey!** Dell/Yearling Books, 1984. 86 p. ISBN 0-440-43371-1.

The minute Harvey Smucker enters eighth grade, he's up to his ears in problems. He discovers he likes Lisa Keller, but so does his best friend. The new orchestra director doesn't recognize Harvey's obvious talent for the flute. And Jon Jamison will stop at nothing to get Harvey. Can Harvey hang on long enough to survive eighth grade?

Hopper, Nancy J. **The Truth or Dare Trap.** E. P. Dutton, 1985. 106 p. ISBN 0-525-44218-9.

Truth or Dare is "just a game" made up by Angie, who is pretty and popular. Megan wants to be Angie's best friend and goes along with the game until it becomes dangerous. A dare to go into a fireworks factory and the discovery that fireworks are being illegally sold to teenagers make this a deadly game.

Howe, Norma. **In with the Out Crowd.** Houghton Mifflin, 1986. 196 p. ISBN 0-395-40490-8.

Robin has always been with the "in crowd," the crowd that seems to run the school. Now the group's standards seem different from

Robin's, and her best friend, Jennifer, is urging her to do things she doesn't think are right. Robin begins to pay more attention to the other kids at her school. Where does she belong?

Jones, Rebecca C. **Germy Blew It.** E. P. Dutton, 1987. 105 p. ISBN 0-525-44294-4.

Jeremy Bluett really did blow it this time. It was his idea to strike to protest school budget cuts. How did he know he'd be the only kid to see it through and the only one to miss being on TV? Jeremy is devastated — but not for long. He sets out to win his share of the limelight. But there's a surprising discovery for Jeremy along the way.

Krensky, Stephen. **The Wilder Summer.** Atheneum, 1984. 164 p. ISBN 0-689-30990-2.

Charlie Wilder is at summer camp but not because he wants to be. Then he sees Lydia Travers and sets out to attract her attention. But that has its problems, too. Janis Shaw and Willoughby Cavendish continually get in Charlie's way. The course of true love may never run smoothly, but only Charlie would find himself with as many hurdles to jump as he does. Sequel to *The Wilder Plot.*

Leroe, Ellen W. **The Plot against the Pom-Pom Queen.** Berkley Books/Pacer Books, 1986. 134 p. ISBN 0-425-08867-7.

Meet the Pig Woman of Balboa High, better known as junior Kelsey Marshall, member of the Ugly Ducklings and a bit overweight. See how she plots revenge against Taffy Foster, queen of the Pretty People, and uses the secrets from Magic Male Grabbers to pursue Balboa's Mr. Wonderful. Then share Kelsey's heartache as she realizes true friendship is not based on looks or attained through tricks.

Lowry, Lois. **Anastasia's Chosen Career.** Houghton Mifflin, 1987. 142 p. ISBN 0-395-42506-9.

Anastasia Krupnik is back, and she's agonizing again. A seventh-grade assignment requires her to choose a future career. How can you do that when you're thirteen? Anastasia enrolls in a modeling school, collecting a unique cast of characters along the way. She pairs up with a dazzling new friend and continues to share her adventures and discoveries with a funny, lovable family.

Meyer, Carolyn. **The Luck of Texas McCoy.** Atheneum/Margaret K. McElderry Books, 1984. 183 p. ISBN 0-689-50312-1.

At sixteen, Texas inherits her grandfather's ranch and starts to make a success of it. She can break a horse as well as any man can. She even teaches a movie star to ride. But Texas is lonely. The rest of her family moved to town when she refused to sell the ranch, and she has no close friends. Discover how Texas solves her problem of loneliness.

Mills, Claudia. **The One and Only Cynthia Jane Thornton.** Macmillan, 1986. 110 p. ISBN 0-02-767090-2.

How can Cynthia be unique when her own sister starts a book? Cynthia is the writer in the family! It is bad enough to dress alike and go everywhere together, but the book is just too much. Join fifth-grader Cynthia as she learns to appreciate the things that really make a person unique.

Milton, Joyce. **Save the Loonies.** Four Winds Press, 1983. 151 p. ISBN 0-590-07857-7.

Family competition and wilderness mysteries await teenage Jenny when she goes camping in New Hampshire with best friend, Nicole. By pressuring everyone to be a winner, Nicole's father has forced his son to run away. Jenny helps solve the problem of the missing boy while helping the local wildlife rangers.

Mines, Jeanette. **Another Chance.** Avon Books/Flare Books, 1985. 112 p. ISBN 0-380-89705-9.

Does Dave deserve another chance? In his rush to impress Anne, he lost his temper when she beat him in tennis. He stole a car and caused the first wreck in the history of the school's driver education class. Now he desperately needs Anne to come to help him sort out his problems. Does he deserve another chance?

Newton, Suzanne. **An End to Perfect.** Viking Penguin/Viking Kestrel, 1984. 212 p. ISBN 0-670-29487-X.

Twelve-year-old Arden learns that nothing perfect can last. Even though she loves the family's new home in Haverlee, her brother, Hill, decides to move back to the city. Then DorJo, Arden's best friend, contemplates leaving her home with Arden and returning to live with her mother, who keeps disappearing. Will this be still another loss for Arden to bear?

Nielsen, Shelly. **Just Victoria.** David C. Cook/Chariot Books, 1986. 120 p. ISBN 0-89191-609-1.

Victoria Hope Mahoney has heard enough details about seventh grade to ruin her summer vacation. But she has a habit of underestimating her own potential. The summer brings a lot of change, but Vic is equal to it as she learns more about her faith, friendship, and growing up.

Nielsen, Shelly. **More Victoria.** David C. Cook/Chariot Books, 1986. 140 p. ISBN 0-89191-453-6.

Vic can see there will be nothing dull about seventh grade — if she can survive it. She is the victim of anonymous notes, supposedly from Corey Talbott, the rowdiest and most popular guy in seventh grade. Thanks to the mysterious note sender, Vic gets sent to the principal's office — the first time in her life. What will her parents say?

Nielsen, Shelly. **Only Kidding, Victoria.** David C. Cook/Chariot Books, 1986. 127 p. ISBN 0-89191-474-9.

Vic is not excited about spending the summer at a resort lodge. But there are surprises at Little Raccoon Lake — like Nina, who doesn't like rules, and the pang that comes with every letter from Chelsie, reminding Vic of what she's missing back home. But the biggest surprise is Vic's discovery of some things that have been right under her nose all along.

Nielsen, Shelly. **Take a Bow, Victoria.** David C. Cook/Chariot Books, 1986. 127 p. ISBN 0-89191-470-6.

Why can't Vic's hugely pregnant mother stay at home till the baby arrives, instead of waddling into the auditorium in full view of all of Vic's friends? Why does her grandmother, Isadora, need to be so flashy and do such strange things? Vic is struggling with her own confusing wish to be a star — and to stay safely hidden backstage.

Park, Barbara. **Buddies.** Alfred A. Knopf/Borzoi Books, 1985. 135 p. ISBN 0-394-86934-6 (0-394-96934-0, library binding).

Thirteen-year-old Dinah Feeney sees her stay at Camp Miniwawa as a chance to change her image from befriender of the underdog to a member of the "in crowd." While Cassandra and Marilyn seem the perfect pair to aid in Dinah's transformation, Fern Wadley, a classic nerd, threatens to ruin Dinah's plans.

Pascal, Francine. **Love and Betrayal and Hold the Mayo!** Viking Penguin/Viking Kestrel, 1985. 210 p. ISBN 0-670-80547-5.

Sixteen-year-old Torrie is thrilled by the chance to spend all summer as a camper-waiter with her best friend, Steffi. Then she sees the shack she is to live in, drops food all over the campers she serves, and falls in love with Steffi's boyfriend. Can all of this be straightened out in time for Torrie to enjoy some of her summer at camp? Sequel to *My First Love and Other Disasters.*

Peck, Richard. **Princess Ashley.** Delacorte Press, 1987. 208 p. ISBN 0-385-29561-8.

As a new student, Chelsea is surprised when beautiful and powerful Ashley Packard picks her as a member of the "in-group." Chelsea is overwhelmed by Ashley and believes that her mother is never right and Ashley is never wrong. One terrible night Chelsea is involved in a tragedy that lets her see she is not meant to be a follower.

Pfeffer, Susan Beth. **Truth or Dare.** Scholastic/Apple Paperbacks, 1983. 169 p. ISBN 0-590-32529-9.

Cathy Wakefield knows sixth grade in the new junior high will be the worst year of her life. Her two best friends won't be going with her. Then Cathy meets Jessica, the most sophisticated girl in sixth grade, and knows life will be perfect. But Jessica couldn't care less about Cathy. And everyone knows it — except Cathy.

Pike, Christopher. **Chain Letter.** Avon Books/Flare Books, 1986. 185 p. ISBN 0-380-89968-X.

Following a bizarre accident that all of them have kept secret, seven high school friends begin getting chain letters advising them to complete the specified task or be punished. Fires, kidnappings, and murders are part of the consequences. Who is sending these letters?

Provost, Gary, and Gail Levine-Provost. **Popcorn.** Bradbury Press, 1985. 147 p. ISBN 0-02-774960-6.

Twelve-year-olds Richard, Missy, and Mark learn that talent isn't enough to zoom you to the top of the record charts. It requires hard work, sacrifice, rejection, guts, and, most of all, perseverance. At last the trio gets a chance to play at Central Park. But can they face the *New York Times* reviews?

Rae, Judie. **Boyfriend Blues.** Dell/Laurel-Leaf Books, 1985. 139 p. ISBN 0-440-90728-4.

Lizzy feels deserted when her best friend starts to date. Then Lizzy meets Henry. Henry shares her interests in music and the environment, but he doesn't seem to be romantically interested in her. Has Lizzy gone too far in establishing herself as an independent activist?

Roberts, Rachel Sherwood. **Crisis at Pemberton Dike.** Herald Press, 1984. 150 p. ISBN 0-8361-3350-1.

So many feelings to sort out! Fifteen-year-old Carol is like a barometer — warm and sunny one day, cold and angry the next. Carol has trouble understanding these changes in herself and the feelings of love, hate, and jealousy she has for her friends and little sister. Carol learns more about herself while helping victims of the 1982 flood in Fort Wayne, Indiana.

Rockwell, Thomas. **How to Fight a Girl.** Illustrated by Gioia Fiammenghi. Franklin Watts, 1987. 112 p. ISBN 0-531-15082-8 (0-531-10140-1, library binding).

Billy Forrester is really proud when he eats fifteen worms to win a bet. Then Alan and his friend Joe are determined to get even. Billy must protect his reputation and his good name. Even more important, he must get a reprieve from his mother and save his trail bike. After all, he ate the fifteen worms to get the bike in the first place.

Roos, Stephen. **Confessions of a Wayward Preppie.** Delacorte Press, 1986. 135 p. ISBN 0-385-29454-9.

Cary Carmichael is a freshman at an exclusive prep school. He must learn to deal with his feuding roommates, social prejudices, and pressure from upperclassmen.

Roos, Stephen. **My Secret Admirer.** Illustrated by Carol Newsom. Dell/Yearling Books, 1985. 117 p. ISBN 0-440-45950-8.

Claire VanKemp knows she's a shoo-in for the Junior Achievement Award for starting New Eden's first and only video game parlor. She's sure being in business is better than having the boy-crazies like the other girls. But when Claire receives a mystery valentine, she can't rest till she finds out who her secret admirer is.

Sachar, Louis. **There's a Boy in the Girls' Bathroom.** Alfred A. Knopf/Borzoi Books, 1987. 195 p. ISBN 0-394-88570-8 (0-394-88570-2, library binding).

Everyone at school hates Bradley Chalkers. The teachers talk about his "serious behavior problem," the girls think he's a monster, and the boys know he's a bully. But Carla, the new counselor, thinks he's sensitive, generous, and honest. With Carla's help, Bradley tries to change. But not everyone is ready for the "new" Bradley.

Sachs, Elizabeth-Ann. **Where Are You, Cow Patty?** Atheneum, 1984. 146 p. ISBN 0-689-31057-9.

Janie feels lonely and neglected when her two friends begin dating and she doesn't. But watching a calf being born gives her a new outlook on life and a new sense of maturity. Janie realizes that dating will come in its own good time.

Sachs, Marilyn. **Fourteen.** Avon Books/Flare Books, 1985. 116 p. ISBN 0-380-69842-0.

Rebecca, at fourteen, has a unique problem — she has watched her own progress through childhood in the books her mother writes. How embarrassing for her, although her mother insists the books are not really about Rebecca at all. Soon Rebecca forgets her own dilemma as she and the new boy, Jason, undertake the mission of finding Jason's father.

Schoch, Tim. **Creeps.** Avon Books/Camelot Books, 1985. 156 p. ISBN 0-380-89852-7.

Kaybee Keeper comes to school in a wild dress with fish and bubbles on it. The kids laugh at her, and Jeff Moody says they are creeps. But Kaybee gets weirder and weirder until Jeff begins to think that Kaybee is an alien on a secret mission from outer space. Jeff's friends think he's crazy, but what if he is right?

Schwartz, Joel L. **Best Friends Don't Come in Threes.** Illustrated by Bruce Degen. Dell/Yearling Books, 1985. 126 p. ISBN 0-440-40603-X.

When Richie returns from camp, he can't wait to see his best friend, Paul, and begin to make plans for a great first year of high school. But Paul has a new friend, Tony, who is just as good as Richie at basketball and soccer. Richie's not certain where he fits in and wonders if a tight twosome can become a close trio.

Sefton, Catherine. **Island of the Strangers.** Harcourt Brace Jovanovich, 1985. 118 p. ISBN 0-15-239100-2.

When a busload of disadvantaged kids from Belfast camps on a nearby island, thirteen-year-old Nora knows there will be serious trouble between them and the local bullies in her Northern Ireland village. Forced to choose between joining the trouble or being deserted by her friends, what will Nora do?

Sharmat, Marjorie Weinman. **The Son of the Slime Who Ate Cleveland.** Illustrated by Rodney Pate. Dell/Yearling Books, 1985. 108 p. ISBN 0-440-48086-8.

Frank and Jack and Lee are good friends who hang around together so much they are called the Sticky Three. Frank knows that he has to pay a price for having unusual ideas and for being different. Although he dreams of a future in show business, right now Frank's busy playing pranks to help his two best friends.

Shura, Mary Frances. **The Josie Gambit.** Dodd, Mead, 1986. 160 p. ISBN 0-396-08810-4.

During a six-month visit with his grandmother, twelve-year-old Greg Farrell renews his friendship with Josie Nolan and meets the beautiful but cruel Tory Mitchell. Chess champion Greg discovers that people sometimes manipulate others like pawns on a chessboard.

Sommer, Karen. **Satch and the Motormouth.** David C. Cook/Chariot Books, 1987. ISBN 1-55513-063-1.

Satch, a sixth grader, thinks he has only one problem — Motormouth Marcie Cook. Why must he sit by her? Why do they always end up in the same groups? He thinks Marcie is responsible for the anonymous valentines he's getting. He has to rethink this relationship after he learns some startling news about her mother and his father.

Swallow, Pamela Curtis. **Leave It to Christy.** G. P. Putnam's Sons, 1987. 160 p. ISBN 0-399-21482-8.

Christy Swan faces many challenges in the seventh grade: a demanding science teacher, the lead role in *Peter Pan,* and the romantic attention of Jeff. Then she decides to tackle the challenge of solving the problems of Michael, a boy who can play the piano brilliantly, but whose classroom behavior is getting him into trouble.

Taylor, William. **Paradise Lane.** Scholastic, 1987. 165 p. ISBN 0-590-41013-X.

Rosie Perkins, fifteen, is used to being an outcast in her New Zealand town, but when Michael Geraghty and his comrades shower her with dead opossums, she is devastated. As she and the repentant Michael become friends, Rosie learns to cope with her mother's illness, her father's cruelty, and even the death of Plum, her pet opossum.

Ure, Jean. **You Two.** Illustrated by Ellen Eagle. William Morrow, 1984. 184 p. ISBN 0-688-03857-3.

Elizabeth has always attended an exclusive prep school. But when her family moves, Elizabeth goes to the noisy, sprawling Gladeside Intermediate. Since Paddy Dewar wants to be her friend, Elizabeth is spared the awkwardness of being an outsider and enjoys a newfound sense of fun and adventure. Her mother, however, has different ideas about her perfect friends.

Wallace, Bill. **Ferret in the Bedroom, Lizards in the Fridge.** Holiday House, 1986. 132 p. ISBN 0-8234-0600-8.

Liz's father is a zoologist, and their home is filled with homeless animals — two turtles, a hawk, an ibex, a ferret, and lizards. Liz, who is running for class president, invites her friends to her house. The animals are not very cooperative, so Liz angrily tells her father that their pets are ruining her life. When he takes them away, Liz learns something about life's priorities.

Wersba, Barbara. **Crazy Vanilla.** Harper and Row/Charlotte Zolotow Books, 1986. 184 p. ISBN 0-06-026368-7 (0-06-026369-5, library binding).

When Tyler, a well-to-do fourteen-year-old wildlife photographer, meets Mitzi, a streetwise, tough fifteen-year-old waitress, things begin to happen. Tyler's mother has a drinking problem, his father is distant, and his older brother has been banished from the family. Mitzi sets out to help Tyler change his relationship with his family, especially with his brother, before the summer ends and they go their separate ways.

Weyn, Suzanne. **The Makeover Club.** Avon Books/Flare Books, 1986. 121 p. ISBN 0-380-75007-4.

Marsha, Clarissa, and Sara organize the Makeover Club with the goals of becoming beautiful, becoming popular, and finding boy-friends. Are their goals farfetched, or will they be successful?

Willey, Margaret. **Finding David Dolores.** Harper and Row, 1986. 150 p. ISBN 0-06-026483-7 (0-06-026484-5, library binding).

Thirteen-year-old Arly has secretly been following and spying on a handsome older boy, David Dolores. When she meets exotic, sophisticated Regina and shares her feelings of alienation and restlessness, she thinks she has found a real friend. The girls meet David's mother, and Regina adopts her as her own mother. Regina's demands on their friendship soon force Arly to distance herself from Regina and to begin to stand up for her own point of view.

Wilson, Gina. **All Ends Up.** Faber and Faber, 1984. 159 p. ISBN 0-571-13196-4.

Claudia and Anna are fourteen-year-old friends in a city in England. When the new girl, Sylvie, becomes their friend, it always seems that two of the three are friends and one person is left out. Claudia's mother is young and pretty and has never been married. Wilf Smee, a local, middle-aged librarian, has plans to change Claudia's family life by marrying her mother.

Windsor, Patricia. **How a Weirdo and a Ghost Can Change Your Entire Life.** Illustrated by Jacqueline Rogers. Delacorte Press, 1986. 123 p. ISBN 0-385-29479-4.

Martha and Jenny are best friends until Martha becomes sick with strep throat. Then Martha vows not to have a friend again. She certainly doesn't expect to become a friend of Teddy the Windbag, who brings her the assignments. Everyone in the class thinks he's weird, but Martha finds out there's more to him than she thought.

Growing Up Female

Anderson, Mary. **Who Says Nobody's Perfect?** Delacorte Press, 1987. 158 p. ISBN 0-385-29582-0.

Fifteen-year-old Jenny is certain that it will be great to be rid of her perfect sister, Carolyn. How could she foresee that she's only trading one model person for another? The Norwegian exchange student who comes to stay with Jenny's family turns out to be Jenny's superior in everything from academics to athletic prowess to boy catching.

Balis, Andrea, and Robert Reiser. **P.J.** Dell/Yearling Books, 1987. 150 p. ISBN 0-440-468805-9.

P.J. is Perfect Jessica. No normal young teenager wants to have that nickname, so P.J. sets out to prove everyone wrong. P.J. experiences funny situations and heartbreaking ones, and she winds up the school year with a disaster that haunts her all summer.

Betancourt, Jeanne. **Puppy Love.** Avon Books/Camelot Books, 1986. 89 p. ISBN 0-380-89958-2.

Eighth grade for Aviva is not much different from seventh grade for Aviva, but her life outside of school has really changed. Her mother has a new husband and a new baby. Her father has a girlfriend — Miriam the Moron. Aviva wants to be Bob Hanley's number one, but he is interested in Joanne Richards. And Josh? Who cares whether the class bully likes you or not?

Blume, Judy. **Just as Long as We're Together.** Orchard Books, 1987. 296 p. ISBN 0-531-05729-1 (0-531-08329-2, library binding).

Almost thirteen, Stephanie has always been an optimist. But her outlook and attitude change as she becomes suspicious that her parents aren't leveling with her about their relationship. Rachel and Alison try to help, but until Steph is willing to face her problems, what can even best friends do?

Branscum, Robbie. **Johnny May Grows Up.** Illustrated by Bob Marstall. Harper and Row, 1987. 88 p. ISBN 0-06-020606-3 (0-06-020607-1, library binding).

Thirteen-year-old Johnny May is afraid she is losing her friend Aaron because he goes on to high school after eighth grade and she cannot afford to. Somehow she must manage to lose weight, impress Aaron and his new friends, do the farm work, take care of Grandma and Grandpa, and come up with enough money by September to go to high school. Sequel to *The Adventures of Johnny May.*

Cavanna, Betty. **Storm in Her Heart.** Westminster Press, 1983. 92 p. ISBN 0-664-32700-1.

Anne is spending the school year in Florida to be with her grandmother, a recovering alcoholic with an interest in ecology. When a hurricane strikes during her mother's visit, Anne demonstrates a strong commitment to helping the victims of the storm.

Conford, Ellen. **You Never Can Tell.** Little, Brown, 1984. 160 p. ISBN 0-316-15267-6.

Why would sensible, logical Kate Bennett fall head over heels over Brick Preston, star of the soap "Lonely Days, Restless Nights"? Incredibly, Brick enrolls in her school, and sixteen-year-old Kate has to decide which is more important — reality or fantasy.

DeClements, Barthe. **How Do You Lose Those Ninth Grade Blues?** Scholastic/Point Books, 1983. 137 p. ISBN 0-590-33195-7.

Elsie Edward, star of *Nothing's Fair in Fifth Grade,* has slimmed down and is going out with Craddoc, one of the cutest boys in school. But her family life leaves much to be desired, and Elsie doesn't have enough confidence in herself to accept Craddoc's interest.

Emerson, Kathy Lynn. **Julia's Mending.** Orchard Books, 1987. 135 p. ISBN 0-531-05719-4 (0-531-08319-5, library binding).

Julia Applebee is twelve and spoiled. When her missionary parents go to China and Julia is forced to spend the summer of 1887 with her country cousins, she has no intention of changing her expectations or her lifestyle. An accident and unexpected associations with her new family bring surprising changes as well as a time of mending and maturing.

Eyerly, Jeannette. **Someone to Love Me.** J. B. Lippincott, 1987. 168 p. ISBN 0-397-32205-4 (0-397-32206-2, library binding).

Patrice, a fifteen-year-old sophomore, is pleased by the attention from Lance, a senior, even though he already has a girlfriend. Their relationship soon becomes intimate, and before she realizes it, Patrice is three months pregnant. By the time she tells her horrified mother, abortion is out. The bodily changes, examinations, tests, and even birth are described as Patrice goes through her pregnancy.

First, Julia. **The Absolute, Ultimate End.** Franklin Watts, 1985. 156 p. ISBN 0-531-10075-8.

Expectations for junior high seem to fall apart for Maggie Thayer and her best friend, Eloise. Neither does well in her chosen extracurricular activity, and Maggie finds herself being an unwilling reader for a blind girl. Then Maggie's father runs for the school board with a campaign to cut funds for extra school activities.

Greenberg, Jan. **Bye, Bye, Miss American Pie.** Farrar, Straus and Giroux, 1985. 150 p. ISBN 0-374-31012-2.

Beth has always been a good student and quite unlike her sister, Louisa, who is always in trouble with their parents. Then Beth is attracted to Jason Teasdale, who rides a motorcycle, has been thrown out of prep school, and shoplifts. Beth ignores Louisa's warnings that she could be headed for trouble, for she feels Louisa is merely jealous.

Greenwald, Sheila. **Valentine Rosy.** Atlantic Monthly Press, 1984. 89 p. ISBN 0-316-32708-5.

Eleven-year-old Rosy Cole is sick of being a baby. Lately her punk older sisters seem to be ruining her "happy family" ideal, and to Rosy, growing up is the pits. To top it all, how can she compete with Christi McCurry, the Christi-Belles, and Christi's very grown-up valentine party?

Gulley, Judie. **Rodeo Summer.** Houghton Mifflin, 1984. 146 p. ISBN 0-395-36174-5.

Janet's sister, Jackie, is gorgeous, and her twin brothers, Jon and Jim, are daredevils. Everyone is a prize-winning rider, except

Janet. Janet decides to change that and buys a spunky little bay as a barrel horse. But Crow has been mistreated, and Janet must win his trust. Her friend David is jealous of the time she spends with Crow. Then comes the accident, and Crow is condemned to death.

Hall, Lynn. **The Giver.** Charles Scribner's Sons, 1985. 119 p. ISBN 0-684-18312-9.

James Flicket, fifteen-year-old Mary McNeal's homeroom teacher, notices that she tries to be "invisible." Mary feels that she is unattractive and that no one will ever love her. James and Mary find each other, but they worry that the difference in their ages and stations in life could cause irreparable damage to both.

Hurwitz, Johanna. **Hurricane Elaine.** Illustrated by Diane De Groat. William Morrow, 1986. 99 p. ISBN 0-688-06461-2.

Fifteen-year-old Elaine is going through the usual teenage ups and downs — a romantic crush on a teacher, the trauma of getting her ears pierced, and coping with flea-carrying pets of younger siblings. Then her quick temper leads to a family crisis.

Klass, Sheila Solomon. **The Bennington Stitch.** Bantam Books, 1986. 134 p. ISBN 0-553-26049-9.

Amy's mother has definite plans for her daughter — Amy is to attend the exclusive Bennington College where she herself had longed to study twenty years ago. How can seventeen-year-old Amy convince her English-teacher mother that college isn't for everyone? Staunch supporters, boyfriend Rob, and counselor Mr. O help Amy discover her own unique creativity, which the SAT's couldn't measure.

Leroe, Ellen. **Confessions of a Teenage TV Addict.** E. P. Dutton/ Lodestar Books, 1983. 138 p. ISBN 0-525-66909-4.

Jennifer Warrens, sixteen, is addicted to TV. She even wears a TV-band transistor radio on her wrist so she can listen to her favorite soap operas during class in Miss Baird's School for Girls. When she transfers to a coed high school, Jennifer feels as if her life is becoming a soap opera. Troubled by the attention of her best friend's boyfriend, sinister notes on her locker, disagreements with her mother, and her addiction to TV, Jennifer struggles to become a part of "real life."

Levinson, Nancy Smiler. **The Ruthie Greene Show.** E. P. Dutton/Lodestar Books, 1985. 122 p. ISBN 0-525-67172-2.

Ruthie Greene feels totally left out. Her family is absorbed in plans for her sister's wedding, her Spanish group considers her ideas for a skit weird, and, worst of all, gorgeous Mark doesn't know she's alive. But when fifteen-year-old Ruthie meets a real Hollywood producer who becomes her mentor, she begins to see herself in a different light.

Lowry, Lois. **Anastasia Has the Answers.** Dell/Yearling Books, 1987. 123 p. ISBN 0-440-40087-2.

Everybody, including her parents and Ms. Willoughby's entire eighth-grade gym class, can climb ropes. Everybody, that is, except Anastasia Krupnik. An aspiring journalist, Anastasia applies the who, what, when, where, and why test and eventually finds the solution to this and other adolescent dilemmas.

McDonnell, Christine. **Count Me In.** Viking Penguin/Viking Kestrel, 1986. 173 p. ISBN 0-670-80417-7.

Eighth-grader Katie hates being a "fifth wheel." Her mother and stepfather are expecting a baby, her best friend Ruth has discovered boys, and her father has a girlfriend. But during a visit with Grandma at her beach house, Katie meets Paul, who gives her a new view of growing up. Later, an "egg-sperience" helps Katie better understand parenting.

Martin, Ann M. **Slam Book.** Holiday House, 1987. 154 p. ISBN 0-0834-0666-0.

Anna is terrified at the thought of starting high school in the fall. So she and her best friends from junior high start a slam book and soon find themselves the center of attention at school. But the game turns dangerous when unpopular Cheryl Sutphin becomes the tragic victim of the slam book.

Meyer, Carolyn. **The Summer I Learned about Life.** Atheneum/Margaret K. McElderry Books, 1983. 198 p. ISBN 0-689-50285-0.

The year is 1928, and girls are trained to make proper wives. But fifteen-year-old Teddie would rather be another Amelia Earhart than a housewife. Her brother's romance and her friend Julie's troubles teach her that a "woman's place" is more complex than she imagined.

Myers, Walter Dean. **Crystal.** Viking Penguin/Viking Kestrel, 1987. 198 p. ISBN 0-670-80426-6.

Sixteen-year-old Crystal — black, beautiful, and with the look high-fashion photographers want — is on her way to becoming a celebrity. Already on the cover of fashion magazines, in perfume advertisements, and appearing on late-night TV talk shows, Crystal is now being considered for a movie role. She attempts to keep her personal and school life from being overwhelmed by the adult world of glamour and excitement.

Park, Barbara. **Beanpole.** Avon Books/Flare Books, 1984. 147 p. ISBN 0-380-69840-4.

By second grade, Lillian was two inches taller than her classmates. Now, at age thirteen, Lillian is still stuck with the look and nickname of "Beanpole." For her thirteenth birthday she makes three wishes, and the first two come true, sort of. Lillian then begins to wonder if she really wants that third wish.

Pfeffer, Susan Beth. **Getting Even.** Berkley Books/Pacer Books, 1987. 188 p. ISBN 0-425-09779-X.

Annie is sure that her summer job in glamorous New York City as an intern on a famous magazine will land her the job as editor of her high school paper. When she doesn't get the position, Annie is shocked and hurt, and then she resolves to get even.

Pitts, Paul. **For a Good Time, Don't Call Claudia.** Avon Books/Flare Books, 1986. 115 p. ISBN 0-380-75117-8.

Fourteen-year-old Claudia and her mother move to an apartment following the death of her father and brother in an accident. Money is tight, and Claudia has to struggle to have a decent wardrobe and to keep her weight down. Then her life improves when she gets a job at a pet store and her mother lets her keep a ferret. But why is she getting these phone calls?

Quin-Harkin, Janet. **Wanted: Date for Saturday Night.** Pacer Books, 1985. 152 p. ISBN 0-399-21150-0.

Up to now, Julie has not cared much about boys, but suddenly it seems very important that she find somebody special to take her to the freshman formal. When her older cousin, Danny, visits for the weekend and the "in crowd" at school thinks he's her college boyfriend, Julie must take drastic measures to save her new reputation.

Rinaldi, Ann. **The Good Side of My Heart.** Holiday House, 1987. 284 p. ISBN 0-8234-0648-2.

Sixteen-year-old Brie begins to date Josh, a high school senior. Even though Josh is handsome and considerate, he has a bad reputation — he was kicked out of military school because of a scandal. Brie worries about her older brother, Kevin, a priest who's expressing doubts about his vocation. She is also having troubles with her father, who is a strict but loving disciplinarian. Depressed, Brie can't seem to deal with any of the men in her life.

Ryan, Mary C. **Frankie's Run.** Little, Brown, 1987. 127 p. ISBN 0-316-76370-5.

Thirteen-year-old Mary Frances's best friend is beginning to get interested in boys. However, Mary Frances is not sure she is ready for dating. She wonders if she should follow her friend's lead or just be herself.

Rylant, Cynthia. **A Blue-Eyed Daisy.** Bradbury Press, 1985. 99 p. ISBN 0-02-777960-2.

Eleven-year-old Ellie, one of Okey Farley's five daughters, is the only one interested in Bullet, the beagle. The others have boys on their minds. During this year in her West Virginia coal-mining town, Ellie has an uncle go off to war, sees a boy in her class have a fit, is saddened when another boy is accidentally killed — but still she finds a best friend, gets kissed for the first time, and turns twelve.

Sachs, Marilyn. **Baby Sister.** E. P. Dutton, 1986. 147 p. ISBN 0-525-44213-8.

Fifteen-year-old Penny finds living in the shadow of her flamboyant sister, Cass, at once exciting and impossible. As Cass's efforts to enliven Penny's existence fall through, Penny discovers her own surprising abilities. To complicate matters, the brother-sister relationship she's always had with Rick, Cass's boyfriend, begins to change.

Shyer, Marlene Fanta. **Adorable Sunday.** Charles Scribner's Sons, 1983. 182 p. ISBN 0-684-17848-6.

Sunday Donaldson is adorable, which leads to a career as a TV model. However, stardom has its price. Sunday is continually juggling auditions, filming, callbacks, friends, her boyfriend, and all the other activities of junior high. But more importantly, Sunday must face the darker side of stardom, a side that proves to be less than adorable.

Snyder, Carol. **The Leftover Kid.** Berkley Books/Pacer Books, 1987. 158 p. ISBN 0-425-09709-9.

Wendy is the only child at home now and really has it made. She has a room to herself and the nearly undivided attention of her parents. But first her brother, his wife, and their newborn baby move in, and then Wendy's grandparents move in. Even though Wendy is known for her sense of humor, she finds her patience wearing thin.

Snyder, Zilpha Keatley. **And Condors Danced.** Delacorte Press, 1987. 211 p. ISBN 0-385-29575-8.

It's 1907. Carly Hartwich is eleven and imagines herself to be invisible. She prefers to spend her time in the lively home of her great-aunt Mehitabel rather than be at home, where her mother is ill and her father overly stern. Growing up is forced on Carly as unexpected tragedies come her way.

Springstubb, Tricia. **Eunice Bottlieb and the Unwhitewashed Truth about Life.** Delacorte Press, 1987. 177 p. ISBN 0-385-29552-9.

Eunice and Joy are set for a great, prosperous summer when they open their own catering business, Have Your Cake. Complications arise when Joy's focus shifts away from the business toward a cute ninth grader, Robert. And when Reggie, a total reject, tries to horn into the longtime friendship between Eunice and Joy, thirteen-year-old Eunice discovers it's time to readjust her outlook.

Stanek, Lou Willett. **Megan's Beat.** Dial Books for Young Readers, 1983. 201 p. ISBN 0-8037-5201-6.

Megan Morgan did not realize that being a farm girl and a "bus kid" was going to set her apart from the popular "town kids" at the high school. Writing for the school newspaper offers her a way to break into the "in group." But then Megan must choose between her new friends and her childhood friends — especially Tom, who lives on the adjoining farm.

Tolles, Martha. **Darci and the Dance Contest.** E. P. Dutton/Lodestar Books, 1985. 99 p. ISBN 0-525-67166-8.

Darci, who is in sixth grade and has moved from California to the East Coast, is having trouble making friends. She wants to enter the school's dance contest, but where can she find a partner? Her brother's three-foot snake further complicates her efforts to be popular. Sequel to *Who's Reading Darci's Diary?*

Windsor, M. A. **Pretty Saro.** Atheneum, 1986. 200 p. ISBN 0-689-31277-6.

Winning the state championship for Best of Show with her pony, Moonlight Rhythm, is the most important thing in the world to fourteen-year-old Sara Jean Banks. Or at least it is before a hearing loss, a revelation of family secrets, and the discovery of new friends make her reconsider her priorities.

Growing Up Male

Adler, C. S. **Roadside Valentine.** Macmillan, 1983. 185 p. ISBN 0-02-700350-7.

Jamie, a high school senior, has been a loner since his mother left him at the age of nine. Now the arguments with his father have gotten worse, and Jamie turns to arcade games, gymnastics, and Louisa, who regards him as only a friend until Valentine's Day sparks Jamie's creative abilities. Then his father prompts Jamie to leave home.

Anderson, Mary. **That's Not My Style.** Atheneum, 1983. 162 p. ISBN 0-689-30968-6.

John Sandor, sixteen, wishes that adults would just stop bugging him about not annoying the neighbors and completing his English assignments so that he can achieve his lifelong ambition — to become as great a novelist as Ernest Hemingway. Will association with a "real" writer, his family's butcher business, and a girl help John discover how to channel his talents?

Andrews, Wendy. **Are We There Yet?** Pacer Books, 1985. 122 p. ISBN 0-448-47758-0.

While on vacation with his family in Dallas, fifteen-year-old Ted is pursued by two rich girls at the same time. Dallas is the last stop on their vacation, and it's Ted's last hope for a fabulous time. He's tired of waiting to be grown-up. Could this be his chance?

Bates, Betty. **Ask Me Tomorrow.** Holiday House, 1987. 135 p. ISBN 0-8234-0659-8.

Instead of taking over his family's apple orchard business, Paige Truitt wants to go to Boston and become a detective or a TV news correspondent. Fifteen-year-old Paige feels trapped, but he does not want to hurt his father's feelings. Paige makes friends with thirteen-year-old Abby Winch, who is visiting her grandparents. Seeing his world through her eyes only makes his decision more difficult.

Carter, Alden R. **Wart, Son of Toad.** Berkley Books/Pacer Books, 1986. 190 p. ISBN 0-425-08885-5.

Steve Michaels struggles with the dilemma of trying to please his father, one of the most unpopular teachers at the high school Steve attends, and with his desire to take an auto mechanics course. Being called Wart, son of Toad, also bothers Steve. His only friend who seems to understand him is Trish, but she might be in love with someone else.

Conford, Ellen. **Why Me?** Little, Brown, 1985. 145 p. ISBN 0-316-15326-5.

Hobie is thirteen and crazy about Darlene. His dreams come true when the poems he writes about her win her affection. But there are complications. G.G., a brainy redhead, plots to ensnare him, and Hobie discovers that the adoring Darlene just may have an ulterior motive.

Hall, Barbara. **Skeeball and the Secret of the Universe.** Orchard Books, 1987. 232 p. ISBN 0-531-05722-4 (0-531-08322-5, library binding).

Matty Collier wants one last fling before the end of high school. He feels out of place in his small southern hometown. He feels more in tune with his movie idol, James Dean — star of *Rebel without a Cause.* He hopes he will discover the meaning of life before he has to grow up, get married, and go to work.

Halvorson, Marilyn. **Cowboys Don't Cry.** Dell/Laurel-Leaf Books, 1986. 160 p. ISBN 0-440-91303-9.

Cowboys don't cry, not even when their drunk fathers embarrass them in front of their new friends. Always on the move, Shane has finally found a school and friends he likes. He is even on the cross-country team. But can he cope with his father's drinking and running away from problems?

Halvorson, Marilyn. **Let It Go.** Delacorte Press, 1986. 235 p. ISBN 0-385-29484-0.

When fifteen-year-old Red Cantrell moves to a small Canadian community, he meets Lance Ducharme from a nearby ranch. Although they become fast friends, each boy is hiding a family secret. These secrets test the boys' friendship as they are led through danger and adventure involving Red's mother, Lance's father, and a drug pusher.

Janeczko, Paul B. **Bridges to Cross.** Macmillan, 1986. 162 p. ISBN 0-02-747940-4.

James Marchuk is about to enter high school and wants to attend the public school. His mother, who insists that he live by a rigid set of rules, says that he must go to the Catholic school. James rebels, but not seriously until he is driven by his teachers' behavior and attitude and his mother's close rein.

Johnston, Norma. **Timewarp Summer.** Atheneum, 1983. 161 p. ISBN 0-689-30960-0.

It's the summer before Scott's senior year, and he takes on an all-consuming project — the creation of a science fiction movie, *Timewarp.* His girlfriend, Julie, his neighbor, Bettina, and Dr. Laura Weller, a scientist ten years Scott's senior, are caught up with him in what proves to be his obsession.

Kemp, Gene. **Charlie Lewis Plays for Time.** Illustrated by Vanessa Julian-Ottie. Faber and Faber, 1984. 132 p. ISBN 571-13248-0.

Charlie Lewis, the son of renowned English concert pianist Marian Forrest, divides his time between music practice, school, and the unruly Moffet clan while his mother is on tour. The clan members want to spend their last term at Cricklepit Combined with their favorite teacher, Mr. Merchant. But an accident befalls Mr. Merchant, and he is replaced by the strict, serious, and unjust Mr. Carter.

Klein, Norma. **The Cheerleader.** Alfred A. Knopf/Borzoi Books, 1985. 134 p. ISBN 0-394-87577-X (0-394-97577-4, library binding).

Eighth-grader Evan Siegal is pursued by two girls: no-nonsense Laurie and popular cheerleader Rachel. Complications arise when Evan's best friend, Karim, confides that *he* worships Rachel. A plot to give Karim a new image and a chance to win Rachel's affection shocks the boys' peers into taking a new look at "equal rights."

Kroll, Steven. **Take It Easy.** Scholastic/Point Paperbacks, 1983. 138 p. ISBN 0-590-32306-7.

Fifteen-year-old Nick Warner knows that being talented academically and athletically is not enough to create happiness. He must struggle to cope with the pain and realities of growing up.

Maloney, Ray. **The Impact Zone.** Delacorte Press, 1986. 246 p. ISBN 0-385-29447-6.

Teenager Jim Nichols thinks that he will solve his problems by running away from his mother and an unbearable stepfather to live with his father. After all, his father leads a glamorous life as a surfer and photographer in Hawaii. But Jim's utopia soon turns to resentment, and he learns that problems must be faced and resolved.

Meyer, Carolyn. **Elliott and Win.** Atheneum/Margaret K. McElderry Books, 1986. 193 p. ISBN 0-689-50368-7.

Fourteen-year-old Win's mother has signed him up for the Los Amigos program, which provides older male friends for fatherless boys. Elliott is not the "amigo" Win would have chosen, but he finds that Elliott can help him deal with the problems in his life. Complications arise when Win's friend Paul suggests that Elliott is a homosexual.

Okimoto, Jean Davies. **Jason's Women.** Atlantic Monthly Press, 1986. 210 p. ISBN 0-87113-061-0.

Jason, sixteen, has always been a wimp, reveling in a fantasy world and dreaming about the women who run provocative ads in the personal column. Then his friendship with eighty-year-old Bertha Jane Fillmore and her Vietnamese prodigy, Thao, helps him appreciate his own special gift of compassion.

Petersen, P. J. **Good-bye to Good Ol' Charlie.** Delacorte Press, 1987. 155 p. ISBN 0-385-29483-2.

Tired of being a reliable "nice guy," sixteen-year-old Charlie uses his move from L.A. to Cascade to change his image. The problem is, who does he want to be — Cowboy Chet, tough guy Chip, or poetic Chad?

Petersen, P. J. **Here's to the Sophomores.** Dell/Laurel-Leaf Books, 1985. 181 p. ISBN 0-440-93394-3.

What can be worse than starting your sophomore year by breaking a leg during football practice? As Mike Parker and his friends Warren and Arnold settle in at Hendley High, they suffer several unlucky breaks. Can Mike balance it all — Warren's staunch defiance of the status quo, Arnold's delinquent tendencies, and the fact that Margaret Olsen suddenly considers Mike more than a friend?

Potter, Marian. **Mark Makes His Move.** William Morrow, 1986. 184 p. ISBN 0-688-06220-2.

Eleven-year-old Mark Frye has always been a bighearted but timid boy, so everyone is surprised when he tackles some challenges in both his home and in the neighborhood. Sometimes his schemes backfire and he has to regroup, but Mark finds strengths he didn't know he had.

Seidler, Tor. **The Tar Pit.** Farrar, Straus and Giroux, 1987. 153 p. ISBN 0-374-37383-3.

Edward Small, Jr., does not get along well with his father or with his classmates. He's not good at sports or at much of anything else. His only friend besides his mother and sister is an imaginary dinosaur who resides in a tar pit.

Spinelli, Jerry. **Jason and Marceline.** Little, Brown, 1986. 228 p. ISBN 0-316-80719-2.

Ninth-grader Jason Herkimer is learning about life, love, and hormones. If only Marceline would cooperate — but she feels a relationship should be based on more than physical attraction. The novel includes a frank discussion of sexual discovery. Sequel to *Space Station Seventh Grade.*

Stine, R. L. **Blind Date.** Scholastic/Point Paperbacks, 1986. 200 p. ISBN 0-590-40326-5.

When Kerry accidentally breaks the leg of the star quarterback on his own football team, it is the "straw that breaks the camel's back." Earlier in the year Kerry and his brother had been in an automobile accident, after which his brother disappeared. Now Kerry receives a series of phone threats, until there is a call that appears to be friendly — or is it?

Stolz, Mary. **The Explorer of Barkham Street.** Illustrated by Emily Arnold McCully. Harper and Row, 1985. 179 p. ISBN 0-06-025976-0 (0-06-025977-9, library binding).

Thirteen-year-old Martin Hastings, a reformed bully, fills his life with fantasies of heroic exploits as an explorer and a sports star. He also dreams about having a better home situation and a better image of himself, of having his dog Rufus back, and of being successful at something. His new circle of friends and growing self-confidence at home make real life as exciting as his daydreams.

Sweeney, Joyce. **Center Line.** Dell/Laurel-Leaf Books, 1985. 246 p. ISBN 0-440-91127-3.

Five motherless teenage boys run away to escape the abuse of their alcoholic father. Money runs low, and sibling quarrels, rivalries, and jealousies arise. Shawn, the eldest brother, feels most responsible for avoiding sickness, finding food and shelter, and trying to keep the family together. He begins to wonder if he has led his brothers into a better life, or if he has condemned them to being fugitives.

Zalben, Jane Breskin. **Here's Looking at You, Kid.** Farrar, Straus and Giroux, 1985. 136 p. ISBN 0-374-33055-7.

When seventeen-year-old Eric Fine moves with his family to Long Island, he finds that making friends and falling in love can be very confusing. Enid is smart and serious and shares Eric's love of writing. Kimberly is beautiful, with all the right packaging and full of life. Should friendship suffer at the expense of love?

Historical Novels

American

Angell, Judie. **One-Way to Ansonia.** Bradbury Press, 1985. 183 p. ISBN 0-02-705860-3.

Ten-year-old Rose Olshansky leaves her homeland of Russia and arrives in New York in 1893. At thirteen, she is working twelve hours a day in the Griffin Cap Factory and thinking that there must be a better way to live her life. Rose begins to play the piano, attend night school, and get involved in the union's activities. She also wonders if she should yield to family pressure and marry her stepmother's wealthy brother.

Avi. **The Fighting Ground.** J. B. Lippincott, 1984. 157 p. ISBN 0-397-32073-6 (0-397-32074-4, library binding).

Thirteen-year-old Jonathan lives near Trenton, New Jersey, in 1778 and becomes caught up in the Revolutionary War. When he is taken prisoner by three Hessian soldiers, Jonathan changes his understanding of war and life forever. The real war, he discovers, is being fought within himself.

Beatty, Patricia. **Turn Homeward, Hannalee.** William Morrow, 1984. 193 p. ISBN 0-688-03871-9.

Hannalee Reed is twelve and a bobbin girl in a Georgia mill during the Civil War. When the Yankees arrive, they round up all the millworkers, including Hannalee, and ship them north to work in the mills there. Mama's special gift brings Hanalee solace in her new life in Indiana, but she wonders whether the persimmon button will help her make her way southward to Georgia and what she will find there if she does arrive.

Clapp, Patricia. **The Tamarack Tree.** Lothrop, Lee and Shepard Books, 1986. 213 p. ISBN 0-688-02852-7.

Rosemary Leigh, a thirteen-year-old orphan from England, loves Vicksburg, Mississippi, when she arrives in 1859 to live with her older brother, Derek. Quickly she becomes part of the city's social life, though her views of slavery set her at odds with the Vicksburg community. Then the Civil War breaks out, and Rosemary needs her every ounce of courage to survive.

Clapp, Patricia. **Witches' Children: A Story of Salem.** Viking Penguin/ Puffin Books, 1987. 159 p. ISBN 0-14-032407-0.

In this novel based on the Salem witch-hunt and trials of 1692, Mary Warren is one of ten young girls who seem to be possessed by the devil. Tituba, the servant Reverend Parris brought to Salem from the islands of Barbados, excites the girls with her stories of life in Barbados — the warmth, the magic, the superstition, the witchcraft. Soon the girls are involved in making their own magic. Their fits of screaming and strange visions lead the people of Salem to believe the girls are the witches' children.

Climo, Shirley. **A Month of Seven Days.** Thomas Y. Crowell, 1987. 151 p. ISBN 0-690-04658-8 (0-690-04656-1, library binding).

Yankee soldiers are camped in the fields below twelve-year-old Zoe's home in Georgia during the Civil War. The captain has taken over her parents' bedroom for himself. Finding out that he is superstitious, Zoe determines to convince the captain that the house is haunted and to get rid of him before her father, a Confederate soldier, returns.

Conrad, Pam. **Prairie Songs.** Illustrated by Darryl S. Zudeck. Harper and Row, 1985. 167 p. ISBN 0-06-021336-1 (0-06-021337-X, library binding).

Louisa's life in a loving pioneer family on the Nebraska prairie is altered by the arrival of a new doctor and his beautiful but frail wife, Emmeline. Louisa is thrilled when Emmeline gives her and her brother, Lester, reading lessons. But as Louisa's love for poetry blossoms, and as Lester slowly begins to come out of his shell, Emmeline fades into a silent, baffling world of madness and despair.

DeFord, Deborah H., and Harry S. Stout. **An Enemy among Them.** Houghton Mifflin, 1987. 203 p. ISBN 0-395-44239-7.

A young Hessian soldier fights on the British side during the American Revolutionary War. Questions of loyalty arise when he is taken prisoner by a German-American family from Pennsylvania.

Ferry, Charles. **One More Time!** Houghton Mifflin, 1985. 171 p. ISBN 0-395-36692-5.

It is 1941, and bandleader Gene Markam has just received a commission in the army. After one more trip, the band will break up. Through the eyes of one musician, nineteen-year-old Skeets Sinclair, the reader is taken on a whirlwind last tour and learns of the many personality conflicts between the band members, harsh travel by bus, and romance with the band's young singer.

Kassem, Lou. **Listen for Rachel.** Macmillan/Margaret K. McElderry Books, 1986. 164 p. ISBN 0-689-50396-2.

After her parents die in a fire, Rachel goes to live with her maternal grandparents in the Appalachian Mountains and to help her grandfather raise horses. She gets to know Granny Sharp, the local healer, and begins to learn about the art of healing with plants and herbs. When the Civil War breaks out, Rachel helps with the sick and injured of both sides. While caring for a young wounded Yankee soldier, Rachel falls in love. Then she must make a difficult decision. Should she stay in the mountains, where her knowledge of healing is needed, or should she marry the Yankee and move to Pennsylvania with him?

Kherdian, David. **Bridger: The Story of a Mountain Man.** Greenwillow Books, 1987. 146 p. ISBN 0-688-06510-4.

In this fictionalized account of a true story, eighteen-year-old Jim Bridger leaves civilization behind and spends the years 1822–1824 on the American frontier. He signs on with General Ashley to "ascend the river Missouri," a journey that brings unbelievable hardships and danger. Many explorers in the party are killed, and many desert the expedition.

Lasky, Kathryn. **Beyond the Divide.** Macmillan, 1983. 254 p. ISBN 0-02-751670-9.

In 1849 Meribah Simon and her father leave their Amish community in Pennsylvania and join a wagon train headed west to find gold. As the terrain becomes more hazardous, the harmony of the group fades and is replaced with petty quarrels, bitterness, and rivalry. When her father's illness prevents their continuing with the wagon train, Meribah must learn to encounter the elements and rely on her own courage. (Literary merit)

Moore, Ruth Nulton. **In Search of Liberty.** Illustrated by James Converse. Herald Press, 1983. 173 p. ISBN 0-8361-3340-4.

Just before undergoing serious surgery, fourteen-year-old Jon Reed receives a 1794 penny from his father. Through the centuries, this Liberty coin had changed hands many times, bringing luck to those who held it. Now Jon desperately hopes that it will bring good luck to him. While hospitalized, Jon learns of the penny's past adventures and makes a crucial decision about its future.

Murrow, Liza Ketchum. **West against the Wind.** Holiday House, 1987. 232 p. ISBN 0-8234-0668-7.

When fourteen-year-old Abigail Parker and her family set out to find her father in the gold mines of Yuba City, California, in 1850, they can only imagine the hardships they will encounter. As she travels from Ohio to the West Coast, Abby matures physically and emotionally and even falls in love with the handsome young stranger, Matthew Reed. (Literary merit)

Nixon, Joan Lowery. **Caught in the Act.** Bantam Books/Starfire Books, 1988. 150 p. ISBN 0-553-05443-0.

Eleven-year-old Mike Kelly is chosen from the Orphan Train by the Friedrichs only because they want someone to work long hours for room and board. Their son, Gunter, makes every effort to get Mike into trouble so that his parents will send Mike back to New York's Tombs Prison. Mike overhears bits and pieces of information that lead him to believe that Mr. Friedrich has killed a man. Book two in the Orphan Train Quartet.

Nixon, Joan Lowery. **A Family Apart.** Bantam Books/Starfire Books, 1987. 162 p. ISBN 0-553-05432-5.

The six Kelly children and their mother struggle to stay alive in New York City in 1860 following the death of the children's father. In spite of every effort, the boys are leaning toward lives of crime, so Mrs. Kelly decides she must put the children up for adoption. They board a train to Missouri, where prospective parents will select the children they wish to adopt. This book focuses on the new life of the oldest Kelly child, thirteen-year-old Frances Mary. Book one in the Orphan Train Quartet. (Literary merit)

O'Dell, Scott. **The Serpent Never Sleeps.** Illustrated by Ted Lewin. Houghton Mifflin, 1987. 227 p. ISBN 0-395-44242-7.

As Serena Lynn sets sail in 1609 for the new settlement in Jamestown, Virginia, she is leaving behind Foxcroft Castle and pursuing a romantic dream of life with handsome young Anthony Foxcroft. In the New World she survives a shipwreck off Bermuda, becomes involved with the conflicts of the settlers, meets Pocahontas, and plays an exciting role in the development of the new colony.

Paige, Harry W. **Shadow on the Sun.** Frederick Warne, 1984. 181 p. ISBN 0-7232-6258-6.

When fourteen-year-old Billy Wade learns that he is the son of Billy the Kid, he finds his values suddenly challenged. Faced with the choice of getting revenge on Pat Garrett, his father's killer, or pursuing a career in photography, Billy makes yet another discovery: the fine line between loyalty and obsession. The story is set in the harsh New Mexico Territory of 1892.

Perez, N. A. **One Special Year.** Houghton Mifflin, 1985. 200 p. ISBN 0-395-36693-3.

From New Year's Day to Christmas, the year 1900 brings many changes for thirteen-year-old Jen McAlister. In her small New York hometown, Jen observes her seventeen-year-old brother, Luke, become close friends with a young widow, and she experiences the highs and lows of her own first love. Jen witnesses rising tension between her dapper father and moody mother and discovers a disturbing secret from the past. Overall, the start of the century proves to be one special year indeed.

Perez, N. A. **The Slopes of War.** Houghton Mifflin, 1984. 202 p. ISBN 0-395-35642-3.

Buck Summerhill is a young private in the Army of the Potomac during the Civil War. He and his sister, Bekah, experience the Battle of Gettysburg and the terrible agony of war — the lack of food and supplies, the weariness of long marches and battles, the sadness of parting from loved ones, and the horror of seeing death everywhere. (Literary merit)

Rappaport, Doreen. **Trouble at the Mines.** Illustrated by Joan Sandin. Thomas Y. Crowell, 1987. 81 p. ISBN 0-690-04445-3 (0-690-04446-1, library binding).

In 1899 Rosie's father, brothers, and other relatives work in the coal mines in Arnot, Pennsylvania. Her father leads the miners in a year-long strike to gain safer working conditions and higher pay. Union organizer Mother Jones arrives to help convince the women and children that they have an important job helping the men. The novel is based on real events.

Rinaldi, Ann. **Time Enough for Drums.** Holiday House, 1986. 249 p. ISBN 0-8234-0603-2.

Fifteen-year-old Jemima Emerson struggles to sort out her feelings about the Revolutionary War and the effects it has on her family. Jem must grow up quickly when her brothers are scattered by the war and her Tory older sister marries a British officer. She must also deal with her growing love for a spy.

Rostkowski, Margaret I. **After the Dancing Days.** Harper and Row, 1986. 217 p. ISBN 0-06-025077-1 (0-06-025078-X, library binding).

Thirteen-year-old Annie's father is a physician working at the veterans' hospital in Kansas City after World War I. Annie goes there often and meets a badly burned young veteran, Andrew, who is bitter and withdrawn. Undaunted by his unfriendliness, Annie keeps coming to visit Andrew, slowly drawing him back into an awareness of the world and helping him see that life is worth living.

Sanders, Scott R. **Bad Man Ballad.** Bradbury Press, 1986. 241 p. ISBN 0-02-778230-1.

In the forests of Ohio in 1813, three unlikely partners, a young backwoods boy named Ely, a Philadelphia lawyer, and a halfbreed girl join to search for a huge man who has murdered a dwarf. Across the countryside the three chase this creature, a being so large his footprint in the mud will hold both of Ely's boots. Each one is driven by a private reason for wanting to find the murderer.

Shore, Laura Jan. **The Sacred Moon Tree.** Bradbury Press, 1986. 209 p. ISBN 0-02-782790-9.

Phoebe Sands is an eleven-year-old girl hungering for adventure in 1863. She hears that the Rebels have captured her friend Jotham's brother, and she is determined to go to Richmond to rescue him. Phoebe disguises herself as a boy, and she and Jotham see more of the war than they really want to on their trip from Pennsylvania to Virginia.

Speare, Elizabeth George. **The Sign of the Beaver.** Houghton Mifflin, 1983. 135 p. ISBN 0-395-33890-5.

Matt will be thirteen while his father's gone, and he'll celebrate his birthday alone while he cares for the wilderness cabin and garden in eighteenth-century Maine. In six weeks his father will return with the rest of the family. Following a terrible encounter with a swarm of bees, Matt is healed by the Indian Saknis and his grandson, Attean. Matt tries to teach Attean to read, and Attean teaches Matt the ways of Indian life and survival in the wilderness. (Literary merit)

Stolz, Mary. **Ivy Larkin.** Harcourt Brace Jovanovich, 1986. 226 p. ISBN 0-15-239366-8.

The Larkins are hard hit by the Depression of 1929, and fourteen-year-old Ivy can't understand why she has to attend the expensive, private Holland School, where all the girls know she is on a scholarship given to poor, but bright, students. Will Ivy let her pride interfere with her parents' dreams of success?

Tamar, Erika. **Good-bye, Glamour Girl.** New American Library/Signet Vista Books, 1985. 151 p. ISBN 0-451-14019-2.

Liesl Rosen's family flees Hitler's Germany in the 1940s, and her physician father finds setting up a new practice in New York very difficult. But Liesl has to have her dreams, and if she can't be another Rita Hayworth, she can at least have Billy — or can she?

Turner, Ann. **Third Girl from the Left.** Macmillan, 1986. 153 p. ISBN 0-02-789510-6.

In 1855 Sarah Goodhue says good-bye to her boring Maine life and heads for the wilderness of a Montana cattle farm as a mail-order bride for Alex Proud. Montana life is hard, and living on a ranch is lonesome, but Sarah refuses to admit defeat. Then Alex dies in an accident, and Sarah has to decide whether to stay in Montana or return to Maine.

Wisler, G. Clifton. **Thunder on the Tennessee.** E. P. Dutton/Lodestar Books, 1983. 153 p. ISBN 0-525-67144-7.

Sixteen-year-old Willie Delamer is determined to fight side-by-side with his father against the Yankees. It is 1862, and Willie is ready for adventure, but nothing has prepared him for the realities of war. At Shiloh Church, Willie learns that courage and honor are only words, and that the real word is survival. (Literary merit)

Yep, Laurence. **Mountain Light.** Harper and Row, 1985. 282 p. ISBN 0-06-026758-5.

Swept up in one of the local rebellions against the Manchus in nineteenth-century China, nineteen-year-old Squeaky travels to America to seek his fortune among the gold fields of California. But the stories told in the villages in China about America do nothing to prepare Squeaky for the reality of what he will face — a reality filled with jealousy, corruption, brutality, and danger. Sequel to *The Serpent's Children.*

World

Atterton, Julian. **The Last Harper.** Julia MacRae Books, 1983. 114 p. ISBN 0-531-03767-3.

In the late sixth century, northern Britain was a jigsaw puzzle of small Celtic kingdoms. It was a time of savage war. Urien, king of Rheged, tried to unify the northern tribes and planned a daring attack on their enemy, the advancing Sea Wolves. Urien is remembered because he had a harper whose songs about the king survived long enough to be written down.

Bawden, Nina. **The Finding.** Lothrop, Lee and Shepard Books, 1985. 153 p. ISBN 0-688-04979-6.

As an infant, Alex was found in swaddling clothes in the arms of the Sphinx. His eleven years in London have been exciting. Everyone loves him, especially Gram. But when her friend Mrs. Angel dies and Alex is to inherit her money, his world changes forever.

Calvert, Patricia. **Hadder MacColl.** Charles Scribner's Sons, 1985. 134 p. ISBN 0-684-18447-8.

Hadder MacColl, the fourteen-year-old daughter of Big Archibald MacColl, gets involved in a bloody war between the clans of Scotland and the English in the 1740s. Her brother, Leofwin, who has been studying in Edinburgh for three years, returns with new ideas about the clans and the return from exile of Bonnie Prince Charlie. Hadder has problems accepting the change in her brother and the fierce devotion of her father to the Jacobite cause.

Carter, Dorothy Sharp. **His Majesty, Queen Hatshepsut.** Illustrated by Michele Chessare. J. B. Lippincott, 1987. 248 p. ISBN 0-397-32178-3 (0-397-32179-1, library binding).

At fourteen, Hatshepsut becomes queen regent of Egypt when her husband, the king, dies. She shares the throne with her husband's son, a child born to another woman. Queen Regent Hatshepsut decides that for the good of Egypt she will name herself pharaoh, up to this time a position held only by men. This is a fictional account of a real queen who ruled Upper and Lower Egypt from 1495 to 1475 B.C.

Cross, Gilbert B. **A Hanging at Tyburn.** Atheneum, 1983. 233 p. ISBN 0-689-31107-2.

Fourteen-year-old George Found, an orphan, tries to survive on his own in England in 1759. Rescued by the Duke of Bridgewater after a disastrous tour with an acting company, George soon becomes an invaluable aide and the designer of a clever plan to build a canal for the duke to use to sell his coal. All goes well until some foes of the duke and of the canal unjustly charge George for theft — an offense punishable only by hanging.

Eger, Jeffrey. **The Statue in the Harbor: A Story of Two Apprentices.** Illustrated by Paula Goodman. Silver Burdett, 1986. 124 p. ISBN 0-382-09146-9 (0-382-09145-0, library binding).

The story of the creation and construction of the Statue of Liberty is told through the eyes of two young apprentices — Philippe Peden, a coppersmith in Paris, and Vincent Tomaso, a stonemason in New York. The story begins in Paris with Philippe working alongside his father, a master coppersmith at the foundry where sculptor Frédéric Auguste Bartholdi's statue is being created. Back in New York, Vincent and his father are working on the pedestal for the statue.

Frank, Rudolf (translated by Patricia Crampton). **No Hero for the Kaiser.** Illustrated by Klaus Steffens. Lothrop, Lee and Shepard Books, 1986. 222 p. ISBN 0-688-06093-5.

Fourteen-year-old Jan Kubitz and his dog are the only survivors of the German attack on his Polish village in 1914, and both are made to follow the fleeing Russians. During the next few years Jan sees war firsthand and demonstrates his courage. This book was originally published in 1931. The author was imprisoned by

Hitler in 1933, and the book was burned in public. (Literary merit)

Geras, Adèle. **Voyage.** Atheneum, 1985. 193 p. ISBN 0-689-30955-4.

In 1904, the *Danzig* sails from Eastern Europe, crammed with Jewish emigrants seeking safety in America. Still a teenager, Minna has to care for her sickly younger brother, Eli, and her mother, who seems ready to collapse. Golda, a young mother, knows that her husband awaits her arrival, but how will she ever face him if she lets their baby die? And Rachel knows that the new land holds no happiness for her — or is she wrong?

Haugaard, Erik Christian. **The Samurai's Tale.** Houghton Mifflin, 1984. 234 p. ISBN 0-395-34559-6.

Taro, a Japanese orphan from humble beginnings, is a servant in the household of a noble, Lord Akiyama. He grows into a trusted, creative aide and eventually becomes a skilled samurai fighting for the enemies of his dead family.

Hilgartner, Beth. **A Murder for Her Majesty.** Houghton Mifflin, 1986. 241 p. ISBN 0 395-41341-2.

When her father is murdered, Alice Tuckfield finds herself an orphan in sixteenth-century England. Now she hears rumors that is was Queen Elizabeth I who wanted Sir Henry Tuckfield killed. Alice is befriended by some boys in the York Minster Boys' Choir and takes refuge in their dormitory. She soon finds out that her own life is in danger.

Howard, Ellen. **When Daylight Comes.** Atheneum, 1985. 210 p. ISBN 0-689-31133-8.

Granddaughter of the Danish governor of St. John Island in the Virgin Islands, young Helena Sødtmann lives a privileged life being cared for by a number of black slaves. Suddenly she is caught in their uprising, taken prisoner, and forced to become a slave herself. In her bondage, Helena receives a prophecy from Queen Lodama. "In time to come, you a brave-hearted woman with hands strong for doing what must be done." (Literary merit)

Langford, Sondra Gordon. **Red Bird of Ireland.** Atheneum/Margaret K. McElderry Books, 1983. 175 p. ISBN 0-689-50270-2.

Thirteen-year-old Aderyn loves her life in Ireland. But in 1846 her father is falsely accused of a crime and is forced to flee Ireland.

Aderyn's mother, Kincora, replaces her husband as a leader in the village, and during the potato famine she tries to lead their neighbors to a new life in America. Aderyn wonders if they can survive the journey.

McCutcheon, Elsie. **Storm Bird.** Farrar, Straus and Giroux, 1987. 176 p. ISBN 0-374-37269-1.

After her father is swindled out of business in 1905, twelve-year-old Jenny Lovett moves to the English seaside town of Newbrigg to live with Aunt Clara. To Jenny's disgust, she becomes a kitchen maid. Her life improves when she befriends a boy who teaches her all about the birds along the marshes. Jenny discovers that there are many ghosts of Newbrigg's past to dig up, but her attention focuses on her father when his ship is lost at sea.

Magorian, Michelle. **Back Home.** Harper and Row, 1984. 375 p. ISBN 0-06-024103-9.

Five years after being sent to America to escape World War II, twelve-year-old Rusty returns to England to a mother who insists she behave like a lady — a mother who is cold and reserved, not at all like her foster mother in America. Sent away to boarding school, Rusty finds refuge from the ridicule of her schoolmates in an abandoned cabin near the school. When her hideout is discovered, Rusty decides the only thing to do is run away to America — to go back home.

O'Dell, Scott. **The Road to Damietta.** Houghton Mifflin, 1985. 230 p. ISBN 0-395-38923-2.

Ricca di Montanaro grows up with Francis Bernardone in their thirteenth-century Italian village and even thinks she is in love with him. Francis, known for his wild and outrageous antics, undergoes a drastic change. He rejects his life of privilege and wears a crude robe and sandals while preaching a gospel of virtue. Together, Ricca and Francis join the Fifth Crusade and seek to deliver their message of peace to the Sultan of Egypt and Syria. Francis is known to us today as St. Francis of Assisi.

Overton, Jenny. **The Ship from Simnel Street.** Greenwillow Books, 1986. 144 p. ISBN 0-688-06182-6.

Polly Oliver's mother wants only the best for her daughters, but Polly decides that she must leave London and follow her beloved, a soldier in the king's army during the Peninsular War in Spain.

As Polly's father searches for her, her mother and sister, Suky, begin an intriguing project involving the family bakery. During the long time Polly is gone, her mother, father, and sister change, as does Polly.

Paterson, Katherine. **Rebels of the Heavenly Kingdom.** E. P. Dutton/Lodestar Books, 1983. 227 p. ISBN 0-525-66911-6.

Fifteen-year-old Wang Lee is stolen by bandits and sold as a slave in China during the 1850s. He is bought and freed by Mei Lin, a young Chinese girl who is a religious rebel and a member of the Taiping Tienkuo, a group that wishes to establish the Heavenly Kingdom of Great Peace. This group plots to overthrow the Manchu government, and both Wang Lee and Mei Lin participate in the battles and intrigue.

Vander Els, Betty. **The Bombers' Moon.** Farrar, Straus and Giroux, 1985. 167 p. ISBN 0-374-30864-0.

Wartime living is dangerous for Ruthie and her younger brother during the Japanese invasion of China in 1942. First they are separated from their missionary parents and sent to boarding school. From there they have a perilous journey to India and eventually travel from Calcutta to Shanghai, with Ruthie having always to be the "good" older sister.

Vogel, Ilse-Margret. **Tikhon.** Illustrations by the author. Harper and Row, 1984. 112 p. ISBN 0-06-026328-8 (0-06-026329-6, library binding).

Tikhon is a young Russian soldier who is trapped in Germany after World War I. Several people hide him before he comes to live with Inge's family. The little girl and the soldier become good friends, learning from each other and sharing their love for the nearby Zobten Mountain. When Tikhon is arrested by the police, Inge is afraid she has lost her friend forever.

Watkins, Yoko Kawashima. **So Far from the Bamboo Grove.** Lothrop, Lee and Shepard Books, 1986. 183 p. ISBN 0-688-06110-9.

During World War II, home to eleven-year-old Yoko Kawashima is Korea. Suddenly she and her family are forced to flee, hoping to return eventually to their homeland of Japan. To escape, Yoko travels for a while disguised as a boy and must earn money to support herself along the way. This is a fictionalized account of the author's childhood.

Yep, Laurence. **The Serpent's Children.** Harper and Row, 1984. 277 p. ISBN 0-06-026809-3 (0-06-026812-3, library binding).

In nineteenth-century China, Cassia and her brother are called "the serpent's children" as an insult. Cassia doesn't mind because legend says that when a serpent sets her mind on something, she doesn't give up. This legend helps Cassia when she finds herself fighting a war against famine, bandits, and the conflict between her father and her brother.

Humor and Satire

Conford, Ellen. **A Royal Pain.** Scholastic, 1986. 171 p. ISBN 0-590-33269-4.

A switch in babies in the hospital of a tiny country in Europe provides the basis for this comedy. Abby Adams, who lives in Kansas, is delighted, at first, to find she is a princess. But she changes her mind when she discovers that she has been betrothed to Prince Casmir since she was a baby, and that she must follow strict rules and regulations.

David, Peter. **Knight Life.** Ace Fantasy Books, 1987. 193 p. ISBN 0-441-45130-6.

King Arthur is back — in our time, in New York City. He's known as Arthur Penn, and he wants to be elected the mayor of New York. Gwen DeVere heads his election campaign, and his business manager is Percy Vale. Because Merlin ages backwards, he appears as an eight-year-old boy. All the familiar conflicts with Morgan and Moe Dred are included.

Goldsmith, Ruth M. **Phoebe Takes Charge.** Atheneum/Margaret K. McElderry Books, 1983. 241 p. ISBN 0-689-50266-4.

When Judge Mayhew leaves his eldest daughter, Phoebe, in charge while he is away on business in 1926, she embarks on a mission to modernize the Mayhew family. She plans to redecorate the house, to host an elaborate dinner party with her father's long-lost eccentric uncle and his Indian friends, and to run off to Boston to seek her fortune. But Phoebe's plans backfire and lead her into a series of chaotic and often hilarious events.

Greene, Constance C. **Just Plain Al.** Viking Penguin/Viking Kestrel, 1986. 134 p. ISBN 0-670-81250-1.

When you turn fourteen, you can't be just plain Al. How about Alex? Zandra? Zandi? With the help of her friend Polly, Al is determined to work on self-improvement, to become a free spirit, and to help humankind. But how can she juggle all those conflicting desires?

Holland, Isabelle. **Green Andrew Green.** Illustrated by Pat Steiner. Westminster Press, 1984. 79 p. ISBN 0-664-32714-1.

Ten-year-old Andrew Green is green and getting greener every day. While staying with Aunt Jessica and Uncle Robert at the shore, he discovered that he could enter an all-green world through his television set. Inside he meets Mr. Fishermen, who teaches Andrew about caring for others.

Keller, Beverly. **Rosebud, with Fangs.** Lothrop, Lee and Shepard Books, 1985. 156 p. ISBN 0-688-03747-X.

Harry used to be a troublesome five-year-old boy. But he's been changed into a huge hairy beast by a madman who wants to use him to get control of the world. Rosebud, as Harry now calls himself, teams up with his sensible sister, Aggie, to undo the damage. But his other two sisters wait for Mama and normalcy to return.

• Korman, Gordon. **Don't Care High.** Scholastic, 1985. 243 p. ISBN 0-590-33322-4.

Paul Abrams is fifteen years old and a new student at Don't Care, I mean Don Carey, High School in New York City. At this school, no one goes out for sports, or joins clubs, or runs for any office. Then Paul meets Sheldon, who has a plan to get Don't Care High caring again by having bizarre Mike Otis run for student body president. Mike doesn't even know that he's in the running, but that doesn't stop Paul and Sheldon or even slow them down.

Korman, Gordon. **A Semester in the Life of a Garbage Bag.** Scholastic, 1987. 257 p. ISBN 0-590-40694-9.

Two eleventh-grade boys, Raymond Jardine and Sean Delancey, set out to change their image by winning a trip to an exotic Greek island. They persuade Sean's grandfather to pose as a dead, obscure Canadian poet, but the plan backfires when the poet becomes an area celebrity.

Livingston, Myra Cohn, compiler. **A Learical Lexicon.** Illustrated by Joseph Low. Atheneum/Margaret K. McElderry Books, 1985. 60 p. ISBN 0-689-50318-0.

If you like humorous and nonsense words, unusual spellings, and hidden meanings, this book is likely to interest you. This glossary is selected from the writings of Edward Lear, the nineteenth-century British landscape painter and humorist. Low's witty illustrations heighten the delightful absurdity of the words.

Manes, Stephen. **Chicken Trek.** Illustrated by Ron Barrett. E. P. Dutton, 1987. 111 p. ISBN 0-525-44312-6.

Oscar Noodleman owes his cousin $49,462.37 and decides the only way to get that much money is to win the Bagful o' Cash prize in a coast-to-coast chicken-eating contest. Traveling cross-country in the Picklemobile, Oscar eats two hundred chicken meals, only to find he is being challenged in the contest by an evil seer with a huge appetite.

Phillips, Louis. **How Do You Get a Horse out of the Bathtub?** Illustrated by James Stevenson. Viking Press, 1983. 71 p. ISBN 0-670-38119-5.

Do you know how to get a horse out of the bathtub or why a flamingo stands on only one leg? Did you ever wonder if rain ever gets up after it falls or if there is an animal that can jump higher than the Empire State Building? Profound answers to these and other preposterous questions can be found in this humorous book.

Pinkwater, Daniel. **The Moosepire.** Little, Brown, 1986. 44 p. ISBN 0-316-70811-9.

The author himself tries to find out the secret of the Moosepire, a vampire moose. His investigation leads to the public library in Yellowtooth. There Pinkwater finds the journal of the Blue Moose, who also attempted to uncover the mystery of the dreaded Moosepire.

Pinkwater, Daniel. **The Snarkout Boys and the Baconburg Horror.** New American Library/Signet Vista Books, 1985. 175 p. ISBN 0-451-13581-4.

Snarkout Boys Walter Galt, Winston Bongo, and Rat (who's a girl, but it's not her fault) continue their adventures in the town of Baconburg. It appears that a werewolf looms in the shadows of the town and that hardened criminal Wallace Nussbaum has escaped his imprisonment on Devil's Island. Is either of them eating up the sidewalks or turning over the cars? Sequel to *The Snarkout Boys and the Avocado of Death.*

Rosenbloom, Joseph. **Wacky Insults and Terrible Jokes.** Illustrated by Sandy Hoffman. Sterling Publishing, 1985. 124 p. ISBN 0-8069-7992-5 (0-8069-4675-X, library binding).

Wrinkle your nose and give a twisted smile, or even a belly laugh, as you read this collection of goofy insults, sick jokes, riddles, verses, and quips. The fifteen sections include both new and old-time favorites, such as "Exercising with Dumbbells," "Quacking Up," "Meanies but Goodies," and "I Love Monkeys, Too."

Schwartz, Alvin, retold by. **Tales of Trickery from the Land of Spoof.** Illustrated by David Christiana. Farrar, Straus and Giroux, 1985. 87 p. ISBN 0-374-37378-7.

Some of the best tricks ever perpetrated are retold here, including "The Organ That Brayed like a Donkey," "Footprints on the Ceiling," and "The Case of the Royal Arabian Jewels."

Mental and Emotional Problems

Ames, Mildred. **The Silver Link, the Silken Tie.** Charles Scribner's Sons, 1984. 215 p. ISBN 0-684-18065-0.

Felice and Tim, two sophomores at an expensive private school in California, both had childhoods marked with disaster, and they have responded by setting themselves apart from the world. Gradually, they grow to trust each other, but before they can resolve their differences, they must deal with a sect devoted to thought control and with their own telepathic powers.

Carrick, Carol. **Stay Away from Simon!** Illustrated by Donald Carrick. Clarion Books, 1985. 63 p. ISBN 0-89919-343-9.

Set in Martha's Vineyard in the 1830s, this book is about a mentally handicapped young man named Simon who doesn't attend school and whose size causes concern on the part of some parents. The children have all been told not to play with Simon. But Simon appears in the schoolyard one day, laughing and playing in the falling snow. On the way home that afternoon, Lucy and her younger brother hear Simon following them and wonder what they should do.

Cassedy, Sylvia. **M.E. and Morton.** Thomas Y. Crowell, 1987. 312 p. ISBN 0-690-04560-3 (0-690-04562-X, library binding).

Eleven-year-old Mary Ellen, M.E., finally has a best friend named Polly. Polly is not like anyone else M.E. knows. She wears old clothes that are too big for her, and she doesn't care what others think. She even talks to and likes M.E.'s brother, Morton, who is a slow learner. Through Polly's influence, M.E. begins to like things about herself and the people around her, including Morton.

Cavallaro, Ann. **Blimp.** E. P. Dutton/Lodestar Books, 1983. 166 p. ISBN 0-525-67139-0.

Kim Lunde is a 186-pound high school junior. She can't believe her good fortune when Gary, the handsome new guy at school, becomes her friend and wants to spend time with her. Kim knows that being overweight is a real problem and resolves to do something about it. She discovers that her problem isn't nearly as significant as the problem Gary is facing.

Crutcher, Chris. **The Crazy Horse Electric Game.** Greenwillow Books, 1987. 215 p. ISBN 0-688-06683-6.

Willie Weaver has everything going for him as a star athlete — until the accident. Betrayed by his body, his father, and his girl, he runs away. But Willie fights back when he finds himself in a world of street toughs and pimps, and he finds additional strength when he enrolls in a special school.

Evernden, Margery. **The Kite Song.** Illustrated by Cindy Wheeler. Lothrop, Lee and Shepard Books, 1984. 186 p. ISBN 0-688-01200-0.

Eleven-year-old Jamie, upset by the death of his mother, rarely speaks to anyone except Clem, his older cousin. Considered stupid because he doesn't talk, Jamie is left to the terrors of his mind until a teacher, Clem, and a poem about a kite unlock those terrors and help him face the past.

Greenwald, Sheila. **Will the Real Gertrude Hollings Please Stand Up?** Dell/Yearling Books, 1985. 162 p. ISBN 0-440-49553-9.

Gertrude Hollings, who is labeled "dumb" by the kids at school and "learning disabled" by her teachers, finds comfort at home with understanding parents and her stuffed owls with whom she creates imaginative adventures. When her parents leave for a three-week business trip to Greece, Gertrude goes to stay with her cousin Albert. Albert, the brain, is the center of his parents' attention, and he is selfish, rude, and hateful toward Gertrude. But Gertrude discovers that Albert doesn't know everything.

Hall, Lynn. **Just One Friend.** Charles Scribner's Sons, 1985. 118 p. ISBN 0-684-18471-0.

Having a friend like Robin to help her through the hard times at her new school is all that sixteen-year-old Dory wants. This year Dory, who is learning disabled, will be "mainstreamed" into a regular class. She hopes she can count on Robin to help her with riding the bus and finding her way around a new building. But Meredith is Robin's friend, and the two pretty and popular girls certainly won't want someone around with learning disabilities.

Hill, Donna. **First Your Penny.** Atheneum, 1985. 207 p. ISBN 0-689-31093-5.

Leading your own life is a difficult challenge for anyone. Sixteen-year-old Richard Downing, however, has an extra strike against him: he's mentally handicapped. Though he lives in New York City, his mother has successfully shut him off from the world. Now that he's growing up, Dicky wants to be independent. The progress that he makes in achieving his goals demonstrates the power of determination.

Hopper, Nancy J. **Ape Ears and Beaky.** E. P. Dutton, 1984. 102 p. ISBN 0-525-44105-0.

At the start, Scott Pritchard only wants to smash Beaky's face for calling him names. But these middle school boys soon are forced to join together once they witness thieves at work at the new condos. Along the way, Scott has to learn to control his temper so it doesn't control him.

Hyland, Betty. **The Girl with the Crazy Brother.** Franklin Watts, 1987. 137 p. ISBN 0-531-10345-5.

A new home, school, and friends aren't the only things that high school sophomore Dana McAllister must adjust to. Her older brother, Bill, is acting weird — he eats oranges to keep himself from turning blue and he says he hears voices. Then one night Bill wildly pleads for Dana's help, but she can do nothing but watch as hospital attendants take him away. When Bill is diagnosed as schizophrenic, Dana is concerned about him, her parents, and herself. What will the kids at school think of the girl with the crazy brother?

LeVert, John. **The Flight of the Cassowary.** Atlantic Monthly Press, 1986. 298 p. ISBN 0-87113-059-9.

Paul, a junior in high school, faces the usual problems of adolescence — parents, girls, football. As the year goes on, he becomes intrigued with the idea that humans can take on characteristics of other animals. He then discovers these animal-like behaviors within himself. Drawing the line between reality and fantasy now becomes almost impossible for Paul.

Lowry, Lois. **Rabble Starkey.** Houghton Mifflin, 1987. 192 p. ISBN 0-395-42506-9.

Twelve-year-old Rabble Starkey's grandmother selected her name, Parable Ann, as well as her mother's name, Sweet Hosanna, right from the Bible. Sweet Hosanna was only fourteen when Rabble was born, and now they both stay with the Bigelows, where Sweet Ho works. When Mrs. Bigelow is admitted to a distant mental hospital, Rabble feels that she and her mother will become a permanent part of the remaining Bigelow family, the family she's always wanted.

Namovicz, Gene Inyart. **To Talk in Time.** Four Winds Press, 1987. 154 p. ISBN 0-02-768170-X.

Twelve-year-old Luke sees a stranger get bitten by a dog that later turns out to be rabid. Luke has trouble speaking to anyone he doesn't know well. Now, however, he must talk in order to save the stranger from rabies.

Nielsen, Shelly. **Autograph, Please, Victoria.** David C. Cook/Chariot Books, 1987. 126 p. ISBN 1-55513-216-2.

How can you have a normal life when your little brother acts totally weird? Eighth-grader Victoria Mahoney becomes an instant celebrity when she wins a national writing contest, but she finds her enthusiasm shadowed by Matt's learning disability. Book three in the Victoria Mahoney series.

Potter, Dan. **Crazy Moon Zoo.** Franklin Watts, 1985. 151 p. ISBN 0-531-10076-6.

Is he crazy, really crazy? That's what Jory Hall wants to know. For a long time seventeen-year-old Jory has known that something inside him set him apart. He certainly isn't like his older brother, Reeve, who is perfect in every way. And why does he care so for the poor animals? Jory feels that if only he can understand why he is different, he'd be able to stop running away from everyone and everything.

Riley, Jocelyn. **Crazy Quilt.** William Morrow, 1984. 215 p. ISBN 0-688-03873-5.

Thirteen-year-old Merle, her brother, and her sister are living with their grandmother in Chicago. They are upset and confused by their mother's mental illness. Merle also finds that her friends at school are changing and that her grandmother is involved in a romance. Sequel to *Only My Mouth Is Smiling.*

Schwartz, Joel L. **Shrink.** Dell/Yearling Books, 1986. 119 p. ISBN 0-440-47687-9.

Ninth-grader Mike Brooks is not doing well in school. His guidance counselor suggests that he see a psychiatrist. Mike's grandfather's illness, coupled with his poor grades, weighs heavily on him. Mike doesn't want to go to a "shrink," but Dr. Rhodes isn't as bad as he expects. Through his relationship with Dr. Rhodes, Mike is able to focus on his schoolwork and to discover that every kid needs someone to talk to.

Shreve, Susan. **Lucy Forever and Miss Rosetree, Shrinks.** Henry Holt, 1987. 121 p. ISBN 0-8050-0340-1.

Lucy and Rosie are sixth-grade psychiatrists at Shrinks, Inc. in the basement of Lucy's house. Inspired by Lucy's father, a real psychiatrist, the girls work on imaginary cases. But can they cope when Cinder — a real little girl being treated by Lucy's father — walks into their office with eyes full of terror and a bright red scar across her throat?

Silsbee, Peter. **The Big Way Out.** Bradbury Press, 1984. 180 p. ISBN 0-02-782670-8.

Fourteen-year-old Paul has a father who is charming one minute, violent the next. Paul's brother, Tim, denies the danger, and Paul's mother tries to protect her husband. Finally, even she flees from California to New York and takes Paul with her. Alone with a telescopic rifle in his hands, Paul sits on the rim of a ten-story water tower and waits for his dad and brother to show up after a cross-country pursuit.

Slepian, Jan. **The Night of the Bozos.** E. P. Dutton, 1983. 152 p. ISBN 0-525-44070-4.

Thirteen-year-old George Weiss and his Uncle Hibbie pick up a hitchhiker, Lolly, who works with her family in carnivals. George and Hibbie find themselves drawn to the carnival life. Hibbie decides to become a Bozo, the heckler at the top of a water tank. This leads to a strange night for all.

Talbert, Marc. **Toby.** Dial Books for Young Readers, 1987. 168 p. ISBN 0-8037-0441-0.

From the womblike security of his hiding place under the porch, ten-year-old Toby learns that the Reverend Olson thinks he should be taken away from his brain-damaged mother and retarded father. Toby struggles against class bullies, the Reverend, the next-door neighbor, and even his own maternal grandparents to stay with his parents, who say they have "more love than brains."

Teague, Sam. **The King of Hearts' Heart.** Little, Brown, 1987. 186 p. ISBN 0-316-83427-0.

Neighbors Harold and Billy were born in the same month in the same hospital and did everything together, including falling out of the same tire swing at the same time at the age of four. However, Billy was brain-damaged in the fall. Now thirteen, the boys are no longer together constantly as Harold has discovered Kate and track and thinks Billy is a pain in the neck. Then a change of heart leads Harold to decide that he will help Billy become a track champion in the International Summer Special Olympics.

White, Ellen Emerson. **Life without Friends.** Scholastic, 1987. 250 p. ISBN 0-590-33781-5.

Seventeen-year-old Beverly will never forgive herself for not telling someone about her boyfriend, Tim, who was responsible for the deaths of two high school students. It's over now, but Beverly continues to blame herself. She spends all her time alone, cut off from her family, friends, and doctor. A chance meeting with Derek helps her come to terms with the past and look toward the future.

Mysteries

Arden, William. **The Three Investigators in The Mystery of Wrecker's Rock.** Random House, 1986. 184 p. ISBN 0-394-87375-0.

When the Three Investigators go fishing, they pause to photograph a bizarre family reunion on the island of Wrecker's Rock. Accidentally, the young sleuths open a deadly can of worms. They are plagued night and day by masked hoodlums, ancient ghosts, and even a werewolf as they reel in a whopping solution to the mystery of these fiends. Part of the Three Investigators Mystery series.

Avi. **Wolf Rider: A Tale of Terror.** Bradbury Press, 1986. 202 p. ISBN 0-02-707760-8.

Fifteen-year-old Andy and his friend Paul are on their way to a party when the phone rings. The caller says he has just stabbed a girl and asks for help. The man gives his name as Zeke, describes the dead girl and her car, and explains why he killed her. No one believes them, so Andy and Paul begin the search for the girl, hoping Zeke has not really killed her yet.

Bellairs, John. **The Curse of the Blue Figurine.** Dial Books for Young Readers, 1983. 200 p. ISBN 0-8037-1119-0 (0-8037-1265-0, library binding).

When Johnny Dixon sneaks the blue statue from the church, he inherits its curse. Father Baart's ghost appears and tries to kill Johnny and take over his body. Can Johnny save himself?

Bellairs, John. **The Mummy, the Will, and the Crypt.** Dial Books for Young Readers, 1983. 168 p. ISBN 0-8037-0029-6 (0-8037-0030-X, library binding).

When twelve-year-old Johnny Dixon sets out to find the will of a bizarre cereal magnate, he chooses the path to adventure. Magic spells, a demonic guardian, and diabolical relatives of the magnate try to stop him.

Bellairs, John. **The Revenge of the Wizard's Ghost.** Dial Books for Young Readers, 1985. 147 p. ISBN 0-8037-0170-5 (0-8037-0177-2, library binding).

There seems to be little hope for thirteen-year-old Johnny Dixon since the ghost of Warren Windrow has possessed his body. His friends, Fergie and Professor Childermass, follow an eerie trail of clues to free Johnny from the spell. But can they outsmart the wily spirit in time to save Johnny's life?

Bellairs, John. **The Spell of the Sorcerer's Skull.** Dial Books for Young Readers, 1984. 170 p. ISBN 0-8037-0120-9 (0-8037-0122-5, library binding).

After many strange happenings, Professor Childermass disappears — right before thirteen-year-old Johnny Dixon's eyes. Johnny and his friends, Fergie and Father Higgins, follow the professor's clues: an antique family clock, a drawing found in his office, and a mysterious skull that Johnny took from the clock. What power does the skull hold?

Bennett, Jay. **The Death Ticket.** Avon Books/Flare Books, 1985. 128 p. ISBN 0-380-89597-8.

Gil's older brother, Gareth, is a dwarf. Estranged from the aunt and uncle who raised them, the two boys are on their own. After Gareth sends Gil the torn half of a lottery ticket, trouble follows Gil as he searches for his brother and the answers to many questions. Can he trust anyone?

Bennett, Jay. **The Skeleton Man.** Franklin Watts, 1986. 170 p. ISBN 0-531-15031-3.

Can you keep a secret? Ray Bond thinks he can when he promises not to tell anyone that his uncle gave him $30,000 for his college education. But when his uncle is found dead and Ray's own life is drawn into a web of gambling, corruption, and murder, Ray struggles with the decision to reveal his secret.

Bennett, Jay. **To Be a Killer.** Scholastic/Point Paperbacks, 1985. 153 p. ISBN 0-590-33208-2.

Paul Moore had it all — talent, brains, and athletic ability. But somebody didn't want it all for Paul. Now Paul is going to get his revenge in the simplest way he knows — Paul is going to be a killer.

Brett, Simon. **The Three Detectives and the Missing Superstar.** Charles Scribner's Sons, 1986. 179 p. ISBN 0-684-18708-6.

Emma doesn't realize that her autograph from rock star Dazzleman is really a code to lead to his kidnappers. But when the Three Detectives decide to unravel the case of the missing star, the autograph becomes a significant clue. Join Emma and her teenage detective friends in their dangerous attempts to locate the star. Part of the Three Detectives Mystery series.

Brown, Irene Bennett. **Answer Me, Answer Me.** Atheneum, 1985. 196 p. ISBN 0-689-31114-1.

After the death of her grandmother, Bryn Kinney is determined to find out who her parents are. Her only clue is an old newspaper clipping from a small town in Kansas. Bryn's search proves to be more difficult, frustrating, and hostile than she imagined. But there are a few bright spots, like a boy named Romney Elliot and a chattery old woman named Birdella Lamb. As the puzzle pieces begin to fit, Bryn sees a legacy that she is proud to call her own.

Carey, M. V. **The Three Investigators in The Mystery of the Cranky Collector.** Random House, 1987. 182 p. ISBN 0-394-89153-8 (0-394-99153-2, library binding).

Who wants to harm Jeremy Pilcher? Who doesn't? The book collector has many enemies. When the nasty old man is kidnapped, the detectives don't know whom to question first. The solution to the kidnapping is buried deep in Pilcher's collection of books, in his secret computer files, in his mysterious past. The Three Investigators must search through each to find the missing man. Part of the Three Investigators Mystery series.

Caroselli, Remus F. **Mystery at Long Crescent Marsh.** Holt, Rinehart and Winston, 1985. 152 p. ISBN 0-03-001414-X.

Twelve-year-old Drum Smith does not like his name because Zinger Simpson and the other kids beat on him, making fun of the name. To get even, Drum begins to follow Zinger around, hoping to discover him doing something wrong. He enlists the aid of his older sister, and together they discover more about Zinger than they should know.

Corbett, Scott. **The Trouble with Diamonds.** Illustrated by Bert Dodson. E. P. Dutton, 1985. 100 p. ISBN 0-525-44190-5.

Jeff Adams's attempts at being an amateur sleuth lead to a comedy of errors. His employer, Ambrose Bunker, who owns a summer resort, believes one of his guests is plotting to steal the jewels that belong to another guest. Solving the mystery involves mistaken identities, chase scenes, and other muddled mishaps.

Cross, Gillian. **On the Edge.** Holiday House, 1985. 169 p. ISBN 0-8234-0599-1.

Fourteen-year-old Tug regains consciousness after being kidnapped by a group of extremists intent on destroying the family unit. "Mr. and Mrs. Doyle" insist that Tug is their son Philip and try to convince him through beatings and brainwashings. Jinny, a local girl, doesn't believe their story. She plots a dangerous rescue attempt, one that will involve great inner strength on her part and Tug's. (Literary merit)

Duncan, Lois. **Locked in Time.** Little, Brown, 1985. 210 p. ISBN 0-316-19555-3.

Nore Robbins is to spend the summer on a Louisiana plantation with her father and her beautiful new stepmother, Lisette. Nore finds herself drawn to her handsome stepbrother, but there is something bizarre going on. There is something very odd about the whole family. Nore feels locked in time and struggles to find the key to the lock.

Dunlop, Eileen. **The House on the Hill.** Holiday House, 1987. 147 p. ISBN 0-8234-0658-X.

What is the mystery of the empty room at the Mount, the creepy Scottish mansion owned by Philip's great-aunt Jane Gilmore? As Philip and his cousin Susan set about to uncover family secrets, they also unlock the somber Jane's remarkable personality and Philip's belief in his own potential.

Eisenberg, Lisa. **Mystery at Snowshoe Mountain Lodge.** Dial Books for Young Readers, 1987. 167 p. ISBN 0-8037-0359-7.

When fourteen-year-old Kate Clancy goes on a ski trip, she expects to find snowy slopes and fun. Instead, her possessions disappear mysteriously, and the other guests and staff behave bizarrely. A surprising friendship with fellow sleuth Bobby Berman makes Kate's stay exciting and challenging.

Farley, Carol. **Mystery of the Melted Diamonds.** Illustrated by Tom Newsom. Avon Books/Camelot Books, 1986. 96 p. ISBN 0-380-89865-9.

Larry's unexciting visit with his cousin Kipper in Kansas changes the night of the big snowstorm. They are forced to take shelter in the abandoned old Morgansterne house, but someone has left the lights blazing and the stove burning! The next morning everyone in town is talking about the big jewelry store robbery. Soon Larry and Kipper are smack in the middle of an investigation.

Garden, Nancy. **Mystery of the Night Raiders.** Farrar, Straus and Giroux, 1987. 167 p. ISBN 0-374-35221-6.

When Brian visits his grandparents' farm, he finds that all is not well. The cows are dying one by one, and the vet can't determine the cause. With his friends Numbles and Darcy, Brian determines to find out what is wrong. Each clue takes them closer to an explanation so terrifying that the three of them must act before it is too late.

Garfield, Leon. **The December Rose.** Viking Penguin/Viking Kestrel, 1987. 208 p. ISBN 0-670-81054-1.

When young Barnacle, a chimney sweep, falls down the wrong chimney into the midst of a conspiracy, he is terrified and runs. In his panic, Barnacle grabs a vital pair of clues, and Inspector Creaker is soon on his trail.

Guy, Rosa. **And I Heard a Bird Sing.** Delacorte Press, 1987. 232 p. ISBN 0-385-29563-4.

Imamu Jones, eighteen, has grown up in Brooklyn, New York, and has withstood much heartache with his alcoholic mother. In this third book that chronicles his life, Imamu has found a kind foster family, a safe place for his recovering mother, and a new job. He enters a new world containing a different kind of love and unfamiliar wealth. But the mysteries that await Imamu inside the Maldoon mansion threaten the tranquility of his new life.

Helldorfer, M. C. **Almost Home.** Bradbury Press, 1987. 211 p. ISBN 0-02-743512-1.

Jessica Laerd and her older brother have been banished to Maine for the summer while their mother attends law school. There Jessie becomes acquainted with the grandfather she hardly knows and discovers Carmen, a young practitioner of magic. As Jessie explores the mystery of pirate Wishbone Jack, she unravels her own dilemmas, too.

Hildick, E. W. **The Case of the Muttering Mummy.** Illustrated by Blanche Sims. Macmillan, 1986. 154 p. ISBN 0-02-743960-7.

The McGurk Detective Organization is at it again! When newest member Mari imitates a mummy's voice, she activates a "curse" that leads the group to unravel a bizarre mystery at a museum. Part of the McGurk Mystery series.

Hildick, E. W. **The Ghost Squad and the Ghoul of Grünberg.** E. P. Dutton, 1986. 186 p. ISBN 0-525-44229-4.

The teenage Ghost Squad is warned that someone threatens the secret of the squad itself. The ghosts immediately go on red alert, setting up their own surveillance of the stranger. Their investigations lead to a nearby computer camp and the mystery of a missing camper, culminating in an international hunt for a Nazi war criminal, the Ghoul of Grünberg. A Ghost Squad book.

Hildick, E. W. **The Ghost Squad and the Halloween Conspiracy.** E. P. Dutton, 1985. 170 p. ISBN 0-525-44111-5.

The Ghost Squad consists of the ghosts of four teenagers who have died and have now formed a group to solve problems. When they discover that Vinnie Boyars, stepson of a senator, is about to poison the trick-or-treat candy that the senator plans to give out at the party for disadvantaged youngsters, the ghosts swing into action. A Ghost Squad book.

Hildick, E. W. **The Ghost Squad Breaks Through.** E. P. Dutton, 1984. 138 p. ISBN 0-525-44097-6.

The Ghost Squad has four ghosts and two live members. Their efforts to thwart a local bully and a daring heist — helped and hindered by the advantages and limitations of ghosthood — make for a suspenseful and hilarious adventure in this first book in a series. A Ghost Squad book.

Hildick, E. W. **The Ghost Squad Flies Concorde.** E. P. Dutton, 1985. 186 p. ISBN 0-525-44191-3.

The Ghost Squad goes international. A fortune hunter has designs on ghost Danny's newly rich mother, and the squad attempts to unmask him. The ghosts go to England on a Concorde jet to investigate his background. Back at home, the squad's two living members are having a difficult time keeping tabs on the fortune hunter. They must resort to drastic, even dangerous, measures. A Ghost Squad book.

Howe, James. **What Eric Knew.** Avon Books/Flare Books, 1986. 138 p. ISBN 0-380-70171-5.

Things around town are dull for Sebastian after his good friend, Eric, moves away. Eric knew a lot about the history of the town, so when Sebastian begins to get coded messages from Eric, he decides he had better investigate. The dark figure in the cemetery complicates the intrigue. Part of the Sebastian Barth Mystery series.

Kidd, Ronald. **Sizzle and Splat.** E. P. Dutton/Lodestar Books, 1983. 122 p. ISBN 0-525-66917-5.

Why would anyone kidnap Buckminster Brody, chief sponsor of the Pirelli Youth Orchestra? Sizzle (Prudence Szyznowski), the seventeen-year-old lead trumpet player, and Splat (Arthur Hadley Reavis Pauling III), the weird but witty tuba player, decide to solve the mystery and learn why their world premier concert has been nixed.

Klaveness, Jan O'Donnell. **The Griffin Legacy.** Macmillan, 1983. 184 p. ISBN 0-02-750760-2.

Thirteen-year-old Amy Enfield goes to live with her grandmother and great-aunt Matilda for a year in their historic New England home. In the living room, a portrait of Lucy Griffin hangs on the wall. Amy and her friends, Ben and Betsy, spend the year unraveling the secret of Lucy Griffin, a loyalist minister named Seth Howes, and a long-lost chalice and paten, all dating from the time of the American Revolution.

Levin, Betty. **A Binding Spell.** E. P. Dutton/Lodestar Books, 1984. 179 p. ISBN 0-525-67151-X.

Wren and her brothers are staying on an isolated farm in Maine with their great-aunt Tebbie. Strange things happen, such as tracks that only Wren sees and a horse-shaped mist. These events seem to be connected with Axel, an old man who lives in a boarded-up house nearby. Wren befriends Axel and finds that his past dovetails with the present.

Moore, Ruth Nulton. **Ghost Town Mystery.** Illustrated by Sibyl Graber Gerig. Herald Press, 1987. 140 p. ISBN 0-8361-3445-1.

Teenage twins Sara and Sam visit Silver Canyon, a Nevada ghost town said to be deserted. But while exploring the old buildings, the twins begin to wonder if there is someone else around. Sara and Sam make friends with an Indian boy from the Paiute reservation, and when they learn about a treasure of gold nuggets mentioned in an old letter found in a miner's trunk, they try to locate the elusive sack of gold. Book five in the Sara and Sam series.

Moore, Ruth Nulton. **Mystery at Camp Ichthus.** Illustrated by Sibyl Graber Gerig. Herald Press, 1986. 127 p. ISBN 0-8361-3421-4.

There is an unsolved mystery at Camp Ichthus, where teenage twins Sara and Sam are junior counselors. How does food disappear from the camp storeroom when the door is locked and guarded by a watchdog? Where does the fiddle playing come from that is heard in the pine woods? Can the twins unravel the mystery? Book four in the Sara and Sam series.

Moore, Ruth Nulton. **Mystery of the Lost Heirloom.** Illustrated by James Converse. Herald Press, 1986. 141 p. ISBN 0-8361-3408-7.

When twins Sara and Sam try to locate a 200-year-old heirloom, their adventure takes them to the Endless Mountains of Pennsylvania. In the course of tracking down the thief who stole a valuable fleur-de-lis pendant from an Indian princess, the twins escape by canoe down the Susquehanna River, make a perilous climb up a steep river bluff, and encounter a ghost at Spirit Lake. Book three in the Sara and Sam series.

Moore, Ruth Nulton. **Mystery of the Missing Stallions.** Illustrated by James Converse. Herald Press, 1984. 133 p. ISBN 0-8361-3376-5.

Sara and Sam are fourteen-year-old twins who have just moved with their family to an old house in Maplewood. The neighboring farm has a riding stable, but someone has been stealing its prize-winning American saddlebreds. The twins discover a Vietnamese refugee living in an abandoned cabin. Is he the thief, or is it someone else? Book one in the Sara and Sam series.

Moore, Ruth Nulton. **Mystery of the Secret Code.** Illustrated by James Converse. Herald Press, 1985. 123 p. ISBN 0-8361-3394-3.

Moving to a new area and school is bad enough, but then Sara must come up with a social studies project that involves researching a historical event in her new community. Classmate Amy Goodwin, into whose house Sara and her family have moved, provides the project, one that turns into an adventure with a secret code and other students pursuing their trail. Book two in the Sara and Sam series.

Murray, Marguerite. **The Sea Bears.** Atheneum, 1984. 170 p. ISBN 0-689-31050-1.

Jeanine and her family plan to spend a quiet summer at the seacoast. Her father mixes business and pleasure when he becomes involved in a top military project. Jeanine discovers two bear-shaped rocks that seem to signal her that a spy in her father's office is passing information to passing submarines. As time progresses, Jeanine and her father's close relationship is tested while they try to locate the spy.

Muskopf, Elizabeth. **The Revenge of Jeremiah Plum.** Illustrated by David Christiana. Henry Holt, 1987. 212 p. ISBN 0-8050-0203-0.

Darcy Kensmore thought that her summer would be dull. But then she moves into her great-aunt Prunella's boarding house and meets Jeremiah Plum, who is a ghost. Darcy learns that Jeremiah was murdered in Aunt Prunella's house and that now, fifty years later, he is determined to find the culprit.

Myers, Walter Dean. **Duel in the Desert.** Viking Penguin/Puffin Books, 1986. 90 p. ISBN 0-14-032101-2.

Brothers Chris and Ken Arrow find themselves on their own for a few days in the Sahara Desert. Their mother, an anthropologist, must finish up a project for a fellow researcher. The two boys uncover the largest theft in Moroccan history, and as they try to solve the mystery, they find themselves racing camels, fleeing through the desert by jeep, and fighting a duel to the death.

Nixon, Joan Lowery. **The Stalker.** Dell/Laurel-Leaf Books, 1987. 180 p. ISBN 0-44-97753-3.

Jennifer Wilcox is shocked to hear that Stella Tray, the mother of her best friend, has been strangled. She's even more horrified to learn that Bobbie, Stella's daughter, has been accused of the crime. When Jennifer, with the help of a retired police detective, sets out to prove Bobbie's innocence, she discovers that the killer has been stalking her.

Paige, Harry W. **The Summer War.** Fredrick Warne, 1983. 167 p. ISBN 0-7232-6223-3.

Ely Justin, an overweight teenager, arrives at summer camp ready to lose weight and win a trophy in a sport. While on a hike, he finds the skeleton of Hans Muller, a German immigrant who disappeared in the 1940s. In trying to learn more information about the immigrant, Ely uncovers secrets that the townspeople would prefer to keep hidden. Then another murder is committed, and Ely himself is in danger.

Parish, Peggy. **The Ghost of Cougar Island.** Illustrated by Deborah Chebrian. Dell/Yearling Books, 1986. 136 p. ISBN 0-440-42872-6.

Three young sleuths are on vacation and are itching for some way to practice their abilities to solve mysteries. While on Cougar Island, they find a private property sign warning that any trespassers will be haunted forever. Whether these legends are true or false, Liza, Bill, and Jed are determined to solve the mystery.

Pearce, Philippa. **The Way to Sattin Shore.** Illustrated by Charlotte Voake. Viking Penguin/Puffin Books, 1985. 176 p. ISBN 0-14-031644-2.

Ten-year-old Kate Tranter lives with her mother, grandmother, and two older brothers. Her favorite companion, however, is her cat, Syrup. When her father's tombstone disappears from the cemetery, Kate is drawn into learning more about her past and the father she never knew.

Pullman, Philip. **The Ruby in the Smoke.** Alfred A. Knopf/Borzoi Books, 1985. 230 p. ISBN 0-394-88826-X (0-394-98826-4, library binding).

Sally Lockhart, orphaned at the age of sixteen, is sent to London in the 1870s to live with an older woman who is a distant cousin. When Sally visits her father's ex-partner and asks him if he ever heard of the "Seven Blessings," the man falls to the floor, dead. Sally finds herself in the middle of a "penny mystery" that takes her to many interesting places in London.

Rodgers, Raboo. **Island of Peril.** Houghton Mifflin, 1987. 175 p. ISBN 0-395-43082-8.

A devil ship, evil monsters, and stolen Mayan art treasures are parts of the mystery that Jeri and Ben try to unravel. But their attempts to piece together the clues lead the two teenagers to the brink of death.

Roos, Kelley, and Stephen Roos. **The Incredible Cat Caper.** Illustrated by Katherine Coville. Dell/Yearling Books, 1986. 136 p. ISBN 0-440-44084-X.

Jessie expects trouble when she smuggles Simba, her Siamese cat, into her parents' Florida condo, where pets aren't allowed. But Jessie is surprised when she hears that another cat — a cat burglar — is robbing a different resident every night. Together with two friends, Herman and Carlos, she sets out to trap the burglar.

Shaw, Diana. **Lessons in Fear.** Little, Brown/Joy Street Books, 1987. 172 p. ISBN 0-316-78341-2.

It's Carter Colborn to the rescue when the unpopular ninth-grade biology teacher is found unconscious in a storage room. Carter's detective skills lead her into danger as she uncovers a culprit whose identity shocks the whole school. A Carter Colborn Mystery.

Singer, Marilyn. **The Case of the Sabotaged School Play.** Illustrated by Judy Glasser. Harper and Row, 1984. 60 p. ISBN 0-06-025794-6 (0-06-025795-4, library binding).

Everyone in the Drama Club agrees that Mary Ellen Moseby's play is the pits. But when it becomes the target of anonymous notes and bad-natured pranks, no one seems to know who might be responsible. Unraveling this mystery is the first case for Sam and Dave.

Smith, Alison. **A Trap of Gold.** Dodd, Mead, 1985. 176 p. ISBN 0-396-08721-3.

No one ever believes Margaret. Only her diary knows that someone is stalking her. When Margaret and her friend George accidentally discover a room of gold in an abandoned mine, they are accused of trespassing. It is when Margaret returns to the mine to help George find his dog that she must confront her mysterious hunter.

Tenny, Dixie. **Call the Darkness Down.** Atheneum/Margaret K. McElderry Books, 1984. 185 p. ISBN 0-689-50289-3.

Morfa Owen is an American teenager studying at a small college in Wales. While searching for information about her Welsh grandparents, Morfa receives a series of mysterious messages. Then she realizes that someone or something is trying to kill her. Morfa and her friends Laney, Arianwen, Rhys, and Gareth attempt to untangle the mystery.

Terris, Susan. **Octopus Pie.** Farrar, Straus and Giroux, 1983. 166 p. ISBN 0-374-35571-1.

Kristin Hart puts up with an octopus in her bedroom because she and her sister Mari can take care of it together. Kristin adores Mari, but she discovers that Mari is more interested in sharing the spotlight with Octopet than in sharing the work with her. When Octopet is octonapped, the girls have to join forces to solve the mystery.

Townsend, John Rowe. **Tom Tiddler's Ground.** J. B. Lippincott, 1986. 170 p. ISBN 0-397-32190-2 (0-397-32191-0, library binding).

Amid the backwater canals of an English industrial town, five children discover the half-sunken skeleton of an old canal boat. They fix up the cabin and make it into gang headquarters. Then the clubhouse is broken into, and two evil-looking men chase them away. The five children begin a race against time to unravel the fifty-year-old mystery of Tom Tiddler's Ground.

Vogt, Esther Loewen. **The Shiny Dragon.** Illustrated by James Converse. Herald Press, 1983. 108 p. ISBN 0-8361-3348-X.

Twelve-year-old Brad never intended to take his cousin, Harry, or his pesky neighbor, Margaret, to the haunted house to see the dragon. But they talk him into it, and he is forced to reveal that the dragon is really only a lizard. Several clues point to mysterious happenings at the old house, and Brad gets into a predicament that only his faith in God can help him through.

Voigt, Cynthia. **The Callender Papers.** Atheneum, 1983. 214 p. ISBN 0-689-30971-6.

"Think carefully" was always the guiding principle of Jean Wainwright's guardian, Aunt Constance. This principle becomes Jean's motto as she begins her unusual employment of sorting out the family papers of Mr. Thiel's late wife. The papers reveal the cruel past of Irene Callender Thiel, which shook their peaceful nineteenth-century village of Marlborough, Massachusetts. The closer Jean comes to the truth, the more danger she faces. (Literary merit)

Wells, Rosemary. **The Man in the Woods.** Dial Books for Young Readers, 1984. 217 p. ISBN 0-8037-0071-7.

Fifteen-year-old Helen Curragh sees a man run into the woods after throwing a rock that causes an auto accident. As Helen and

Pinky Levy, her only friend at New Bedford High, gather evidence that the "Punk Rock Thrower" is only a dupe and that the real criminal is still at large, clever but unmistakable threats are made against Helen.

Yep, Laurence. **The Tom Sawyer Fires.** William Morrow, 1984. 135 p. ISBN 0-688-03861-1.

The fifteen-year-old Duke of Baywater is actually only a street kid with visions of grandeur. He teams up with newspaper reporter Mark Twain and a fireman named Tom Sawyer to solve the mystery of unexplained explosions and fires in San Francisco during the 1860s. The story is full of historically accurate information about early fire-fighting equipment and the city of San Francisco. Sequel to *The Mark Twain Murders.*

Native American Experiences

Collura, Mary-Ellen Lang. **Winners.** Dial Books, 1984. 129 p. ISBN 0-8037-0011-3.

Fifteen-year-old Jordy Threebears has never lived on an Indian reservation. Then he is sent to a Blackfoot reservation to live with his grandfather, Joe, who has recently been released from prison and whom Jordy barely knows. Jordy wonders if he will ever experience real freedom. Christmas brings a present as wild and untamed as the new life that Jordy finds himself living.

Highwater, Jamake. **The Ceremony of Innocence.** Harper and Row/ Charlotte Zolotow Books, 1985. 186 p. ISBN 0-06-022301-4 (0-06-022302-2, library binding).

This is the tragic story of the struggle between Amana, a mother with too many memories, and Jemina, a daughter with too few. Alone and destitute after the death of her husband, Amana finds friendship, love, and finally disillusionment when she strives to give her daughter and grandchildren a sense of pride in their Indian heritage. Part two of the Ghost Horse Cycle.

Highwater, Jamake. **Eyes of Darkness.** Lothrop, Lee and Shepard, 1985. 189 p. ISBN 0-688-41993-3.

Yesa, a Santee Sioux, is raised by his grandmother during the 1800s after his father and two brothers are killed by whites. To avoid further exploitation, Yesa's tribe leaves Minnesota to live in Canada. There Yesa is educated as a doctor by whites, but the slaughter of his people at Wounded Knee causes him to reconsider his life's purpose. (Literary merit)

Highwater, Jamake. **I Wear the Morning Star.** Harper and Row/ Charlotte Zolotow Books, 1986. 148 p. ISBN 0-06-022355-3 (0-06-022356-1, library binding).

Amana's youngest grandson, Sitko, is sent to a foster home, beaten by the teachers, and ridiculed by the students. In his new home he persists in remembering and telling the Indian myths he learned from his grandmother. Rejected by his older brother, Reno, Sitko becomes a painter and finds an outlet for expressing his almost-lost Indian heritage. Part three of the Ghost Horse Cycle.

Highwater, Jamake. **Legend Days.** Harper and Row/Charlotte Zolotow Books, 1984. 147 p. ISBN 0-06-022303-0 (0-06-022304-9, library binding).

Eleven-year-old Amana, orphaned in a smallpox epidemic, is abandoned in the wilderness, where she makes friends with a fox. With its help, she develops the courage of a warrior and learns to hunt. When she returns to her tribe, her duties are to learn to cook, sew, and care for her family. Amana must also watch helplessly as her native land is taken over by whites and Indian traditions are lost. Part one of the Ghost Horse Cycle, which traces the lives of three generations of a Northern Plains Indian family.

Morris, Neil, and Ting Morris. **Featherboy and the Buffalo.** Illustrated by Anna Clarke. Silver Burdett, 1984. 23 p. ISBN 0-382-06894-7 (0-382-06890-4, library binding).

The tribe of Featherboy, a young Sioux, has moved to its summer camp, but something seems wrong. Featherboy overhears some adults discussing that the buffalo cannot be found. Featherboy is determined to locate the herd. The novel includes information pages on the Plains Indians.

Morris, Neil, and Ting Morris. **Little Bear and the White Horse.** Illustrated by Anna Clarke. Silver Burdett, 1984. 23 p. ISBN 0-382-06895-5 (0-382-06891-2, library binding).

Little Bear, a member of the Crow tribe, goes with a raiding party to the Blackfoot camp. He has been visited by the Spirit and hopes to avenge his father's death at the hands of the Blackfoot warriors. The novel includes information pages on the Crows.

Morris, Neil, and Ting Morris. **Morning Sun and the Lost Girl.** Illustrated by Anna Clarke. Silver Burdett, 1984. 23 p. ISBN 0-382-06896-3 (0-382-06892-0, library binding).

An Iroquois tale tells how the chief's daughter is lost in the forest during a berry-picking expedition. Morning Sun feels it is her fault and leaves early the next morning to search for Silver Shell. The novel includes information pages on the Iroquois nation.

Morris, Neil, and Ting Morris. **Taku and the Fishing Canoe.** Illustrated by Anna Clarke. Silver Burdett, 1984. 23 p. ISBN 0-382-06897-1 (0-382-06893-9, library binding).

Taku was too young to go out fishing with the village fishermen, so he made his own canoe and went out with his sister, Sawa. They made a great catch, but then a storm brought disaster to the children. The novel includes information pages on the Northwest Coast Indians.

O'Dell, Scott. **Streams to the River, River to the Sea.** Houghton Mifflin, 1986. 191 p. ISBN 0-395-40430-4.

Sacagawea was a young Shoshone maiden who was kidnapped from her people in the late 1700s. She eventually married a French trapper, Charbonneau. The two, with their infant son, led Lewis and Clark in 1804–1806 as they traveled the northern part of the United States in search of a land route to the Pacific. This fictionalized account is told from Sacagawea's point of view.

Paulsen, Gary. **Sentries.** Bradbury Press, 1986. 165 p. ISBN 0-02-770100-X.

Like sentries who watch and wait, the teenagers in these three stories await a change in their lives from the familiar to the unexpected. All come from different backgrounds — an Ojibway, an illegal Mexican migrant worker, and a sheep rancher's daughter — but some of their experiences are similar. Interspersed with their stories are the war experiences of three young veterans.

Wallin, Luke. **Ceremony of the Panther.** Bradbury Press, 1987. 124 p. ISBN 0-02-792310-X.

Sixteen-year-old John Raincrow has some bad friends and some bad habits like drinking and using drugs. His father takes him to the Miccosukee reservation in the Florida Everglades to stay with Grandmother Mary, where John and his father hunt panthers and deer to acquire the medicine used in the past by their people. John must decide if he will follow the medicine path taken by his father or select another way of life.

Wisler, G. Clifton. **Buffalo Moon.** E. P. Dutton/Lodestar Books, 1984. 105 p. ISBN 0-525-67146-3.

Fourteen-year-old Willie Delamer has lived a rough life on his father's Texas ranch. When his parents plan to send him to school in New Orleans to "smooth out the edges," he runs off to survive on his own and spends months with his Comanche friend, Red Wolf, and Chief Yellow Shirt. (Literary merit)

Wisler, G. Clifton. **The Wolf's Tooth.** E. P. Dutton/Lodestar Books, 1987. 119 p. ISBN 0-525-67197-8.

Elias does not know how he will survive the isolated Indian reservation where his father is a schoolteacher. The hard work and the threat of Comanche attacks are more than he can bear. When wolves steal several of their chickens, Elias decides to hunt the wolves with Thomas Three Feathers. This begins an adventure that changes his life and earns Elias a new name and a new friendship.

Wosmek, Frances. **A Brown Bird Singing.** Illustrated by Ted Lewin. Lothrop, Lee and Shepard Books, 1986. 120 p. ISBN 0-688-06251-2.

Fifth-grader Anego is a Chippewa who was left by her father to grow up with the white Veselka family in Minnesota many years ago. But now various messages arrive that her father, Hamigeesek, will return for her. Anego barely remembers him and considers the Veselkas her family now.

Physical Disabilities

Blos, Joan W. **Brothers of the Heart: A Story of the Old Northwest, 1837–1838.** Charles Scribner's Sons, 1985. 162 p. ISBN 0-684-18452-4.

Fourteen-year-old Shem has been crippled from birth. This handicap forces his father to give up their Ohio home and to move to Millfield, Michigan. But nothing is right about the move — not the house and not his father's job. Shortly after they arrive, father and son quarrel heatedly, and Shem flees Millfield. He begins a life of adventure traveling in the Michigan wilderness in the 1830s, and eventually he and an old Indian woman become brothers of the heart.

Christian, Mary Blount. **Growin' Pains.** Macmillan, 1985. 179 p. ISBN 0-02-718490-0.

Twelve-year-old Ginny Ruth Grover misses her laughing father and feels the same urge he did to leave her dying town, Clemmons, Texas. Her no-nonsense mother does not understand Ginny Ruth, and Ginny Ruth turns to writing and to the physically impaired Mr. Billy for solace. A near tragedy causes many emotions to surface in those close to Ginny Ruth.

Clifford, Eth. **The Man Who Sang in the Dark.** Illustrated by Mary Beth Owens. Houghton Mifflin, 1987. 96 p. ISBN 0-395-43664-8.

Ten-year-old Leah is frightened by the sightless stranger who shares the apartment building where she, her mother, and her brother, Daniel, find themselves living after her father's death. Set against the Great Depression of the 1930s, this story combines acceptance, family loyalty, and a touching romance.

DeClements, Barthe. **Sixth Grade Can Really Kill You.** Viking Penguin/Viking Kestrel, 1985. 146 p. ISBN 0-670-80656-0.

Is "Bad Helen's" love of practical jokes the result of her "badness" or a cover-up technique designed to protect the sensitive feelings of a nonreader? Follow Helen's antics through her sixth-grade year as she at last comes to terms with her problem and directs her energies toward overcoming her handicap.

Gorman, Carol. **Chelsey and the Green-Haired Kid.** Houghton Mifflin, 1987. 110 p. ISBN 0-395-41854-2.

Chelsey, a paraplegic confined to a wheelchair, witnesses a murder during a basketball game at her high school. Jack, the green-haired new kid at school, seems to know more than he lets on. When Chelsey knows she is being followed, she confronts Jack.

Gould, Marilyn. **The Twelfth of June.** J. B. Lippincott, 1986. 183 p. ISBN 0-397-32130-9 (0-397-32131-7, library binding).

Even though twelve-year-old Janis has cerebral palsy, she wants to be like other girls and maybe even have a boyfriend too. Her best friend, Barney, is being pressured by his mother, his violin teacher, and his religious adviser as he approaches his bar mitzvah. Janis finds she is not as handicapped by her illness as are those who react to it by trying to protect her. Sequel to *Golden Daffodils.*

Graber, Richard. **Doc.** Harper and Row/Charlotte Zolotow Books, 1986. 151 p. ISBN 0-06-022064-3 (0-06-022094-5, library binding).

Doc is a frustrated, angry old man with advanced Alzheimer's disease. His grandson Brad blindly worships the old doctor as he used to be, and refuses to recognize that his grandfather is becoming senile. With the help of his three-generation family, Brad learns that there is a time to hold on and a time to let go.

Greenberg, Jan. **No Dragons to Slay.** Farrar, Straus and Giroux, 1983. 119 p. ISBN 0-374-45509-0 (0-374-35528-2, library binding).

Thomas Newman is a prominent figure of strength and ability. He is popular with the girls and a talented member of the soccer team. All of this changes when Thomas learns that he has a malignant tumor. The next several months involve painful medication, tests, and treatments. Through all this, Thomas learns that you don't have to have cancer to be faced with a life-threatening situation.

Hamilton, Dorothy. **Last One Chosen.** Illustrated by James L. Converse. Herald Press, 1982. 106 p. ISBN 0-8361-3306-4.

As a result of a farm accident, one of eleven-year-old Scott Hardesty's legs is shorter than the other. His father feels responsible for the accident and carries his guilt silently. Scott wishes he could play ball as well as the other boys — not because he likes ball so much, but because he hates being the last one chosen.

Howe, James. **A Night without Stars.** Avon Books/Flare Books, 1985. 178 p. ISBN 0-380-69877-3.

Eleven-year-old Maria is frightened when she learns that she is to have open-heart surgery. Her parents and the doctors and nurses really can't answer all the questions she has. That's when she goes to talk with Donald, a boy the other kids in the hospital call "Monster Man" because he was burned and disfigured by a fire years ago. Donald needs a friend too, and they are able to help each other over some rough times.

Kerr, M. E. **Night Kites.** Harper and Row/Charlotte Zolotow Books, 1986. 216 p. ISBN 0-06-023253-6 (0-06-023254-4, library binding).

Several years ago Erick's brother, Pete, built a kite with lights so that he could fly it at night. Pete told him night kites aren't afraid to be different, and some people are different also. Now, at seventeen, Erick must face the fact that his brother has AIDS. An MTV fan and Madonna imitator, Erick's girlfriend, Nicki, is also different. Erick doesn't want his family to find out he has been dating her, and Nicki's goal seems to be to get Erick to like her so she can dump him.

Klein, Norma. **Going Backwards.** Scholastic, 1986. 182 p. ISBN 0-590-40328-1.

Charles, a senior in high school, finds it difficult to lead a normal life after his grandmother moves in. Grandmother Gustel has Alzheimer's disease and can no longer care for herself. To further complicate matters, Charlie's father refuses to see that there is a problem.

Levy, Marilyn. **The Girl in the Plastic Cage.** Ballantine Books/Fawcett Juniper Books, 1982. 190 p. ISBN 0-449-70030-5.

Thirteen-year-old Lori, a talented gymnast, meets the older, hazel-eyed Kurt in her doctor's office, where she discovers she has scoliosis, or curvature of the spine. Kurt's cast is soon off, while Lori's body brace threatens her future as a gymnast, her relationship with Kurt and her friends, and her own fragile self-image.

The "plastic cage" designed to straighten her body may twist her spirit.

Miklowitz, Gloria D. **Good-bye Tomorrow.** Delacorte Press, 1987. 150 p. ISBN 0-385-29562-6.

High school junior Alex received blood transfusions following an auto accident several years ago. Now he's fighting off round after round of flu-like symptoms. Blood tests reveal that Alex has ARC, or AIDS-related complex, and that his immune system is very weak. His girlfriend, friends, and family react in a variety of ways to Alex's illness.

Phelan, Terry Wolfe. **Making Half Whole.** New American Library/ Signet Vista Books, 1985. 159 p. ISBN 0-451-13630-6.

Allison has accepted her life as a "Navy brat," but now she has been transplanted from California to a New Jersey suburb with no ocean. She quickly makes friends with twin sisters Jane and Marnia, but then she has to face Marnia's struggle with a life-threatening kidney disease.

Radley, Gail. **CF in His Corner.** Four Winds Press, 1984. 134 p. ISBN 0-590-07901-8.

Fourteen-year-old Jeff must spend the summer taking care of his seven-year-old brother, Scotty, while their mom works. Scotty's not a typical seven year old. He eats a lot but stays small. He must take vitamins with every meal and sleep with a vaporizer on every night. All these clues spell something more serious than just asthma — it's cystic fibrosis. Jeff thinks Scotty should know the truth about his illness, but his mom disagrees.

Richmond, Sandra. **Wheels for Walking.** Atlantic Monthly Press, 1985. 195 p. ISBN 0-87113-041-6.

A head-on collision leaves eighteen-year-old Sally Parker paralyzed from the chest down. Fighting to regain control of her body and her life seems too big a task for a fun-loving girl. While boyfriend Brian, fellow quadriplegic Jake, and therapist Michael all play a part in her battle, it is up to Sally to win the battle.

Rickett, Frances, and Steven McGraw. **Totaled.** Ballantine Books, 1983. 201 p. ISBN 0-345-30468-3.

When eighteen-year-old Christopher Reilly is profoundly injured in an auto accident, his future looks bleak. Long before Chris gains any real awareness, his older brother, Frank, who is an honors graduate of the University of Notre Dame, and his friend, seventeen-year-old Laurie Carpenter, begin what will become a two-year battle to bring Christopher back to a meaningful life.

Talbert, Marc. **Thin Ice.** Little, Brown, 1986. 207 p. ISBN 0-316-83133-6.

Sixth-grader Martin Enders feels his life is on "thin ice" — his dad has moved to Alaska, his mother is busy with her job, his diabetic sister depends on him for her insulin injections, and, worst of all, his teacher begins sticking his nose into their family affairs. Could Mr. Raven be as lonely as Martin?

Ure, Jean. **After Thursday.** Delacorte Press, 1987. 181 p. ISBN 0-385-29548-0.

Seventeen-year-old Marianne and pianist Abe have a great relationship. Then Abe, who is blind, prepares to leave London for Manchester to help another girl with her recitals. Marianne worries about what she will do with Abe gone. Will he come back to her?

Voigt, Cynthia. **Izzy, Willy-Nilly.** Atheneum, 1986. 258 p. ISBN 0-689-31202-4.

Fifteen-year-old Izzy Lingard is in an auto accident on the way home from a party. As a result, her leg is amputated below the knee. Izzy spends the next three months learning to live without a perfect body in a world that prefers perfection. Her new life completely changes her relationships with family, friends, and school acquaintances.

Religious Experiences

Arrick, Fran. **God's Radar.** Bradbury Press, 1983. 224 p. ISBN 0-02-705710-0.

Roxie and her family move from New York to a Southern community that focuses its activities around the Stafford Hill Baptist Church and the television ministry of Dr. Clement Caraman. Their neighbors gradually involve Roxie and her parents in their church and its ministries. When Glenna, Roxie's sister, comes home for Thanksgiving, she's concerned that their lives are being taken over by this religious community. Roxie is torn between acceptance of her new life and a desire to return to the old way.

Gaeddert, LouAnn. **Daffodils in the Snow.** E. P. Dutton, 1984. 114 p. ISBN 0-525-44150-6.

Marianne's father keeps an especially close eye on his daughter, making certain that no young man comes too near. So it's especially surprising that Marianne is pregnant and will say only that her baby is God's child. This is the story of a contemporary town's reaction to an event similar to one that occurred in Bethlehem more than 2000 years ago.

Holland, Isabelle. **Abbie's God Book.** Illustrated by James McLaughlin. Westminster Press, 1982. 80 p. ISBN 0-664-32688-9.

Almost twelve, Abbie is trying to understand God. Until recently, God wasn't a problem; He was just somebody who reserved a special place of safety on His "lap" for Abbie. As Abbie searches for God's identity, she discovers more about her parents' wisdom, the real value of friendship and forgiveness, and, most importantly, her own special place in God's world.

Howe, Norma. **God, the Universe, and Hot Fudge Sundaes.** Houghton Mifflin, 1984. 182 p. ISBN 0-395-35483-8.

Sixteen-year-old Alfie's caught in the middle between her religious mother and her skeptical father. She's torn in yet another direction when she meets Kurt, a college student who supports the scientists at a trial that focuses on how science will be taught in schools. Should evolution be taught exclusively, or should the biblical version of creation be included in science classes? Meanwhile, Alfie's little sister, Francie, is dying, and Alfie holds out hope that there's something better in store for Francie.

Leeson, Muriel. **The Bedford Adventure.** Illustrated by James Ponter. Herald Press, 1987. 132 p. ISBN 0-8361-3448-6.

Pete Murray, thirteen, is a timid Christian. When he and his family travel to Bedford, England, they visit the home of John Bunyan, author of *Pilgrim's Progress.* Inspired by the example of Bunyan and impressed with his courage as a Christian, Pete becomes involved in a police mystery where he is threatened physically and falsely accused of robbery.

Pinkwater, Jill. **The Disappearance of Sister Perfect.** E. P. Dutton, 1987. 149 p. ISBN 0-525-44278-2.

Sherelee Holmes may be barely thirteen, yet she's following devotedly in the footsteps of her imagined great-grandfather, Sherlock Holmes. When her sister disappears into the scary world of the "Perfect's" cult, Sherelee attempts a brilliant rescue, assisted by an aging chauffeur, an eccentric aunt, and a reluctant "Watson."

Provost, Gary, and Gail Levine-Freidus. **Good If It Goes.** Bradbury Press, 1984. 146 p. ISBN 0-02-774950-9.

On his thirteenth birthday, David Newman will celebrate his bar mitzvah. But how can he find time for basketball practice, preparing for his bar mitzvah, and a new girlfriend? His life becomes very hectic, and David is confronted with some important choices.

Rylant, Cynthia. **A Fine White Dust.** Bradbury Press, 1986. 106 p. ISBN 0-02-777240-3.

Thirteen-year-old Pete's life changes the summer of the revival. It is also the summer that the Preacher Man visits Pete's small North Carolina town. The Preacher Man seems to cast a spell over Pete — enough to make Pete want to leave his family and friends and to go on the road to do God's work. (Literary merit)

Smith, Doris Buchanan. **Laura Upside-Down.** Viking Penguin/Puffin Books, 1986. 148 p. ISBN 0-14-032085-7.

To ten-year-old Laura, her lack of religious training has never been a problem — that is, until now as she compares the beliefs of her two friends, Anna, who is a Christian, and Zipporah, who is a Jew. And when Laura gets to know Daurice, a strange woman who may prove to be a witch, Laura's lack of faith becomes crucial.

Wojciechowska, Maia. **How God Got Christian into Trouble.** Westminster Press, 1984. 80 p. ISBN 0-664-32717-6.

Eleven-year-old Christian Wolny often gets into lots of trouble, but with a name like Christian, what could posssibly go wrong? One day Christian finds himself talking to God about one of his problems and indicates that things could be a lot easier if God would stop being invisible. So God decides to become a Puerto Rican child and to hang around with Christian for a few days.

Science Fiction and the Future

Angell, Judie. **The Weird Disappearance of Jordan Hall.** Orchard Books, 1987. 121 p. ISBN 0-531-08327-6.

Sixteen-year-old Jordan Hall lands a job working in the New York City magic store of Emma Major's parents. Jordan feels that Emma is the best part of the job. The excitement starts when Jordan chases a cat into the famous Louis Langhorn's disappearing box, and he becomes invisible. Emma and Jordan, who want only to be alone together, suddenly cannot be farther apart.

Benoit, Hendra. **Hendra's Book.** Scholastic/Point Paperbacks, 1985. 137 p. ISBN 0-590-33202-3.

Hendra and two other teenagers, Max and Sal, made a big mistake when they touched a piece of satellite that dropped through the roof of the mall. Now they all have superpowers and are supposed to be a team, but they can't stand each other. Hendra just wants to be a Ninja, one of those ancient Japanese warriors. She's a gymnast, and her psionic powers have given her ideas. Max says it isn't safe to use her powers by herself, but she's tempted to do so. Part of the Psi Patrol trilogy.

Danziger, Paula. **This Place Has No Atmosphere.** Delacorte Press, 1986. 156 p. ISBN 0-385-29489-1.

Teenager Aurora is devastated to learn that her parents have decided to become pioneers in the twenty-first century and to live in a colony on the moon. The worst part for Aurora is that she must go with them. Aurora learns to adapt to the people and way of life in a colony where everyone must count on one another for survival.

DeWeese, Gene. **The Calvin Nullifier.** G. P. Putnam's Sons, 1987. 142 p. ISBN 0-399-21466-6.

A UFO, with a cat interstellar secret spy on board, lands in twelve-year-old Calvin's backyard. Calvin's father worked on *Trailblazer,* a space probe headed for Uranus that went dead just hours before reaching its goal. Calvin, his friend Kathy, and the cat from the UFO soon find themselves in space trying to rescue *Trailblazer.*

Etchemendy, Nancy. **The Crystal City.** Avon Books/Camelot Books, 1985. 173 p. ISBN 0-380-89699-0.

Maggie's brother, William, saves the doomed starship *Genesis* and leads the space travelers to safety on Earth II. But then they're caught in a copper dust storm and accosted by a huge and terrifying spider creature. Are the spider beasts in the Crystal City friendly or deadly? Sequel to *The Watcher of Space.*

Forrester, John. **Bestiary Mountain.** Bradbury Press, 1985. 140 p. ISBN 0-02-735530-6.

Sixteen-year-old twins Tamara and Drewyn Langstorm have grown up as part of the moon colony. Their parents moved to the moon after Old Earth's chemical wars in the 2130s. But when the twins were small, their mother returned to Old Earth to encourage the rebirth of Earth's animals. Now the twins were also going there to escape the oppression of the Overones. Book one of the Bestiary trilogy.

Forrester, John. **The Secret of the Round Beast.** Bradbury Press, 1986. 145 p. ISBN 0-02-735380-X.

Twins Tamara and Drewyn arrive on Old Earth to be with their mother, but Tamara's friend Saraj is discovered to be part human and part robot. Their mother's hybrid, Kana, who is part cat and part human, and the twins' friend from Luna, Jaric, decide to join the evil Gorid in the struggle for control of Old Earth. Book two of the Bestiary trilogy.

Fradin, Dennis Brindell. **How I Saved the World.** Dillon Press/Gemstone Books, 1986. 160 p. ISBN 0-87518-355-7.

Thirteen-year-old Shelley and his Uncle Myron spot blue light under a flying saucer as they watch the night sky in northern Michigan. Of course, no one believes them when they tell their story. But several weeks later, a once-abandoned copper-mining town is reinhabited by people who look and talk like characters seen in reruns on television.

Gardiner, John Reynolds. **Top Secret.** Illustrated by Marc Simont. Little, Brown, 1984. 110 p. ISBN 0-316-30368-2.

Nine-year-old Allen Brewster has an idea for his science project — human photosynthesis. The trouble is, nobody except Gramps will take him seriously. Allen concocts and consumes a special formula, and suddenly he begins to turn green. Allen realizes he has made the big time when a presidential adviser visits him and he is given top-secret status for his discovery.

Haas, Dorothy. **The Secret Life of Dilly McBean.** Bradbury Press, 1986. 202 p. ISBN 0-02-738200-1.

Dilly McBean, orphaned at an early age, has spent years in boarding schools. He has never told anyone about his extraordinary magnetic powers. Then Dilly begins a new life in the small town of Hennessey Depot. There he is kidnapped by an evil madman who wishes to control the world with a computer.

Haynes, Mary. **Wordchanger.** Illustrated by Eric Jon Nones. Dell/Laurel-Leaf Books, 1985. 252 p. ISBN 0-440-99671-6.

Twelve-year-old William's stepfather, Bruno, is a physicist who has developed a machine that can change words on a page — wherever they're written. Realizing the danger of this machine, William and his mother take it and flee. This begins a bizarre cross-country chase, with Bruno in close pursuit of William, the machine, and a stowaway — Lily — who has problems of her own.

Hill, Douglas. **Alien Citadel.** Atheneum/Margaret K. McElderry Books and Argo Books, 1984. 124 p. ISBN 0-689-50281-8.

Finn Ferral, along with other warriors of the Wasteland, continues the fight against the alien Slavers who now rule Earth and who are trying to exterminate the warriors. Finn is captured and taken to the Citadel, a huge underground fortress from which there is no escape. Finn must somehow find the secret of the Citadel and destroy it before it destroys him. Sequel to *The Huntsman* and *The Warriors of the Wasteland.*

Hill, Douglas. **The Caves of Klydor.** Atheneum/Margaret K. McElderry Books, 1985. 118 p. ISBN 0-689-50320-2.

A broad river sweeps along under the orange sun of the planet Klydor. On either side, the land is rugged and silent. Then around the bend floats a crude raft, carrying five teenagers from Earth. They had been exiled to Klydor by the evil ColSec, the Colonization Section of Earth's government. Can they adjust to this new world? Sequel to *Exiles of ColSec.*

Hill, Douglas. **ColSec Rebellion.** Atheneum/Margaret K. McElderry Books and Argo Books, 1985. 121 p. ISBN 0-689-50360-1.

Cord MaKiy and other teenagers from Earth have been exiled to the planet Klydor. There they decide to fight back, to try to overthrow the Colonization Section of Earth's government. ColSec colonizes planets by grabbing unwilling teenagers and shipping them into outer space. Determined to put an end to ColSec, Cord and his friends return to Earth to recruit members of street gangs to fight against the government. Betrayed, Cord and his friends face prison and possible execution.

Hill, Douglas. **Warriors of the Wasteland.** Atheneum/Margaret K. McElderry Books and Argo Books, 1983. 130 p. ISBN 0-689-50269-9.

Twenty-year-old Finn Ferral and his Bloodkin friend, Baer, hunt for Finn's adopted sister in the Wasteland of America after the atomic bomb is detonated. In their search they encounter the Slavers, who are the alien rulers of America, renegade humans, and the evil Claw. Finn also discovers American Indian descendants who ask him to make a difficult decision about his future. Sequel to *The Huntsman.*

Hoover, H. M. **Orvis.** Viking Penguin/Viking Kestrel, 1987. 186 p. ISBN 0-670-81117-3.

Twelve-year-old Toby, unhappy because she must leave school on Earth to attend one on Mars, discovers an obsolete robot, Orvis, who has been sent to a nearby dump. Toby, determined to save the robot, sets off across the country with Orvis and her friend Thaddeus, hoping to reach Toby's grandmother's farm and safety. Along the way they encounter thieves, renegades, wild animals, and the law.

Hoover, H. M. **The Shepherd Moon.** Viking Press, 1984. 149 p. ISBN 0-670-63977-X.

Thirteen-year-old Merry seems to be the only one who observed the arrival of Mikel Goodman, a colonist from an artificial moon. Everyone denies that there are colonists there. But Mikel is a dangerous person who has been created and raised only in a laboratory environment. He can destroy anything by rearranging its atoms, and to do so, he must only touch it with his hands. How can Merry defend her people against such powers?

Hughes, Monica. **The Isis Pedlar.** Atheneum/Argo Books, 1983. 121 p. ISBN 0-689-30988-0.

Fifteen-year-old Moira accompanies her father as he flies around the galaxy, cheating and tricking those he meets. When their spaceship breaks down on Isis, Moira, with the aid of a young man and a robot called "Guardian," tries to keep her father from interfering with life on the planet.

Hurley, Maxwell. **Max's Book.** Scholastic/Point Paperbacks, 1985. 151 p. ISBN 0-590-33203-1.

Teenagers Max, Sal, and Hendra wouldn't be caught dead together. But then all three touch a piece of satellite and soon discover they have superhuman powers. In this book, Max tells his version of the wild and zany problems faced by the Psi Patrol. Ten-foot-long arms and extrasensory perception are just the beginning of their discoveries. Part of the Psi Patrol trilogy.

Johnson, Annabel, and Edgar Johnson. **A Memory of Dragons.** Atheneum/Argo Books, 1986. 170 p. ISBN 0-689-31263-6.

Paul Killian, recently graduated from Vocational High School, is employed as a technician by the nation's largest defense center in the West. He is a genius with tools and finds himself caught up in a struggle between those who want the western states to secede and those who want the United States to remain whole. Paul also has a past that haunts and eludes him — memories of an abusive father and a violent murder.

Karl, Jean E. **Strange Tomorrow.** E. P. Dutton, 1985. 135 p. ISBN 0-525-44162-X.

Thirteen-year-old Janie reluctantly accompanies her father as he checks the secret underground retreat for government leaders. After the attack from Clord, she is thankful for her safe location. In the second part of this story, another Janie sets out several generations later with a small group of colonists to reclaim a lost portion of Earth in Zeta valley.

Kiesel, Stanley. **Skinny Malinky Leads the War for Kidness.** E. P. Dutton/Lodestar Books, 1984. 163 p. ISBN 0-525-66918-3.

There is trouble at Scratchland. The kids have taken over the schools, and Mr. Foreclosure, a powerful mutant red ant who hates kids, is plotting to capture their leader, Skinny Malinky. Most of Skinny's friends have become Young People through the

Status Quo Solidifier. Skinny must convince the kids that he is on their side.

Leroe, Ellen W. **Robot Raiders.** Harper and Row, 1987. 181 p. ISBN 0-06-023835-6.

Sixteen-year-old computer genius Bixby Wyler has been asked to help NASA with its Mars Mission. Bixby has created the first female humanoid, and NASA wants to use her for their Mars Mission. In trying to complete the project, Bixby comes up against anticomputer fanatics and a killer robot.

Liquori, Sal. **Sal's Book.** Scholastic/Point Paperbacks, 1985. 148 p. ISBN 0-590-33201-5.

When a huge meteor-like object falls through the mall ceiling into the fountain, Sal, along with Hendra and Max, touches it. Sal soon discovers that the satellite has given the three teenagers psionic powers. Sal, Hendra, and Max normally wouldn't be caught dead together, but now they form the Psi Patrol. Part of the Psi Patrol trilogy.

McKillip, Patricia A. **The Moon and the Face.** Atheneum/Argo Books, 1985. 146 p. ISBN 0-689-31158-3.

Four Moon-Flashes have passed since Kyreol and Terje left Riverworld for Dome City. But now each of them must make a separate journey. Kyreol will travel to a planet far beyond the Dome to observe the inhabitants of another world. Terje will return as an observer to the Riverworld. They both discover that though their journeys and lives separate, their dreams are still the same. Sequel to *Moon-Flash.*

McKillip, Patricia A. **Moon-Flash.** Atheneum/Argo Books, 1984. 150 p. ISBN 0-689-31049-8.

Kyreol lives in a clearly defined world on the river, but she is filled with questions about her own life. Where did her mother go when she left the Riverworld? Why doesn't her father mourn her mother as dead? Kyreol and her friend Terje dare to take a trip to the Fourteen Falls, which mark the edge of Riverworld. There they are caught in the rapids and pass through to a world far different from Riverworld. The Hunter must protect them from danger but permits them to explore this new world.

Melling, O. R. **The Druid's Tune.** Penguin Books/Puffin Books, 1983. 236 p. ISBN 0-14-03-1778-3.

Rosemary, seventeen, and her sixteen-year-old brother, Jimmy, are taken from the twentieth century to another time and another place — the battle camp of a Celtic warrior queen. A wizard druid also arrives out of the mists of time. A battle awaits, treachery abounds, and death is all around. Then the druid disappears. Will Rosemary and Jimmy ever get back to their own world?

Norton, Andre. **The Gate of the Cat.** Ace Books, 1987. 243 p. ISBN 0-441-27376-9.

A hunted wildcat and Kelsie McBlair fall through a gate in the Scottish highlands. They enter a world where fearsome creatures abound, witches rule supreme, and the forces of the Dark ravage the countryside. Kelsie holds the key to Witch World's future.

Sargent, Pamela. **Eye of the Comet.** Harper and Row, 1984. 275 p. ISBN 0-06-025196-4 (0-06-025197-2, library binding).

Lydee, who lives on a comet world, must visit Earth, the primitive planet that was once the home of the comet dwellers. Because both worlds need each other desperately now, Lydee must become a bridge between the comet worlds and Earth, whether she wants to or not.

Senn, Steve. **Ralph Fozbek and the Amazing Black Hole Patrol.** Illustrated by the author. Avon Books/Camelot Books, 1986. 102 p. ISBN 0-380-89905-1.

Ralph Fozbek is ready for a boring summer in Fogville. But then a black hole escapes from the laboratory of Dr. Krebnickel, the town's daffy genius. Ralph agrees to help chase the runaway hole and soon finds himself in outer space — and in the middle of a lot of trouble. A Big Bang is about to destroy the entire universe. Only Ralph, with the help of a new friend, can stop it.

Service, Pamela F. **A Question of Destiny.** Atheneum, 1986. 160 p. ISBN 0-689-31181-8.

Dan Stratton's father is running for president. During the campaign, fourteen-year-old Dan becomes suspicious about David Green, one of his father's advisers. Dan does some research and discovers something shocking. Confronted with the information, David proves who he is and what he needs to do. To Dan's surprise, he himself becomes a willing participant and helps David.

Sleator, William. **Interstellar Pig.** E. P. Dutton, 1984. 197 p. ISBN 0-525-44098-4.

Sixteen-year-old Barney fears that his summer vacation at a beach cottage on the East Coast will be a bore without kids his age around. But at the beginning of the second week, a strange group moves in next door, and soon Barney has joined them in a board game called Interstellar Pig. As the neighbors seek more and more information from Barney about the cottage where he's staying, he begins to notice the resemblance between these people and the characters in the game. (Literary merit)

Sleator, William. **Singularity.** E. P. Dutton, 1985. 170 p. ISBN 0-525-44161-1.

Sixteen-year-old twins Harry and Barry convince their parents to let them spend some time alone at their deceased great-uncle's farm, where farm animals belonging to local people have met strange deaths. The twins discover a bizarre house and playhouse at Uncle Ambrose's farm. Inside the playhouse, time passes much more quickly than outside. Harry and Barry each plot to be the older twin — but not without penalties.

Stoff, Joshua. **The Voyage of the Ruslan: The First Manned Exploration of Mars.** Illustrated by the author. Atheneum, 1986. 104 p. ISBN 0-689-31191-5.

Projecting from known scientific facts, this book portrays an imaginary voyage to Mars by the Soviets in the 1990s. Join with the crew of the *Ruslan* as they fly through space, land on Mars, describe the appearance of the planet, and discover plant life on Mars.

Walker, Irma. **Portal to E'ewere.** Atheneum/Argo Books, 1983. 159 p. ISBN 0-689-30998-8.

Sixteen-year-old AMity lives in the N'Eastern States of America in the twenty-first century. Due to overpopulation, people live in swarms and are never alone. When AMity discovers a new world inhabited by fairy-like creatures, she decides to rescue her grandfather, brother, and best friend and to transport them there.

Weaver, Lydia. **Splashman.** New American Library/Signet Vista Books, 1985. 190 p. ISBN 0-451-14020-6.

A rainy, boring vacation at the seashore turns into an exciting underwater adventure with the elements of a nightmare. A sea monster creates havoc with a terrifying storm and then lures the children of the seaside village to take an underwater trip with Peter as the leader. Peter claims that his mother is a mermaid and that he must find her.

Webb, Sharon. **Ram Song.** Illustrated by Thomas Deitz. Atheneum/Argo Books, 1984. 218 p. ISBN 0-689-31058-7.

On the planet Aulos, a strange beam that disorients people is interrupting a yearly festival. The immortal Kurt Kraus is called upon to meet this emergency with the help of three unsuspecting mortals of quite differing backgrounds. What is bringing them together and why? Sequel to *Earthchild* and *Earth Song.*

Space and Time

Cooper, Susan. **Seaward.** Atheneum/Margaret K. McElderry Books and Argo Books, 1984. 167 p. ISBN 0-689-50275-3.

Calliope and Westerly leave the world of reality behind to find themselves together in a world filled with perils orchestrated by the beautiful Lady Taranis. Without understanding why, they know they must journey to the sea. The two meet the Stone People and others who try to prevent them from completing that journey; they also meet Lugan and Snake, who help them. As Calliope and Westerly journey, they make important discoveries about themselves.

Cresswell, Helen. **Moondial.** Macmillan, 1987. 202 p. ISBN 0-02-725370-8.

While staying with her aunt Mary for the summer, Minty hears two children crying to be set free from the house next door. They turn out to be the ghosts of an abused Victorian kitchen boy and a little girl from an earlier period of time. Through the power of a mysterious sundial, Minty eventually meets the children by traveling back in time and tries to help them.

Johnson, Annabel, and Edgar Johnson. **The Danger Quotient.** Harper and Row, 1984. 216 p. ISBN 0-06-022852-0 (0-06-022853-9, library binding).

Eighteen-year-old Casey is one of a group of supergeniuses in a small underground colony built after the face of Earth was blighted by nuclear war. The survivors are slowly and mysteriously dying. Casey must travel back through time to the twentieth century to find out how to save the remaining survivors.

Kennemore, Tim. **Changing Times.** Faber and Faber, 1984. 149 p. ISBN 0-571-13285-5.

An alarm clock that doesn't work and a mirror — gifts that cold, disdainful Victoria chose for her fifteenth birthday — prove to be almost more than she can handle. Strange journeys through time hold the key to Victoria's "bratty" behavior and help Victoria understand her parent's unhappiness.

Kittleman, Laurence R. **Canyons beyond the Sky.** Atheneum, 1985. 212 p. ISBN 0-689-31138-9.

The last place Evan Ferguson wants to spend his twelfth summer is Antelope Spring, where his father is heading an archeological expedition. Aided by geologist George Foster and young Cee-Jay Kohler, Evan gains toughness and desert savvy. Then he is mysteriously transported 5,000 years back in time, where he befriends an Indian boy from the ancient culture that his father is studying. It is this incredible journey that finally wins his father's respect and ensures Evan's own self-confidence.

Lindbergh, Anne. **The Hunky-Dory Dairy.** Illustrated by Julie Brinckloe. Harcourt Brace Jovanovich, 1986. 147 p. ISBN 0-15-237449-3.

Traveling back in time, eleven-year-old Zannah finds the perfect man for her mother and new friends for herself when she befriends the residents of a dairy that has been transported back to the twelfth century. But how can she bring the two worlds together without being accused of witchcraft?

Lindbergh, Anne. **The Shadow on the Dial.** Harper and Row, 1987. 153 p. ISBN 0-06-023882-3 (0-06-023883-6, library binding).

Twelve-year-old Dawn and her younger brother, Marcus, go to visit their uncle Doo in Florida. As they make the long trip, they are followed by a van with an ad on the side saying, "Your Heart's Desire JUST DIAL." When they find a sundial in Uncle Doo's garden, the children turn the sundial. Mr. Bros appears and asks them their heart's desire. The children decide to give their uncle what he said he always wanted — to be a flute player. By traveling back in time, they hope to change the future.

Payne, Bernal C., Jr. **It's About Time.** Macmillan, 1984. 170 p. ISBN 0-02-770230-8.

Have you ever wanted to go back in time? Chris and Gail, two teenagers, transport themselves back to 1955 by looking at an old photograph of their teenage parents. Gail interrupts the future by causing their parents not to meet, which suspends her brother and herself in time. They devise a plan to unite their parents so they will be able to return to 1983.

Peck, Richard. **Blossom Culp and the Sleep of Death.** Delacorte Press, 1986. 185 p. ISBN 0-385-29433-6.

This fourth episode with Blossom and Alexander involves the restoration of an Egyptian princess, dead for 3,500 years, to her rightful tomb. To complicate the escapade, certain Egyptian artifacts have fallen into the nasty hands of Lettie Shambaugh's mother. Retrieving these artifacts proves to be a comic and spooky adventure.

Pryor, Bonnie. **Mr. Z and the Time Clock.** Dillon Press/Gemstone Books, 1986. 117 p. ISBN 0-87518-328-X.

When twelve-year-old Julie's antique clock turns out to be a time machine, she and her twin brother take some unusual trips into the past and future. Once they accidentally bring travelers from another time period home with them. Join the twins as they learn to appreciate the important values shared by all people, regardless of their place in history.

Purtill, Richard. **Enchantment at Delphi.** Harcourt Brace Jovanovich/Gulliver Books, 1986. 149 p. ISBN 0-15-200447-5.

Eighteen-year-old Alice Grant is in the ancient Greek town of Delphi as part of a special university study project. She stumbles onto a "line of power" that enables her to travel in time on a series of visits to Apollo, Dionysus, and Athena. While in present time, Alice falls in love with a young Greek, and together they make one final trip along the "line of power."

Rodowsky, Colby. **Keeping Time.** Farrar, Straus and Giroux, 1983. 137 p. ISBN 0-374-34061-7.

Drew wants to go with his friends to watch the Orioles play the Yankees, but he has to practice with his "family" of street performers. One night down at the harbor while playing "Greensleeves," Drew is mysteriously transported to Elizabethan London. There he meets Symon Ives, and their adventures and friendship begin.

Singer, Marilyn. **Horsemaster.** Atheneum/Argo Books, 1985. 179 p. ISBN 0-689-31102-8.

Fourteen-year-old Jessica and her friend Jack are running away from their Wisconsin homes. They stop for shelter at a deserted farmhouse where an unusual tapestry of a horse is hanging. The tapestry has special powers that project the two across time to an ancient culture. There the horse god is seeking a horsemaster who will lead the people through times of war to a time of peace.

Sports

Avi. **S.O.R. Losers.** Bradbury Press, 1984. 90 p. ISBN 0-02-793410-1.

South Orange River Middle School requires its students to play one sport a year, but Ed Sitrow and ten other nonjocks had "better" things to do last year, like study art, play poker, and write. This year they can't escape the rules. With Mr. Lester, their optimistic history teacher, as coach, Ed and his friends form a seventh-grade soccer team that becomes as famous as the school's past all-stars, but for different reasons. The S.O.R. Losers' unforgettable season is related here as a hilarious declaration of independence.

Christopher, Matt. **The Hockey Machine.** Illustrated by Richard Schroeppel. Little, Brown, 1986. 137 p. ISBN 0-316-14055-4.

Steve Crandell is a talented young hockey player, so talented that he is sought out for a special "young players" team that will play professional hockey clubs. When he arrives at the training center, Steve discovers that he must play — in order to survive.

Christopher, Matt. **Red-Hot Hightops.** Illustrated by Paul D. Mock. Little, Brown, 1987. 148 p. ISBN 0-316-14056-2.

Kelly is able to shoot baskets just fine when playing with her friends, but she freezes up during actual games. Then Kelly finds a pair of red high-top shoes in her locker with a note wishing her good luck. Mysteriously, when Kelly wears the shoes, she no longer freezes up during games and becomes a star player. But where did the shoes come from? Will Kelly ever be able to play ball without wearing them?

Christopher, Matt. **Supercharged Infield.** Illustrated by Julie Downing. Little, Brown, 1985. 120 p. ISBN 0-316-13983-1.

Penny Farrell, captain and third-base player of the softball team, is faced with a unique dilemma. Two of the infielders have turned into super athletes — just what the team needs. But at the same time they have become cold and emotionless. Can there be a link between her friends' new abilities and their association with Harold Dempsey, the team's scorekeeper?

Crutcher, Chris. **Stotan!** Greenwillow Books, 1986. 183 p. ISBN 0-688-05715-2.

Seventeen-year-old swimmer Walker Dupree and his three best friends have the opportunity to become stotans, athletes who are a cross between a stoic and a spartan. The four teenagers comprise the high school swim team in a Washington town, and stotan week is planned just for the four of them by their coach, Max Il Song. The coach is determined to make them physically and mentally ready for anything. (Literary merit)

Dygard, Thomas J. **Halfback Tough.** William Morrow, 1986. 210 p. ISBN 0-688-05925-2.

When Joe becomes a football hero at his new high school, he thinks he has left his past behind. But old chums show up, vandalize the school, and cause Joe's principal and new friends to suspect his good intentions. Joe has to decide who he really is — a troublemaker or a team player.

Dygard, Thomas J. **Tournament Upstart.** William Morrow, 1984. 199 p. ISBN 0-688-02761-X.

The Falcons, from tiny Cedar Grove High in the Ozark foothills, decide they are ready to move up from the Class B basketball tournament to play Class A teams. But their star player now thinks he is too good for this "hick" team. The coach and the townspeople begin to doubt that the Falcons can play well against the big-city schools.

Howe, Fanny. **Race of the Radical.** Viking Penguin/Viking Kestrel, 1985. 150 p. ISBN 0-670-80557-2.

Alex Porter loves bike racing so much that his father decides to build him a BMX-type bike that is lighter than air. Alex feels the bike is a surefire ticket to the pros, and names it "the Radical." The bike proves successful, but it captures the attention of someone else. Soon the chase is on to discover who has stolen the Radical.

Kelly, Jeffrey. **The Basement Baseball Club.** Houghton Mifflin, 1987. 175 p. ISBN 0-395-40774-5.

The McCarthy Roaders have lost nine games in a row to their arch rivals, the Hemlock Street Poisons. They blame their losses on Bull Reilly, the new pitcher for the Poisons. The Roaders' hopes soar when a big kid moves into their neighborhood, but he says he won't play baseball. How can they change his mind?

Klass, David. **The Atami Dragons.** Charles Scribner's Sons, 1984. 134 p. ISBN 0-684-18223-8.

Jerry's plans of playing on a winning summer baseball team are crushed when his father announces that they will be spending the summer in Japan. Although Jerry understands his father's hopes that a change of scenery may heal the emotional wounds left by the recent death of Jerry's mother, the cultural shock and loneliness of a foreign land hit him hard. Only when Jerry meets the Atami Dragons baseball team does his summer begin to have meaning.

Knudson, R. R. **Rinehart Shouts.** Farrar, Straus and Giroux, 1987. 115 p. ISBN 0-374-36296-3.

Arthur Rinehart spends the summer bird watching and trying to overcome his fear of water. He wants to try his racing shell, *Read More,* against the other racing shells on the river, but first he needs some confidence in his own abilities.

Knudson, R. R. **Zan Hagen's Marathon.** Farrar, Straus and Giroux, 1984. 183 p. ISBN 0-374-38811-3.

Zan Hagen is very sure of herself, perhaps too sure. In deciding to try for the U. S. Olympic team in track events, Zan refuses to listen to the advice and coaching of her longtime friend, Arthur Rinehart. Her stubborness and her distrust of fellow competitors work together to produce one of the most humiliating experiences in her life.

Larsen, Rebecca. **Slow as a Panda.** Dillon Press/Gemstone Books, 1986. 136 p. ISBN 0-87518-327-1.

A twelve-year-old competitive swimmer tries to keep the swim team from falling apart by getting rid of her delusions about the coach. She tries to overcome her own feelings of inadequacy and self-doubt about her abilities.

Montgomery, Robert. **Rabbit Ears.** New American Library/Signet Vista Books, 1985. 159 p. ISBN 0-451-13631-4.

The new player nicknamed "the Kid" promises to be the best pitcher Jason's team has ever had. But the Kid's "rabbit ears" prove to be too distracting. He goes to pieces when he hears razzing from the opposing team and when he picks up bad vibes about his girlfriend and his very ill father. Jason and the Kid learn to help each other on and off the playing field.

Myers, Walter Dean. **The Outside Shot.** Dell/Laurel-Leaf Books, 1987. 185 p. ISBN 0-440-96784-8.

Lonnie Jackson leaves Harlem on a basketball scholarship to a small midwestern college. Lonnie is poorly prepared for the academic classes, the pressures of college ball, and the temptation to fix games for local gamblers. In addition, he meets Sherry, who wants to be a track star. Lonnie finds he is as confused about their relationship as he is about college. Sequel to *Hoops.*

Smith, Doris Buchanan. **Karate Dancer.** G. P. Putnam's Sons, 1987. 175 p. ISBN 0-399-21464-X.

Fourteen-year-old Troy Matthews draws cartoons for the local newspaper and is working toward his black belt in karate. He wants his disapproving parents to understand his love for karate. At a karate demonstration to benefit victims of muscular dystrophy, Troy discovers how he feels about those closest to him.

Voigt, Cynthia. **The Runner.** Atheneum, 1985. 181 p. ISBN 0-689-31069-2.

His name is Bullet because he runs like one, with running consuming his life. He is a solitary runner, not part of anything, not even his family. To his father, he is a disgrace; to his coach, a lonely winner; to his few friends, a mystery. His black teammate, Tamer Shipp, understands Bullet because they are alike. Despite Tamer's offer of friendship and the friendship of his boss, Patrice, Bullet remains a solitary figure, apparently caring only for one other person.

The Supernatural

Avi. **Devil's Race.** J. B. Lippincott, 1984. 152 p. ISBN 0-397-32094-9 (0-397-32095-7, library binding).

Sixteen-year-old John Proud is tormented by the ghost of an evil ancestor who shares his own name and looks like him and who was hanged in 1854 for being a demon. There is only one person who can help John in his desperate battle with the dark side of his mind — his pretty cousin Ann. But can he trust her? Or is she in a conspiracy with a fiend?

Battles, Edith. **The Witch in Room 6.** Harper and Row, 1987. 151 p. ISBN 0-06-020412-5 (0-06-020413-3, library binding).

Sean has trouble with reading, spelling, football, and baseball until apprentice witch Cheryl Suzanne Endor joins his fifth-grade class. With her help, Sean soon excels at what used to trouble him. He in turn tries to help Cheryl fit in with the popular crowd and make a difficult decision for an eleven-year-old girl — whether to continue to become a witch or to give up and be like everyone else.

Bellairs, John. **The Dark Secret of Weatherend.** Dial Books for Young Readers, 1984. 182 p. ISBN 0-8037-0072-5 (0-8037-0074-1, library binding).

Fourteen-year-old Anthony Monday and Miss Eells, the librarian at Hoosac, Minnesota, find a diary written by J. K. Borkman. It appears to be the writings of a crazy man. Then Borkman's sons move into an old house, once the Borkman family home, and strange things begin to happen — violent hailstorms and blizzards. Anthony and Miss Eells face great danger as they trace the source of these violent weather conditions.

Bonham, Frank. **Premonitions.** Holt, Rinehart and Winston, 1984. 166 p. ISBN 0-03-071306-4.

High school newspaper editor Kevin Spicer thinks he's a sixteen-year-old klutz — so much so that he is afraid to ask out Anni, a

French girl in his class. But Anni calls Kevin, and a relationship develops. Kevin finds himself entangled in the mystery surrounding Anni's clairvoyance and the death of her brother a year before. What is Anni hiding? Why does she insist that their love will never work?

Brittain, Bill. **Dr. Dredd's Wagon of Wonders.** Illustrated by Andrew Glass. Harper and Row, 1987. 179 p. ISBN 0-06-020713-2 (0-06-020714-0, library binding).

The town of Coven Tree has been hit by a drought that dries up wells, causes animals to suffer, and prevents the sowing of crops. Enter Dr. Dredd and his Wagon of Wonders, including a young boy, Bufu the Rainmaker, who demonstrates that he can make it rain. Dr. Dredd will allow Bufu to make it rain, but will the community be willing to pay the price? With the help of fourteen-year-old Ellen McCabe, Bufu runs away, leaving the town open to the wrath and sinister powers of Dr. Hugo Dredd.

Brittain, Bill. **Who Knew There'd Be Ghosts?** Illustrated by Michele Chessare. Harper and Row, 1985. 119 p. ISBN 0-06-020699-3 (0-06-020700-0, library binding).

Tommy, Books, and Harry the Blimp have used the old deserted Parnell House and surrounding grounds as a playground. Now Avery Katkus, a crooked antique dealer who wants to buy the house, plans to tear it down board by board to look for something valuable. The boys, with the help of two ghostly allies, set out to turn the tables on Avery Katkus by uncovering the secrets that Parnell House has kept hidden for the last hundred years.

Carris, Joan. **Witch-Cat.** Illustrated by Beth Peck. Dell/Yearling Books, 1986. 154 p. ISBN 0-440-49477-X.

It's up to Rosetta, an experienced witch-cat, to teach young Gwen Markham how to understand and use her special witch powers right in her hometown of Hampshire, Ohio. But Gwen is a science buff who likes to find answers to everything — she is an unlikely candidate for the age-old order of witches. Will Rosetta have any success?

Cassedy, Sylvia. **Behind the Attic Wall.** Avon Books/Camelot Books, 1985. 315 p. ISBN 0-380-69843-9.

At twelve, Maggie has been thrown out of more boarding schools than she cares to remember. Now she is to live in a bleak old house with her great-aunts, who with Uncle Morris are her only living relatives. From behind the closet door in the great and gloomy house, Maggie hears whisperings and beckoning voices. In this forbidding house of her ancestors, Maggie finds magic — the kind that for once lets the lonely girl love and be loved.

Cross, Gillian. **Roscoe's Leap.** Holiday House, 1987. 160 p. ISBN 0-8234-0669-5.

A strange house, dubbed Roscoe's Leap, is falling apart from neglect. Its occupants, descendants of Samuel Roscoe, barely tolerate each other. Twelve-year-old Stephen, Samuel's great-great-grandson, starts on a thrilling adventure when the old collection of wind-up toys reveals the dark secrets of the family's past.

DeClements, Barthe, and Christopher Greimes. **Double Trouble.** Viking Penguin/Viking Kestrel, 1987. 168 p. ISBN 0-670-81567-5.

Orphan twins Faith and Phillip are placed in different foster homes. They write to each other, but are almost able to communicate mentally with one another. Faith lives with their aunt, who thinks Faith isn't grateful for being taken in by her, while Phillip lives with a couple who belong to a strange religious sect and who want to make him a member. When Faith feels threatened by her social studies teacher's illegal activities, she contacts Phillip for help.

Duncan, Lois. **Locked in Time.** Little, Brown, 1985. 210 p. ISBN 0-316-19555-3.

Nore Robbins is disconcerted by being summoned to the Louisiana plantation where her father and new stepmother live. She is even more troubled by Lisette and her three children. Lisette's beauty has a chilling, ageless quality that unnerves Nore. As her father pleads for her to accept Lisette, Nore searches ancient journals for the secret of the inhabitants of Shadow Grove.

Duncan, Lois. **The Third Eye.** Dell/Laurel-Leaf Books, 1985. 220 p. ISBN 0-440-98720-2.

Karen is a senior in high school before she realizes she has been born with a third eye — a unique power that lets her see and help find missing children. When twelve babies are kidnapped from the child care center where she works, Karen endangers her own life by following the kidnappers. Fortunately, help comes from a very unexpected and surprising source.

Gormley, Beatrice. **The Ghastly Glasses.** Illustrated by Emily Arnold McCully. Avon Books/Camelot Books, 1987. 117 p. ISBN 0-380-70262-2.

Fifth-grader Andrea Reve is having difficulty seeing, but she gets more than she bargains for with her first pair of glasses. She is suspicious when she sees the creepy eye painted on the building where she goes for her glasses, and despite Aunt Bets's comments, Andrea is quite sure that the white-coated woman is not an eye doctor. Andrea is right. Looking through the glasses gives her the spooky power of mind control over her family and friends. Her experiments soon get out of hand.

Hahn, Mary Downing. **Wait Till Helen Comes.** Clarion Books, 1986. 184 p. ISBN 0-89919-453-2.

Molly and Michael have a new father and seven-year-old stepsister, Heather, who is hateful and tells lies about them. The family moves to a converted church in the country. When Heather, who saw her own mother die in a fire, discovers a small gravestone with her initials on it, she becomes possessed by the ghost of a little girl whose mother died in a fire in the 1880s. Molly must somehow save Heather from the ghost before it leads Heather to her own death.

Hoobler, Thomas. **Dr. Chill's Project.** G. P. Putnam's Sons, 1987. 188 p. ISBN 0-399-21480-1.

Fifteen-year-old Allie, who can move objects just by thinking, is part of Dr. Chill's secret project along with other young people who also have unusual abilities. A strange man sometimes watches the young people perform experiments set up by Dr. Chill. But what is the ultimate goal of these experiments? When one of the young people disappears, the others join together to run away to safety.

Horowitz, Anthony. **The Devil's Door-Bell.** Holt, Rinehart and Winston, 1984. 159 p. ISBN 0-03-063813-5.

After his parents are killed, thirteen-year-old Martin Hopkins is taken to a farm in Yorkshire, England, by a strange old woman. Martin is mistreated and fears for his life. He discovers an abandoned nuclear power plant in the forest nearby and becomes caught up in the strange happenings connected with the plant.

Horowitz, Anthony. **The Night of the Scorpion.** Pacer Books, 1984. 159 p. ISBN 0-448-47751-3.

Martin Hopkins, a thirteen-year-old English boy, foresees the crash of a petrol truck into his school, so he is able to save his classmates. Recognizing a diary with the mark of the Old Ones, Martin and his guardian trace the diary to Peru. There they begin a new battle against the powers of evil. Sequel to *The Devil's Door-Bell.*

Horowitz, Anthony. **The Silver Citadel.** Berkley Books/Pacer Books, 1986. 150 p. ISBN 0-425-08890-1.

Beware — don't read this book if you are afraid of the supernatural. What appear to be ordinary brothers unite with other children who possess supernatural powers in an effort to save the world from the Old Ones. Horrible adventures await them as they become entangled in a web of evil.

Johnson, Annabel, and Edgar Johnson. **Prisoner of PSI.** Atheneum/Argo Books, 1985. 149 p. ISBN 0-689-31132-X.

Only one thing could tempt Tristan out of hiding. He has learned of the approaching death of his father, who exploited the psychic powers of the father-son team on national television to the point that Tristan, even at age thirteen, could take it no longer. Now, five years later, Tristan must decide whether or not to help save his father from international terrorists.

Katz, Welwyn Wilton. **Witchery Hill.** Atheneum/Margaret K. McElderry Books, 1984. 244 p. ISBN 0-689-50309-1.

Fourteen-year-old Mike Lewis is, as usual, spending his summer vacation with his father, but this year they are staying on the English Channel Island of Guernsey, where nothing else is at all usual. Mike must decide whether to accept his father's judgment that witchcraft is illogical and therefore nonexistent, or whether to help his friend Lisa fight a coven of witches to save her father's life.

Kilgore, Kathleen. **The Ghost-Maker.** Houghton Mifflin, 1984. 206 p. ISBN 0-395-35383-1.

After he is expelled from school, sixteen-year-old Lee is packed off to Florida to live with his grandmother and to await his parents' divorce. When he meets May, a certified medium, his exile takes a new turn. Lee becomes her apprentice, but his newly found powers bring conflict and his world becomes full of mystery and danger.

Klein, Robin. **Games. . . .** Illustrated by Melissa Webb. Viking Penguin/ Viking Kestrel, 1987. 150 p. ISBN 0-670-81403-2.

Three girls spend a weekend in an isolated country house that has an intriguing past. The girls hold a séance, but what begins as fun soon gets out of hand — and their foolish game plunges them into a night of terror.

Kushner, Donn. **Uncle Jacob's Ghost Story.** Illustrated by Christopher Manson. Holt, Rinehart and Winston, 1986. 132 p. ISBN 0-03-006502-X.

Paul asks about his great-uncle Jacob, for whenever anyone talks about Jacob, they speak in "hushed, disapproving voices" about the family's outcast. Paul's grandfather and his friend, Mr. Eisbein, finally tell Paul the story of Jacob, who is really a warm, caring man, and the ghosts who followed him from Poland to America.

McGinnis, Lila. **Auras and Other Rainbow Secrets.** Hastings House, 1984. 109 p. ISBN 0-8038-0551-9.

Eleven-year-old Nora has a strange talent. She has inherited her mother's ability to see colors around people — auras that tell her about their feelings. Whenever Nora mentions anything about the colors, her father becomes very angry. But seeing auras is as natural to Nora as breathing. Can it really be bad? Why does Nora's ESP ability anger her father?

Mahy, Margaret. **The Changeover.** Scholastic/Point Paperbacks, 1984. 263 p. ISBN 0-590-33798-X.

Only Laura knows that Sorenson Carlisle is a witch. When Laura's brother, Jacko, becomes possessed, she turns to Sorenson for help. The ultimate solution requires Laura to become a witch and to face the demon who is draining the life from Jacko. While he lies lifeless in a New Zealand hospital, Laura must decide if she is strong enough to save him by risking her life and mortality to change over to the world of the supernatural.

Nelson, Theresa. **Devil Storm.** Orchard Books, 1987. 212 p. ISBN 0-531-05711-9 (0-531-08311-X, library binding).

Thirteen-year-old Walter Carroll and his younger sister, Alice, have been raised on tales of Old Tom, the supposedly crazy old black man who haunts the coast of Bolivar, stealing and conjuring. But when the Devil Storm he predicted invades the peninsula of Texas in 1900, can even Tom save them?

Norton, Andre, and Phyllis Miller. **House of Shadows.** Atheneum/Margaret K. McElderry Books, 1985. 201 p. ISBN 0-689-50298-2.

Mike, Susan, and six-year-old Tucker are taken to live with their great-aunt Hendrika in New York until their parents can send for them. Aunt Hendrika's house, built before the Revolutionary War, seems to be haunted by the ghosts of three young children who disappeared during an Indian raid. Susan, Mike, and Tucker attempt to clear up the mystery.

Place, Marian T. **The First Astrowitches.** Illustrated by Tom O'Sullivan. Avon Books/Camelot Books, 1985. 155 p. ISBN 0-380-70056-5.

The Organization of American Witches sent a spaceship to probe outer space for a pollution-free planet where witches could live in good health. But the spacecraft party has not been heard from in years. Witchard and Witcheena are concerned since his parents and her parents are aboard. Witchard decides that Witcheena and he will stow away on NASA's new space shuttle and will try to contact their parents from outer space.

Rabinowitz, Ann. **Knight on Horseback.** Macmillan, 1987. 197 p. ISBN 0-02-775660-2.

When he is on his own for a day in London while traveling with his family in England, thirteen-year-old Eddie steals a wooden toy — a knight on horseback. A mysterious stranger in a cape begins to turn up wherever Eddie goes. Could it really be the ghost of Richard III? Through the magic of the toy, Eddie learns much about the love of fathers for sons. (Literary merit)

Roth, David. **A World for Joey Carr.** Ballantine Books/Fawcett Juniper Books, 1984. 149 p. ISBN 0-449-70048-8.

Ever since fourteen-year-old Joey's mom died, his dad has been removed and barely speaks. Joey finds a dog in the park, but his dad refuses to let Joey keep him. That night Joey decides to start out on foot for his grandparents' home in northern Vermont. On the way he meets Hannah, a dying woman who claims to be a witch seeking a cure for her cancer. Together they experience some very strange adventures.

Rundle, Anne. **Moonbranches.** Macmillan, 1986. 163 p. ISBN 0-02-777190-3.

In the early days of World War I, fourteen-year-old Frances spends the summer in Scotland with her aunt, the housekeeper at a house with a violent past. The house seems familiar to Frances, but she doesn't know why. She is taunted by Martin, the youthful heir to this Scottish estate, and retreats to the woods, the graveyard, and the dusty attic to avoid him. She dreams of Martin's twin brother, Simon, who drowned years before. Then from the past Simon calls to Frances to help him.

Singer, Marilyn. **Ghost Host.** Harper and Row, 1987. 182 p. ISBN 0-06-025623-0 (0-06-025624-9, library binding).

Sixteen-year-old football player Bart Hawkins discovers that a nasty poltergeist named Stryker has invaded his house. Not only is he concerned, but so are the nine friendly ghosts who live there. One ghost, pretty young Millicent, offers to help Bart's football team if he will get rid of Stryker. But how can he trap a poltergeist?

Sobol, Donald J. **The Amazing Power of Ashur Fine.** Macmillan, 1986. 114 p. ISBN 0-02-786270-4.

When sixteen-year-old Ashur Fine sets out on a cross-country trip to find his aunt's mugger, he becomes involved in a mysterious theft and kidnapping case. Using the extrasensory powers he obtained from an ancient African elephant, Ashur should be able to solve the case easily. But can he?

Twohill, Maggie. **Jeeter, Mason and the Magic Headset.** Bradbury Press, 1985. 103 p. ISBN 0-02-789530-0.

Jeeter Huff likes rock music loud, so her family gives her a radio and headset for her tenth birthday. The next afternoon Jeeter hears a mystery message over the headset from someone named Mason. She begins listening every day for more messages. Who is this mysterious Mason?

VanOosting, James. **Maxie's Ghost.** Farrar, Straus and Giroux, 1987. 118 p. ISBN 0-374-34873-1.

Even though fourth-grader Maxie hates Halloween, the director of the orphanage sends him to school dressed as a ghost. The class returns to the orphanage to entertain the preschoolers. While there, Maxie and his friend Judy mysteriously fly off on an adventure where Maxie meets a special ghost of his own.

Wolitzer, Meg. **The Dream Book.** Greenwillow Books, 1986. 148 p. ISBN 0-688-05148-0.

Two girls, "Danger" Roth and Claudia Lemmon, share many things — telephone calls, afternoon snacks, and matching dreams. How is this happening? Is it ESP or magic? The dreams seem to be unraveling the mystery of Claudia's missing father. But they also involve the strange Dr. Byrd, who lives in an upstairs apartment.

Wright, Betty Ren. **Christina's Ghost.** Holiday House, 1985. 105 p. ISBN 0-8234-0581-8.

Christina is disappointed that she must spend her summer with her grumpy uncle. However, her summer turns out to be filled with adventure, mystery — and even ghosts. And as the summer progresses, Christina and her uncle learn that time changes all things, especially people.

Wright, Betty Ren. **A Ghost in the Window.** Holiday House, 1987. 152 p. ISBN 0-8234-0661-X.

Fourteen-year-old Meg Korshak is furious when she has to give up playing the part of Princess Running Deer in summer theater in order to visit her father in a rooming house. When her "real" dreams, those predicting coming events, begin again, she is terrified, although her special gift may help her new friend, Caleb. Sequel to *A Secret Window.*

Survival

Ashley, Bernard. **High Pavement Blues.** Julia MacRae Books, 1983. 176 p. ISBN 0-531-04607-9.

Buckingham Palace, Big Ben, the Tower of London — all are stops on the tourists' map, but few will ever see the vendor's stall on the "high pavement" along the Thames River that fifteen-year-old Kevin and his mother call home. Learning to survive in a single-parent household and along the pavement where bullies make the rules is very difficult for Keith because of his poor self-image.

Dekkers, Midas. **Arctic Adventure.** Orchard Books, 1987. 158 p. ISBN 0-531-08304-7 (0-531-05704-6, library binding).

Dutch brothers Menno and Adrian go to the Arctic in search of relics from seventeenth-century whaling voyages. When they are shipwrecked on an island off Greenland, they discover a whale in a hidden inland lake. The brothers develop a deep attachment to Anouk the whale, but they put the whale and themselves in danger from the crew of a whaling boat when they radio for help.

Ferris, Jean. **Amen, Moses Gardenia.** Farrar, Straus and Giroux, 1985. 200 p. ISBN 0-374-30252-9.

Why can't things work out in the real world like they do in her dream world? Fifteen-year-old Farrell has everything money can buy, but what she really wants is a family and friends to love her. Farrell's depression leads her to the brink of suicide. Can her counselor and friends help her get back on the right track?

Forman, James D. **Doomsday Plus Twelve.** Charles Scribner's Sons, 1984. 230 p. ISBN 0-684-18221-1.

In the year 2000, the nuclear holocaust known as Doomsday is twelve years past. But the same forces, ideas, and prejudices that caused the first destruction of most of the Earth and its people are now threatening the final destruction of everything and everyone remaining. A group of Oregon teenagers, led by Valerie

Tucker and a strange assortment of friends, marches on a crusade to prevent another nuclear war.

Grant, Cynthia D. **Kumquat May, I'll Always Love You.** Atheneum, 1986. 206 p. ISBN 0-689-31198-2.

Seventeen-year-old Livvy is totally alone. Her drunken father died, her grandmother died, and her mother went out for margarine and never returned. Livvy has been alone for two years except for the companionship of her best friend, Rosella. But then Livvy's friend Raymond returns to town, and her life becomes even more confusing.

Hall, Lynn. **The Solitary.** Charles Scribner's Sons, 1986. 121 p. ISBN 0-684-18724-8.

Seventeen-year-old Jane returns to the home of her childhood nightmare. Her mother is now in prison for the murder of her father. Jane is determined to make a success of herself and her business of breeding rabbits, but can she do it alone?

Holman, Felice. **The Wild Children.** Viking Penguin/Puffin Books, 1985. 149 p. ISBN 0-14-031930-1.

Be ready for an incredible adventure story if you pick up this book. When Russian troops arrest his parents and sister following the Bolshevik Revolution of 1917, twelve-year-old Alex joins a group of other homeless boys who must live underground and steal to survive. They encounter terrible hardships as they move around the country, searching for food and safety. Will Alex, like so many of the wild children, finally give up and die, or will he succeed in finding a better life?

Hyde, Dayton O. **Island of the Loons.** Atheneum, 1984. 155 p. ISBN 0-689-31047-1.

Fourteen-year-old Jimmy tries several times to escape from the island in Lake Superior where he is being held prisoner, but each time the escaped convict catches him. He has to cook for the man and cut logs to build a cabin for winter. At last comes the day when the convict slips on the ice and breaks his leg, and Jimmy gets his chance for freedom.

Lawrence, Louise. **Children of the Dust.** Harper and Row, 1985. 183 p. ISBN 0-06-023738-4 (0-06-023739-2, library binding).

After a nuclear war devastates the Earth, a small band of people struggles to survive. The children in this new world, created by the radioactive dust that almost destroyed humankind, are born with mutations. With their strange eyes and even stranger beliefs and ways, can they be the world's hope for the future?

Mathieson, David. **Trial by Wilderness.** Houghton Mifflin, 1985. 171 p. ISBN 0-395-37697-1.

Have you ever wondered if you could survive in the wilderness without food, shelter, tools, or weapons? Seventeen-year-old Elena Bradbury is put to the test when the small plane in which she is a passenger crashes off the coast of British Columbia. Alone in the wilderness, she must rely on Stone Age techniques and her own ingenuity to gather food, create shelter, kindle fire, and ultimately rescue herself.

Mayhar, Ardath. **Medicine Walk.** Atheneum, 1985. 83 p. ISBN 0-689-31135-4.

Burr celebrates his twelfth birthday alone in the desert following a plane crash in which his father, the pilot, is killed. The remains of the plane are hidden under the trees, and the crash occurred outside their flight plan, so Burr knows his only chance for survival is to walk for help. Throughout his journey he relies on advice that he remembers hearing from Nachito, an Apache foreman on the family ranch. But can Burr survive alone in the desert?

Mazer, Harry. **Cave under the City.** Thomas Y. Crowell, 1986. 152 p. ISBN 0-690-04557-3 (0-690-04559-X, library binding).

Toby and his five-year-old brother live in New York City. When their father goes off to find work and their mother is taken to a hospital, the boys are left to fend for themselves. They take to the streets of New York to escape being sent to a children's shelter.

Miklowitz, Gloria. **After the Bomb.** Scholastic/Point Paperbacks, 1985. 156 p. ISBN 0-590-33287-2.

The city is in chaos, but the underground shelter from the 1960s saved their lives. Matt assumes control, carries his injured mom to the hospital, and worries about his dad's whereabouts. Life will never be the same for him after the destruction caused by the bomb and the lesson he learns from the Russians and Americans.

Moeri, Louise. **Downwind.** E. P. Dutton, 1984. 121 p. ISBN 0-525-44096-8.

While fleeing a possible radiation leak from a nuclear power plant, twelve-year-old Ephraim and his family learn that radiation is not the only danger when people panic. Ephraim comes "outside the backyard fence" as he helps his father deal with the terrifying problems that threaten all the family members.

Naylor, Phyllis Reynolds. **The Dark of the Tunnel.** Atheneum, 1985. 207 p. ISBN 0-689-31098-6.

High school senior Craig Sheldon, his mother, and his brother, Lonnie, have lived with their father's brother, Big Jim, since their father was killed in a coal-mining accident. Craig worries about his mother's failing health and also about Big Jim's job as county civil defense chief. Big Jim is to plan for the safety of their rural community in a mock nuclear attack, but many of the directives he must follow are just absurd. The family members must face their problems with courage and humor.

Paulsen, Gary. **Hatchet.** Bradbury Press, 1987. 195 p. ISBN 0-02-770130-1.

Thirteen-year-old Brian Robeson is on his way to visit his father, a mechanical engineer working in the Canadian wilderness, for the first time since his parents' divorce. Brian knows why his mother left his father, and he has become obsessed by his knowledge of the Secret. Then the single-engine plane crashes after the pilot suffers a heart attack, and Brian is the lone survivor in a desolate area. He has just his wits and a hatchet that his mother gave him as a going-away gift. (Literary merit)

Petersen, P. J. **Going for the Big One.** Delacorte Press, 1986. 178 p. ISBN 0-385-29453-0.

When their stepmother leaves and takes everything with her, the three Bates teenagers decide to hike across the mountains to a small town where they can wait for their father, who is looking for work in Alaska. They soon discover that there is more danger in the woods than just the bears and the weather. The teenagers must decide whether they should stay together or split up, a decision that will determine whether or not they will survive.

Phipson, Joan. **Hit and Run.** Atheneum/Margaret K. McElderry Books, 1985. 119 p. ISBN 0-689-50362-8.

The pressures from an overbearing father and family wealth almost smother sixteen-year-old Roland Fleming. Responding to the teasing of other boys, he steals a Ferrari. But on his joyride, Roland hits a baby carriage, panics, and flees into the wild Australian countryside. By running away from the accident, Roland appears to be throwing away his life. However, the decisions he makes after that accident show how helpful a disaster can be.

Richter, Hans Peter (translated by Edite Kroll). **Friedrich.** Viking Penguin/Puffin Books, 1987. 149 p. ISBN 0-14-032205-1.

The story of Friedrich, a young German Jewish boy, is told by a German friend who lived in the same apartment house. After Hitler comes to power in the 1930s, Friedrich is expelled from school, his mother dies, and his father is deported. Although the two boys remain friends, Friedrich is left on his own to hide from the Nazis, and he is even denied entry to a shelter during a bombing raid in 1942.

Richter, Hans Peter (translated by Edite Kroll). **I Was There.** Viking Penguin/Puffin Books, 1987. 204 p. ISBN 0-14-032206-X.

The narrator and his two friends are members of the Hitler Youth movement in Nazi Germany during the 1930s. Richter recounts the day-to-day events and attitudes of young German people under Hitler.

Ruckman, Ivy. **Night of the Twisters.** Thomas Y. Crowell, 1984. 153 p. ISBN 0-690-04408-9 (0-690-04409-7, library binding).

Twelve-year-old Dan, his baby brother, and his best friend take shelter in the basement when devastating tornadoes hit their town. Coping with a natural disaster is explored in this fictional account of the tornadoes that struck Grand Island, Nebraska, in 1980.

Skurzynski, Gloria. **Caught in the Moving Mountains.** Illustrated by Ellen Thompson. Lothrop, Lee and Shepard Books, 1984. 143 p. ISBN 0-688-01635-9.

Paul and Lance, two thirteen-year-old brothers by adoption, take a three-day hiking trip into Idaho's White Cloud Mountains. Their father hopes the excursion will toughen them up. Everything goes smoothly the first day, but that night a drug smuggler crashes nearby in a stolen airplane. Then an earthquake strikes. Paul and Lance must use all their skills to survive.

Strieber, Whitley. **Wolf of Shadows.** Alfred A. Knopf/Borzoi Books and Sierra Club Books, 1985. 105 p. ISBN 0-394-97224-X (0-394-97224-4, library binding).

Wolf of Shadows has always been an outcast from the pack because of his size and color. The other wolves merely tolerate his existence on the fringe of their lives. One day a great flash of light and a mushroom cloud fill up the skies. A human woman and her cubs arrive in a great metal bird, and Wolf of Shadows knows that all must band together for survival.

Swindells, Robert. **Brother in the Land.** Holiday House, 1985. 151 p. ISBN 0-8234-0556-7.

Life is normal for English teenager Danny until a nuclear war breaks out, and he is faced with Black Rain, the search for food, ruthless marauders, and, worst of all, the dreaded Purples. Danny relates, in journal form, the horrible experiences that he encounters and their shattering effects on those who are left. His friendship with Kim reinforces the knowledge that the need for giving and receiving love cannot be destroyed.

Thrasher, Crystal. **A Taste of Daylight.** Atheneum/Margaret K. McElderry Books, 1985. 204 p. ISBN 0-689-50313-X.

The Depression of 1929, the death of her father, and moving to the city are problems encountered by seventeen-year-old Seely in this fifth and final book about the Robinson family. The family encounters a day-to-day struggle for survival but discovers there is a ray of hope.

Yolen, Jane. **Children of the Wolf.** Viking Press, 1984. 136 p. ISBN 0-670-21763-8.

Tales of ghosts haunt the Indian village of Godamuri until Mohandas, a fourteen-year-old Indian boy, and Mr. Welles, a missionary from the orphanage, decide to investigate. To their surprise, the ghosts are really two young girls who have been raised by wolves. They capture the girls, and Mohandas tries desperately to teach the girls words and human habits.

War

Burchard, Peter. **Sea Change.** Farrar, Straus and Giroux, 1984. 117 p. ISBN 0-374-36460-5.

This three-part novel portrays special mother-daughter relationships over three generations. Each woman is faced with the crisis of war and its emotional trauma. Throughout, as Alice, Anne, and Lisa grow into adults and have daughters of their own, they learn to face up to the realities of war, and as a result, they strengthen the bonds of their family. A new awareness of life and the values it holds begins to develop.

Ferry, Charles. **Raspberry One.** Houghton Mifflin, 1983. 232 p. ISBN 0-395-34069-1.

During World War II, two young airmen, Nick and Hildy, are flying bombing support for the Allied fleet in the Pacific. When they are faced with Japan's kamikaze offensive, they are devastated at first by the horrors of war, but ultimately their war experience strengthens them.

Gehrts, Barbara (translated by Elizabeth D. Crawford). **Don't Say a Word.** Macmillan/Margaret K. McElderry Books, 1986. 169 p. ISBN 0-689-50412-8.

Anna is a teenager living in Berlin during World War II. Her father, an officer in the Luftwaffe, opposes Hitler's policies. Soon her world changes: her first love is sent to the Soviet Union, where he is killed, and her best friend, a Jew, loses her freedom. Then Anna's father is declared a traitor. Through the ordeal, her mother tries to provide a stable family life.

Hall, Lynn. **If Winter Comes.** Charles Scribner's Sons, 1986. 119 p. ISBN 0-684-18575-X.

Meredith McCoy, her friends, and her family face thirty hours that may in fact be the last hours for them all. An ultimatum has been issued threatening the firing of atomic missiles at the

United States. Meredith examines her present and future through new eyes as the threat of nuclear warfare becomes imminent.

Hough, Richard. **Razor Eyes.** E. P. Dutton/Lodestar Books, 1983. 115 p. ISBN 0-525-66916-7.

More than forty years after the fact, Mick Boyd, now a farmer in New Zealand, recounts his experiences as a British pilot in World War II. Blessed with exceptional eyesight, Mick was called "Razor Eyes" and was sent on a dangerous secret mission into enemy territory. There, facing his fears and trying to survive against all odds, Mick encountered the ultimate test of his courage. This is a fictionalized account of the author's wartime experiences.

McCutcheon, Elsie. **Summer of the Zeppelin.** Farrar, Straus and Giroux, 1985. 168 p. ISBN 0-374-37294-2.

To Elvira Preston, the war looms large in England in 1918. Her father has gone off to war, and she is left with her unloving, never-satisfied stepmother and her baby brother. Suddenly, in the midst of a nearby thicket, Elvira and a friend discovered a ruined house, which becomes their "Sanctuary." But matters turn complicated when they find a German prisoner of war hiding in the Sanctuary. (Literary merit)

Orlev, Uri (translated by Hillel Halkin). **The Island on Bird Street.** Houghton Mifflin, 1983. 162 p. ISBN 0-395-33887-5.

Alex, an eleven-year-old Jewish boy, is all alone in the Warsaw Ghetto during World War II. His mother was snatched away by the Germans, and now his father is gone, too. Alex and his tiny pet mouse are on their own, without food and shelter. He wonders if he can escape from the Germans by hiding. How long could he last? Most of all, Alex wonders whether his father will return as he promised.

Ossowski, Leonie (translated by Ruth Crowley). **Star without a Sky.** Lerner Publications, 1985. 214 p. ISBN 0-8225-0771-4.

What will the five do when they find Abiram, a young Jewish boy, hiding in the cellar during World War II? One is a girl, without family except for a grandfather who is now in disfavor with the Nazis. The other four are students at the local boarding school. Should the five obey the German law and turn Abiram in to the authorities or should they protect their cache of food and save him as well?

Southall, Ivan. **The Long Night Watch.** Farrar, Straus and Giroux, 1984. 160 p. ISBN 0-374-34644-5.

In an attempt to preserve the democratic Western civilization during World War II, one hundred Australians band together under a powerful leader, General Matthew Palmer, and set up an outpost on a deserted South Pacific island. Jon Griffiths, a sixteen year old with a strong fear of war, goes with the group and becomes a lookout in an isolated area. Can he overcome his fears and handle this responsibility?

Drama

Carlson, Bernice Wells. **Let's Find the Big Idea.** Illustrated by Bettye Beach. Abingdon Press, 1982. 128 p. ISBN 0-687-21430-0.

The nineteen fables and stories in this collection have been dramatized into skits, playlets, and plays you can produce almost any place with very little practice and simple props. The purpose of the book is to find the underlying truth in each fable. And that's where the audience comes in. At the end of each presentation, the storyteller will ask, "What's the big idea?"

Kamerman, Sylvia E., editor. **Christmas Play Favorites for Young People.** Plays, 1983. 283 p. ISBN 0-8238-0257-4.

Eighteen royalty-free, one-act plays for the Christmas season are presented in this collection. The plays are appropriate for elementary, junior high, and high school students and are both humorous and serious. They range from contemporary stories of mixed-up presents to classics like "A Christmas Carol" and "Little Women." Production notes for each play and a section on creative dramatics are included.

Kamerman, Sylvia E., editor. **Holiday Plays round the Year.** Plays, 1985. 291 p. ISBN 0-8238-0261-2.

Twenty-seven one-act, royalty-free plays are presented for such holidays as Christmas, Thanksgiving, Halloween, Lincoln's Birthday, Washington's Birthday, Valentine's Day, Book Week, St. Patrick's Day, Columbus Day, Black History Week, Easter, and Mother's Day. Production notes are included for all plays.

Korty, Carol. **Writing Your Own Plays.** Charles Scribner's Sons, 1986. 116 p. ISBN 0-684-18470-2.

Tony Awards are given for the outstanding Broadway plays each year, and every well-known actor and actress hopes to receive that prestigious trophy. But suppose being backstage or offstage is more your forte. If that is the case, this book could be your guide to writing an award-winning play. The author gives guidelines, suggestions, and examples for choosing a story, developing ideas, writing a first draft, adapting and revising, and preparing the final script.

Nolan, Paul T. **Folk Tale Plays round the World.** Plays, 1984. 240 p. ISBN 0-8238-0253-1.

These sixteen plays convey the folklore, customs, and national characteristics of countries in Asia, Europe, and the Americas. Many are favorites — such as "A Leak in the Dike" from Holland, "Stanislow and the Wolf" from Poland, and "Johnny Appleseed" from the United States. Background information accompanies each play, and the directions make it easy for young people to perform and present each play before audiences.

Steinhorn, Harriet. **Shadows of the Holocaust: Plays, Readings, and Program Resources.** Kar-Ben Copies, 1983. 80 p. ISBN 0-930494-25-3.

Steinhorn, a survivor of the Holocaust, offers a series of original plays, music, and poems on this theme. The collection commemorates the Jewish victims of the Holocaust and offers hope to contemporary victims of many lands caught in the struggle for human rights.

Picture Books for Older Readers

Aiken, Joan. **The Moon's Revenge.** Illustrated by Alan Lee. Alfred A. Knopf/Borzoi Books, 1987. 32 p. ISBN 0-394-89380-8 (0-394-99380-2, library binding).

Sep, the seventh son of a seventh son, wants to learn how to play the fiddle. A mysterious voice tells him to throw a shoe at the moon seven nights in a row. The moon, enraged with the dirty marks left by the shoe on its face, curses Sep to go without shoes, among other things, for seven years. Learning to play the fiddle is only one of the challenges he faces while the moon gets its revenge.

Anderson, Joan. **The Glorious Fourth at Prairietown.** Photographs by George Ancona. William Morrow, 1986. 44 p. ISBN 0-688-06246-6 (0-688-06247-4, library binding).

The Carpenter family moves from Westmoreland County, Pennsylvania, to a new farm in Prairietown, Indiana. There they take part in their frontier community's celebration of the Fourth of July in 1836.

Baylor, Byrd. **The Best Town in the World.** Illustrated by Ronald Himler. Charles Scribner's Sons, 1983. 30 p. ISBN 0-684-18035-9.

The best town in the world could be your town. It's the place where dogs are smarter, chickens lay prettier eggs, wildflowers grow taller and thicker, and people know how to make the best chocolate cakes and toys in the world. This Texas hill town is enchantingly brought to life by both author and illustrator. (Literary merit)

Bernbaum, Israel. **My Brother's Keeper: The Holocaust through the Eyes of an Artist.** Illustrated by the author. G. P. Putnam's Sons, 1985. 63 p. ISBN 0-399-21242-6.

Bernbaum's five very large paintings tell the story of the Holocaust. They focus on the Warsaw Ghetto in Poland, which eventually became home to more than 500,000 Jews in 1941. In the text, Bernbaum tells the reader about life in the Warsaw Ghetto and explains the detail and symbolism in his paintings. His message is that we all have a responsibility for one another. (Literary merit)

Carey, Valerie Scho. **The Devil and Mother Crump.** Illustrated by Arnold Lobel. Harper and Row, 1987. 39 p. ISBN 0-06-020982-8 (0-06-020983-6, library binding).

In this tale, Mother Crump is a feisty old baker. Many say that she is meaner than the Devil himself. The Devil decides to teach her a lesson, but instead he learns a few things from her.

Gerstein, Mordicai. **The Mountains of Tibet.** Illustrated by the author. Harper and Row, 1987. 32 p. ISBN 0-06-022144-5 (0-06-022149-6, library binding).

All his life a woodcutter longs to travel and see the world. But he grows old without ever leaving his valley in the mountains of Tibet. When he dies, he is suddenly offered the chance to live again, in any form and in any place he likes. The woodcutter must decide which choice would be the most rewarding.

Hawkey, Raymond. **Evolution: The Story of the Origins of Humankind.** Illustrated by the author. G. P. Putnam's Sons, 1987. 12 p. ISBN 0-399-21437-2.

The story of the evolution of humankind is told in animated three-dimensional illustrations. In far earlier eras we see a prehistoric volcano that spouts smoke and flames and an air-breathing fish that hauls itself from the primeval mud. Representative of contemporary times, an astronaut walks on the moon.

Hirsh, Marilyn. **I Love Passover.** Illustrated by the author. Holiday House, 1985. 28 p. ISBN 0-8234-0549-4.

As Passover approaches, Sarah has many questions to ask. Why does her family celebrate the Passover? Why must they eat the flat, hard matzo, the bitter herbs dipped in salt water, and the haroseth? Why are children rewarded for returning the afikomen they have taken to hide? Sarah's patient mother answers these and other questions about the Passover holiday.

Hoban, Russell. **The Marzipan Pig.** Illustrated by Quentin Blake. Farrar, Straus and Giroux, 1987. 40 p. ISBN 0-374-34859-6.

The marzipan pig made of almond candy is lost behind the couch until a mouse finds and eats it. This causes the mouse to think new thoughts. She falls in love with the grandfather clock, but unfortunately she is soon eaten by an owl, who, in turn, is affected by the candy pig's thoughts. The story moves on to involve a bee, a hibiscus flower, and another mouse.

Holder, Heidi, editor. **Crows: An Old Rhyme.** Illustrated by the editor. Farrar, Straus and Giroux, 1987. ISBN 0-374-31660-0.

In this visual interpretation, the twelve omens of the rhyme about the crows reflect the unusual love story of a faithful mink and an adventurous weasel. Notes on the text and a key to the symbols are included.

Hughes, Jill. **Vikings.** Illustrated by Ivan Lapper. Gloucester Press, 1984. 32 p. ISBN 0-531-03481-X.

The Vikings of Scandinavia explored the coasts of what is now the United States, Greenland, Iceland, the British Isles, and the Soviet Union, as well as other distant lands, in the eighth to tenth centuries. They were great seafarers, wood and metal workers, and traders. This short, colorful book documents the Vikings' travels through the world and their impact upon it.

Kurelek, William, with additional text by Margaret S. Engelhart. **They Sought a New World: The Story of European Immigration to North America.** Illustrated by the author. Tundra Books, 1985. 48 p. ISBN 0-88776-172-0.

Immigrants have come to North America from all parts of the world. This book looks at what it was like to be a European immigrant to our continent. It is based on the paintings and writings of William Kurelek, who was the son of such an immigrant. (Literary merit)

Lopez, Donald S. **Flight: Great Planes of the Century.** Illustrated by William S. Phillips. Viking Penguin, 1985. 16 p. ISBN 0-670-80585-8.

The great planes of the twentieth century seem to fly from the pages of this three-dimensional book. Detailed paintings and an informative text trace the development of the history of airplanes — from the brief lift-off of the Wright Brothers' *Flyer* to the supersonic journeys of the Concorde.

Macaulay, David. **Mill.** Illustrated by the author. Houghton Mifflin, 1983. 128 p. ISBN 0-395-34830-7.

This fictional account, with detailed pen-and-ink drawings, brings to life the planning, construction, and operation of New England mills throughout the nineteenth century and well into the twentieth century. The imaginary mill town of Wicksbridge demonstrates the typical pattern of a mill's transition from water power to electricity to closing for a condominium development. The town's social, economic, and architectural history are detailed.

Miller, Jonathan. **The Human Body.** Illustrated by Harry Willock. Viking Press/Studio Books, 1983. 12 p. ISBN 0-670-38605-7.

Three-dimensional, movable illustrations demonstrate the workings of the human body. By operating the scale models, the reader can make a heart beat, lungs breathe, and muscles contract. The illustrations clearly show how we think, see, hear, move, and stay alive.

Miller, Jonathan, and David Pelham. **The Facts of Life.** Viking Penguin, 1984. 12 p. ISBN 0-670-30465-4.

Intricate three-dimensional illustrations depict the development of a baby from conception to birth. Pull-tabs help unravel the mysteries of chromosomes and show the changes the fertilized egg undergoes. Pop-up illustrations show the male and female reproductive organs, the growth of the fetus within the uterus, and the process of birth.

Palin, Michael. **Mirrorstone.** Illustrated by Alan Lee. Alfred A. Knopf/Borzoi Books, 1986. 30 p. ISBN 0-394-88353-5.

English schoolboy Paul looks in the bathroom mirror but sees another figure, not his own reflection. He is transported back in time to the medieval laboratory of the wizard Salaman, who sends Paul on an underwater quest for the mirrorstone. This book is uniquely designed with mirrorlike pieces inserted in the illustrations.

Van Allsburg, Chris. **The Mysteries of Harris Burdick.** Illustrated by the author. Houghton Mifflin, 1984. 14 p. ISBN 0-395-35393-9.

"He had warned her about the book. Now it was too late." This is one of the fourteen captions accompanying intriguing drawings in this book that will inspire you to write your own stories. You can also try to figure out why Harris Burdick, the original author and illustrator, disappeared and why he drew what he drew. The book invites you to use your imagination to solve the mysteries.

van der Meer, Ron, and Alan McGowan. **Sailing Ships.** Illustrated by Borje Svensson. Viking Penguin, 1984. 12 p. ISBN 0-670-61529-3.

With their sails hoisted high, three-dimensional ships travel across the pages. Paintings, text, diagrams, and drawings trace the development of sailing ships through the past five thousand years.

Winthrop, Elizabeth, adapter. **He Is Risen: The Easter Story.** Illustrated by Charles Mikolaycak. Holiday House, 1985. 27 p. ISBN 0-8234-0547-8.

Taken from the gospels of Matthew and Luke in the King James Version of the Bible, this adaptation highlights the events that led to the crucifixion and resurrection of Christ. The expressions on the faces in the illustrations reflect the varied emotions of those involved.

Poetry

Cassedy, Sylvia. **Roomrimes.** Illustrated by Michele Chessare. Thomas Y. Crowell, 1987. 71 p. ISBN 0-690-04466-6 (0-690-04467-4, library binding).

Here is a poem about every letter of the alphabet from *A* to *Z*. Each poem describes a room or place, ranging from attic and greenhouse to roof, vestibule, and zoo.

Chamberlain, William. **The Policeman's Beard Is Half Constructed.** Illustrated by Joan Hall. Warner Books, 1984. 108 p. ISBN 0-446-38051-2.

A computer called Racter wrote the poetry in this collection. The programmer worked in BASIC on a Z89 micro with 64K of RAM to include syntax directives as well as words and phrases. The results are quite pleasing to both the ear and the mind, and you'll quickly forget that this writing was done by a machine. The black-and-white illustrations are unique and well suited to this unusual writing.

Eliot, T. S. **Growltiger's Last Stand and Other Poems.** Illustrated by Errol Le Cain. Farrar, Straus and Giroux/Harcourt Brace Jovanovich (copublisher), 1987. 32 p. ISBN 0-374-32809-9.

This book contains three poems taken from T. S. Eliot's *Old Possum's Book of Practical Cats.* Besides the title poem, the collection features "The Pekes and the Pollicles" and "The Song of the Jellicles."

Esbensen, Barbara Juster. **Cold Stars and Fireflies: Poems of the Four Seasons.** Illustrated by Susan Bonners. Thomas Y. Crowell, 1984. 70 p. ISBN 0-690-04362-7 (0-690-04363-5, library binding).

Poems about nature and the changing seasons are grouped according to season, beginning with autumn.

Farber, Norma, and Myra Cohn Livingston, compilers. **These Small Stones.** Harper and Row/Charlotte Zolotow Books, 1987. 84 p. ISBN 0-06-024013-X (0-06-024014-8, library binding).

The title for this collection of poems comes from a poem by Lilian Moore, "Beach Stones." Each poem was chosen because it shows how the small things of the world change if you look closely at them. The poems are grouped according to where these things are found — on the ground, in the air.

Fleischman, Paul. **I Am Phoenix: Poems for Two Voices.** Illustrated by Ken Nutt. Harper and Row/Charlotte Zolotow Books, 1985. 51 p. ISBN 0-06-021881-9 (0-06-021882-7, library binding).

This collection of fifteen poems about birds — the sound, the sense, and the essence of birds — is designed to be read aloud by two voices. From "The Wandering Albatross" to "The Common Egret," the poems are illustrated with detailed pen-and-ink drawings.

Gordon, Ruth, compiler. **Under All Silences: Shades of Love.** Harper and Row/Charlotte Zolotow Books, 1987. 78 p. ISBN 0-06-022154-2 (0-06-022155-0, library binding).

Here is a collection of love poems tracing love from the first meeting, to discovery, to passion, to knowledge, and beyond. Included are poems by such poets as Maya Angelou, Emily Dickinson, May Sarton, Karl Shapiro, and e. e. cummings.

Hopkins, Lee Bennett, compiler. **Munching: Poems about Eating.** Illustrated by Nelle Davis. Little, Brown, 1985. 44 p. ISBN 0-316-37169-2.

These poems by American and English poets highlight the pleasures of eating. Included are poems by Lewis Carroll, Edward Lear, Ogden Nash, David McCord, and Arnold Adoff. Bright and delicious artwork accompanies each poem.

Hughes, Langston. **The Dream Keeper and Other Poems.** Illustrated by Helen Sewell. Alfred A. Knopf/Borzoi Books, 1986. 77 p. ISBN 0-394-91096-6.

This collection, originally published in 1932, was selected by the poet to include lyrical poems, songs, and blues. Many explore the experience of being black. The fifty-nine poems are arranged according to theme: "The Dream Keeper," "Sea Charm," "Dressed Up," "Feet O' Jesus," and "Walkers with the Dawn." Storyteller

Augusta Baker introduces the collection, and Sewell's woodcuts accompany the poems. (Literary merit)

Janeczko, Paul B., compiler. **Going Over to Your Place: Poems for Each Other.** Bradbury Press, 1987. 151 p. ISBN 0-02-747670-7.

This collection of one hundred thirty-two poems reflects impressions of everyday love and loss by such poets as Adrienne Rich, May Swenson, John Ciardi, and Stanley Kunitz. Topics range from the opening poem by Peter Meinke, "The Heart's Location," to a first kiss, to arm wrestling, to shooting crows, to a belly dancer, to the final poem by Ted Kooser, "At Midnight."

Janeczko, Paul B., compiler. **Pocket Poems: Selected for a Journey.** Bradbury Press, 1985. 127 p. ISBN 0-02-747820-3.

The one hundred twenty poems in this collection were written by eighty American poets, such as William Cole, Eugene Field, Paul Zimmer, Ogden Nash, X. J. Kennedy, and John Updike. The poems are short and cover a wide variety of subjects. As the title suggests, the book is small and can easily be placed in the pocket of a traveler or others on the move. (Literary merit)

Janeczko, Paul B., compiler. **Poetspeak: In Their Work, about Their Work.** Bradbury Press, 1983. 228 p. ISBN 0-02-747770-3.

This is more than a collection of one hundred forty-eight poems by sixty-two living poets. It also includes the poets' thoughts about how a poem is written and about the influence of people, places, and experiences on their poetry. The poems focus on family and friends, love, dreams, war, and growing up. (Literary merit)

Janeczko, Paul B., compiler. **Strings: A Gathering of Family Poems.** Bradbury Press, 1984. 153 p. ISBN 0-02-747790-8.

These one hundred twenty-five poems by numerous American poets celebrate the various relationships within families — parents and children, brothers and sisters, husbands and wives, grandparents and grandchildren. They express humor, inspiration, remembrance, or regret. The poems are suitable for age groups ranging from young teen to adult. All are not easy to read, however, and many require close reading.

Janeczko, Paul B., compiler. **This Delicious Day.** Orchard Books, 1987. 77 p. ISBN 0-531-05724-0 (0-531-08324-1, library binding).

Here are poems featuring all kinds of meals and food. Sixty-five short poems provide treats for the eye, the ear, the tongue, the funny bone, and the mind. The compiler even invites the reader to come back for seconds.

Koch, Kenneth, and Kate Farrell, compilers. **Talking to the Sun: An Illustrated Anthology of Poems for Young People.** Metropolitan Museum of Art and Holt, Rinehart and Winston, 1985. 112 p. ISBN 0-87099-436-0 (0-03-005849-X, Holt, Rinehart and Winston).

Poets Kenneth Koch and Kate Farrell have chosen poems ranging from African chants and European lullabies to Japanese haiku and Native American verse. The poems are illustrated by works of art from the Metropolitan Museum of Art in New York. The collection is organized by theme, and there are brief introductions to each section and explanatory sentences accompanying some poems.

Larrick, Nancy, compiler. **Tambourines! Tambourines to Glory! Prayers and Poems.** Illustrated by Geri Greinke. Westminster Press, 1982. 101 p. ISBN 0-664-32689-7.

This collection of children's prayers in poem form includes poems from other cultures and eras. Included are works by Madeleine L'Engle, Victor Hugo, Robert Browning, and individual boys and girls.

Lewis, Claudia. **Long Ago in Oregon.** Illustrated by Joel Fontaine. Harper and Row/Charlotte Zolotow Books, 1987. 54 p. ISBN 0-06-023839-9 (0-06-023840-2, library binding).

These poems describe one year in the life of a young girl in a small Oregon town in 1917. Family, neighbors, school, World War I, and moving to a new house are among the topics touched on by the poems.

Livingston, Myra Cohn, compiler. **Cat Poems.** Illustrated by Trina Schart Hyman. Holiday House, 1987. 32 p. ISBN 0-8234-0631-8.

New and old poems by Karla Kuskin, John Ciardi, and others describe cats hunting, washing, sleeping, and playing. Tomcats, kittens, "jellicle" cats, cats that turn into princesses — this book is a celebration of all kinds of cats. (Literary merit)

Livingston, Myra Cohn. **Celebrations.** Illustrated by Leonard Everett Fisher. Holiday House, 1985. 32 p. ISBN 0-8234-0550-8.

Sixteen holidays are celebrated in this collection — from New Year's Day to Christmas Eve and including Martin Luther King,

Jr., Day, Passover, Labor Day, and Halloween. Enhancing the sometimes serious, sometimes light, and often informative poetry are vivid illustrations. A special day is saved for the reader to enjoy as his or her very own — the Birthday.

Livingston, Myra Cohn. **Earth Songs.** Illustrated by Leonard Everett Fisher. Holiday House, 1986. 26 p. ISBN 0-8234-0615-6.

Thirteen poems and large full-color paintings celebrate the features of the Earth, including the continents, mountains, forests, water, and volcanoes. A companion book to *Sea Songs* and *Sky Songs.*

Livingston, Myra Cohn, compiler. **Easter Poems.** Illustrated by John Wallner. Holiday House, 1985. 32 p. ISBN 0-8234-0546-X.

From "The Easter Bunny" and "Grandma's Easter Bonnet" to "These Three" and "The Cherry-Tree Carol," this book contains eighteen poems related to the Easter theme. Among the featured poets are Joan Aiken, John Ciardi, and X. J. Kennedy; also included are poems translated from Russian and German. Wallner's illustrations make this book a treat for the eyes as well as for the ears.

Livingston, Myra Cohn. **Monkey Puzzle and Other Poems.** Illustrated by Antonio Frasconi. Atheneum/Margaret K. McElderry Books, 1984. 34 p. ISBN 0-689-50310-5.

From the white birches of New England to the redwoods along the Pacific Coast, trees are the topic of this poetry collection. Trees of different appearance and projecting different personalities are paraded before the reader in words and woodcuts. Perhaps your favorite tree is here.

Livingston, Myra Cohn, compiler. **New Year's Poems.** Illustrated by Margot Tomes. Holiday House, 1987. 32 p. ISBN 0-8234-0641-5.

These seventeen poems celebrate the first holiday of the year. The first poem, David McCord's "January One," is followed by one on the Chinese New Year, Julia Fields's "The Bell Hill," a poem of Cornish superstitions about New Year's Day, and Ruth Whitman's "Beginning a New Year Means."

Livingston, Myra Cohn, compiler. **Poems for Jewish Holidays.** Illustrated by Lloyd Bloom. Holiday House, 1986. 32 p. ISBN 0-8234-0606-7.

Sixteen poems by twelve contemporary authors celebrate such Jewish holidays as Yom Kippur and Purim. The collection includes poems by Valerie Worth, Richard Margolis, Meyer Hahn, and R. H. Marks.

Livingston, Myra Cohn, compiler. **Poems of Lewis Carroll.** Illustrated by John Tenniel, Harry Furniss, Henry Holiday, Arthur B. Frost, and Lewis Carroll. Thomas Y. Crowell, 1973. 149 p. ISBN 0-690-00178-9 (0-690-04540-9, library binding).

This collection features poems, parodies, puzzles, acrostics, and riddles by Lewis Carroll, the author of *Alice in Wonderland.* Poems from the Alice books are included, along with those from *Sylvia and Bruno* and the entire *The Hunting of the Snark.* Also included are notes on the poems, an index of titles, and an index of first lines. Part of the Crowell Poets series.

McCullough, Frances, editor. **Love Is Like the Lion's Tooth: An Anthology of Love Poems.** Harper and Row, 1984. 80 p. ISBN 0-06-024138-1 (0-06-024139-X, library binding).

The many faces of love throughout the world and throughout time are presented in this collection of poems. Such poets as William Butler Yeats, Walt Whitman, e. e. cummings, and Edna St. Vincent Millay are featured.

Merriam, Eve. **Fresh Paint.** Illustrated by David Frampton. Macmillan, 1986. 32 p. ISBN 0-02-766860-6.

Eve Merriam's poetry is unrhymed, and the images in her poems create vivid pictures in the reader's mind. This collection of new poems includes title poem "Fresh Paint," "A New Pencil," "Giving Thanks," and "A Throw of Threes." Woodcuts nicely complement the poems. (Literary merit)

Morrison, Lillian. **The Break Dance Kids: Poems of Sport, Motion, and Locomotion.** Lothrop, Lee and Shepard Books, 1985. 63 p. ISBN 0-688-04553-7 (0-688-04554-5, library binding).

Physical activity is the theme of this poetry collection. Poems celebrate the movements and motion of sports and dance and explore the silence of self-reflection after a hard-fought competition.

Powell, Lawrence Clark, compiler. **Poems of Walt Whitman: Leaves of Grass.** Illustrated by John Ross and Clare Romano Ross. Thomas Y. Crowell, 1964. 169 p. ISBN 0-690-64430-2 (0-690-64431-0, library binding).

Powell has selected those poems by Walt Whitman that he finds to be the most intense and powerful. Short poems appear in their entirety, while excerpts from some of the longer poems are included. The poems are arranged by such headings as America the Beautiful, Love Poems, and War Poems. Also included are a reading list, an index of titles, and an index of first lines.

Rylant, Cynthia. **Waiting to Waltz: A Childhood.** Illustrated by Stephen Gammell. Bradbury Press, 1984. 47 p. ISBN 0-02-778000-7.

A young girl's growing up in a small Appalachian town is creatively told in these thirty poems. The appropriate and precise pencil drawings by Gammell amplify the text. You will identify with these characters and places whether you have ever lived in a small town or not. (Literary merit)

Short Story Collections

Aiken, Joan. **Up the Chimney Down and Other Stories.** Harper and Row/Charlotte Zolotow Books, 1985. 248 p. ISBN 0-06-020036-7 (0-06-02037-5, library binding).

These stories involve the world of magic, whimsy, farce, and domestic comedy. There are macabre touches and splendidly eccentric characters, such as Mrs. McMurk, who has just eaten her last servant and is looking for a replacement; Miss Hooting, who gets revenge by giving a family a pair of robots; and a lion cub who should be wearing a "buyer beware" sign on its mane.

Alcock, Vivien. **Ghostly Companions: A Feast of Chilling Tales.** Delacorte Press, 1987. 132 p. ISBN 0-385-29559-6.

Scissors destroying a dress? A statue that stares through wooden eyes? Here are ten scary tales, set in England, that will delight and frighten ghost-story lovers. Each story presents a chilling tale of ghosts interfering in the lives of normal human beings.

Asimov, Isaac, Martin H. Greenberg, and Charles G. Waugh, editors. **Caught in the Organ Draft: Biology in Science Fiction.** Farrar, Straus and Giroux, 1983. 276 p. ISBN 0-374-31228-1.

These twelve science fiction stories all deal with the study of life itself — biology. Each author has taken a biological theme and developed it far beyond what we might imagine and often far beyond our worst fears. Mutants, biological experimentation, plagues, germ warfare, and hostile organisms are only some of the topics found in this collection. Included are stories by Isaac Asimov, Ray Bradbury, and Ursula LeGuin.

Asimov, Isaac, Martin H. Greenberg, and Charles G. Waugh, editors. **Young Extraterrestrials.** Harper and Row, 1984. 240 p. ISBN 0-06-020167-3 (0-06-020168-1, library binding).

Piers Anthony and R. A. Lafferty are two of the contributors to this collection of eleven short stories about children who are extraterrestrials. None is from Earth; none is human. Some are obviously aliens, while others seem no different from human children. Some are here as ambassadors of peace, while others are here for more selfish and more frightening reasons.

Asimov, Isaac, Martin H. Greenberg, and Charles G. Waugh, editors. **Young Ghosts.** Harper and Row, 1985. 210 p. ISBN 0-06-020171-1 (0-06-020172-X, library binding).

Twelve stories by such authors as Ray Bradbury and Madeleine L'Engle feature characters who are all young ghosts. Some want revenge, some are searching for peace, some come to warn the living, and others try to draw the living to the land of the dead.

Asimov, Isaac, Martin H. Greenberg, and Charles G. Waugh, editors. **Young Monsters.** Harper and Row, 1985. 213 p. ISBN 0-06-020169-X (0-06-020170-3, library binding).

The young monsters in these fourteen short stories by such authors as Ray Bradbury, Stephen King, and Jane Yolen are horrid, or grotesque, or unusual, and often terribly clever. Some of the stories are humorous, while some are truly frightening.

Asimov, Isaac, Martin H. Greenberg, and Charles G. Waugh, editors. **Young Mutants.** Harper and Row, 1984. 256 p. ISBN 0-06-020157-6 (0-06-020156-8, library binding).

These short stories feature children with one common characteristic — they are all mutants. Some of the children have strange powers, which they use for good purposes, or for bad. Some are more than mere geniuses. Some of the children can control their mutations, some of them can't. Some of the mutations are terrifying — and one of the mutants isn't human at all. Included are stories by Ray Bradbury, Alan E. Nourse, and Zenna Henderson.

Asimov, Isaac, Martin H. Greenberg, and Charles G. Waugh, editors. **Young Star Travelers.** Harper and Row, 1986. 209 p. ISBN 0-06-020178-9 (0-06-020179-7, library binding).

The characters in each of these stories are young star travelers. Some have never been to Earth, some can remember what Earth was like, some live on strange planets, while others live inside artificial worlds with only robots for companionship. Included are stories by such authors as Arthur C. Clarke, Andre Norton, and Ray Bradbury.

Asimov, Isaac, Martin H. Greenberg, and Charles G. Waugh, editors. **Young Witches and Warlocks.** Harper and Row, 1987. 207 p. ISBN 0-06-020183-5 (0-06-020184-3, library binding).

The children in these ten short stories are all young witches or warlocks. All have amazing powers to use for good or evil, to be playful and mischievous or cruel and ruthless. The stories, full of mystery and magic, are by such authors as Isaac Asimov, Ray Bradbury, and Elizabeth Coatsworth.

Babbitt, Natalie. **The Devil's Other Storybook.** Illustrated by the author. Farrar, Straus and Giroux/Michael di Capua Books, 1987. 82 p. ISBN 0-374-31767-4.

The ten stories in this collection are about the devil. He is full of vanity and other human failings, and he hasn't gotten it through his head that a good soul is hard to come by.

Barrett, Peter A., editor. **To Break the Silence: Thirteen Short Stories for Young Readers.** Dell/Laurel-Leaf Books, 1986. 221 p. ISBN 0-440-98807-1.

These outstanding short stories have been gathered especially for young readers. Written by celebrated British and American authors, the stories entertain and enrich while offering insights into the elements of short fiction. Authors include Philippa Pearce, Langston Hughes, E. L. Konigsburg, and Nicholasa Mohr.

Chambers, Aidan, and others. **A Haunt of Ghosts.** Harper and Row/Charlotte Zolotow Books, 1987. 177 p. ISBN 0-06-021206-3 (0-06-021207-1, library binding).

This collection of stories about ghosts includes five by Aidan Chambers and five by such authors as Joan Aiken and Jan Mark. The stories vary from the eerie to the frightening. All affirm that ghosts have control over the living. Some stories are based on real events or folk legends, but some are pure invention, such as John Gordon's story of the ghost made of ice, or Jan Mark's story of the dangers of vanity and long hair.

Chambers, Aidan, compiler. **Out of Time.** Harper and Row/Charlotte Zolotow Books, 1985. 186 p. ISBN 0-06-021201-2 (0-06-021202-0, library binding).

This collection of ten science fiction stories for young readers includes stories about a hologram with the wrong voice, a forbidden love, and a young man whose reactions to a test determine the fate of humankind. Monica Hughes, Douglas Hill, and Jill Paton Walsh are a few of the authors whose works are included.

Chambers, Aidan, compiler. **Shades of Dark.** Harper and Row/Charlotte Zolotow Books, 1986. 126 p. ISBN 0-06-021247-0 (0-06-021248-9, library binding).

In this collection of ghost stories, the reader will encounter ghosts who dispense justice, pursue revenge, wreak havoc, and render comfort. Here are eight original tales by such authors as Helen Cresswell, John Gordon, and Jan Mark about the denizens of the supernatural world doing what they do best — making sure that the living keep a proper respect for the dead and for those shades of dark in-between.

Conford, Ellen. **If This Is Love, I'll Take Spaghetti.** Scholastic, 1983. 165 p. ISBN 0-590-32338-5.

Dieting, first love, rock singers, phone addiction, and advice columns are featured in this collection of nine short stories. Readers will identify with many of the situations and enjoy the humorous way each story is presented.

Fleischman, Paul. **Coming-and-Going Men: Four Tales.** Illustrated by Randy Gaul. Harper and Row/Charlotte Zolotow Books, 1985. 147 p. ISBN 0-06-021883-5 (0-06-021884-3, library binding).

Four short stories present the adventures of traveling artisans and tradesmiths as they pass through the small town of New Canaan, Connecticut, in the year 1800. Each of these coming-and-going men changes — or is changed by — his customers.

Gallo, Donald R., editor. **Sixteen: Short Stories by Outstanding Writers for Young Adults.** Dell/Laurel-Leaf Books, 1985. 179 p. ISBN 0-440-97757-6.

Original short stories by such well-known writers as Robin F. Brancato, Robert Cormier, Bette Greene, M. E. Kerr, Norma Fox Mazer, and Richard Peck are compiled in this rich collection. The stories range from science fiction to realistic fiction and are arranged in five categories: Friendships, Turmoils, Loves, Decisions, and Families. Questions at the end of the book allow the reader to explore each story in more depth. (Literary merit)

Gallo, Donald R., editor. **Visions: Nineteen Short Stories by Outstanding Writers for Young Adults.** Delacorte Press, 1987. 228 p. ISBN 0-385-29588-X.

These nineteen short stories dealing with teenage concerns were written especially for this collection. Topics vary from a story about a girl who loves ghosts, to a Chinese girl charting the progress of her family toward becoming Americans, to a story of death and new beginnings. Such authors as Joan Aiken, Norma Fox Mazer, Richard Peck, and Sue Ellen Bridgers are included. A short biographical sketch of the author follows each story.

Gorog, Judith. **No Swimming in Dark Pond and Other Chilling Tales.** Philomel Books, 1987. 111 p. ISBN 0-399-21418-6.

These thirteen horror stories range from the commonplace to the bizarre, from grandmother's cozy kitchen to a dark, forgotten cellar in the Middle East.

Hoke, Helen, compiler. **Spirits, Spooks, and Other Sinister Creatures.** Franklin Watts, 1984. 136 p. ISBN 0-531-04769-5.

Disembodied spirits, visitors from the past, and creatures bringing nothing but danger come alive in this collection of short tales. The settings range from the house next door to spooky old castles, and the creatures are sometimes humorous, and sometimes frightening.

Howker, Janni. **Badger on the Barge and Other Stories.** Greenwillow Books, 1984. 291 p. ISBN 0-688-04215-5.

A gallery of characters stars in these five stories. Each story describes a significant encounter between two people — one young, one old.

Kahn, Joan, compiler. **Handle with Care: Frightening Stories.** Greenwillow Books, 1985. 209 p. ISBN 0-688-04663-0.

If you love eerie, puzzling tales, this book's for you. The fourteen stories will set you delightfully, chillingly on edge. Featured are such mystery greats as Agatha Christie, Isak Dinesen, and Ellery Queen.

Lively, Penelope. **Uninvited Ghosts and Other Stories.** Illustrated by John Lawrence. E. P. Dutton, 1985. 120 p. ISBN 0-525-44165-4.

Are you fascinated by the unimaginable? If so, you will enjoy this collection of eight supernatural tales. In each story, young

British children are caught in fairy tales that come to life, or become mixed up with supernatural beings. Martians, ghosts, dragons, talking clocks, and gryphons all make an appearance in this collection.

MacIntosh-Schechner, Samuel, and Richard Schechner. **The Engleburt Stories: North to the Tropics.** Illustrated by Samuel MacIntosh-Schechner. PAJ Publications, 1987. 109 p. ISBN 1-55554-024-4.

A wonderful assortment of animal and human characters is introduced in these adventures of little Engleburt, a penguin who dreams of warmer climates and a community of penguins in the Caribbean waters.

McKinley, Robin, editor. **Imaginary Lands.** Greenwillow Books, 1986. 246 p. ISBN 0-688-05213-4.

This collection of nine fantastic tales features a strong sense of place, ranging from the California landscape to the imaginary land of Damar. From dragons to fairies and from myth to magic, it's all here for readers to enjoy.

Pearce, Philippa. **Who's Afraid? and Other Strange Stories.** Greenwillow Books, 1987. 152 p. ISBN 0-688-06895-2.

Here are eleven stories of the unexpected and the threatening. There is one tale about Samantha's discovery of a fat old ghost in a bathrobe at the top of her grandparents' apple tree and another about an evil kitchen boy who prepares a deadly plum pudding. Two teachers who vanish from a playground in an explosive fireball and a ghostly dog are other characters appearing in this spooky collection.

Poe, Edgar Allan (compiled by Neil Waldman). **Tales of Terror.** Illustrated by Neil Waldman. Prentice-Hall, 1985. 186 p. ISBN 0-13-884214-0.

Ten of Poe's best and most terrifying tales are collected in this book. These stories are as spine-chilling today as when they first appeared in the 1800s. Such tales as "The Pit and the Pendulum," "The Black Cat," and "The Cask of Amontillado" will haunt your imagination and tingle your spine.

Price, Susan. **Ghosts at Large.** Illustrated by Alison Price. Faber and Faber, 1984. 90 p. ISBN 0-571-13282-0.

In these twelve traditional ghost stories, the ghosts are continually on the move: looking after their ill-gotten riches, fulfilling promises they made in life, or just being hyperactive. Mortals too are given to journeying in these tales.

Rylant, Cynthia. **Children of Christmas: Stories for the Season.** Illustrated by S. D. Schindler. Orchard Books, 1987. 38 p. ISBN 0-531-05706-2 (0-531-08306-3, library binding).

These six short stories portray the lives of six people during the Christmas season. Included are the man who lives alone and raises Christmas trees, a young girl and her father who visit a diner on Christmas eve, and a little boy and his grandfather who spend their Christmas together for the first time. You'll want to read these special stories more than once. (Literary merit)

Rylant, Cynthia. **Every Living Thing.** Illustrated by S. D. Schindler. Bradbury Press, 1985. 81 p. ISBN 0-02-777200-4.

Animals ranging from parrots to boars are featured in this collection. Many of the twelve stories have an unexpected twist and pair unusual pets with unlikely masters. For example, a turtle helps the boy who takes care of him finish first, and robins build their nest in an old man's ivy plant, becoming a symbol of hope to his ill wife.

Sanders, Scott R. **Hear the Wind Blow: American Folk Songs Retold.** Illustrated by Ponder Goembel. Bradbury Press, 1985. 202 p. ISBN 0-02-778140-2.

American folksongs relate events in American history: immigration and settlement, the Revolutionary War, the heyday of whaling, mountain life, the Civil War, the invention of various machines, the building of the railroad, and the daily lives of lumberjacks, outlaws, and cowboys. This illustrated book takes the lyrics of twenty American folksongs and retells them as short stories.

Schwartz, Alvin, retold by. **More Scary Stories to Tell in the Dark.** Illustrated by Stephen Gammell. J. B. Lippincott, 1984. 99 p. ISBN 0-397-32081-7 (0-397-32082-5, library binding).

These scary stories, collected from folklore, involve ghosts, witches, and vampires, and include "jump" stories and scary songs. Creepy drawings add to the ominous mood of the book. There are over two dozen scary stories, all just right for reading alone or for telling aloud in the dark.

Segel, Elizabeth, compiler. **Short Takes: A Short Story Collection for Young Readers.** Illustrated by Jos. A. Smith. Lothrop, Lee and Shepard Books, 1986. 158 p. ISBN 0-688-06092-7.

In each of these nine short stories, or "takes," a young person's life is about to change. A question or short commentary introduces each tale. Included are stories by such authors as Constance Greene, Philippa Pearce, Lois Lowry, E. L. Konigsburg, and Robert Cormier. (Literary merit)

Simon, Seymour. **Einstein Anderson Sees through the Invisible Man.** Illustrated by Fred Winkowski. Viking Press, 1983. 74 p. ISBN 0-670-29065-3.

Armed with his extensive knowledge of science and a repertoire of puns, America's premier child scientist tackles ten mysteries in this book. Einstein Anderson uses his knowledge of light and optics, water pressure, vision, space science, inertia, atmospherics and pollution, chemistry, animal behavior, and fluid physics to solve the cases.

Vivelo, Jackie. **A Trick of the Light: Stories to Read at Dusk.** G. P. Putnam's Sons, 1987. 124 p. ISBN 0-399-21468-2.

These nine short stories relate chilling or unnatural happenings. Read them at dusk, just as it is beginning to be dark and mysterious outside — but be sure to have a light close by to chase away the shadows.

Yolen, Jane, Martin H. Greenberg, and Charles G. Waugh, editors. **Dragons and Dreams: A New Collection of Fantasy and Science Fiction Stories.** Harper and Row, 1986. 178 p. ISBN 0-06-026792-5 (0-06-026793-3, library binding).

These ten original fantasy and science fiction stories create a colorful mosaic of fantasy and wonder and inspire a sense of the impossible, of surprise, and of magic. Imagination is the common element, and subjects range from dragon lore to magical subway rides through time. Featured are works by such authors as Zilpha Keatley Snyder, Patricia MacLachlan, Patricia A. McKillip, and Jane Yolen.

Yolen, Jane, Martin H. Greenberg, and Charles G. Waugh, editors. **Spaceships and Spells.** Harper and Row, 1987. 182 p. ISBN 0-06-026796-8.

This collection of thirteen original fantasy and science fiction stories makes one wonder what is reality and what is magic. One story is about a boy who plays a fantasy game before he reads the instructions and learns the price that he will have to pay for doing so. In another story, a young boy is looking for little green men but finds something else. The book includes stories by such authors as Robert Lawson, Bruce Coville, Isaac Asimov, and Jane Yolen.

Zolotow, Charlotte, compiler. **Early Sorrow: Ten Stories of Youth.** Harper and Row/Ursula Nordstrom Books, 1986. 212 p. ISBN 0-06-026936-7 (0-06-026937-5, library binding).

The ten stories in this collection deal with loss, separation, unrequited or unspoken love, and divorce or death of a loved one — painful experiences that hasten the transition from adolescence to adulthood. Each main character must find a way to deal with his or her sorrow. Included are stories by Carson McCullers, Stephen Vincent Benet, and Katherine Mansfield.

Animals and Pets

Ahlstrom, Mark E. (edited by Howard Schroeder). **The Black Bear.** Crestwood House, 1985. 47 p. ISBN 0-89686-276-3.

Did you know that some black bears are pure white, and that others are dark blue? That it is the only North American bear that can easily climb trees? That pork is the black bear's favorite food, but that it will also eat ants and apples? Find out about the physical characteristics, habits, and environment of the black bear in this book. Part of the Wildlife Habits and Habitat series.

Ahlstrom, Mark E. (edited by Howard Schroeder). **The Coyote.** Crestwood House, 1985. 47 p. ISBN 0-89686-277-1.

Despite humans' determined efforts to get rid of them, there are more coyotes now than there ever were before. These wolf-like animals use other animals to help catch their prey, and a single coyote can cover an area of one hundred square miles while searching for food. Other facts about the coyote's habits and its physical characteristics and environment are described in this book. Part of the Wildlife Habits and Habitat series.

Ahlstrom, Mark E. (edited by Howard Schroeder). **The Elk.** Crestwood House, 1985. 47 p. ISBN 0-89686-278-X.

Elk once lived across much of North America, but today they thrive only in the western mountains. An elk herd is usually led by an old female, and some herds migrate more than a hundred miles each fall and spring. This book describes the life cycle of the elk, its characteristics, habitat, and predators, and its place in the world today. Part of the Wildlife Habits and Habitat series.

Ahlstrom, Mark E. (edited by Howard Schroeder). **The Moose.** Crestwood House, 1985. 47 p. ISBN 0-89686-279-8.

A bull moose, the largest deer in the world, has the largest antlers of all North American animals. This huge creature loves to eat water lilies, but because of their size, moose have to kneel down to eat grass. Other details about the moose's physical characteristics, habits, and habitat can be found in this book. Part of the Wildlife Habits and Habitat series.

Ancona, George. **Sheep Dog.** Photographs by the author. Lothrop, Lee and Shepard Books, 1985. ISBN 0-688-04118-3 (0-688-04119-1, library binding).

Sheep dogs are trained to watch for lost and hurt sheep and for situations that may cause harm to their flocks. The Welsh corgi, Border collie, and Australian kelpie are described in this book. It also explains how to raise and train sheep dogs.

Barton, Miles. **Animal Rights.** Gloucester Press, 1987. 32 p. ISBN 0-531-17045-4.

Human beings have long made use of animals. Recently, many people have expressed their concern about the treatment of animals in laboratories, in slaughterhouses, and even in homes as pets. This book offers thought-provoking answers to the question of whether animals have the right to a pain-free and humane existence.

Blumberg, Leda. **Pets: A Reference First Book.** Franklin Watts, 1983. 67 p. ISBN 0-531-04649-4.

Whether your pet preference is canine, feline, or more exotic, you will enjoy reading about many kinds and breeds of animals that can add comfort and enjoyment to human lives. Learn how to choose the perfect horse, gerbil, spider, or snake and how to care for your pet.

Brown, Fern G. **Horses and Foals.** Franklin Watts, 1986. 88 p. ISBN 0-531-10118-5.

This introductory book describes the physical characteristics of horses and foals, their care and training, and the history of the different breeds of horses. The book is useful for beginning riders, new horse owners, or those readers wanting to learn more about horses.

Butler, Beverly. **Maggie by My Side.** Dodd, Mead, 1987. 96 p. ISBN 0-396-08862-7.

The author describes the challenges, hazards, and joys of training with Maggie, her fifth guide dog since she lost her sight at age fourteen, and the quirks and devotion of the guide dogs who preceded Maggie. This well-written narrative also discusses the history of guide dogs and how to become a trainer.

Casey, Denise. **Black-Footed Ferret.** Photographs by Tim W. Clark. Dodd, Mead/Skylight Books, 1985. 64 p. ISBN 0-396-08625-X.

This is a first-hand account of the study of the black-footed ferret, including its physical characteristics, life cycle, history, habits, hunting practices, and method of raising its young, along with an important look at its future. This small animal may be the rarest mammal in North America.

Curtis, Patricia. **All Wild Creatures Welcome.** Photographs by David Cupp. E. P. Dutton/Lodestar Books, 1985. 130 p. ISBN 0-525-67164-1.

Where can you take an injured racoon, an orphaned bobcat, or a sick deer? Lifeline for Wildlife in Stony Point, New York, is one of numerous animal hospitals and rehabilitation centers across the country where hundreds of such animal and bird casualties are cared for and then released, if possible. The interesting and varied daily work of this dedicated staff is described, and you are told just what to do if you find an injured, orphaned, or sick animal.

Dewey, Jennifer Owings. **Clem: The Story of a Raven.** Illustrated by the author. Dodd, Mead, 1986. 127 p. ISBN 0-396-08728-0.

The author tells the story of Clem, a raven who was blown from its nest as a baby and rescued by the author's husband. Clem becomes part of their household, along with a burrowing owl and the author's baby. The raven adapts to indoor living and has many strange and often humorous encounters with animals around their house and neighboring farms before returning to the wild. (Literary merit)

Emert, Phyllis Raybin (edited by Howard Schroeder). **Guide Dogs.** Crestwood House, 1985. 47 p. ISBN 0-89686-282-8.

Can you imagine what it would be like to cross a busy street if you were blind? This book will tell you how guide dogs are trained to assist the blind in such situations. The author discusses guide dogs in history, breeds used as guide dogs, training methods, and other general information. A glossary of terms is included. Part of the Working Dogs series.

Emert, Phyllis Raybin (edited by Howard Schroeder). **Hearing-Ear Dogs.** Crestwood House, 1985. 47 p. ISBN 0-89686-283-6.

Did you know a dog can be trained to alert deaf people to the sound of alarm clocks, doorbells, and other noises? The tasks performed by these amazing canines are described, and there is a description of the necessary requirements, the breeds of dogs used, several training methods, and general information. A glossary of terms is included. Part of the Working Dogs series.

Emert, Phyllis Raybin (edited by Howard Schroeder). **Law Enforcement Dogs.** Crestwood House, 1985. 47 p. ISBN 0-89686-284-4.

Dogs are used in police departments around the world to find and catch criminals "in the act." This volume describes the use of dogs in law enforcement, the breeds of dogs suitable for such work, and training methods. A glossary of terms is included. Part of the Working Dogs series.

Emert, Phyllis Raybin (edited by Howard Schroeder). **Military Dogs.** Crestwood House, 1985. 47 p. ISBN 0-89686-286-0.

Did you know dogs are trained to save soldiers' lives? This book discusses requirements for military dogs and the breeds used. Military dogs in the past are described and compared with the military dog today. A glossary of terms is included. Part of the Working Dogs series.

Emert, Phyllis Raybin (edited by Howard Schroeder). **Search and Rescue Dogs.** Crestwood House, 1985. 47 p. ISBN 0-89686-285-2.

Dogs can be taught to follow the trail of a missing person. This book explains the training that a dog undergoes to find a person lost in a wilderness area. The various breeds of dogs used, requirements for search and rescue dogs, training methods, and general information are discussed. A glossary of terms is included. Part of the Working Dogs series.

Emert, Phyllis Raybin (edited by Howard Schroeder). **Sled Dogs.** Crestwood House, 1985. 47 p. ISBN 0-89686-288-7.

Sled dogs can pull heavy loads over hundreds of miles of snow and ice. The author discusses sled dogs in history, suitable dog breeds, equipment, training methods, and sporting events. A glossary of terms is included. Part of the Working Dogs series.

Fitzpatrick, Michael. **A Closer Look at Apes.** Illustrated by Richard Orr. Gloucester Press, 1987. 32 p. ISBN 0-531-17038-1.

Intelligent, distinctive, and fascinating, apes seem the most humanlike of all animal species. Read about several members of the primate family — including gorillas, chimpanzees, and orangutans — and their particular characteristics, habitats, and habits. A glossary of terms is included.

Foster, Rory C. **I Never Met an Animal I Didn't Like.** Franklin Watts, 1987. 201 p. ISBN 0-531-15041-0.

Dr. Foster, the founder of the Northwoods Wildlife Center in Minocqua, Wisconsin, treated and rehabilitated sick and injured wildlife until 1984, when he was diagnosed as having Lou Gehrig's disease and was forced to relinquish his work at the wildlife center. In this book he shares with readers his many experiences treating wild animals and small pets and cautions readers to avoid abandonment of and cruelty toward animals.

Freedman, Russell. **Can Bears Predict Earthquakes? Unsolved Mysteries of Animal Behavior.** Prentice-Hall, 1982. 82 p. ISBN 0-13-114009-4.

Can bears predict earthquakes? How smart are dolphins? Mystery monsters of the deep and elephants' "burial" of their dead are just a few of the fascinating puzzles of animal behavior explored in this book. It covers questions about animal behavior that have been asked for years. In an entertaining style, pictures highlight the possible answers to these intriguing questions, along with facts and figures from the animal world.

Freedman, Russell. **Sharks.** Holiday House, 1985. 40 p. ISBN 0-8234-0582-6.

There are three hundred fifty different kinds of sharks, and fewer than a dozen of these are the larger sharks considered a menace by humans. They account for about twenty-eight serious shark attacks around the world each year. This book describes some of the varieties of sharks, their methods of hunting, details of birth, their living habits, and their usefulness to humans.

Green, Carl R., and William R. Sanford (edited by Howard Schroeder). **The Bison.** Crestwood House, 1985. 47 p. ISBN 0-89686-275-5.

Did you know that the bison, or buffalo, once lived in large herds from Florida to Alaska, and from New York to the Rocky

Mountains? Once there were over fifty million bison roaming North America. Today, while there are no free-roaming bison left, conservation efforts have restored the herds of North America's largest land animal. The details of these and other facts about the bison can be found in this book. Part of the Wildlife Habits and Habitat series.

Green, Carl R., and William R. Sanford (edited by Howard Schroeder). **The Great White Shark.** Crestwood House, 1985. 47 p. ISBN 0-89686-281-X.

Learn more about great white sharks from this book: They don't have many teeth, although they do hunt sea lions and sea turtles. They don't have any bones. Their skin was once used as sandpaper. And they have been known to attack small fishing boats. Part of the Wildlife Habits and Habitat series.

Green, Carl R., and William R. Sanford (edited by Howard Schroeder). **The Humpback Whale.** Crestwood House, 1985. 47 p. ISBN 0-89686-274-7.

Although named the humpback whale, this whale does not have a hump on its back. It is a playful mammal that can do somersaults, and it communicates with other humpbacks by making singing sounds. Each humpback can be identified by the distinctive markings on its tail. These details and others about the appearance, behavior, and life cycle of the humpback whale are discussed in this book. Part of the Wildlife Habits and Habitat series.

Green, Carl R., and William R. Sanford (edited by Howard Schroeder). **The Porcupine.** Crestwood House, 1985. 47 p. ISBN 0-89686-280-1.

Contrary to popular belief, a porcupine does not "shoot" its quills. When threatened, it erects its quills and attempts to back into its enemy. The quills are stubbornly imbedded and can kill another animal. The porcupine can also kill trees by removing the bark. Its teeth never stop growing. Other facts about the characteristics, habits, and habitat of the second largest rodent in North America can be found in this book. Part of the Wildlife Habits and Habitat series.

Hall, Lynn. **Tazo and Me.** Photographs by Jan Hall. Charles Scribner's Sons, 1985. 42 p. ISBN 0-684-18305-6.

The author describes how she chose and trained her particular breed of horse, a Paso Fino, and the expectations that she had for the horse. She relates how she discovered that pleasure riding was more enjoyable for her than formal competitions.

Hewett, Joan. **When You Fight the Tiger.** Photographs by Richard Hewett. Little, Brown, 1984. 90 p. ISBN 0-316-35956-4.

You might be surprised to learn that many of the wild animals appearing on television or in movies have received special rearing and training. Gentle Jungle is a California ranch that gets animals ready for their acting roles and prepares humans to work with them. The text and photographs in this book depict a typical day on the ranch.

Hirschi, Ron. **Headgear.** Photographs by Galen Burrell. Dodd, Mead, 1986. 63 p. ISBN 0-396-08673-X.

Do horns and antlers help animals coexist in peace, or are they dangerous weapons? This book discusses the characteristics and habitats of North American animals with horns and antlers, including the elk, big horn, prong horn, moose, caribou, deer, and mountain goat. It looks at why female caribou have antlers while cow moose do not, describes how young animals learn to use their headgear, and presents some of the folklore associated with animals' horns and antlers. Illustrated with magnificent color photographs.

Johnson, Sylvia A., and Alice Aamodt. **Wolf Pack: Tracking Wolves in the Wild.** Lerner Publications, 1985. 96 p. ISBN 0-8225-1577-6.

The latest scientific information on the life of a wolf pack and the strong family ties that bind its members together is presented in this book. Readers will discover that there is much social interaction among the wolves in a pack as they share the work of hunting, maintaining territory, and raising their young. The book also explores traditional stories about the wolf and the troubled relationship that has long existed between wolves and humans.

Kaplan, Elizabeth, and Michael A. Kaplan. **Good Cats: The Complete Guide to Cat Training.** Illustrated by John Canemaker. Putnam/Perigee Books, 1985. 125 p. ISBN 0-399-51117-2.

This thorough guide to cat training would be a great book for a new kitten or cat owner. It explains litter training, how to keep your cat from clawing the furniture and drapes, how to train your cat to walk on a leash, and many more helpful hints for a cat owner.

Koebner, Linda. **Forgotten Animals: The Rehabilitation of Laboratory Primates.** E. P. Dutton/Lodestar Books, 1984. 116 p. ISBN 0-525-66773-3.

Chimpanzees, the laboratory animals most like humans, are at the heart of the controversy over whether animals should be used for research and how they should be treated. The author describes what animal-rights groups are doing to save these animals and suggests some alternatives to using live animals in scientific research.

Lampton, Christopher. **Dinosaurs and the Age of Reptiles.** Franklin Watts/First Books, 1983. 90 p. ISBN 0-531-04526-9.

Here is a look at the origin of dinosaurs, how they lived, and why they disappeared. The book also discusses the discovery and investigation of dinosaur fossils and those of other reptiles from the dinosaurs' time period. A glossary of terms is included.

Leder, Jane Mersky (edited by Howard Schroeder). **Stunt Dogs.** Crestwood House, 1985. 47 p. ISBN 0-89686-289-5.

Nipper, Rin Tin Tin, Asta, Lassie, and Benji are some of the famous stunt dogs used in television and movies. This book discusses how stunt dogs are trained and describes some beginning and advanced stunts. A glossary of terms is included.

MacClintock, Dorcas. **African Images.** Illustrated by Ugo Mochi. Charles Scribner's Sons, 1984. 142 p. ISBN 0-684-18089-8.

Detailed silhouettes cut from a single sheet of black paper highlight this book about the animals of Africa. It is organized around their habitats: the forests, the rivers and lakes, the swamps and marshes, the bush, the savannas, and the grasslands.

Milani, Myrna M. **The Invisible Leash: A Better Way to Communicate with Your Dog.** New American Library/Signet Books, 1986. 204 p. ISBN 0-451-14613-1.

Dr. Milani discusses the world of dog senses — how they work, which ones are the most important, and how they're related to the way a dog acts, communicates, and responds (or doesn't respond) to commands.

Newman, Matthew (edited by Howard Schroeder). **Watch/Guard Dogs.** Crestwood House, 1985. 47 p. ISBN 0-89686-287-9.

Some dogs work very quietly day and night, guarding people and businesses. This book tells their story, with information on who needs a professional watchdog, which breeds are suitable, how watchdogs are trained, and how their rights can be protected. A glossary of terms is included. Part of the Working Dogs series.

Ostrow, Marshall. **Goldfish: Everything about Aquariums, Varieties, Care, Nutrition, Diseases, and Breeding.** Barron's Educational Series, 1985. 87 p. ISBN 0-8120-2975-5.

Most everyone enjoys seeing a few goldfish swimming in a bowl, but if you're serious about goldfish, this is the book for you. It includes selecting and establishing aquarium equipment, selecting and buying goldfish, recognizing and treating diseases, breeding goldfish, and establishing a goldfish pool outside. Perhaps the book might suggest some possible projects for a science fair.

Patent, Dorothy Hinshaw. **All about Whales.** Holiday House, 1987. 48 p. ISBN 0-8234-0644-X.

The answers to many questions often asked about whales (Do humpbacks really sing? What whale has the longest flippers?) fill this introduction to the world's largest animals. The author enthusiastically discusses the whale's appearance, as well as what it eats, how it communicates, and the several different kinds of whales.

Patent, Dorothy Hinshaw. **Buffalo: The American Bison Today.** Photographs by William Muñoz. Clarion Books, 1986. 73 p. ISBN 0-89919-345-5.

At one time millions of bison grazed the prairies, but no more do the buffalo roam. Today the 100,000 or so American bison live in parks and preserves or on privately owned ranches, and their numbers are carefully controlled. This book describes the life of the buffalo according to the season of the year — courtship, birth, and survival during the winter. What people are doing to see that this symbol of strength and freedom survives is also discussed.

Patent, Dorothy Hinshaw. **Dolphins and Porpoises.** Holiday House, 1987. 86 p. ISBN 0-8234-0663-6.

Dolphins and porpoises are small members of the whale family. Their intelligence, playfulness, and friendliness have made them a source of interest and fascination to humans since earliest times, and people have learned to communicate with them. This book is an introduction to the different species of dolphins and porpoises and their physical characteristics, feeding habits, sonar systems, and social behavior.

Patent, Dorothy Hinshaw. **Draft Horses.** Photographs by William Muñoz. Holiday House, 1986. 86 p. ISBN 0-8234-0597-4.

Belgian and Clydesdale horses are two breeds whose strength and endurance make them well suited to drawing heavy loads. Such draft horses have been in use in various parts of the world since the Middle Ages. The physical traits, origins, breeds, uses, and care of draft horses are examined in this book.

Patent, Dorothy Hinshaw. **The Way of the Grizzly.** Photographs by William Muñoz. Clarion Books, 1987. 65 p. ISBN 0-89919-383-8.

This close look at the grizzly bear tells us what they eat, where they live, how they hibernate, how they give birth and rear their cubs, and how humans have threatened their survival.

Patterson, Francine. **Koko's Kitten.** Photographs by Ronald H. Cohn. Scholastic, 1985. 30 p. ISBN 0-590-33811-0.

Dr. Patterson taught a female gorilla, Koko, how to communicate using the American Sign Language. When Koko was asked what present she wanted for her twelfth birthday, she signed "Cat." This is the story of Koko and the kitten, fully documented with photographs.

Peters, David. **Giants of Land, Sea and Air: Past and Present.** Illustrated by the author. Alfred A. Knopf/Borzoi Books and Sierra Club Books, 1986. 73 p. ISBN 0-394-87805-1 (0-394-97805-6, library binding).

This is a book about giants — about many of the biggest animals ever to inhabit the Earth's land, seas, and air. The giants are grouped according to either type or shape so that their similarities, differences, and peculiarities can easily be seen. Seventy-one of the largest animals of all time are compared to humans and to each other in full-color paintings, all drawn to the same scale.

Pope, Joyce. **A Closer Look at Horses.** Illustrated by Peter Barrett. Gloucester Press, 1987. 32 p. ISBN 0-531-17039-X.

Zebras, donkeys, wild horses, and domesticated horses are given a closer look in this book. The author examines the physical characteristics, habits, habitats, and uses of the many different types of horses.

Pope, Joyce. **A Closer Look at Reptiles.** Illustrated by Gary Hincks, Alan Male, and Phil Weare. Gloucester Press, 1985. 32 p. ISBN 0-531-17014-4.

Lizards, crocodiles, alligators, turtles, tortoises, and snakes are all examples of reptiles. Some are similar — crocodiles and alligators; some are not — turtles and snakes. Yet, as this book explains, all have certain common features that place them in the same animal family.

Pope, Joyce. **Taking Care of Your Cat.** Photographs by Sally Anne Thompson and R. T. Willbie/Animal Photography. Franklin Watts, 1986. 32 p. ISBN 0-531-10159-2.

This book is specially designed for young cat owners. Practical instructions on feline care cover the basics of choosing the right breed for you, successfully house training your kitten, and feeding and caring for your pet.

Pope, Joyce. **Taking Care of Your Dog.** Photographs by Sally Anne Thompson and R. T. Willbie/Animal Photography. Franklin Watts, 1986. 32 p. ISBN 0-531-10160-6.

Everybody loves a puppy, but not everyone knows how to take care of one properly, or even how to choose the breed that will best fit the family's needs and lifestyle. Written for young dog owners, this book will help with all those choices and decisions.

Poynter, Margaret. **What's One More?** Illustrated by Elise Primavera. Atheneum, 1985. 117 p. ISBN 0-689-31083-8.

The author didn't consciously decide to run an adoption and nursing service for unwanted dogs. She had only one dog of her own when family members left their dog "for a while," neighbors abandoned their pet, and strays found their way to her door. She found herself caring for ill, injured, and abused dogs, as well as wanted ones, and struggled to reduce animal euthanasia by finding permanent homes for the dogs.

Pringle, Laurence. **Animals at Play.** Harcourt Brace Jovanovich, 1985. 70 p. ISBN 0-15-203554-0.

A noted science author describes many types of animal play, ranging from mock battles on the ground to aerial acrobatics in the trees. Is it just for fun? Does play somehow aid the survival of a species? Readers will learn how scientists study and debate these questions.

Pringle, Laurence. **Feral: Tame Animals Gone Wild.** Macmillan, 1983. 110 p. ISBN 0-03-775420-0.

This book gives information about the habits and lifestyles of those animals that were once tame or domesticated by humans and that now have become wild. Discussed are feral birds, pigs, dogs, cats, burros, and horses and their impact on people and on the environment.

Rahn, Joan Elma. **Animals That Changed History.** Illustrated by the author. Atheneum, 1986. 109 p. ISBN 0-689-31137-0.

Some animals have played important roles in our history. Horses have used their strength and power to perform much of the work of peace and war through the years; black rats and fleas have served as the carriers of the plague, which completely changed European society in the mid-1300s; and the American beaver led European traders to explore virtually all of Canada in their greed for beaver skins. This book shows how seemingly insignificant events can have a ripple effect on larger events.

Rankin, Chrissy. **How Life Begins: A Look at Birth and Care in the Animal World.** Photographs by Oxford Scientific films. G. P. Putnam's Sons, 1985. 64 p. ISBN 0-399-21199-3.

Starting with creatures that are born by simple cell division, this book goes on to show us insects, reptiles, birds, and mammals, each with its own unique way of reproducing offspring. The varied role of parents is also explored.

Reed, Don C. **Sevengill: The Shark and Me.** Illustrated by Pamela Ford Johnson. Alfred A. Knopf/Borzoi Books and Sierra Club Books, 1986. 125 p. ISBN 0-394-86926-5 (0-394-96926-X, library binding).

Imagine having as a work partner a huge shark named Sevengill! Author Reed did just that in his work as head diver at Marine World. The two developed a special relationship as the writer spent thousands of hours in Sevengill's territory under some very dangerous conditions. Reed describes their experiences in this book.

Sattler, Helen Roney. **Fish Facts and Bird Brains: Animal Intelligence.** Illustrated by Giulio Maestro. E. P. Dutton/Lodestar Books, 1984. 113 p. ISBN 0-525-66915-9.

Animal intelligence is demonstrated by fish, birds, wild animals, apes and monkeys, and even flat worms. What scientists have discovered about animal intelligence can help us know more about human learning. This book includes intelligence tests that you can give to your pet, and may suggest some ideas for a science project.

Scott, Jack Denton. **Swans.** Photographs by Ozzie Sweet. G. P. Putnam's Sons, 1987. 64 p. ISBN 0-399-21406-2.

Swans can fly as fast as 55 miles per hour and may have as many as 25,000 feathers. These and other facts and figures about the seven species of swans are presented in this book. Swimming habits, nesting practices, and care of the young, which are called *cygnets,* are also explained. The many pictures illustrate aspects of swans that most of us never have a chance to see.

Seuling, Barbara. **Elephants Can't Jump and Other Freaky Facts about Animals.** E. P. Dutton/Lodestar Books, 1985. 72 p. ISBN 0-525-67155-2.

Many strange-but-true facts about animals will delight and amuse animal lovers everywhere. These curious and captivating facts — about how animals live, eat, sleep, move, play, communicate, reproduce, raise babies, and survive — make for entertaining and informative reading.

Smith, Elizabeth Simpson. **A Dolphin Goes to School: The Story of Squirt, a Trained Dolphin.** Illustrated by Ted Lewin. William Morrow, 1986. 85 p. ISBN 0-688-04815-3 (0-688-04816-1, library binding).

If you have ever marveled at the antics of trained dolphins, you'll enjoy this story of a real-life dolphin, Squirt, and the trainer who teaches him to be a star performer. The book provides details about the capture and training of dolphins.

Smith, Jack. **Cats, Dogs, and Other Strangers at My Door.** Franklin Watts, 1984. 275 p. ISBN 0-531-09751-X.

One way to keep track of your life is through the animals that share it. In the course of author Smith's life on Mount Washington in Los Angeles, he has encountered the usual poodles and Airedales, but he has also spotted exotic hummingbirds and coyotes. All became an important part of his family.

Strachan, Elizabeth. **A Closer Look at Whales and Dolphins.** Illustrated by Norman Weaver. Gloucester Press, 1985. 32 p. ISBN 0-531-17015-2.

Giants of the deep and playful dolphins and porpoises are described in this beautifully illustrated book. It explains how these animals differ from fish, and discusses their physical characteristics, habits, habitats, patterns of migration, and reproduction.

Wakefield, Pat A. (with Larry Carrara). **A Moose for Jessica.** Photographs by Larry Carrara. E. P. Dutton, 1987. ISBN 0-525-44342-8.

In this true story, a bull moose falls in love with a cow named Jessica. The story takes place on the Carrara farm in Vermont and starts with the appearance of the moose at the cow pasture one October morning. The moose returns to visit the pudgy hereford, Jessica, for the next seventy-six days. The moose then disappears, but the story ends with the hope that he will return the next October.

Zallinger, Peter. **Dinosaurs and Other Archosaurs.** Random House, 1986. 96 p. ISBN 0-394-84421-1 (0-394-94421-6, library binding).

Full-page photographs and text describe several of the prehistoric dinosaurs and other reptiles that once roamed the land. Physical characteristics, habits, habitats, and individual species are discussed. A glossary of terms is included.

Biography and Autobiography

American Figures

Adler, David A. **Martin Luther King, Jr.: Free at Last.** Illustrated by Robert Casilla. Holiday House, 1986. 48 p. ISBN 0-8234-0618-0.

Martin Luther King, Jr., dreamed of a world free of prejudice, hate, and violence and worked to bring equality to American blacks. In 1968, at the young age of thirty-nine, King was gunned down, yet the marker on his grave reads, "free at last." King's accomplishments and dreams live on and continue to provide inspiration to whites and blacks alike.

Banfield, Susan. **James Madison.** Franklin Watts/First Books, 1986. 72 p. ISBN 0-531-10217-3.

Soon after James Madison completed his studies at Princeton University, the American colonies won the war with England and became a new country needing a system of government. This book tells how Madison helped by contributing ideas for the Constitution and Bill of Rights. Later, he served as our fourth president.

Bruce, Preston. **From the Door of the White House.** Lothrop, Lee and Shepard Books, 1984. 176 p. ISBN 0-688-00883-6.

A doorman's job involves much more than openings and closings when one is on the personal staff of the president of the United States. When Preston Bruce landed the job at the White House, he was very surprised to find himself the confidant of presidents Eisenhower, Kennedy, Johnson, Nixon, and Ford. He provides an insider's perspective on their personal and professional lives and tells of his role in such momentous events as the funeral of John F. Kennedy and the resignation of Richard M. Nixon.

Chaplik, Dorothy. **Up with Hope: A Biography of Jesse Jackson.** Dillon Press/People in Focus Books, 1986. 128 p. ISBN 0-87518-347-6.

This book highlights the life of Jesse Jackson and his attempt to become the first black president of the United States. It covers his childhood in South Carolina, his education, and his influential work in the civil rights movement.

Cohen, Daniel. **Carl Sagan: Superstar Scientist.** Dodd, Mead, 1987. 168 p. ISBN 0-396-08776-0.

Carl Sagan is a well-known astronomer, educator, and author. His fame has spread outside of the scientific community because of his ability and desire to communicate his ideas and love of science to the general public. The book relates Sagan's life and highlights his involvement with the space probes. You may have seen Sagan on his successful series, "Cosmos."

Cooper, Ilene. **Susan B. Anthony.** Franklin Watts/Impact Biographies, 1984. 111 p. ISBN 0-531-04750-4.

After making fun of her parents and sister for attending a meeting on women's rights and signing a petition in favor of these rights, Susan B. Anthony went on to become a leader in the women's rights movement in the nineteenth century. This is the story of Anthony's lifetime struggle to gain equal rights for America's women and of the many problems she encountered in her struggle.

Faber, Doris. **Eleanor Roosevelt: First Lady of the World.** Illustrated by Donna Ruff. Viking Penguin/Viking Kestrel, 1985. 57 p. ISBN 0-670-80551-3.

Eleanor Roosevelt was America's first lady during the four presidential terms of her husband, Franklin, from 1933 to 1945. She herself had enormous political influence and won respect in the United States and abroad. Part of the Women of Our Times series.

Faber, Doris. **Love and Rivalry: Three Exceptional Pairs of Sisters.** Viking Press, 1983. 200 p. ISBN 0-670-44221-6.

This book reveals the lives of three nineteenth-century women: writer Harriet Beecher Stowe, actress Charlotte Cushman, and poet Emily Dickinson. The future of each of these women was affected by the love and rivalry they shared with their sisters. Other influences on their lives included religion, society, and how they coped with personal trauma.

Freedman, Russell. **Indian Chiefs.** Holiday House, 1987. 149 p. ISBN 0-8234-0625-3.

If invaders threatened your home, family, and food supply, would you move on or stand and fight? Each of the six great Indian chiefs featured here had to resolve just that question when white pioneers encroached on their hunting grounds. The stories of Red Cloud, Sitting Bull, Santana, and others are told truthfully and simply. Included are black-and-white photographs and replicas.

Freedman, Russell. **Lincoln: A Photobiography.** Clarion Books, 1987. 150 p. ISBN 0-89919-380-3.

Freedman's biography of Abraham Lincoln contains numerous photographs, prints, newspaper clippings, and copies of actual letters written by Lincoln. The author follows Lincoln from his boyhood, to his years as a lawyer, to his marriage to Mary Todd, to his political life, to his years as president, and finally to his assassination. The book also includes a sampling of Lincoln's writings and a list of Lincoln historical sites, with addresses to write for more information. (Literary merit — Newbery Award, 1987)

Gross, David C. **A Justice for All the People: Louis D. Brandeis.** E. P. Dutton/Lodestar Books, 1987. 116 p. ISBN 0-525-67194-3.

Louis Brandeis, the first Jewish Supreme Court justice, served on the court from 1916 to 1939. Born in Kentucky and educated in Europe, Brandeis studied law at Harvard and then began his law practice in Boston. He became a philanthropist who championed issues benefiting the public good. This book relates his life and shows how his cornerstone on all issues was that he be morally correct and that he serve humankind. Part of the Jewish Biography series. (Literary merit)

Harris, Jacqueline L. **Henry Ford.** Franklin Watts/Impact Biographies, 1984. 110 p. ISBN 0-531-04754-7.

Henry Ford dreamed of a car that everyone could own. In 1908, his first Model T rolled off the assembly line. Getting twenty miles per gallon at speeds up to forty-five miles per hour, the Model T became the car of the common person. This biography tells of Ford's successes and failures in developing his early cars and in creating the Ford Motor Company.

Harris, Jacqueline L. **Martin Luther King, Jr.** Franklin Watts/Impact Biographies, 1983. 110 p. ISBN 0-531-04588-9.

This biography of Martin Luther King, Jr., describes the events that molded his life: his first encounters with bigotry, his and his family's involvement in the civil rights movement, and, most importantly, his commitment to Mahatma Gandhi's philosophy of nonviolent protest against injustice. The book chronicles King's travels, speeches and rallies, winning of the Nobel Peace Prize, and assassination in 1968.

Keller, Mollie. **Alexander Hamilton.** Franklin Watts/First Books, 1986. 72 p. ISBN 0-531-10214-9.

Alexander Hamilton, the first secretary of the treasury, started life as a poor person with no advantages. But he set high goals for himself and became a successful lawyer and politician. He was a hero in the Revolutionary War and an aide and adviser to George Washington. He was a framer of the Constitution and set up our first bank.

Lee, Martin. **Paul Revere.** Franklin Watts/First Books, 1987. 95 p. ISBN 0-531-10312-9.

Silversmith Paul Revere is best known for his midnight ride to warn American colonists that the British were coming. This biography provides a look at his life in context of the emerging nation. A time-line, list of additional reading, and black-and-white reproductions and photographs are included.

Lowry, Timothy S. **And Brave Men, Too.** Crown, 1985. 246 p. ISBN 0-517-55707-X.

Fourteen Congressional Medal of Honor recipients from the Vietnam War tell their experiences in the war, including some current reflections as they look back to that time. The author has provided much description and background about life in the United States during the war in Vietnam.

Ludel, Jacqueline. **Margaret Mead.** Franklin Watts/Impact Biographies, 1983. 118 p. ISBN 0-531-04590-0.

Margaret Mead became one of the world's most respected and well-known anthropologists through her studies of primitive cultures. This book details her study of the people of Samoa and her work with the Manus of New Guinea in the 1920s through

1950s. Mead's concern for maintaining cultural diversity is evident in this book.

McClung, Robert M. **The True Adventures of Grizzly Adams.** William Morrow, 1985. 200 p. ISBN 0-688-05794-2.

John Adams, better known as Grizzly Adams, was one of the Old West's most famous frontiersmen during the mid-1800s. He was among the most adventuresome of all the colorful '49ers who flocked to California during the gold rush. He was soon disillusioned with the greed and corruption in the gold fields, so he turned his back on society and found a new life and refuge in the vast Western wilderness.

Meltzer, Milton. **Betty Friedan: A Voice for Women's Rights.** Illustrated by Stephen Marchesi. Viking Penguin/Viking Kestrel, 1985. 57 p. ISBN 0-670-80786-9.

Betty Friedan is one of the leaders of the women's movement. Her 1963 book, *The Feminine Mystique,* questioned whether raising children and keeping house were women's only source of fulfillment, and in 1966 she founded the National Organization for Women. This book focuses on Friedan's childhood and youth and how these early years influenced her adult accomplishments. Part of the Women of Our Times series.

Meltzer, Milton. **George Washington and the Birth of Our Nation.** Franklin Watts, 1986. 189 p. ISBN 0-531-10253-X.

Although he had little formal education, George Washington learned much from the world around him. He became the commander in chief of the colonial forces and our first president. He had the job of setting up a new country and of selecting the people to run it. This biography covers Washington's childhood in Virginia and extends to his death at Mount Vernon in 1799.

Metzer, Larry. **Abraham Lincoln.** Franklin Watts/First Books, 1987. 93 p. ISBN 0-531-10307-2.

Abraham Lincoln — log splitter and lawyer, farmer and sixteenth president — played a central role in one of the most exciting and decisive periods in American history, the Civil War, which freed the black population from slavery. Simply written and illustrated, this biography gives all the facts about Lincoln's life in a readable format.

Monchieri, Lino (translated by Mary Lee Grisanti). **Abraham Lincoln.** Silver Burdett, 1985. 64 p. ISBN 0-382-06855-6 (0-382-06985-4, library binding).

Abraham Lincoln withstood a difficult childhood on the frontier in Kentucky and Indiana, became a country lawyer, and developed into one of the most famous presidents of the United States, serving during the Civil War. This biography recounts Lincoln's life from his birth to his assassination in 1865. Part of the Why They Became Famous series.

Montgomery, M. R. **In Search of L. L. Bean.** Illustrated by Mary F. Rhinelander. New American Library/Plume Books, 1985. 244 p. ISBN 0-452-25751-4.

L. L. Bean, who was born in 1872, was close to forty when he started his mail-order business in hunting and fishing equipment. This book looks not only at Bean's successes and failures but also at the L. L. Bean myth that was created by Bean himself. It includes an examination of catalogs and marketing techniques in the mail-order business.

Morrison, Dorothy Nafus. **Under a Strong Wind: The Adventures of Jessie Benton Frémont.** Atheneum, 1983. 176 p. ISBN 0-689-31004-8.

In 1864, John Frémont was asked to run for president of the United States. If he had run, he would have split the Republican party, thus costing Abraham Lincoln the presidential election and perhaps preventing the North from winning the Civil War and the slaves from obtaining their freedom. It was Frémont's wife, Jessie, who talked him out of running for president. From the time she eloped with John at age seventeen, Jessie gave him her advice and help. This is the story of her years as Mrs. Frémont and of the adventures and hardships she experienced.

Peavy, Linda, and Ursula Smith. **Dreams into Deeds: Nine Women Who Dared.** Charles Scribner's Sons, 1985. 148 p. ISBN 0-684-18484-2.

This book gives a detailed account of the lives of nine women, all of whom dared to do something to make the world a better place. Because of their accomplishments, each of these women has been named to the National Women's Hall of Fame. The book investigates their lives as children and their determination to meet their goals.

Peavy, Linda, and Ursula Smith. **Women Who Changed Things.** Charles Scribner's Sons, 1983. 187 p. ISBN 0-684-17849-4.

This collective biography presents the lives of nine women who dared to make changes in society — to question society's discriminatory ethics against women, children, the poor, and minorities. The women were active between 1880 and 1930 and made contributions to such fields as medicine, religion, politics, business, education, and athletics. An important event in each woman's life is highlighted at the beginning of each biography.

Randolph, Blythe. **Amelia Earhart.** Franklin Watts/Impact Biographies, 1987. 114 p. ISBN 0-531-10331-5.

Amelia Earhart is still considered by most people to be America's most famous female aviator. Earhart made history in 1928, when she became the first woman to fly across the Atlantic, and in 1932, when she was the first woman to make a solo flight across the Atlantic. In 1937, Earhart disappeared during an attempted flight around the world, and although theories exist about her fate, the mystery has never been solved.

Reische, Diana. **Patrick Henry.** Franklin Watts/First Books, 1987. 92 p. ISBN 0-531-10305-6.

Famous for his statement, "Give me liberty or give me death," Patrick Henry contributed a feisty spirit as well as political leadership to the emerging United States. This biography traces the highlights of his life and career as orator, lawyer, statesman, and framer of the Bill of Rights. The book includes sources, a bibliography, and excellent black-and-white photographs and reproductions.

Richards, Norman. **Dreamers and Doers: Inventors Who Changed Our World.** Atheneum, 1984. 153 p. ISBN 0-689-30914-7.

Here is a look at the lives and achievements of four men who developed their dreams into inventions that have changed our lives. Robert H. Goddard made space flight possible. Charles Goodyear made rubber into a usable product. Thomas Edison invented the incandescent light bulb. And George Eastman devised a process for developing and printing pictures.

Roosevelt, Elliott. **Eleanor Roosevelt, with Love: A Centenary Remembrance.** E. P. Dutton/Lodestar Books, 1984. 166 p. ISBN 0-525-67147-1.

Elliott Roosevelt describes the more personal side of his mother: the trials of her childhood, adolescence, and domineering mother-in-law and her discovery that her husband, Franklin, was having an affair. As first lady, Eleanor traveled the world, caring and listening to those around her and winning respect for her concern for human welfare. Yet she still kept in close contact with her family and worked to keep her family together, despite the pressures of life in the White House.

Scheader, Catherine. **Contributions of Women: Music.** Dillon Press, 1985. 136 p. ISBN 0-87518-274-7.

The lives of five remarkable women, all trendsetters in the field of music, are explored here. Popular opera star Beverly Sills is one of the five included in this well-written, documented look at the early lives, dreams, and achievements of these women. Brief biographies of other women in the field are included.

Smith, Gene. **Lee and Grant: A Dual Biography.** New American Library/Meridian Books, 1984. 412 p. ISBN 0-452-00773-9.

Vivid, interwoven biographical portraits explore the lives of two opposing generals in the Civil War. One was the personification of the ideal Southern gentleman; the other was a graceless, unprepossessing, small-town Midwesterner. The two illuminate and define each other's greatness and give human meaning to the vast conflict between the North and the South.

Story, Bettie Wilson. **Gospel Trailblazer: The Exciting Story of Francis Asbury.** Illustrated by Charles Cox. Abingdon Press, 1984. 125 p. ISBN 0-687-15652-1.

The establishment of Methodism in the American colonies in the 1770s and after the American Revolution required dedication and self-sacrifice. Francis Asbury committed his life to his faith, and through his long trips on horseback up and down the length of the Eastern seaboard, he played an important role in the growth of Methodism. This biography tells the story of his hardships and his final success as one of American Methodism's first bishops.

Sullivan, George. **Mr. President: A Book of U.S. Presidents.** Dodd, Mead, 1984. 158 p. ISBN 0-396-08737-X.

Forty men have served as president of the United States during the last two hundred years. This book describes where and when each man was born, his political party, his term of office, the hottest political issues of the day, and a summary of the major events of his term of office.

Topalian, Elyse. **Margaret Sanger.** Franklin Watts/Impact Biographies, 1984. 122 p. ISBN 0-531-04763-6.

Margaret Sanger was a crusader in the early 1900s, a period when women were supposed to be seen and not heard. Her foes were powerful: the medical profession, the law, and the Catholic Church. At first, few people supported her belief that birth-control information should be made available to all women, rich and poor. But as Sanger's supporters increased, so did her problems. This book describes her life and her achievements.

Wilson, Dorothy Clarke. **I *Will* Be a Doctor! The Story of America's First Woman Physician.** Abingdon Press, 1985. 160 p. ISBN 0-687-19727-9.

Even as a small child, Elizabeth Blackwell knew she was "different." When her father's business difficulties in England prompted a move to the United States in the mid-1800s, Blackwell began to exert her amazing energies in helping care for her family. The need for a consuming challenge led her to the study of medicine, a field then closed to women. She went on to found the New York Infirmary and Women's Medical College and also did pioneering work in the areas of sanitation, hygiene, and individual knowledge of the body. This biography emphasizes the hardships Blackwell endured in becoming a doctor and in practicing medicine.

Wolcott, Leonard T., and Carolyn E. Wolcott. **Wilderness Rider.** Abingdon Press, 1984. 144 p. ISBN 0-687-45570-7.

Noah Fidler, the subject of this biography, was a Methodist circuit rider — that is, a traveling minister — in the late 1700s and early 1800s. His territory was the sparsely settled areas of western Pennsylvania, Ohio, Maryland, Virginia, and West Virginia. He traveled from settlement to settlement, where people gathered for church services every few weeks. Fidler traveled daily in all weather, stayed with families along the way, and sometimes slept in the open.

Woods, Harold, and Geraldine Woods. **Equal Justice: A Biography of Sandra Day O'Connor.** Dillon Press/Reaching Out Books, 1985. 127 p. ISBN 0-87518-292-5.

Sandra Day O'Connor is the first woman Supreme Court justice. This biography describes her childhood, her early legal career, and her life since appointment to the Supreme Court.

Artists and Writers

Baldwin, Neil. **To All Gentleness: William Carlos Williams, the Doctor-Poet.** Atheneum, 1984. 199 p. ISBN 0-689-31030-7.

William Carlos Williams held two full-time jobs. He was a physician in Rutherford, New Jersey, for his entire life, delivering babies, making house calls, and holding office hours. But every moment he could find, even in the middle of the night, he was a writer, both a poet and novelist. When Williams had an idea for his writing, he'd jot it down on a prescription blank. He looked on Walt Whitman as his hero, and like Whitman, he tried to sing the praises of the common person and everyday experiences. (Literary merit)

Blackwood, Alan. **Beethoven.** Illustrated by Richard Hook. Bookwright Press, 1987. 32 p. ISBN 0-531-18131-6.

This brief biography describes the major happenings in the life of German composer Ludwig van Beethoven. He was born in 1770, and his musical talents were recognized at an early age. He studied music in Vienna and went on to become one of the greatest composers who ever lived. The first signs of Beethoven's hearing loss appeared in 1801, and by 1817 he was totally deaf, although he continued to compose music during the ten final years of his life. Part of the Great Lives series.

Bober, Natalie S. **Breaking Tradition: The Story of Louise Nevelson.** Atheneum, 1984. 142 p. ISBN 0-689-31036-6.

Louise Nevelson has been called the greatest living artist in the United States. This book tells of her childhood in Rockland, Maine, and of her familiarity with many areas of the arts, including dance, music, and the theater. Nevelson finally settled on sculpture as her medium and began to earn recognition as an artist in this area only when she was fifty-eight years old. Many photographs of Nevelson's artwork are included.

Dahl, Roald. **Boy: Tales of Childhood.** Farrar, Straus and Giroux, 1984. 160 p. ISBN 0-374-37374-4.

Roald Dahl, author of *Charlie and the Chocolate Factory* and numerous other works of fiction, shares his most memorable experiences of boyhood while attending boarding schools with tough headmasters in England and Norway. He also relates family experiences that led to some delightful adventures.

Erlanger, Ellen. **Isaac Asimov: Scientist and Storyteller.** Lerner Publications, 1986. 55 p. ISBN 0-8225-0482-0.

How Isaac Asimov arrived in the United States from the Soviet Union at the age of three and became a noted scientist and prolific writer of science and science fiction works is a tale worth telling. Asimov, the winner of the Hugo and Nebula awards for distinguished contributions to the field of science fiction, has been writing for over forty years. Part of the Achievers series.

Fritz, Jean. **China Homecoming.** Photographs by Michael Fritz. G. P. Putnam's Sons, 1985. 133 p. ISBN 0-399-21182-9.

Jean Fritz was thirteen years old when she left her home in China in 1928. She described her life as an American child growing up in China and her arrival in the United States in *Homesick, My Own Story.* This companion book is the story of Fritz's first visit back to China in 1984, when she was sixty-nine years old. She looks for her old house, school, and church and makes many new friends in a greatly changed China.

Gherman, Beverly. **Georgia O'Keeffe: The "Wideness and Wonder" of Her World.** Atheneum, 1986. 117 p. ISBN 0-689-31164-8.

Georgia O'Keeffe was born in the 1880s and became a painter at a time when women only taught art, while men became the artists. She grew up in Wisconsin and Virginia and painted in New York, Texas, and New Mexico. O'Keeffe is most well known for her desert landscapes and close-up paintings of flowers and bones. She was independent at a time when it was unusual for women to be in control of their lives. This biography looks at her life and her painting.

Hacker, Jeffrey H. **Carl Sandburg.** Franklin Watts/Impact Biographies, 1984. 121 p. ISBN 0-531-04762-8.

If you want to see the life of a poet, journalist, biographer, novelist, children's writer, and folklorist unfold before your eyes as you read, this is the book for you. The author has imaginatively and sensitively put together the essentials of Sandburg's life and career with many quotations from his works and some well-chosen photographs. (Literary merit)

Kresh, Paul. **Isaac Bashevis Singer: The Story of a Storyteller.** Illustrated by Penrod Scofield. E. P. Dutton/Lodestar Books, 1984. 135 p. ISBN 0-525-67156-0.

Isaac Bashevis Singer, born in Poland in 1904, grew up with a strong love for reading, including those nonreligious books that his father, a rabbi, found objectionable. Singer arrived in the United States in 1935 and wrote essays, reviews, and stories for a Jewish magazine, *Forward.* He was forty-six before he began to receive recognition for his novels and short stories, and in 1978, at age seventy-four, he won the Nobel Prize for literature. Part of the Jewish Biography series.

Lewis, C. S. (edited and compiled by Lyle W. Dorsett and Marjorie Lamp Mead). **Letters to Children.** Macmillan, 1985. 120 p. ISBN 0-02-570830-9.

Here are actual letters written to children by English writer C. S. Lewis, the author of *The Chronicles of Narnia.* Whether he is advising his goddaughter concerning her First Communion and Confirmation or simply acknowledging receipt of original artwork depicting his unforgettable characters, Lewis's words are direct, encouraging, and expressed on a level that young readers can appreciate. (Literary merit)

Mebane, Mary E. **Mary.** Fawcett Juniper Books, 1982. 253 p. ISBN 0-449-70025-9.

Mary E. Mebane, writer and university professor, describes her experiences growing up black and poor in Durham County, North Carolina. Her story covers the time from her early childhood until her graduation from the North Carolina College at Durham in 1954. Mebane had a strong drive to succeed and improve herself despite little encouragement from her family, friends, and teachers. (Literary merit)

Meltzer, Milton. **Dorothea Lange: Life through the Camera.** Illustrated by Donna Diamond; photographs by Dorothea Lange. Viking Penguin/Viking Kestrel, 1985. 57 p. ISBN 0-670-28047-X.

This biography concentrates on the 1930s, when American photographer Dorothea Lange provided a visible record of the effects of the Great Depression. Her simple, direct photographs captured the plight of migrant workers and rural Americans and helped bring about important social reforms. Part of the Women of Our Time series.

St. George, Judith. **The Mount Rushmore Story.** G. P. Putnam's Sons, 1985. 125 p. ISBN 0-399-21117-9.

Before the faces emerged, Mount Rushmore was simply part of the Black Hills of South Dakota. But to Gutzon Borglum, it was the face of a mountain that would show his love for America by giving birth to the faces of four presidents — George Washington, Thomas Jefferson, Abraham Lincoln, and Theodore Roosevelt. From the planning stages, through the fourteen years of carving, to the completion of the monument in 1941, Borglum's exciting adventure is a fast-reading story.

Sendak, Philip (translated and adapted by Seymour Barofsky). **In Grandpa's House.** Illustrated by Maurice Sendak. Harper and Row, 1985. 40 p. ISBN 0-06-025462-9.

Philip Sendak shares with readers the story of his own life — his boyhood in a Polish-Jewish *shtetl* in Poland and his leaving home to come to America, where he met his future wife and raised a family. Then the elder Sendak relates a children's story he heard, he says, from his own father.

Athletes

Allen, Maury. **Jackie Robinson: A Life Remembered.** Franklin Watts, 1987. 260 p. ISBN 0-531-15042-9.

The year 1947 brought about a change in the all-white game of baseball. The man responsible for this change is highlighted in this book. Jackie Robinson stood up to hatred and bigotry. He never lost his composure, even though he was taunted and degraded. As a result, Robinson opened the way for blacks and other minorities to participate in baseball.

Devaney, John. **Where Are They Today? Great Sports Stars of Yesteryear.** Crown, 1985. 217 p. ISBN 0-517-55344-9 (0-517-55345-7, paperback).

This book focuses on fifty-two famous figures from the world of sports during the 1950s and 1960s. The four-page biographies tell about the athletes' careers, their peak performances, and their lives today. Each piece has a "then and now" photograph. The majority of the featured athletes were active in football, baseball, and basketball, but athletes in a few additional sports are also included.

Foyt, A. J. (with William Neely). **A. J.** Warner Books, 1984. 249 p. ISBN 0-446-32418-3.

Race-car driver A. J. Foyt begins his life story with his learning to drive at the age of five, when he won his first race. He closes the biography with the accounts of his recent wins in the 1980s. Foyt traces his early successes to his upbringing by his father, a mechanic, to his natural ability to drive race cars, and to his fierce competitiveness. The picture Foyt gives of himself appears honest and complete.

Frommer, Harvey. **Baseball's Greatest Managers.** Franklin Watts, 1985. 280 p. ISBN 0-531-09779-X.

Throughout the more than one hundred years that baseball has been our national pastime, all types of individuals have been managers of baseball teams. This collection of twenty-one biographies offers a rare inside look at some of the greatest baseball pilots of all time. You will meet such greats as Walter Alston, Leo Durocher, Whitey Herzog, and Dick Williams.

Knudson, R. R. **Babe Didrikson: Athlete of the Century.** Illustrated by Ted Lewin. Viking Penguin/Viking Kestrel, 1985. 57 p. ISBN 0-670-80550-5.

Mildred Didrikson was so small as a child that everyone called her "Babe." But by the sixth grade, she excelled in almost every sport — basketball, tennis, golf, running, jumping, swimming, bowling. Later Didrikson won three medals in the 1932 Olympics and won the Women's U.S. Open golf championship in 1954, just one year after a cancer operation and two years before her death at age forty-three. This biography focuses on Didrikson's early years, at a time when there were few opportunities for female athletes. Part of the Women of Our Time series.

Lee, Bill (with Dick Lally). **The Wrong Stuff.** Viking Penguin/Penguin Books, 1985. 242 p. ISBN 0-14-007941-6.

What do major league pitchers do all day? According to Bill Lee, who played baseball from 1964 to 1979, mostly with the Red Sox, many pitchers enjoy their work, play hard, put up with criticism from the management, and relax by drinking and partying. Lee's book gives an inside picture of the pleasures and difficulties of playing in the major leagues.

Navratilova, Martina (with Mary Carillo). **Tennis My Way.** Photographs by Kimberly Butler. Penguin Books, 1984. 215 p. ISBN 0-14-007183-0.

The basic techniques of playing tennis are explained by the number-one female tennis player, Martina Navratilova. The introduction gives the reader an overview of Martina and her accomplishments. She feels that nutrition and proper conditioning play a big role in developing a successful tennis style, as do mental concentration and attitude.

Silverstein, Herma. **Mary Lou Retton and the New Gymnasts.** Franklin Watts, 1985. 83 p. ISBN 0-531-10053-7.

Mary Lou Retton's dedication, power, self-confidence, flexibility, and desire to win have earned her a place in gymnastic history and a gold medal at the 1984 Olympics. Her accomplishments, along with those of other gymnasts from around the world, are retold in this book. Concluding the book is a description of how to begin gymnastic training and the levels of competition required to reach Olympic status.

Entertainers

Bain, Geri, and Michael Leather. **The Picture Life of Bruce Springsteen.** Franklin Watts, 1986. 47 p. ISBN 0-531-10204-1.

This book describes the life of one of the most popular rock stars of our times, Bruce Springsteen. Photographs of his home and school depict the type of life Bruce had growing up in Freehold, New Jersey. His struggle to stardom was a hard one, but this book describes Bruce as a caring individual who finally made it to the top.

Fornatale, Pete. **The Story of Rock 'n' Roll.** William Morrow, 1987. 210 p. ISBN 0-688-06276-8 (0-688-06277-6, paperback).

Take a look beyond MTV, back to the 1950s to see how rock 'n' roll began, with legends like Chuck Berry and Elvis Presley. Then read on to learn about the exciting scene in the 1960s — Bob Dylan and the roots of folk rock, the British invasion, and the psychedelic sound of Jimi Hendrix and the Doors. Heavy metal, punk, New Wave, the "Boss," and, yes, MTV are all here, too, with over fifty photographs to introduce you to the social trends and artists that helped shape rock as you know it today.

Fulpen, H. V. **The Beatles: An Illustrated Diary.** Putnam/Perigee Books, 1985. 175 p. ISBN 0-399-51123-7.

Follow the Beatles day-by-day throughout their entire career — from their first performances in the late 1950s to their disbanding in 1970. This book documents important events in the lives of George Harrison, John Lennon, Paul McCartney, and Ringo Starr, the recording dates of individual songs, and many facts that will interest any Beatle fan. Besides a daily diary for each year, the book includes many articles on the Beatles and hundreds of photographs.

Haskins, James. **Diana Ross: Star Supreme.** Illustrated by Jim Spence. Viking Penguin/Viking Kestrel, 1985. 56 p. ISBN 0-670-80549-1.

As a tomboy growing up in a poor neighborhood in Detroit, Diana Ross often got into fights with kids twice her age who were picking on her little brothers and sisters. This same fighting spirit helped Diana become a world-famous star, first singing with some high school friends, the Supremes, and then performing as a solo artist and actress.

Love, Robert. **Elvis Presley.** Franklin Watts/Impact Biographies, 1986. 126 p. ISBN 0-531-10239-4.

This book tells of Elvis Presley's life, from his childhood in a ramshackle house in East Tupelo, Mississippi, in the 1930s, to his death at Graceland in Memphis in 1977. The gospel music he heard in church as a young boy influenced his mature musical style. Another strong influence was the rhythm and blues broadcast over Memphis's black radio station. Presley's mother bought him his first guitar when he was eleven, and by the time he made his first recording in 1954, he had fused many distinctive styles.

Saunders, Susan. **Dolly Parton: Country Goin' to Town.** Illustrated by Rodney Pate. Viking Penguin/Viking Kestrel, 1985. 56 p. ISBN 0-670-80787-7.

Dolly Parton, the famous country singer, songwriter, actress, and TV star, was born in a log cabin in the backwoods of Tennessee. There she wrote songs using a homemade guitar and put on "lipstick" with a red crayon to perform up in a tree, pretending it was a stage. Dolly's career, from the Smoky Mountains to the Grand Ole Opry to Hollywood, is recounted in this book.

Tompert, Ann. **The Greatest Showman on Earth: A Biography of P. T. Barnum.** Dillon Press/People in Focus Books, 1987. 120 p. ISBN 0-87518-370-0.

P. T. Barnum is best known for organizing his famous circus, "The Greatest Show on Earth," in 1871. Ten years later he merged his show with a competitor's to form the Barnum and Bailey Circus, which continued for a generation after his death in 1891. Earlier in his life Barnum started his American Museum, which featured such acts as a flea circus, the tiny General Tom Thumb, and Jumbo, the world's largest elephant. He also served in the Connecticut legislature and was the mayor of Bridgeport. In his lifetime, Barnum made, lost, and remade several fortunes.

Wootton, Richard. **Elvis!** Random House, 1985. 122 p. ISBN 0-394-87046-8 (0-394-97046-2, library binding).

Elvis Presley changed popular music when he started performing in the mid-1950s, and rock 'n' roll has never been the same. He was twenty years old when he first achieved success, and the next twenty years brought both ups and downs to his career and his life. Presley died an early death at age forty-two in 1977, but musical historians still refer to him as the "King of Rock 'n' Roll."

Wootton, Richard. **John Lennon.** Random House, 1985. 126 p. ISBN 0-394-87047-6 (0-394-97047-0, library binding).

Here is the story of John Lennon's life, from his childhood in England to his tragic death in New York City at the age of forty in 1980. This biography describes Lennon's schooling and adolescence, the formation and astonishing success of the Beatles, and the group's eventual breakup in 1970. Above all, the book shows Lennon as a musical artist.

World Figures

Aaseng, Nathan. **More with Less: The Future World of Buckminster Fuller.** Lerner Publications, 1986. 80 p. ISBN 0-8225-0498-7.

An imaginative and visionary architect and inventor, Buckminster Fuller is best known for his geodesic dome. Although many discount him as a "lunatic," he posed and answered many questions about where society and technology are taking us, and he used the principles of nature in his designs.

Adler, David A. **Our Golda: The Story of Golda Meir.** Illustrated by Donna Ruff. Viking Press, 1984. 52 p. ISBN 0-670-53107-3.

Golda Mabovitch was born in Russia in 1898, where life was hard for her family under the czar's rule. Her father immigrated to America, and when Meir was eight, she, her mother, and her two sisters joined him in Milwaukee, Wisconsin. Meir was only eleven when she made her first speech on behalf of poor children in Milwaukee. Later she and her husband, Morris, helped build the beginning Jewish homeland in Palestine. As time went on, Golda Meir became a world leader and prime minister of her new country, Israel.

Ansell, Rod, and Rachel Percy. **To Fight the Wild.** Harcourt Brace Jovanovich, 1986. 151 p. ISBN 0-15-289068-8.

A modern-day Robinson Crusoe, Rod Ansell survived for two months in the Australian wilderness. Ansell describes the accident that left him stranded in the wilderness, his establishment of a base camp, how he adapted to the solitude and loneliness, and his eventual rescue.

Atkinson, Linda. **In Kindling Flame: The Story of Hannah Senesh, 1921–1944.** Lothrop, Lee and Shepard Books, 1985. 214 p. ISBN 0-688-02714-8.

Daughter of a famous playwright, Hannah Senesh was destined to lead a life of ease in Hungary. But World War II came, and Hannah's plans to be a writer were changed. Instead, she immigrated to Palestine, worked in a kibbutz, and finally became the only female in a secret resistance movement. Her work allowed her to "light the way for humankind." (Literary merit)

Cheney, Glenn Alan. **Mohandas Gandhi.** Franklin Watts/Impact Biographies, 1983. 114 p. ISBN 0-531-04600-1.

When he died in 1948, Mohandas Gandhi left the world a legacy of nonviolent resistance against social injustice, which has inspired such great leaders as Martin Luther King, Jr. This book traces Gandhi's life and times, including his extensive work in South Africa and his native India to achieve equality of all races and religions. Discover Gandhi's "truth" and his lifelong struggle against injustice in the world.

Cohen, Daniel. **Henry Stanley and the Quest for the Source of the Nile.** M. Evans, 1985. 170 p. ISBN 0-87131-445-2.

John Rowlands was born in Wales in 1841 and spent a terrible childhood in a workhouse. He ran away when he was fifteen and eventually arrived in New Orleans in 1857. There he met Henry Stanley, who adopted him and renamed him with his own name,

Henry Stanley. After he won some journalistic fame, the New York *Herald* gave financial backing for Stanley's successful expedition into Africa to find the missionary Dr. Livingstone. Stanley made two more expeditions into Africa and located the source of the Nile River.

Conner, Edwina. **Marie Curie.** Illustrated by Richard Hook. Bookwright Press, 1987. 32 p. ISBN 0-531-18134-0.

This short biography describes the major happenings in the life of scientist Marie Curie. She was born in Warsaw, Poland, in 1867 and studied and worked as a chemist and physicist in Paris. She is best known for her discovery of the radioactive elements polonium and radium. Curie received the Nobel Prize for physics in 1903 and a second Nobel Prize for chemistry in 1911. Part of the Great Lives series.

Cowen, Ida, and Irene Gunther. **A Spy for Freedom: The Story of Sarah Aaronsohn.** E. P. Dutton/Lodestar Books, 1984. 158 p. ISBN 0-525-67150-1.

This well-written, fast-paced book describes the life of Sarah Aaronsohn, who became the Jewish leader of a secret spy organization called the NILI. During World War I the organization's goal was to help free the Jews of Palestine from the oppression of Turkish rule by giving and receiving information from the British Intelligence. Part of the Jewish Biography series.

Cremaschi, Gabriella (translated by Stephen Thorne). **Albert Schweitzer.** Silver Burdett, 1985. 62 p. ISBN 0-382-06986-2 (0-382-06856-4, library binding).

Albert Schweitzer, born in Germany in 1875, became a missionary doctor in the African country of Gabon. He also achieved fame for being a clergyman, philosopher, and music scholar. This book gives a detailed account of his life and his accomplishments. Part of the Why They Became Famous series.

Currimbhoy, Nayana. **Indira Gandhi.** Franklin Watts/Impact Biographies, 1985. 116 p. ISBN 0-531-10064-2.

Indira Gandhi attended her first political meeting in 1920, when she was three years old, and from then on she was fascinated by the Indian government. Her father, the first prime minister of independent India, made Indira his hostess and counted on her advice. Two years after his death, Indira began her twenty-year reign over this land of 700 million people. This book describes Indira's life and her reign as prime minister.

Faber, Doris. **Margaret Thatcher: Britain's "Iron Lady."** Illustrated by Robert Masheris. Viking Penguin/Viking Kestrel, 1985. 57 p. ISBN 0-670-80785-0.

As a grocer's daughter in a small English town, Margaret Thatcher had to overcome her working-class social standing to become one of today's most powerful politicians. She is the only woman who has ever headed a major European country. This biography details her landslide victory in 1979 as prime minister of Great Britain, her courageous brush with a terrorist's bomb, and her firm control in guiding her country through social, economic, and political strife.

Feinberg, Barbara Silberdick. **Marx and Marxism.** Franklin Watts/Impact Books, 1985. 122 p. ISBN 0-531-10065-0.

Who was this man Karl Marx, one of the most important figures in the development of communism? Where did he come from? What did he think, speak, and write about? How did he influence modern communism and socialism? All these questions and many more are answered in this book that deals with nineteenth-century philosopher Karl Marx, and his political, economic, and social theories.

Fradin, Dennis Brindell. **Remarkable Children: Twenty Who Made History.** Little, Brown, 1987. 207 p. ISBN 0-316-29126-9.

This book presents brief biographies of twenty children from different places and different times. All gained fame in childhood for their unusual talents and remarkable achievements. Included are Wolfgang Amadeus Mozart, John Quincy Adams, Sacagawea, Louis Braille, Helen Keller, Pablo Picasso, Judy Garland, Shirley Temple, Anne Frank, Nadia Comaneci, and Tracy Austin.

Hoobler, Dorothy, and Thomas Hoobler. **Nelson and Winnie Mandela.** Franklin Watts/Impact Biographies, 1987. 128 p. ISBN 0-531-10332-3.

Nelson and Winnie Mandela are a powerful force against apartheid, South Africa's policy of strict racial segregation and discrimination. Nelson, the imprisoned leader of the African National Congress, and Winnie, a political activist in the struggle for black majority rights, remain united in their fight for equality, despite being separated since 1962.

Hunter, Nigel. **Karl Marx.** Illustrated by Chris Higham. Bookwright Press, 1987. 32 p. ISBN 0-531-1833-2.

Karl Marx remains one of the world's most important political theorists. His own personal life was a struggle, but his main concern was the struggle of humankind to free itself from the bonds of misery and oppression. The economic, political, and social theories of this nineteenth-century philosopher remain popular today, and the nations of the world can be classified as either Marxist or anti-Marxist. Part of the Great Lives series.

Keller, Mollie. **Golda Meir.** Franklin Watts/Impact Biographies, 1983. 113 p. ISBN 0-531-04591-9.

When Golda Meir left Russia at the age of seven, she had no idea that she was on the first step toward eventual immigration to and formation of the state of Israel. This book traces the history of Zionism and the political career of this woman who became prime minister of Israel at age seventy.

Keller, Mollie. **Winston Churchill.** Franklin Watts/Impact Biographies, 1984. 120 p. ISBN 0-531-04752-0.

Follow Winston Churchill as he grows up isolated in an aristocratic family during the late 1800s, goes to various private schools, becomes a soldier for his country, pursues a political career as a young man, guides England through World War I and II, and becomes one of the most important "Elder Statesmen" of all time. This book details the role Winston Churchill played in shaping the history of our modern world.

Leitner, Isabella (with Irving A. Leitner). **Saving the Fragments: From Auschwitz to New York.** New American Library/Plume Books, 1986. 131 p. ISBN 0-453-00502-0 (0-452-25868, paperback).

This sequel to *Fragments of Isabella* chronicles the life of Isabella Leitner after the Nazi prison camp Auschwitz is liberated by the Russians. She is eventually reunited with her father, but she finds that this reunion causes more problems since her father cannot understand why she has lost her faith.

Marrin, Albert. **Hitler.** Viking Penguin/Viking Kestrel, 1987. 249 p. ISBN 0-670-81546-2.

Adolf Hitler rose from a penniless tramp to the most powerful man in modern history. He reshaped the mind of the German nation, built an unstoppable army, and committed murder on an unimaginable scale. This book discusses Hitler's childhood with his tyrannical father, his experiences in World War I, his rise to power in the Nazi party, and his leadership of Germany.

Neimark, Anne E. **One Man's Valor: Leo Baeck and the Holocaust.** E. P. Dutton/Lodestar Books, 1986. 113 p. ISBN 0-525-67175-7.

Leo Baeck was a world-renowned rabbi and scholar. His determination and intelligence helped thousands flee Nazi Germany, but he chose to stay "to watch out for those who haven't yet gone." Baeck's strength served as a symbol of hope to others imprisoned with him in Theresienstadt.

Shiels, Barbara. **Winners: Women and the Nobel Prize.** Dillon Press, 1985. 221 p. ISBN 0-87518-293-3.

This book focuses on eight women who have won the Nobel Prize in the fields of literature, peace, physics, chemistry, and physiology/medicine since 1938. An introduction tells the reader about Alfred Nobel and the establishment of the Nobel Prizes. Included are appendixes listing all the women who have won Nobel Prizes, a bibliography, and a suggested reading list.

Siegal, Aranka. **Grace in the Wilderness: After the Liberation, 1945–1948.** Farrar, Straus and Giroux, 1985. 220 p. ISBN 0-374-32760-2.

It's terrible to be homesick, and fifteen-year-old Piri Davidowitz was. She and her sister, Iboya, survived the concentration camp at Bergen-Belsen, but instead of being allowed to return home to Hungary after the end of World War II, the Red Cross sent the girls to Sweden. Here an older couple became Piri's foster parents and provided stability and love. This biography is the sequel to *Upon the Head of the Goat,* which describes Piri's childhood in Hungary and provides another haunting recollection of the Holocaust.

Topalian, Elyse. V. **I. Lenin.** Franklin Watts/Impact Biographies, 1983. 115 p. ISBN 0-531-04589-7.

This biography traces Vladimir Lenin's youth and development as a revolutionary leader and focuses on his role in the revolutionary movement in Russia between 1900 and 1917. When the czar's government was overturned, Lenin became the first head of the new Soviet state.

Turner, Dorothy. **Queen Elizabeth I.** Illustrated by Martin Salisbury. Bookwright Press, 1987. 32 p. ISBN 0-531-18132-4.

This brief biography relates the major happenings in the life of Queen Elizabeth I, who ruled England from 1558 to 1603. This was an eventful period in English history: William Shakespeare was writing and producing his plays, Sir Francis Drake sailed around the world, England became a major European power, and English colonization began. Throughout this era, Elizabeth commanded respect and allegiance from the English people. Part of the Great Lives series.

Weidhorn, Manfred. **Napoleon.** Atheneum, 1986. 212 p. ISBN 0-689-31163-X.

This biography recounts the life of Napoleon Bonaparte, a man familiar for his poses. It shows how the liberal, revolutionary stances of Napoleon's early career in the military became rigid after he crowned himself Emperor of the French and lost touch with the people in his struggle to maintain power. In the early 1800s Napoleon's empire covered most of western and central Europe, and his mark on Europe's geography and laws is still felt today throughout the Western world.

Weinstein, Frida Scheps (translated by Barbara Loeb Kennedy). **A Hidden Childhood, 1942–1945.** Hill and Wang, 1985. 151 p. ISBN 0-8090-5444-2.

With her doll tied securely in a shoebox, some black-market food, and her meager possessions, a young French-Jewish girl was sent to a convent school to avoid being captured by the Germans in 1942. Here Frida became a willing pupil, fascinated by the rituals and mysteries of Catholicism. Frida was spared from persecution during the Holocaust, but as time passed, she realized that she was now totally without family. Her father had fled to Jerusalem, and she feared that her mother had been taken to a concentration camp. What would happen to her when the war ended? This memoir is told in young Frida's words.

Computers and Robotics

Asimov, Isaac, and Karen A. Frenkel. **Robots: Machines in Man's Image.** Harmony Books, 1985. 229 p. ISBN 0-517-55110-1.

A robot is a machine and a computer combined into a piece of equipment that can follow directions and do work. This book gives a historical overview of the myths and reality of robots, and it describes how robots are being used in industry and the inner workings of robots. Research and development as well as the future of robotics are explored, and the book includes photographs, diagrams, a glossary, and addresses of manufacturers and trade associations.

Baldwin, Margaret, and Gary Pack. **Computer Graphics.** Illustrated by Jerry Gregory. Franklin Watts/First Books, 1984. 88 p. ISBN 0-531-04704-0.

Today's new art form is controversial. It is computer art. Some people say it's not an art form because the "art" is produced by a machine, while others believe that the machine is nothing more than a tool in the hand of the artist — just like a paintbrush. Read this book and decide for yourself — and see how computer graphics are used in engineering, business, science, video games, and the home. Part of the Computer-Awareness series.

Baldwin, Margaret, and Gary Pack. **Robots and Robotics.** Illustrated by Jerry Gregory. Franklin Watts/First Books, 1984. 61 p. ISBN 0-531-04705-9.

Robots have clanked their way through human dreams for centuries. Now, they and androids really exist. This book explains what robots are and describes their activities in industry, outer space, and the home. Part of the Computer-Awareness series.

Berger, Melvin. **Data Processing.** Franklin Watts/First Books, 1983. 66 p. ISBN 0-531-04640-0.

This book defines data processing and describes the functions of computer input and output, processing, storage, and programming. The computer has already revolutionized the way facts are gathered and turned into useful information. We are now able to process large quantities of data at speeds that were impossible before the introduction of computer data processing. Part of the Computer-Awareness series.

Berger, Melvin. **Word Processing.** Franklin Watts/First Books, 1984. 66 p. ISBN 0-531-04729-6.

Word processing is a special way of writing that uses a computer to put any text into printed form. With a word processor, you can compose the text, make changes and corrections, and produce any number of identical or similar copies. It is faster, easier, and neater than using a typewriter and can be used to produce letters, articles, reports, memos, books, and other documents. Find out more about using a word processor. Part of the Computer-Awareness series.

Bolognese, Don, and Robert Thornton. **Drawing and Painting with the Computer.** Franklin Watts/How-to-Draw Books, 1983. 71 p. ISBN 0-531-03593-X (0-531-04653-2, library binding).

From the beginning of time, art has been a powerful form of expression. The artist's tools and materials become an important part of each historical age. Today, artists seeking new ways to express their impressions of our civilization have looked for new tools. In our electronic world, one new tool is the computer. Welcome to the world of the paint machines.

Carter, Alden R., and Wayne J. LeBlanc. **Supercomputers.** Franklin Watts/Impact Books, 1985. 114 p. ISBN 0-531-04931-0.

While not for beginners, this book provides a good overview of how a computer works and what different systems are involved: hardware, system and programming languages, and applications. The book also describes the race among nations in developing new computers able to manage large amounts of information in ways that will help people make better and faster decisions. Supercomputers will change our life in many ways that sound almost like science fiction.

Cattoche, Robert J. **Computers for the Disabled.** Franklin Watts/First Books, 1986. 96 p. ISBN 0-531-10212-2.

The computer can be thought of as an extension of the human mind. It can sort, compare, and remember data. It can also be thought of as an extension of the human body for those people unable to control their fingers. About ten million people have disabilities that affect movement. Many of these people have now found hope and independence through the use of computers. Part of the Computer-Awareness series.

Chester, Michael. **Robots: Facts behind the Fiction.** Macmillan, 1983. 90 p. ISBN 0-02-718220-7.

What do Shakey, Timel, Elmer, Elsie, MiniMover 5, TeachMover, The Robot Adversary, Boris Handroid, RhinoCharger, Motionmate, Unimate, PUMA, Robart, Avatar, Quester, R2-D2, Topo, BOB, Hero 1, and Ahmad have in common? They all are working robots. This interesting, informative book gives a detailed description of the history, design, and function of computers and robots, especially those built by amateur hobbyists.

Cooper, Carolyn E. **Creative Computer-Video.** Franklin Watts/First Books, 1985. 59 p. ISBN 0-531-10037-5.

This book explores the possibilities presented by merging computers and video and describes the uses of this combination in education, business, television, and the art world. Included are a glossary and suggestions for computer-video projects. Part of the Computer-Awareness series.

Cooper, Carolyn E. **Electronic Bulletin Boards.** Franklin Watts/First Books, 1985. 66 p. ISBN 0-531-04907-8.

We've all seen or used bulletin boards in our classrooms, supermarkets, or laundromats. It is a convenient way of communicating with many people. Now the invention and popularity of the personal computer have led to a new type of bulletin board. This book describes the functions and operation of computer bulletin boards and the equipment needed. Part of the Computer-Awareness series.

Darling, David J. **Fast, Faster, Fastest: The Story of Supercomputers.** Illustrated by Tom Lund. Dillon Press, 1986. 73 p. ISBN 0-87518-316-6.

Here is a look at present and future uses of supercomputers — the most powerful computers designed. Some of these unbelievable machines can perform more than 500 million calculations per second. Other volumes in the World of Computers series look at the invention of the microchip, computer hardware and software, home computers, and robots.

D'Ignazio, Fred, and Allen L. Wold. **The Science of Artificial Intelligence.** Franklin Watts/First Books, 1984. 87 p. ISBN 0-531-04703-2.

The science of artificial intelligence is barely thirty years old. Artificial intelligence enables a machine to act like a living creature or to do something that would be considered intelligent if a person did it. But the machine can only do what it is told to do. This book explains how artificial intelligence is being used in computer technology and robotics. Part of the Computer-Awareness series.

Elliott, Sharon. **Computers in Action.** Illustrated by David Anstey. Bookwright Press, 1985. 32 p. ISBN 0-531-03829-7.

Computers have become part of everyday life. This brief book explains how computers are being used in the home, in hospitals, in the workplace, and in space. A glossary of terms is included. Part of the Discovering Computers series.

Elliott, Sharon. **The Micro.** Illustrated by David Anstey. Bookwright Press, 1985. 32 p. ISBN 0-531-03827-0.

You know using computers is fun. You can make pictures and music, play games, do calculations, and perform many other tasks. Here you will find out what a microcomputer is, how it works, and what you can make it do. A glossary of terms is included. Part of the Discovering Computers series.

Elliott, Sharon. **What Are Computers?** Illustrated by David Anstey. Bookwright Press, 1985. 32 p. ISBN 0-531-03828-9.

This book describes the different sizes and capabilities of computers, how they work, and what they can be made to do. A glossary of terms is included. Part of the Discovering Computers series.

Francis, Dorothy B. **Computer Crime.** E. P. Dutton/Lodestar Books, 1987. 104 p. ISBN 0-525-67192-7.

Even though many computer criminals are teenage hackers who have never been in trouble before, computer crime is a criminal activity. Computer hackers may be unaware of the damage that can occur when they dial a number at random and enter the data bank of a hospital, school, or bank — the cost of such crimes adds up to millions of dollars each year. This book looks at various types of computer crimes and discusses possible security measures.

Graham, Ian. **Computer: The Inside Story.** Illustrated by Denis Bishop, Chris Forsey, Jim Robins, and Hayward Art Group. Gloucester Press, 1983. 37 p. ISBN 0-531-03462-3.

CRTs, CPUs, RAMs, bits, and bytes are just a few of the computer terms that you will become familiar with in this beginning book of computers. Computer vocabulary, the basic structure and method of operation of computers, the computer revolution, and the importance of computers in our futures are explained in easy-to-understand language.

Greene, Laura. **Computer Pioneers.** Franklin Watts/First Books, 1985. 86 p. ISBN 0-531-04906-X.

This book contains biographies of the men and women who contributed to the evolution of computers and the electronic age, from the seventeenth century to the present. In the early years, people didn't see a need for speedy computing; the old method worked just fine and was cheap. Not until World War II did people begin to recognize the need for speed. Part of the Computer-Awareness series.

Hawkes, Nigel. **Computers: How They Work.** Illustrated by Paul Cooper, Elsa Godfrey, and Rob Shone. Franklin Watts, 1983. 29 p. ISBN 0-531-04679-6.

Computers are electronic machines that handle information. The information can be in the form of facts, figures, words, pictures, or even music. This information, however, is dependent on what we ask the computer to do. This book explains the many things that computers can be asked to do and what the results will be. A glossary of terms and index are included. Part of the Electronic Revolution series.

Hawkes, Nigel. **Computers in Action.** Illustrated by Paul Cooper, Elsa Godfrey, Nick May, and Rob Shone. Franklin Watts, 1983. 29 p. ISBN 0-531-04723-7.

Computer technology is improving all the time, and the impact of computers in everyday life is sure to grow in the future. This book explains the need for keeping track of information so it can be available wherever and whenever we need it. Part of the Electronic Revolution series.

Hawkes, Nigel. **Computers in the Home.** Illustrated by Steve Braund. Franklin Watts, 1984. 29 p. ISBN 0-531-04725-3.

Here is a look at the basic components of a home computer system. The book presents information about electronic games and computerized appliances and provides a look at what computers might do in the future. Part of the Electronic Revolution series.

Hawkes, Nigel. **Robots and Computers.** Illustrated by Steve Braund. Franklin Watts, 1984. 29 p. ISBN 0-531-04816-0.

This book explores the new role of robots in today's world and explains how robots are controlled by computers. Directions are provided for programming robots, and the book gives examples of how robots are used in transportation, industry, and space. A glossary of terms is provided. Part of the Electronic Revolution series.

Herda, D. J. **Computer Maintenance.** Illustrated by Anne Canevari Green. Franklin Watts/First Books, 1985. 66 p. ISBN 0-531-04905-1.

This book describes how a microcomputer works and how to care for it. The author gives helpful suggestions on how to fix a variety of computer problems. Nothing lasts forever; but with a little care and preventive maintenance, your micro can be around and functioning for a long time. Part of the Computer-Awareness series.

Herda, D. J. **Computer Peripherals.** Franklin Watts/First Books, 1985. 68 p. ISBN 0-531-10036-7.

The most useful and most widely available computer peripherals are described in this book. Topics discussed include keyboards and monitors, printers, storage systems, and modems. A glossary of terms is included. Part of the Computer-Awareness series.

Herda, D. J. **Microcomputers.** Franklin Watts/First Books, 1984. 86 p. ISBN 0-531-04730-X.

Computers today are often hidden inside telephones, typewriters, cameras, watches, and even toys and games. They are at work in hospitals, schools, factories, and our homes. This book provides background information about microcomputers and also includes lists of manufacturers' addresses, magazines, and catalogs. Part of the Computer-Awareness series.

Hintz, Sandy, and Martin Hintz. **Computers in Our World, Today and Tomorrow.** Franklin Watts/First Books, 1983. 89 p. ISBN 0-531-04639-7.

The world of the future will be shaped by young thinkers like you. With the help of computers, we can go beyond our wildest dreams. This book looks into the roles of computers in medicine, business, law enforcement, science, entertainment, education, and the home. Part of the Computer-Awareness series.

Irvine, Mat. **Satellites and Computers.** Franklin Watts, 1984. 29 p. ISBN 0-531-04817-9.

What satellites look like, how they get into orbit, and how they are used are described in this book. Photographs, diagrams, and a glossary of terms are provided. Part of the Electronic Revolution series.

Jackson, Peter. **The Chip.** Warwick Press, 1986. 37 p. ISBN 0-531-19006-4.

An encyclopedia approach to various questions concerning the computer chip is offered in this book: what a chip is, how it works, how it is used, types of chips, and its place in the future. Part of the Science in Action series.

Jespersen, James, and Jane Fitz-Randolph. **RAMs, ROMs, and Robots: The Inside Story of Computers.** Illustrated by Bruce Hiscock. Atheneum, 1984. 149 p. ISBN 0-689-31063-3.

This book deals with some of the misconceptions people have about computers by explaining how computers work, their strengths and limitations, their many uses, and their future capabilities.

Lampton, Christopher. **Advanced BASIC.** Franklin Watts/Computer Literacy Skills Books, 1984. 113 p. ISBN 0-531-04848-9.

This book is for the reader who already has an understanding of BASIC but who would like to write more sophisticated programs. By the end of the book, the reader will be able to write a word processing program, a mailing list, and games.

Lampton, Christopher. **Assembly-Language Programming for Radio Shack, Timex Sinclair, Adam, and CP/M Computers.** Franklin Watts/Computer Literacy Skills Books, 1985. 128 p. ISBN 0-531-04924-8.

This book is written for the person who wants to go beyond the restrictions of BASIC computer language and even beyond the higher languages of PASCAL and LOGO. It is for the person who finds these languages frustrating and slow. Assembly-language (or machine-language) programming is the only language that the computer actually understands. It is the language built into the computer's microprocessor chip. Learning this language will also teach more about the inner workings of the computer.

Lampton, Christopher. **BASIC for Beginners.** Franklin Watts/Computer Literacy Skills Books, 1984. 99 p. ISBN 0-531-04745-8.

This book introduces the language of BASIC and how it is used in programming a microcomputer. Included are programming projects to test your knowledge of BASIC and a list of vocabulary terms.

Lampton, Christopher. **COBOL for Beginners.** Franklin Watts/Computer Literacy Skills Books, 1984. 104 p. ISBN 0-531-04746-6.

COBOL is a high-level computer language invented for businesses. This book explains the basics of COBOL and how it aids in running a business operation.

Lampton, Christopher. **Computer Languages.** Franklin Watts/First Books, 1983. 84 p. ISBN 0-531-04638-9.

How do you talk to a computer? The spoken word doesn't work; so the written word must be used. English is too complicated; therefore, the computer's own language — numbers — is used. This book introduces computer programming languages, including FORTRAN, COBOL, BASIC, PASCAL, and LOGO. Part of the Computer-Awareness series.

Lampton, Christopher. **FORTH for Beginners.** Franklin Watts/Computer Literacy Skills Books, 1985. 101 p. ISBN 0-531-04849-7.

FORTH is a computer language that allows for very fast processing. It often takes the form of just one symbol. This book explains how to use FORTH and how to write programs of your own.

Lampton, Christopher. **FORTRAN for Beginners.** Franklin Watts/Computer Literacy Skills Books, 1984. 106 p. ISBN 0-531-04747-4.

FORTRAN, the first high-level computer language, is still used today by scientists, engineers, and mathematicians. This book presents the fundamentals of using FORTRAN, particularly for those students interested in technical disciplines.

Lampton, Christopher. **Graphics and Animation on the TRS-80: Models I, III, and 4.** Franklin Watts/Computer Literacy Skills Books, 1985. 100 p. ISBN 0-531-10143-6.

This book shows you how to create and animate computer graphics on the TRS-80. Several programs and activities are suggested that give the user a chance to experiment with nearly every technique presented. Some knowledge of BASIC language is needed, but you don't have to be an expert programmer.

Lampton, Christopher. **The Micro Dictionary.** Franklin Watts, 1984. 90 p. ISBN 0-531-04840-3.

Here is "computerese" at your fingertips. This simplified pronunciation key and collection of precise definitions will provide you with a handy reference source for all those questions that don't come programmed in your latest software purchase.

Lampton, Christopher. **PASCAL for Beginners.** Franklin Watts/Computer Literacy Skills Books, 1984. 106 p. ISBN 0-531-04748-2.

Even though there is a wide variety of software available, knowing a computer language is a desirable skill. This book suggests learning PASCAL because it is a powerful, structured language and because it encourages a straightforward, disciplined technique in programming.

Lampton, Christopher. **PILOT for Beginners.** Franklin Watts/Computer Literacy Skills Books, 1984. 88 p. ISBN 0-531-04850-0.

With this book you can turn the computer into a teaching machine. It explains the use of the language PILOT, which was first developed as a programming language for educators and which can create interactive tests and dialogues between the user and the machines.

Lampton, Christopher. **Programming in BASIC.** Franklin Watts/First Books, 1983. 66 p. ISBN 0-531-04644-3.

Computers are marvelous machines. They can guide spaceships, prepare grocery lists, help a writer type a novel, or take you on a make-believe trip to Mars. Best of all — a single computer can do all these things; you just have to tell it what you want it to do. The art of programming is what this book is about. It introduces the computer language BASIC, which was originally developed as a tool for teaching computer programming and which can be used for writing sophisticated programs. Part of the Computer-Awareness series.

Litterick, Ian. **Computers and You.** Bookwright Press, 1984. 47 p. ISBN 0-531-04777-6.

The effect of computers on our lives is the topic of this book. It describes some of their advantages and disadvantages and raises questions for the reader about dealing with the computer age. A glossary of terms and a resource list are included. Part of the Age of Computers series.

Litterick, Ian. **Computers in Everyday Life.** Bookwright Press, 1984. 47 p. ISBN 0-531-04776-8.

Computers are rapidly becoming a more and more important part of everyday life in many countries. This book discusses some of the changes taking place as computers become more sophisticated and more widespread. A glossary of terms and a resource list are included. Part of the Age of Computers series.

Litterick, Ian. **How Computers Work.** Bookwright Press, 1984. 47 p. ISBN 0-531-04778-4.

You do not need to know how a computer works to use one. But if you make the effort to understand what goes on inside computers, you will find them easier to use. This book tells you what the various parts of a computer system do, how they work, and how they are made. A glossary of terms and a resource list are included. Part of the Age of Computers series.

Litterick, Ian. **Programming Computers.** Illustrated by David Anstey. Bookwright Press, 1984. 47 p. ISBN 0-531-04774-1.

Computers can do nothing without programs. It is the programs that turn the pieces of silicon, plastic, and metal into data processing systems, video games, or whatever. This book is not a lesson in programming in any particular language or on any particular computer. It explains in general what programming is about, and shows how to tell a good program from a bad one. A glossary of terms and a resource list are included. Part of the Age of Computers series.

Litterick, Ian. **Robots and Intelligent Machines.** Illustrated by David Anstey. Bookwright Press, 1984. 47 p. ISBN 0-531-04773-3.

Will robots take over our work? Will homes have robot servants? Will machines take over our brain work? This book attempts to answer these questions and many more questions people have about robots. A glossary of terms and a resource list are included. Part of the Age of Computers series.

Litterick, Ian. **The Story of Computers.** Bookwright Press, 1984. 47 p. ISBN 0-531-04775-X.

It is only forty years since computers were first built. Their history is the story of people's search for better ways to write, count, and communicate. Computers now form an important part of our lives and affect all aspects of society. Their important and exciting story is told in this book. A glossary of terms and a resource list are included. Part of the Age of Computers series.

McKie, Robin. **Robots.** Illustrated by Hayward Art Group and Gerard Browne. Franklin Watts, 1986. 32 p. ISBN 0-531-10136-3.

Here is a fairly in-depth look at robots, including their construction, programming, and various uses in today's world. Informational charts, a glossary of terms, and an index are included. Part of the Modern Technology series.

McKie, Robin. **Technology.** Illustrated by Chris Forsey, the Maltings Partnership, and Jim Robins. Franklin Watts, 1984. 38 p. ISBN 0-531-04838-1.

This is part of an eight-book series that shows how the different sciences discover answers to many searching questions. Technology begins when engineers and scientists put scientific discoveries to a practical use. The scope of technology is vast, and this book looks only at the more important areas that affect our lives — including electricity, computers, space, manufacturing, and medicine. A glossary of terms is included. Part of the Science World series.

Markle, Sandra. **The Programmer's Guide to the Galaxy.** Illustrated by Stella Ormai. Lothrop, Lee and Shepard Books, 1984. 128 p. ISBN 0-688-01833-5 (0-688-03748-8, library binding).

Designed for the beginning or intermediate computer programmer, this book teaches the programming techniques of BASIC by having the reader follow a robot named PETR and the boy who owns him as they travel through the galaxy. Each planet presents a problem that the reader must solve. Sequel to Kids' Computer Capers.

Marsh, Peter. **Robots.** Warwick Press, 1983. 37 p. ISBN 0-531-09223-2.

Here is a comprehensive account of robots in fact and fiction and a look at their impact on our lives. It explains how robots work, how they can be equipped, and how they will be used in the future, here on Earth and in space. A glossary of terms is included. Part of the Science in Action series.

Megarry, Jacquetta. **Computer World.** Warwick Press/Gateway Fact Books, 1984. 93 p. ISBN 0-531-09228-3.

Is a computer intelligent? What is a microchip? What is a binary system? These and many other questions are answered in this book. Topics discussed in other volumes in the series include flowcharts, microprocessors, input devices, and uses of computers in the present and in the future. Color pictures, diagrams, programs, and descriptions of the most popular microcomputers on today's market show the impact of the computer revolution.

Perry, Robert L. **Computer Crime.** Franklin Watts/First Books, 1986. 65 p. ISBN 0-531-10113-4.

Legal and ethical problems can arise when using a computer, such as the piracy of hardware and software and the theft of information and electronic funds. This book describes computer crimes, how they are committed, and how other people are affected by these crimes. A glossary of terms and a bibliography are included. Part of the Computer-Awareness series.

Pizzey, Steve, and Sheila Snowden. **The Computerized Society.** Bookwright Press, 1986. 48 p. ISBN 0-531-18039-5.

Basic information about the computer is presented in this book. Topics include the computer revolution, what the computer can do, how computers are used in our society, and the growth of the computer industry. Part of the Tomorrow's World series.

Schneiderman, Ron. **Computers: From Babbage to the Fifth Generation.** Franklin Watts, 1986. 58 p. ISBN 0-531-10131-2.

This is a historical look at computers, ranging from the earliest calculating machines to current technology. Included in the discussion are the abacus, Napier's bones, Pascal's Arithmetic Machine, Charles Babbage's nineteenth-century mechanical calculating machine, and the founding of IBM. The book brings the story up-to-date with a look at first- through fifth-generation computers. Part of the History of Science series.

Silverstein, Alvin, and Virginia B. Silverstein. **The Robots Are Here.** Prentice-Hall, 1983. 128 p. ISBN 0-13-782185-9.

If you are interested in the history of robotics, this book is for you. It considers what robots are, what they do, and where this new technology is going. Other topics include robots in the workplace, medical robots, robots in space, robots in the house, building your own robot, and fun and games with robots.

Slater, Don. **Information Technology.** Illustrated by Rob Shone. Franklin Watts, 1986. 32 p. ISBN 0-531-10198-3.

This short book gives a detailed explanation of computers and computer parts. It tells how we use the computer today and predicts future uses. Colorful illustrations lead the reader through the discussion. Part of the Modern Technology series.

Sturridge, Helena. **Micro-Computers.** Warwick Press, 1983. 37 p. ISBN 0-531-09222-4.

This introduction to microcomputers emphasizes how they work. It explains the binary system and looks at the range of peripherals available to microcomputer users. There are sections on the silicon chip, software, and programming. A glossary of terms is included. Part of the Science in Action series.

Taft, David. **Computer Programming.** Illustrated by Hayward Art Group. Warwick Press, 1985. 38 p. ISBN 0-531-19007-2.

This book is based on a fictional story of two people collecting geological samples on the planet Calypso. When they are about to take off, their spaceship fails to fire, and they find themselves stranded. It is now up to them to learn how to program the computer to help them escape the planet. Part of the Science in Action series.

Waldock, Henry, and Robin Betts. **Sound Synthesizer.** Franklin Watts, 1985. ISBN 0-531-17012-8.

An Apple II or Commodore 64 computer can be turned into a musical instrument by using the machine's keyboard like a piano or synthesizer. This book explains how it's done, emphasizing the need for logical steps in building such a program and the importance of timing. Part of the Write Your Own Program series.

White, Jack R. **How Computers Really Work.** Illustrated by Barbara Shannon; photographs by the author. Dodd, Mead, 1986. 112 p. ISBN 0-396-08768-X.

If you are fascinated by computers, discover just how these remarkable mechanical brains really perform their many functions — from games to medical diagnoses. Diagrams and photographs make the explanations understandable, and computer terminology is explained in the text.

Wold, Allen L. **Computer Science.** Franklin Watts, 1984. 122 p. ISBN 0-531-04764-4.

What do you do with a computer once you've mastered the rudiments of computer operation and programming? This book is a guidebook for the student who desires to use a computer in a science project. The student may achieve better results and have a better overall presentation when the computer is involved in the investigation or the analysis of the results. Part of the Projects for Young Scientists series.

Drugs and Drug Abuse

Berger, Gilda. **Crack: The New Drug Epidemic!** Franklin Watts, 1987. 128 p. ISBN 0-531-10410-9.

Crack is a relatively inexpensive, white, powdery substance made from cocaine. It is highly addictive and deadly. A single use can cause death or a coma. Why do people start using this drug? Who is using it? What is being done to treat crack addicts and to stop the crack trade? Answers to these questions are presented in this book.

Berger, Gilda. **Smoking Not Allowed: The Debate.** Franklin Watts/ Impact Books, 1987. 143 p. ISBN 0-531-10420-6.

Both sides of the debate over smoking are examined in this book. It looks at the history of smoking, the proven and possible harmful health effects, changing regulations to discourage smoking in public places, and the individual's right to smoke.

Browne, David. **Crack and Cocaine.** Illustrated by Ron Hayward Associates. Gloucester Press, 1987. 32 p. ISBN 0-531-17047-0.

Crack is a powerful and extremely dangerous form of cocaine. It affects all levels of society, and although the United States is the world's greatest consumer of crack, the drug is sold and used in numerous other countries. This book describes what is being done on the local, national, and world levels to counteract the production and sale of crack and cocaine. Useful addresses are included.

Chomet, Julian. **Cocaine and Crack.** Illustrated by Peter Harper. Franklin Watts, 1987. 62 p. ISBN 0-531-10435-4.

No longer is crack considered the "plaything" of the rich and famous. The drug is becoming available to everyone, and as a result, it is now considered among the most addictive drugs. This book looks at where crack and cocaine come from, and what their effects are on the human body. Part of the Understanding Drugs series.

Cohen, Susan, and Daniel Cohen. **A Six-Pack and a Fake I.D.: Teens Look at the Drinking Question.** M. Evans, 1986. 150 p. ISBN 0-87131-459-2.

Though adults tell teens not to drink alcohol, they themselves often drink. Throughout the country many teens are finding alcohol a central part of their school and after-school life. Using true stories from many teens, this book discusses the role of alcohol in a teen's life, reasons for teen drinking, and physiological effects of alcohol. An excellent summary chapter and information on groups that can help combat teenage drinking are included.

Dolan, Edward F., Jr. **Drugs in Sports.** Franklin Watts, 1986. 122 p. ISBN 0-531-10157-6.

The use and abuse of drugs in the sports world is a topic that has caused much controversy. This book explains how such drugs as anabolic steroids, brake drugs, amphetamines, cocaine, and marijuana affect an athlete's body and mind, and what the sports world is doing to cope with the drug problem.

Edwards, Gabrielle I. **Coping with Drug Abuse.** Illustrated by Nancy Lou Gahan. Rosen Publishing Group, 1983. ISBN 0-8239-0612-4.

The author, a high school science teacher, discusses all aspects of drug abuse, including drugs that are being used, their physiological effects, and attempts to halt drug usage.

Godfrey, Martin. **Heroin.** Illustrated by Peter Harper. Franklin Watts, 1987. 62 p. ISBN 0-531-10436-2.

Here is a look at why people take heroin, its effect on the body, heroin-related illnesses, the cost of addiction, heroin manufacture, trade, and related crime, and sources of help. Part of the Understanding Drugs series.

Godfrey, Martin. **Marijuana.** Illustrated by Peter Harper. Franklin Watts, 1987. 62 p. ISBN 0-531-10437-0.

This book discusses why people take marijuana, how it affects the body, what the plant looks like, the health risks, marijuana manufacture, trade, and related crime, and how to get help. Part of the Understanding Drugs series.

Harris, Jonathan. **Drugged Athletes: The Crisis in American Sports.** Four Winds Press, 1987. 175 p. ISBN 0-02-742740-4.

Athletes are susceptible to drug use for several reasons: they are under intense pressure to compete at high performance levels, minority athletes often feel the added pressure of racism and discrimination, and drug dealers are readily available. This book focuses on remedies being tried at all levels by the sports world and government agencies, the testing programs now in use, and drug prevention and treatment centers.

Hawkes, Nigel. **The Heroin Trail.** Illustrated by Ron Hayward Associates. Gloucester Press, 1986. 32 p. ISBN 0-531-17028-4.

Heroin is derived from the opium poppy, which is grown primarily in Asia and in Mexico. This book discusses the manufacture, sale, and use of heroin and points out the severe consequences for those who become addicted to this drug. Part of the Issues series.

Hughes, Barbara. **Drug-Related Diseases.** Franklin Watts/First Books, 1987. 96 p. ISBN 0-531-10381-1.

Most drugs evolved out of a legitimate desire to deal with or help ease pain. For these purposes, drugs do not usually cause disease. Drug-related diseases occur when drugs are overused or used for purposes not intended. Drug dependency is considered a disease because it disturbs the normal working of the body. This book looks at such drugs as alcohol, cocaine, heroin, and amphetamines, the health problems that may result from their use or abuse, and what can be done to overcome dependency on them.

Porterfield, Kay Marie. **Coping with an Alcoholic Parent.** Rosen Publishing Group, 1985. 134 p. ISBN 0-8239-0662-0.

A family with an alcoholic parent is a troubled family, and youngsters who live in such a family often feel trapped and guilty. If you even suspect your parent of being an alcoholic, read this book. Here are solid ways to help you understand how to "survive and thrive" and how to deal with the numerous problems in such a family. The book includes an excellent reference section.

Pownall, Mark. **Inhalants.** Illustrated by Peter Harper. Franklin Watts, 1987. 62 p. ISBN 0-531-10434-6.

Inhalants are available in the home, school, and office. Such substances as glue, aerosols, and paints give off vapors that can be inhaled into the lungs in concentrated form to give the sensation of being stoned. Inhalants usually produce a change in behavior and can result in impaired health or even death. This book offers valuable information on inhalants and ways to get help if dependency occurs. Part of the Understanding Drugs series.

Stepney, Rob. **Alcohol.** Illustrated by Peter Harper. Franklin Watts, 1987. 62 p. ISBN 0-531-10433-8.

Alcohol is widely consumed and advertised in our society. This book discusses why people drink, what alcohol is, its effects on the body, damage it can cause, safe levels of alcohol, and sources of help. Part of the Understanding Drugs series.

Woods, Geraldine, and Harold Woods. **Cocaine.** Franklin Watts/First Books, 1985. 65 p. ISBN 0-531-10035-9.

Cocaine use in the United States is increasing each year despite the physical and social problems that accompany its abuse. For those people who become dependent on cocaine, getting and using the drug becomes the focus of their lives. Two types of treatment are widely used with cocaine addicts: therapeutic communities and out-patient treatment centers. This book also includes a history of cocaine and how cocaine is grown, processed, and shipped around the world.

Ecology

Cochrane, Jennifer. **Air Ecology.** Illustrated by Cecilia Fitzsimons. Bookwright Press, 1987. 47 p. ISBN 0-531-18151-0.

This activity-based book looks at the ways living things affect and are affected by their environments. Discussions of such topics as air pollution and plants' use of air to disperse seeds are followed by hands-on activities demonstrating the scientific principles involved. Other books in the Project Ecology series focus on land ecology, plant ecology, and water ecology.

Cutchins, Judy, and Ginny Johnston. **The Crocodile and the Crane: Surviving in a Crowded World.** William Morrow, 1986. 54 p. ISBN 0-688-06304-7 (0-688-06305-5, library binding).

As human beings expand cities and factories, the natural habitat of many animal species shrinks. Several are dangerously close to extinction. This book describes how care and breeding in controlled environments have helped protect such animals as the wattled crane, Morelet's crocodile, and the Arabian oryx. Learn about this threat to endangered species and what you can do to help preserve nature's balance. Black-and-white photographs and a glossary of terms are included.

Ehrlich, Anne H., and Paul R. Ehrlich. **Earth.** Franklin Watts, 1987. 258 p. ISBN 0-531-15036-4.

This summary of Earth's environmental predicament looks at the origins, character, and extent of the changes brought about by human action; the dangers of imprudence and the necessity of caution in all operations affecting Earth's life-support systems; and the importance of living in harmony with those systems. A list of additional readings is included.

Finney, Shan. **Noise Pollution.** Illustrated by Anne Canevari Green. Franklin Watts/Impact Books, 1984. 107 p. ISBN 0-531-04855-1.

Noise has been a problem since the first century B.C., when Julius Caesar banned chariots from the streets of Rome. What is noise pollution? What is the difference between sound and noise? Can we really be harmed by noise? What can be done about noise pollution? This book answers these questions and several others about a problem that affects all of us today.

Gay, Kathlyn. **The Greenhouse Effect.** Franklin Watts/Science Impact Books, 1986. 87 p. ISBN 0-531-10154-1.

What is the greenhouse effect and how will it change the temperature of the Earth? This book studies how increasing levels of carbon dioxide in the atmosphere are affecting our environment and how and why scientists study climatic changes.

Gutnik, Martin J. **Ecology.** Franklin Watts, 1984. 111 p. ISBN 0-531-04765-2.

An explanation of ecology and why we must work to conserve our natural environment is the major focus of this book. The scientific method is explained along with how to set up and present your science project and how to write the formal report. The book suggests possible ecology projects involving air, water, soil, and the human population. Part of the Projects for Young Scientists series.

Lambert, Mark. **The Future for the Environment.** Bookwright Press, 1986. 48 p. ISBN 0-531-18075-1.

Our tropical rain forests are being destroyed at the rate of one hundred acres a minute. Five hundred species of animals are in danger of becoming extinct. By the middle of the next century, over 40,000 different kinds of plants will probably have disappeared. This book explains other ways in which our world is rapidly changing and discusses steps being taken to slow down and stop the changes. Part of the Tomorrow's World series.

Lambert, Mark. **Future Sources of Energy.** Bookwright Press, 1986. 48 p. ISBN 0-531-18077-8.

Most sources of energy are nonrenewable, and most will eventually be exhausted. How, then, will we heat and light our homes, run our cars, and cook our food? By reading this book you will learn about the development of new energy sources and how the sources we have now will be used in different ways. Part of the Tomorrow's World series.

McCormick, John. **Acid Rain.** Illustrated by Ron Hayward Associates. Gloucester Press, 1986. 31 p. ISBN 0-531-17016-0.

When the moisture in the air is mixed with the pollution of smoke and fumes given off by factories and cars, acid rain develops. Acid rain affects forests, soil, rivers and lakes, wildlife, buildings, and even people. This book has excellent pictures, charts, maps, and graphs and includes a list of countries and their contributions to the acid rain problem. Part of the Issues series.

Ostmann, Robert, Jr. **Acid Rain: A Plague upon the Waters.** Dillon Press, 1982. 204 p. ISBN 0-87518-224-0.

Pollutants are released into the air from electric power plants and factories by the burning of coal and to a lesser degree by oil and natural gas. These pollutants combine with rain and turn it into acid that can harm lakes, streams, forests, buildings, cars, and people. This book describes the global extent of the problem and a few efforts made to improve the situation. Charts and graphs are included.

Pringle, Laurence. **Here Come the Killer Bees.** William Morrow, 1986. 58 p. ISBN 0-688-04630-4 (0-688-04631-2, library binding).

Are there really "killer bees"? Africanized bees have developed special characteristics through adaptations to climate that make them worthy of the name "killer bees." Learn about these bees and the potential threat to crops and wildlife as they invade our continent from Brazil. Photographs and a bibliography are included.

Simon, Noel. **Vanishing Habitats.** Gloucester Press, 1987. 32 p. ISBN 0-531-17062-4.

As the human population increases and people require more land for urban and agricultural development, more natural areas are destroyed, including wetlands, deserts, forests, rain forests, and grasslands. This is one book in a series that presents a new approach to natural history by looking at wildlife under threat because of our failure to protect the environment. Each book examines the difficulty of preserving wildlife in today's world and offers some solutions to protect and save species from extinction. Part of the Survival series.

Fine Arts

Dance

Castle, Kate. **Ballet Company.** Photographs by Chris Fairclough. Franklin Watts, 1984. 48 p. ISBN 0-531-10023-5.

"Shall we dance?" In bright, bold, beautiful photographs and easy-to-read text, the author tells the reader about one day in the life of a ballet company: the classes, rehearsing, costume fitting, shoes, scenery, wigs, and other details. The story ends with the performance.

Dufort, Antony. **Ballet Steps: Practice to Performance.** Illustrated by the author. Clarkson N. Potter/Phoebe Phillips Editions Books, 1985. 141 p. ISBN 0-517-55522-0.

This book explains in words and pictures the detailed language of ballet, including the five basic positions, exercises at the barre and center work, petit and grand allegro, rehearsals, and pas de deux. Dufort's many beautiful pencil drawings depict a variety of ballet movements, and the book also includes photographs of dancers in well-known ballets.

Finney, Shan. **Dance.** Franklin Watts/First Books, 1983. 64 p. ISBN 0-531-04525-0.

In the 1800s, many people argued that dancing was unhealthy. Today dancing is not only enjoyed by the audience who watches a ballet or other performance, but by an increasing number of people who dance for fitness, entertainment, and emotional and physical therapy. Anyone can dance, and this book shares techniques and ideas for getting started.

Kuklin, Susan. **Reaching for Dreams: A Ballet from Rehearsal to Opening Night.** Lothrop, Lee and Shepard Books, 1987. 128 p. ISBN 0-688-06316-0.

If you've ever wondered what it's like to be a member of a dance company, this book is for you. By interviewing dancers, choreographers, and support people, the author shows how hard work and dreams bring the production of a ballet alive.

Newman, Barbara. **The Nutcracker.** Barron's Educational Series, 1985. 46 p. ISBN 0-8120-5672-8.

The many phases in the creation of *The Nutcracker* ballet are described in this book. It explores the plot as it was created by E.T.A. Hoffmann and modified by Alexandre Dumas *père,* the writing of the libretto, the music composed by Pyotr Ilyich Tchaikovsky, and the choreography by Lev Ivanov and George Balanchine. The book includes designs, photography, and illustrations from many presentations of *The Nutcracker* in several countries. Part of the Stories of the Ballet series.

Switzer, Ellen. **The Nutcracker: A Story and a Ballet.** Photographs by Steven Caras and Costas. Atheneum, 1985. 100 p. ISBN 0-689-31061-7.

This book tells about three versions of *The Nutcracker:* the story by E.T.A. Hoffmann, with music by Pyotr Ilich Tchaikovsky and choreography by Lev Ivanov, the ballet that was first presented in St. Petersburg in 1892, and the ballet created by George Balanchine for presentation in 1954 by the New York City Ballet. Most of the book tells the story of Balanchine's *Nutcracker* in text and full-color photographs. Ten dancers are interviewed to give their interpretations of the characters they depict in *The Nutcracker.*

Painting and Other Art Forms

Bolognese, Don, and Elaine Raphael. **Charcoal and Pastel.** Franklin Watts, 1986. 64 p. ISBN 0-531-10226-2.

The technique of drawing using charcoal and pastel is explained in this book, stressing the importance of texture, line, motion, shapes, and patterns. In the last chapter you'll learn how this medium and technique can be used to make book covers. Part of the Illustrator's Library series.

Bolognese, Don, and Elaine Raphael. **Pen and Ink.** Franklin Watts, 1986. 64 p. ISBN 0-531-10133-9.

This book is designed to help readers become the best storytellers they can be by creating illustrations to describe the story. The technique of pen and ink, choosing pens, keeping a sketchbook, and developing a personal style are described. Part of the Illustrator's Library series.

Bolognese, Don, and Elaine Raphael. **Pencil.** Franklin Watts, 1986. 64 p. ISBN 0-531-10134-7.

Drawing with a pencil involves such techniques as shading, line, and tone. This book explains these techniques and discusses various types of papers, pencils, and erasers that may be used. It emphasizes pencil drawings and sketches as a "peephole" into the artist's mind and gives the reader an understanding of how picture ideas are born and how they are transformed. Part of the Illustrator's Library series.

Frame, Paul. **Drawing Reptiles.** Franklin Watts/How-to-Draw Books, 1986. 64 p. ISBN 0-531-10225-4.

Here is a guide to drawing alligators, crocodiles, lizards, snakes, and other reptiles. The book introduces the reader to the materials needed for drawing and provides exercises for increasing drawing skills. Specific instructions are then given for drawing various types of reptiles, including information on anatomy and shading.

Harris, Nathaniel. **Leonardo and the Renaissance.** Illustrated by Martin Salisbury. Bookwright Press, 1987. 42 p. ISBN 0-531-18137-5.

Leonardo da Vinci was an Italian painter, sculptor, architect, musician, engineer, and scientist who lived from 1452 to 1519. His versatility and wide-ranging creative powers mark him as an excellent example of Renaissance genius. This book examines his life and accomplishments, how he was influenced by the Renaissance, and how the Renaissance influenced Italy and other European countries. Part of the Life and Times series.

Waldron, Ann. **True or False? Amazing Art Forgeries.** Hastings House, 1983. 140 p. ISBN 0-8038-7220-8.

Art detectives and scholars have uncovered forgeries of paintings, drawings, sculpture, jewelry, wood carvings — just about every kind of artwork — in great museums and art collections throughout the world. Behind each forgery is a stranger-than-fiction story full of suspense, fascination, humor, and even tragedy. This collection tells of some of the world's most spectacular fakes and the interesting characters who produced them.

Theater and Music

Fox, Dan, and Claude Marks. **Go in and out the Window: An Illustrated Songbook for Young People.** Metropolitan Museum of Art and Henry Holt, 1987. 144 p. ISBN 0-87099-500-6 (Metropolitan Museum of Art) and 0-8050-0628-1 (Henry Holt).

Sixty-one classic childhood songs from around the world are coupled with photographs of artwork from the Metropolitan Museum of Art. Work songs, play songs, nursery songs, nonsense rhymes, lullabies, and ballads are matched with paintings, sculpture, prints, photographs, objets d'art, textiles, and musical instruments.

Haskins, James. **Black Music in America: A History through Its People.** Thomas Y. Crowell, 1987. 198 p. ISBN 0-690-04460-7 (0-690-04462-3, library binding).

Haskins traces black music from the earliest slave songs and spirituals, through ragtime and the blues, to jazz, bop, soul, disco, modern jazz, and beyond. To tell the story, he "presents vivid, living portraits of the extraordinary men and women who gave the world America's first truly original cultural gift."

Kettelkamp, Larry. **Electronic Musical Instruments.** William Morrow, 1984. 122 p. ISBN 0-688-02781-4.

Through the use of electronics, the world of music has been forever changed. The revolution from traditional musical instruments to electronic music is told by author Larry Kettelkamp, himself a musician. He explains how electronic music is produced, describing oscillators, synthesizers, electronic organs, and sound processors, and provides advice on performing and recording electronic music. Included are photographs and definitions for many electronic terms.

Lasky, Kathryn. **Puppeteer.** Photographs by Christopher G. Knight. Macmillan, 1985. 58 p. ISBN 0-02-751660-1.

Paul Vincent Davis is a puppeteer who frequently performs at the Puppet Show Place in Boston. This book describes in photographs and words the months of preparation for the first performance of *Aladdin and His Wonderful Lamp.* Davis performs all the puppet characters, changes sets and props, operates the music and lights — all himself. Here is a look at how he prepares and performs his show.

Straub, Cindie, and Matthew Straub. **Mime: Basics for Beginners.** Photographs by Jeff Blanton. Plays, 1984. 152 p. ISBN 0-8238-0263-9.

With mime growing in popularity, this book offers detailed instruction to help mimes of all ages master the movements and expressions of this lively art form. This is a workbook that gives step-by-step instructions in how to progress from beginner to confident performer.

Games

D'Ignazio, Fred. **Invent Your Own Computer Games.** Franklin Watts/ First Books, 1983. 90 p. ISBN 0-531-04637-0.

Do you spend a lot of your money on electronic games? If you do, you might like to try your hand at inventing your own games for a microcomputer. This book explains how to create original sports, board, strategy, word, number, and adventure games, and it gives instructions for programming and playing eleven simple computer games. Part of the Computer-Awareness series.

Duck, Mike. **Graphics: Hangman.** Gloucester Press, 1984. 45 p. ISBN 0-531-03483-6.

By following the steps given in this book, you will learn to use graphics commands on your computer. First, you will prepare a program for playing Hangman, a word game you already know. The second program will show you how to make a different section of the hanged man appear each time you give a wrong answer. You will enjoy hours of learning and fun following these directions. Part of the Write Your Own Program series.

Hartnell, Tim. **Tim Hartnell's Giant Book of Computer Games.** Ballantine Books, 1984. 288 p. ISBN 0-345-31609-6.

More than forty computer games are provided in this book to appeal to varied interests and abilities. The range is from classic board games, like chess and simulations, to demanding adventure programs. The book is written so that programs can be adapted or improved. Many games include program breakdowns and background to allow you to practice and improve game-writing skills.

Jeffries, Ron, and Glen Fisher. **Commodore 64 Fun and Games: Volume 2.** Warner Books, 1984. 174 p. ISBN 0-446-38183-7.

Thirty-five computer programs are presented for the Commodore 64 computer. Each program includes a brief summary of what the program will do and how you may use it. Also included are important variables and a description of how the program works. An introduction and symbol summary make this a worthwhile book for the computer enthusiast.

Lampton, Christopher. **How to Create Adventure Games.** Franklin Watts/First Books, 1986. 72 p. ISBN 0-531-10119-3.

This is a good first book on the development of computer games. The book provides instructions for writing a computer program for an adventure game using the language BASIC. Part of the Computer-Awareness series.

Lampton, Christopher. **How to Create Computer Games.** Franklin Watts/First Books, 1986. 86 p. ISBN 0-531-10120-7.

The game of Fish has been turned into a computer game. This book explains how to set up Fish on the computer, how to play it, and, possibly, how to beat the computer. Instructions for this and other computer games are given using BASIC. Part of the Computer-Awareness series.

Marshall, Gary. **Beginning BASIC: Space Journey.** Illustrated by Andy Farmer. Gloucester Press, 1984. 45 p. ISBN 0-531-03482-8.

What an easy way to learn to use your computer! This book explains the computer and its parts and will help you write your own program as you play Shuttle Launch, Asteroids, and Shuttle Landing. A helpful glossary will explain any terms you don't know. The games can be used with Commodore 64 and Apple IIe computers. Part of the Write Your Own Program series.

Sullivan, George. **Screen Play: The Story of Video Games.** Frederick Warne, 1983. 88 p. ISBN 0-7232-6251-9 (0-7232-6254-3, paperback).

Back in 1966, Ralph Baer started it all with the invention and marketing of the Odyssey home game system. Now Pac-Man, Space Invaders, and Donkey Kong are just a few of the numerous video games available in the video arcade or for the home computer. Here is a look at the development of these games.

Zubrowski, Bernie. **Raceways: Having Fun with Balls and Tracks.** Illustrated by Roy Doty. William Morrow/Boston Children's Museum Activity Books, 1985. 80 p. ISBN 0-688-04159-0 (0-688-04160-4, paperback).

Such scientific principles as gravity, momentum, and kinetic energy are illustrated in a wide selection of games to be played or made with balls and tracks. Step-by-step instructions are given for a variety of games and are enhanced by numerous illustrations.

Health and Diseases

Anderson, Madelyn Klein. **Environmental Diseases.** Franklin Watts/First Books, 1987. 60 p. ISBN 0-531-10382-X.

According to this author, every disease is an environmental disease. Most of the time our environment protects us from attack. However, such factors as hazardous chemicals and radiation may attack without us being aware of what is happening. The author discusses a variety of diseases that may result.

Arnold, Caroline. **Pain: What Is It? How Do We Deal With It?** Illustrated by Frank Schwarz. William Morrow, 1986. 86 p. ISBN 0-688-05710-1 (0-688-05711-X, library binding).

Pain, real or imagined, is part of everyone's life from birth to death. From new techniques used to measure pain to ways to relieve and prevent pain, the author makes the reader aware of the many facets of this condition.

Berger, Gilda. **PMS: Premenstrual Syndrome.** Franklin Watts/Impact Books, 1984. 77 p. ISBN 0-531-04857-8.

Premenstrual syndrome is a female medical problem characterized by a group of specific physical and sometimes psychological symptoms that appear before menstruation begins each month. This book helps the reader identify symptoms and learn how to relieve them with proper diet, exercise, and tension reduction. A chapter on professional help for PMS, social and legal issues, a bibliography, and an appendix for sources of information and help are included.

Brown, Fern G. **Hereditary Diseases.** Franklin Watts/First Books, 1987. 80 p. ISBN 0-531-10386-2.

Just what diseases can children inherit from their parents? This book attempts to answer this question by discussing heredity and the causes, symptoms, and treatment of birth defects and such hereditary diseases as cystic fibrosis, sickle cell anemia, Tay-Sachs, and diabetes. It also explores the growing field of genetic counseling.

Eagles, Douglas A. **Nutritional Diseases.** Franklin Watts/First Books, 1987. 80 p. ISBN 0-531-10391-9.

Diseases that are related to nutrition are discussed in this book, including those caused by protein and vitamin deficiencies. The development, symptoms, treatment, and possible prevention of osteoporosis, arteriosclerosis, phenylketonuria, and diabetes are described. The book also explores the eating disorders of anorexia and bulimia, which result in inadequate nutrition.

Ewy, Donna, and Rodger Ewy. **Teen Pregnancy: The Challenges We Faced, the Choices We Made.** Illustrated by Linda Gerrard Ely. New American Library/Signet Books, 1985. 285 p. ISBN 0-451-13915-1.

Specifically written for young readers, this book explains every aspect of pregnancy, from conception through various methods of childbirth, while avoiding talking down to young readers and technical jargon. The confusing and often contradictory emotions that surround teen pregnancies are also explored. This is a book written for teens by other teens who've "been there," and it offers no-nonsense information in a readable format.

Fine, Judylaine. **Afraid to Ask: A Book for Families to Share about Cancer.** Lothrop, Lee and Shepard Books, 1986. 171 p. ISBN 0-688-06196-6 (0-688-06195-8, library binding).

Family doctors are often reluctant to tell cancer patients and their families the whole truth about cancer. This book tells the reader what cancer is, who gets it, how to prevent it, how to treat it, what the symptoms are, and what the survival rates are. Based on actual case histories, the book describes cancers in nineteen different parts of the body.

Hawkes, Nigel. **AIDS.** Illustrated by Ron Hayward Associates. Gloucester Press, 1987. 32 p. ISBN 0-531-17054-3.

The first known case of Acquired Immune Deficiency Syndrome was discovered in 1981. At the time this book was written, over 32,000 cases had been reported in the United States. The disease is transmitted through contaminated needles shared by drug users, homosexual and heterosexual intercourse, blood transfusions, and interuterine contact between an infected woman and her unborn fetus. The disease is described as a time bomb, for as long as unsuspecting and healthy people do not take precautions, the virus will continue to spread. In addition to providing general information about AIDS, this book describes avoiding and preventing AIDS and current treatment programs. Part of the Issues series.

Hyde, Margaret O. **Is This Kid "Crazy"? Understanding Unusual Behavior.** Westminster Press, 1983. 96 p. ISBN 0-664-32707-9.

People who behave differently are often labeled as "crazy." The author discusses many of the problems that set these people apart: emotional illness, hyperactivity, autism, schizophrenia, depression, anorexia nervosa, and bulimia. Also included are a glossary of mental health terms, suggestions for further reading, and a list of names and addresses of service agencies throughout the country.

Kolodny, Nancy J. **When Food's a Foe: How to Confront and Conquer Eating Disorders.** Little, Brown, 1987. 143 p. ISBN 0-316-50167-0.

Kolodny examines the causes and effects of bulimia and anorexia nervosa and discusses ways in which these eating disorders can be prevented. It is a hands-on book that challenges the reader to think and to work by using the checklists, questionnaires, and exercises to find personalized solutions to individual problems.

Landau, Elaine. **Alzheimer's Disease.** Franklin Watts/First Books, 1987. 67 p. ISBN 0-531-10376-5.

Alzheimer's disease is a degenerative, progressive disease of the central nervous system. In the United States alone, over two million adults have been affected. How one copes with this disease, what treatment programs are available, and how the disease affects the families are all discussed in this book. Black-and-white photographs and a bibliography are included.

Metos, Thomas H. **Communicable Diseases.** Franklin Watts/First Books, 1987. 75 p. ISBN 0-531-10380-3.

How are diseases such as the common cold spread? This book explains the causes of communicable diseases — including the plague, sexually transmitted diseases, and the common cold — classifies these diseases, and discusses diagnosis and treatment.

Nourse, Alan E. **AIDS.** Franklin Watts/Impact Books, 1986. 128 p. ISBN 0-531-10235-1.

This is the story of a modern plague that has already killed over twelve thousand Americans. Dr. Nourse explores the possible origins, symptoms, and characteristics of AIDS, chronicles the continuous search for a cure, and addresses popular myths and fears about AIDS. Concluding chapters discuss protection against AIDS and predictions about the future of the disease.

Nourse, Alan E. **Herpes.** Franklin Watts/Impact Books, 1985. 99 p. ISBN 0-531-10069-3.

Genital herpes is a sexually transmitted disease that affects the lives of twenty million people. At present there is no safe effective vaccine for this virus. Dr. Nourse discusses the characteristics of genital herpes and describes ways to protect yourself from this disease.

Powledge, Fred. **You'll Survive!** Charles Scribner's Sons, 1986. 88 p. ISBN 0-684-18632-2.

Adolescence can be the best of times and the worst of times. It can be very rewarding, yet very scary. There are so many stages that one goes through, so many unanswered questions, and so many heartaches. This book discusses the physical and emotional stages of adolescence, explores the relationships between teens and parents, peers, and society in general, and suggests ways of coping with common problems.

Roy, Ron. **Move Over, Wheelchairs Coming Through! Seven Young People in Wheelchairs Talk about Their Lives.** Photographs by Rosmarie Hausherr. Clarion Books, 1985. 83 p. ISBN 0-89919-249-1.

The seven disabled young people in this book use wheelchairs to get around. Lizzy can speak and move her head, but she cannot use her hands, arms, feet, or legs. She operates her wheelchair by a computer, using her chin to give commands. Jose has spina bifida and gets around town by manually wheeling himself. The book focuses on how the young people perform their daily activities and also includes a section with facts about the diseases the young people have and a list of further readings.

Silverstein, Alvin, and Virginia B. Silverstein. **The Story of Your Foot.** Illustrated by Greg Wenzel. G. P. Putnam's Sons, 1987. 80 p. ISBN 0-399-61216-5.

Durable and hard working, yet mistreated and underappreciated — such is the plight of our feet, which log in 115,000 steps a day (about 4 1/2 miles). Besides describing the physical properties of our feet and how they compare with animals' feet, this book describes human feet and their actions — from punting a football, to walking on fire, to helping heal other parts of the body. Learn what to look for in a good pair of running shoes, why women in ancient China bound their feet, and why a flea is a superior jumper.

Ward, Brian R. **Smoking and Health.** Franklin Watts, 1986. 45 p. ISBN 0-531-10180-0.

This book presents basic facts about tobacco: its cultivation and processing, how it affects the body, its effects on the nonsmoker, and special risks to women and children. There are sections on giving up the habit, returning to health, and having the right to choose. A glossary of terms is included. Part of the Life Guides series.

History and Government

American

Ashabranner, Brent, and Melissa Ashabranner. **Into a Strange Land: Unaccompanied Refugee Youth in America.** Dodd, Mead, 1987. 120 p. ISBN 0-396-08841-4.

Many thousands of teens have arrived alone in the United States, refugees from war-torn homelands. This book chronicles the stories of individual Southeast Asian refugees and discusses some of their problems, hopes, and successes.

Boorstin, Daniel J. (with Ruth F. Boorstin). **The Landmark History of the American People: Volume 1, From Plymouth to Appomattox.** Random House, 1987. 218 p. ISBN 0-394-99118-4 (0-394-89120-1, for vols. 1 and 2).

American history from early settlement to the Civil War is covered in this volume. There are five major sections in the book: An Assortment of Plantations, Thirteen States Are Born, American Ways of Growing, Thinking Like Americans, and The Rocky Road to Union. The book concludes with the Declaration of Independence and the Constitution of the United States.

Boorstin, Daniel J. (with Ruth F. Boorstin). **The Landmark History of the American People: Volume 2, From Appomattox to the Moon.** Random House, 1987. 192 p. ISBN 0-394-99119-2 (0-394-89120-1, for vols. 1 and 2).

Volume 2 in this comprehensive look at American history begins with the period following the Civil War and extends to contemporary times. It describes such early go-getters as cattle ranchers, oilmen, and storekeepers, looks at people instrumental to our history, and focuses on such modern events as the several wars, the development of atomic power, and explorations by the astronauts.

Boyer, Edward. **River and Canal.** Illustrated by the author. Holiday House, 1986. 45 p. ISBN 0-8234-0598-2.

The Pocosink Canal and Navigation Company is imaginary, but it is typical of similar companies of the 1800s. Canals and locks were constructed for transportation during this period. Construction could be complex — in this account the owners had to design an inclined railroad and build an aqueduct over the Ohio River. The book also describes life on canal boats and the duties of a lock keeper.

Burchard, Sue. **The Statue of Liberty: Birth to Rebirth.** Harcourt Brace Jovanovich, 1985. 200 p. ISBN 0-15-279969-9.

In celebration of the centennial of the Statue of Liberty, the world's most famous symbol of freedom, the author has traced the history of the statue over a period of 121 years — from the birth of the idea at a French dinner party in 1865 to Liberty's rebirth in 1986 as a restored and refurbished monument. This book covers not only the problems during construction of the statue but also the major physical changes on Liberty and Ellis Island in the past century. This is a comprehensive, up-to-date treatment of the woman who dominates New York Harbor.

Claypool, Jane. **The Worker in America.** Franklin Watts, 1985. 116 p. ISBN 0-531-04933-7.

Early American settlers worked in order to survive. They needed basic skills to clear the land, build a house, and grow crops. Today, workers find that basic skills are not enough. This book discusses social and economic changes that have created the need for more highly skilled workers, the entrance of blacks, women, and immigrants into the labor force, and the growth of unions to protect all workers. Part of the Issues in American History series.

Collier, Christopher, and James Lincoln Collier. **Decision in Philadelphia: The Constitutional Convention of 1787.** Ballantine Books, 1987. 363 p. ISBN 0-345-34652-1.

A detailed account of the drafting of the U.S. Constitution in Philadelphia in 1787 is presented in this book. A biographical sketch of each signer is given, and the book discusses the pro and con arguments for each section of the Constitution. Readers will also gain a look at daily life in eighteenth-century America. A full biography and list of sources are included.

Costabel, Eva Deutsch. **A New England Village.** Illustrated by the author. Atheneum, 1983. 42 p. ISBN 0-689-30972-4.

This book provides an accurate, brief description of life in a New England village in 1830. It covers such crafts as candlemaking, quilting, weaving, printing, and tinsmithing and describes the homes, farms, schools, and shops. Black-and-white drawings reflect early American designs. (Literary merit)

Dolan, Edward F., Jr., and Margaret M. Scariano. **Cuba and the United States: Troubled Neighbors.** Franklin Watts/Impact Books, 1987. 121 p. ISBN 0-531-10327-7.

Here is a look at the history of diplomatic relations between the United States and Cuba from the Revolutionary War to the present day. The book also explains Cuba's current political philosophy under Fidel Castro and how it contrasts with the political philosophy of the United States.

Fisher, Leonard Everett. **The Alamo.** Holiday House, 1987. 64 p. ISBN 0-8234-0646-6.

An exciting group of pictures helps to tell the story of the Alamo and of the adventures that happened within its walls. Originally built as a chapel in the mid-1700s, the Alamo was converted into a fortress. For nearly two weeks in 1836, a mere 180 Texan revolutionaries in the Alamo held off an army of several thousand Mexican soldiers. Although all the Texans perished in the siege, their courage inspired other Texans, who remembered the Alamo as they defeated the Mexicans six weeks later, which made Texas independent of Mexico.

Fisher, Leonard Everett. **Ellis Island: Gateway to the New World.** Holiday House, 1986. 64 p. ISBN 0-8234-0612-1.

Authentic photographs and original scratchboard drawings add interest to this story of Ellis Island in New York Bay. Between 1892 and 1954 this island was the chief immigration station for newcomers to the United States.

Fitzgerald, Merni Ingrassia. **The Voice of America.** Dodd, Mead, 1987. 118 p. ISBN 0-396-98937-2.

The Voice of America has one main purpose: to disseminate truth to the inhabitants of those countries whose governments do not allow free news to appear. This book reviews the history of the VOA operation, shares letters from listeners throughout the world, and discusses special programming, such as children's shows and Radio Marti.

Freedman, Russell. **Cowboys of the Wild West.** Clarion Books, 1985. 103 p. ISBN 0-89919-301-3.

What were the original cowboys like? According to this book, they were young males in their teens or twenties who tended cattle or horses in the late nineteenth century. Included are excerpts from the published recollections of some cowboys and many photographs of the open range, the trails, the ranches, and the cowboys who worked there.

Gorman, Carol. **America's Farm Crisis.** Franklin Watts/Impact Books, 1987. 125 p. ISBN 0-531-10408-7.

One of the pressing problems of the 1980s is the American farm crisis. This book examines important questions about the crisis and considers several solutions to it. Chapters cover a history of farming from the Depression of the 1930s to the 1980s, what farmers want and what the critics say, the emotional toll on farm families, and how they can get help.

Grigoli, Valorie. **Patriotic Holidays and Celebrations.** Franklin Watts/First Books, 1985. 66 p. ISBN 0-531-10044-8.

Patriotic American holidays are examined in this book. There are the national holidays, such as Independence Day and Flag Day; holidays honoring people and personalities, such as the day honoring Martin Luther King, Jr.; military holidays, such as Memorial Day and Veterans' Day; and some regional holidays and celebrations, such as Confederate Memorial Day and Frontier Days in Cheyenne, Wyoming.

Hanmer, Trudy J. **The Advancing Frontier.** Franklin Watts, 1986. 144 p. ISBN 0-531-10267-X.

Americans have always followed the advancing frontier, whether it be the West, Alaska, outer space, or even the world of computers. This book describes some of these frontiers, the adventurers who explored them, and the influence that the idea of an unlimited frontier has had on American thought. Part of the Issues in American History series.

Hanmer, Trudy. **The Growth of Cities.** Franklin Watts, 1985. 120 p. ISBN 0-531-10056-1.

The history of cities in America is complex. In the colonial days, cities began to appear on the frontier. Then, with the Industrial

Revolution, there was great immigration to the cities. Over subsequent years, our large modern cities of today developed. This book looks at the history of American cities and the problems and promises of urbanization.

Harris, Jonathan. **A Statue for America: The First 100 Years of the Statue of Liberty.** Four Winds Press, 1985. 225 p. ISBN 0-02-742730-7.

The Statue of Liberty was proposed by French historian Édouard Laboulaye in 1865 to commemorate the alliance of France with the American colonies during the American Revolution. It was designed by French sculptor Frédéric Bartholdi, constructed of copper in France, shipped to New York City in 1885, and dedicated in 1886.

Hart, William B. **The United States and World Trade.** Franklin Watts/Economics Impact Books, 1985. 103 p. ISBN 0-531-10067-7.

This book examines the reasons for the changing fortunes of the United States in the world marketplace. It discusses how and with whom the United States and other countries trade goods and services, the role the United States plays in world trade, and the impact and effect of world trade on developing nations and global interdependence.

Hilton, Suzanne. **Faster Than a Horse: Moving West with Engine Power.** Westminster Press, 1983. 204 p. ISBN 0-664-32709-5.

The history of the United States is closely tied to the growth in importance of steamboats, railroads, trolleys, and automobiles. Each section of this book presents dramatic accounts of the men and women who helped develop and popularize these machines. An interesting sidelight is the discussion of the disasters that occurred during the machines' development. The book also lists places across the country where you can take a ride in these antique machines.

Hirschfelder, Arlene. **Happily May I Walk: American Indians and Alaska Natives Today.** Charles Scribner's Sons, 1986. 152 p. ISBN 0-684-18624-1.

Through discussion of tribal governments, languages, religion, music and dance, education, and relations with the U.S. government, this book dispels many stereotypes about Native Americans and Alaska Natives. It cites life-changing historical events, such as the army's creation of Indian reservations in the 1800s and the forced relocation of Aleuts during World War II to abandoned mines where they had to sleep in relays, leading to many deaths from pneumonia and tuberculosis. From their ancestral roots to modern-day culture, the lives of contemporary Native Americans and Alaska Natives are presented in this well-illustrated book.

Katz, William Loren. **Black Indians: A Hidden Heritage.** Atheneum, 1986. 198 p. ISBN 0-689-31196-6.

American historians have largely ignored the contributions that black Indians made to the development of our country. This book traces the history of relations between blacks and American Indians and reveals the hidden heritage of the black Indians, beginning with the earliest Spanish explorations of the New World and including the settling of the Wild West.

Kronenwetter, Michael. **Are You a Liberal? Are You a Conservative?** Franklin Watts/Impact Books, 1984. 99 p. ISBN 0-531-04751-2.

The terms *liberal* and *conservative* have a long history in European and American politics, going all the way back to the American and French revolutions. This book shows the political and philosophical factors that gave birth to these positions in the eighteenth and nineteenth centuries and then moves up to the present to show what role these political positions have played in the administrations of Franklin Roosevelt, Lyndon Johnson, and Ronald Reagan.

Lawson, Don. **An Album of the Vietnam War.** Franklin Watts, 1986. 87 p. ISBN 0-531-10139-8.

This book recounts the origins and events of the Vietnam War, focusing on the involvement of the United States from 1961 to 1975. It also discusses the antiwar movement here at home. Graphic black-and-white photographs illustrate scenes from the war.

Lord, Walter. **The Night Lives On.** William Morrow, 1986. 253 p. ISBN 0-688-04939-7.

This book continues to report on Lord's research on the "unsinkable" *Titanic,* which sank off the coast of Newfoundland in 1912, killing more than 2,200 passengers. Lord investigates such issues as whether the captain really knew how to handle the ship, why warnings about icebergs in the area went unheeded, and what the band was really playing. A final question that is posed is whether the *Titanic* can be salvaged. Sequel to *A Night to Remember.*

Mabie, Margot C. J. **Vietnam: There and Here.** Holt, Rinehart and Winston, 1985. 166 p. ISBN 0-03-072067-2.

Beginning with Vietnam's history, this book explains the development of conditions in Southeast Asia that triggered the least understood and most unpopular of all American foreign involvements. Bitter disputes between hawks and doves, and liberals and conservatives kept Americans in turmoil as an ancient civilization was bombarded and eventually destroyed. Careful to present the facts evenly, the writer gives both a concise overview and essential details of the war and the reaction around the globe.

McGowen, Thomas. **Midway and Guadalcanal.** Franklin Watts, 1984. 104 p. ISBN 0-531-04866-7.

At the beginning of World War II, the United States faced its greatest modern military challenge. The next few years of the Pacific war were critical to the course of history for both the United States and Asia. The battles of Midway and Guadalcanal were turning points in that war. This book identifies the key American and Japanese figures and explains crucial events in the war in the Pacific.

Marrin, Albert. **Victory in the Pacific.** Atheneum, 1983. 217 p. ISBN 0-689-30948-1.

Although Pacific means "peaceful," many of the battles of World War II were fought in the Pacific Ocean. This book chronicles American and Japanese naval operations during the war.

Marrin, Albert. **War Clouds in the West: Indians and Cavalrymen, 1860–1890.** Atheneum, 1984. 219 p. ISBN 0-689-31066-8.

The Indian Wars on the Western Plains of the United States took place from approximately 1860 to 1890, as the Native Americans struggled to survive against the increasing numbers of white settlers. This book gives a detailed account of both sides in that struggle. Read about the Cheyenne, the Comanche and General Sherman, the Sioux and Chief Red Cloud, Sitting Bull and General Custer, and Crazy Horse and General Crook.

Meltzer, Milton, editor. **The American Revolutionaries: A History in Their Own Words, 1750–1800.** Thomas Y. Crowell, 1987. 210 p. ISBN 0-690-04641-3 (0-690-04643-X, library binding).

Using actual letters, diaries, memoirs, interviews, ballads, newspaper articles, and speeches of people who lived in the American colonies from 1750 to 1800, Meltzer tells what life was like during this period. He brings a new understanding of the Revolutionary War by using the words of the revolutionaries themselves.

Meltzer, Milton, editor. **The Black Americans: A History in Their Own Words, 1619–1983.** Thomas Y. Crowell, 1984. 306 p. ISBN 0-690-04419-4 (0-690-04418-6, library binding).

Three hundred fifty years of black experiences and opinions — ranging from major literary, political, and social writers to obscure recorders of their own lives and times — fill this book. Maya Angelou, Frederick Douglass, W.E.B. Du Bois, Marcus Garvey, Langston Hughes, Martin Luther King, Jr., David Walker, Ida B. Wells, Richard Wright — all are represented here through their own writings; and hundreds of blacks of note in all fields, including Muhammad Ali and Ralph Abernathy, are written about by others. (Literary merit)

Mercer, Charles. **Statue of Liberty.** G. P. Putnam's Sons, 1985. 96 p. ISBN 0-399-20670-1 (0-399-21231-0, paperback).

Whose idea was the Statue of Liberty? Who built this amazing structure? How long did construction take? What is the statue made of? These and many other questions are answered in this book about our colossal statue. You'll learn that the statue is 151 feet tall and sits atop a 65-foot base. A single fingernail measures 10 by 13 inches, and each eye is 2½ feet across.

Morris, Richard B. **Witnesses at the Creation: Hamilton, Madison, Jay, and the Constitution.** New American Library/Plume Books, 1986. 279 p. ISBN 0-452-25867-7.

The year is 1787, and the reader is transported to colonial America to watch the development of the Constitution. Alexander Hamilton, James Madison, and John Jay are just a few of the framers of this historic document, and all become dramatic characters, not dusty historical figures.

Olmos, David. **National Defense Spending: How Much Is Enough?** Franklin Watts/Impact Books, 1984. 92 p. ISBN 0-531-046758-X.

The Reagan administration proposed spending 1.5 trillion dollars on defense from 1984 to 1988. This is comparable to spending a billion dollars a day every day except Sunday for five years. Those who support this recommendation argue that our national safety demands that we match the Soviets dollar for dollar and weapon for weapon. Critics of this expense feel that there are other ways to protect our country and that spending this much on the military means less money for education, nutrition, and welfare. The book presents both sides in a clear factual manner.

Pascoe, Elaine. **Racial Prejudice.** Franklin Watts, 1985. 118 p. ISBN 0-531-10057-X.

When people discriminate against other people whose skin is a different color, it is called racial prejudice. This book examines the roots of racism in the United States by reviewing the treatment of Blacks, Native Americans, Asians, and Hispanics in America. It also reviews the damaging effects of prejudice and suggests ways to eliminate it. Part of the Issues in American History series.

Ribaroff, Margaret Flesher. **Mexico and the United States Today: Issues between Neighbors.** Franklin Watts/Impact Books 1985. 98 p. ISBN 0-531-04757-1.

Political, social, and economic ties exist between the United States and Mexico, as does some tension. Much of the land in the Western and Southwestern states was originally under Mexican control but became part of the United States, which started the conflict in the nineteenth century. Economic differences between the two nations in the twentieth century have increased the tensions. Nevertheless, these two countries have found ways to overcome their differences and to coexist.

Selden, Bernice. **The Mill Girls: Lucy Larcom, Harriet Hanson Robinson, Sarah G. Bagley.** Atheneum, 1983. 191 p. ISBN 0-689-31005-6.

In the mid-1800s, young women flocked to the cities where new mill jobs provided money to send back home, with a little left over for luxuries. Many women took advantage of the educational opportunities provided by mill owners. But as production increased, working conditions grew worse, and workers united to improve the workplace. In this book you will meet three of these mill workers. Lucy Larcom went on to become a famous poet, and both Harriet Hanson Robinson and Sarah G. Bagley were involved with early union activities.

Shapiro, William E. **The Statue of Liberty.** Franklin Watts/First Books, 1985. 66 p. ISBN 0-531-10047-2.

Here's a look at the huge statue that sits in New York City's harbor. The book describes the creation and construction of the Statue of Liberty, its erection in New York Harbor, and the efforts to modernize and renovate the monument prior to its centennial in 1986. Included are facts and figures on its various names, location, weight, dimensions, and a chronology of its existence.

Sloan, Frank. **Titanic.** Franklin Watts/First Books, 1987. 96 p. ISBN 0-531-10396-X.

Why did the *Titanic* sink in 1912? Did it hit an iceberg? Was there "bad luck" on board? What about the "curse of the mummy"? Were the investigations into the *Titanic*'s sinking complete? This book discusses these questions and reveals how remains of the ship were discovered on the bottom of the Atlantic Ocean in 1985 by oceanographers using a computerized underwater video camera.

Sweeney, James B. **Famous Aviators of World War II.** Franklin Watts/ First Books, 1987. 95 p. ISBN 0-531-10302-1.

This book describes famous aviators during World War II. One was Claire Chennault, whose father hoped he would remain a teacher but who decided to become a pilot. He, like the others mentioned in this book, planned several of the air attacks of the war. Other aviators featured include James Doolittle, Curtis LeMay, Carl Spaatz, and Emmett O'Donnell. A glossary of terms is included.

Whedbee, Charles Harry. **Outer Banks Tales to Remember.** John F. Blair, 1985. 133 p. ISBN 0-89587-044-4.

From the Outer Banks of North Carolina come seventeen tales to amuse, mystify, explain, or tempt. Gathered from the inhabitants of the area, these stories add to the lore of a special part of America and the hardy folks who live there.

Whitney, Sharon, and Tom Raynor. **Women in Politics.** Franklin Watts, 1986. 143 p. ISBN 0-531-10243-2.

From small towns to big cities, from state capitals to Washington, women are now running successfully for office. Beginning with the story of Sojourner Truth, the authors trace the development of women in politics, concentrating on those who have been in the forefront of women's victories.

Windrow, Martin. **The Civil War Rifleman.** Illustrated by Jeffrey Burn. Franklin Watts, 1985. 32 p. ISBN 0-531-10081-2.

There were 3½ million men who wore the uniforms of either the North or South during the struggle between the states. This book compares their uniforms, commands, weapons, and equipment.

Windrow, Martin. **The World War II GI.** Illustrated by Kevin Lyles. Franklin Watts, 1986. 32 p. ISBN 0-531-10084-7.

What was it like to be a soldier back in World War II? Mainly through pictures, this book shows what basic training was like, what uniforms were worn by soldiers at different ranks and in different branches of service, and what equipment they were responsible for operating. A time chart indicates important battles and events of the war.

Wolf, Bernard. **Cowboy.** William Morrow, 1985. 76 p. ISBN 0-688-03877-8 (0-688-03878-6, library binding).

Meet the McRae family, who for three generations have lived on a ranch in Rosebud County, Montana. Wallace McRae is a cowboy. His day starts at 4:30 a.m. and might involve branding cattle and horses, rounding up the cattle in the spring, taking part in the local rodeo, gathering and storing hay, or interacting with the coal workers in town. The cowboys in this community try to maintain their traditional way of life, although there are clear signs that this way of life is threatened.

World

Abells, Chana Byers. **The Children We Remember.** Greenwillow Books, 1986. 44 p. ISBN 0-688-06371-3 (0-688-06372-1, library binding).

Photographs of children killed during the Holocaust vividly demonstrate the horrors of war and the particular cruelty of the Nazis before and during World War II. This book also honors some of the children who were able to survive the Holocaust, either by relying on their own resources or with the help of others.

Arnold, Guy. **Datelines of World History.** Warwick Press, 1983. 93 p. ISBN 0-531-09212-7.

This book views history in stepping stones of time, beginning with the early civilizations of people who lived between 40,000 B.C. and 500 B.C. and concluding with a time block in our modern world from 1840 through 1983. Each block of time is divided into chronological sections that show the development of the major and minor powers, culture, religion, and technology. In addition to the time lines, important political and cultural developments are explained in the text or shown through color pictures and photographs.

Banyard, Peter (edited by John Pimlott). **The Rise of the Dictators, 1919–1939.** Franklin Watts, 1986. 62 p. ISBN 0-531-10233-5.

Such dictators as Italy's Benito Mussolini, Germany's Adolf Hitler, Spain's Francisco Franco, and the Soviet Union's Joseph Stalin are discussed in this book. Chapters focus on the aftermath of war, the pressures of peace, the failure of the League of Nations, and the road to world war. Included are appendixes of personalities, major powers, private armies, land warfare, air warfare, and a chronology of events. Part of the Conflict in the Twentieth Century series.

Baynham, Simon (edited by John Pimlott). **Africa from 1945.** Franklin Watts, 1987. 62 p. ISBN 0-531-10319-6.

Social, economic, and political conflicts are examined in this book about Africa since the end of World War II. It looks at the partition of Africa by European nations, independence for many of the African colonies and territories, and the continent's uncertain future. The appendixes include information on personalities, apartheid, famine, foreign intervention, counter insurgency in Rhodesia, and a chronology of events.

Bentley, Judith. **The Nuclear Freeze Movement.** Franklin Watts, 1984. 122 p. ISBN 0-531-04772-5.

As the number of nuclear weapons in the world has increased, so has the opposition to these weapons. This book examines the history of the nuclear freeze movement — its beginning, the leaders of the movement, why more people are joining, and what the effect of the freeze would be. Historical time charts and race developments make this an easy-to-understand source of information.

Branigan, Keith. **Prehistory.** Illustrated by David Salariya and Shirley Willis. Warwick Press, 1984. 37 p. ISBN 0-531-03745-2.

How did prehistoric people survive without electricity, running water, and all the luxuries we take for granted? Discover how they hunted with flint or stone and clothed themselves with skins and handwoven materials. Read how rituals and art forms developed as people made their world meet their needs. Part of the History as Evidence series.

Braymer, Marjorie. **Atlantis: The Biography of a Legend.** Atheneum/ Margaret K. McElderry Books, 1983. 225 p. ISBN 0-689-50264-8.

Have you heard of the lost continent of Atlantis, a rich and powerful sea nation of the ancient world? It has sparked the imagination of men and women for thousands of years. Various people have developed theories about the location and importance of this lost continent, some placing it in the Atlantic, some in the Mediterranean. Read this biography of a legend and decide for yourself.

Carroll, Raymond. **The Future of the United Nations.** Franklin Watts/ Impact Books, 1985. 119 p. ISBN 0-531-10062-6.

The United Nations was first organized in 1945 to reduce the threat of nuclear war and to improve the life of all people in the world. But over the years there has been much criticism of this organization, especially by the United States, and the spirit of cooperation is often missing. This book examines the history of the U.N., its organization and conflicts, and its prospects for the future.

Carroll, Raymond. **The Palestine Question.** Franklin Watts/Impact Books, 1983. 90 p. ISBN 0-531-04549-8.

The region of land in the Middle East known as Palestine is the topic of this book. It examines the conflict between the Israelis and the Arabs over this land, tracing the history of Palestine and explaining why both groups claim it. The emphasis of the book is on the fate of Palestine in the twentieth century.

Chaikin, Miriam. **A Nightmare in History: The Holocaust, 1933–1945.** Clarion Books, 1987. 150 p. ISBN 0-89919-461-3.

The twelve years of the Nazi regime and its oppression of the Jewish people is retold by Chaikin and by excerpts from diaries and eyewitness accounts. She discusses the prejudice against Jews that existed in Germany long before Hitler rose to power, and describes the imprisonment of Jews, especially in the Warsaw Ghetto, the 1943 Uprising, and the death camps where millions of Jews died. The book also identifies those individuals and nations who helped the Jews.

Coker, Chris (edited by John Pimlott). **Terrorism and Civil Strife.** Franklin Watts, 1987. 62 p. ISBN 0-531-10385-4.

Terrorist acts and civil strife have occurred during the twentieth century in numerous locations around the world, ranging from Chile to Ireland to Lebanon to South Africa to the Philippines. Here is a look at some of the social, economic, and political conflicts that have taken place. The book identifies and analyzes the problems and, when possible, offers solutions.

Corbishley, Mike. **The Romans.** Illustrated by David Salariya and Shirley Willis. Warwick Press, 1983. 37 p. ISBN 0-531-09221-6.

Beginning as a small group of farmers in central Italy, the Romans eventually built an empire that stretched from North Africa to the Black Sea and that lasted roughly from 31 B.C. to the fall of Rome in A.D. 476. This book describes Rome, known for its entertainment, customs, cuisine, and world dominance; Pompeii, a flourishing port and resort until it was destroyed by Mt. Vesuvius in A.D. 79; and Roman forts, provincial towns, and the countryside. A glossary of terms is included. Part of the History as Evidence series.

Dank, Milton. **D-Day.** Franklin Watts, 1984. 106 p. ISBN 0-531-04863-2.

The Allied forces decided that an invasion was necessary to defeat the Germans and end World War II. Operation Overlord was the code name for the plan to land American and British troops on the beaches of Normandy in a surprise attack on German forces in France on June 6, 1944. This book looks at the planning and execution of the invasion, German preparation for defense, and how D-Day became a turning point in the war. It focuses on the personalities of Adolf Hitler and Winston Churchill and their generals. Part of the Turning Points in World War II series.

De Lee, Nigel (edited by John Pimlott). **Rise of the Asian Superpowers from 1945.** Franklin Watts, 1987. 62 p. ISBN 0-531-10407-9.

Asia has undergone great change since the end of World War II. This book focuses on the Maoist revolution in China, the consolidation of power, the Japanese reconstruction after the war, and the fragmented Asian subcontinent. Such personalities as Chiang Kai-shek of Taiwan, Hirohito of Japan, Mao Tse-tung of China, and Jawaharlal Nehru of India are discussed. Included in the appendixes are information on Chinese revolutionary warfare, Chinese tactics in Korea, violence on the Indian subcontinent, the Indian and Pakistani armies, and a chronology of events.

Dolan, Edward F., Jr. **Anti-Semitism.** Franklin Watts, 1985. 135 p. ISBN 0-531-10068-5.

Hatred for the Jews did not begin with Adolf Hitler and did not end with him. It surfaced long ago in the Middle Ages and still flourishes today in the United States, parts of Europe, and the Arab nations. This book explains the roots of anti-Semitism, traces it through history to the 1980s, and explores its effect on the Jewish people.

Dunrea, Olivier. **Skara Brae: The Story of a Prehistoric Village.** Illustrated by the author. Holiday House, 1986. 35 p. ISBN 0-8234-0583-4.

North of Scotland, on one of the Orkney Islands, Neolithic farmers and herders built a village five thousand years ago. At first they built only temporary shelters, but these were followed with houses of rock, whale bone, and sod, and insulated with midden, or refuse. This book tells how these houses were designed and built, how the settlement was discovered in the mid-nineteenth century, and what it reveals about life and culture during this prehistoric period.

Ferrara, Peter L. **East vs. West in the Middle East.** Franklin Watts/Impact Books, 1983. 90 p. ISBN 0-531-04543-9.

This book focuses on the implications of the rivalry in the Middle East as the superpowers of the East and West try to influence nations and events in this region. The enormous oil reserves are part of the superpowers' interest in the Middle East, and the oil-producing nations have tried to resist manipulation and to maintain their independence through OPEC.

Ferrara, Peter L. **NATO: An Entangled Alliance.** Franklin Watts/Impact Books, 1984. 90 p. ISBN 0-531-04759-8.

Can NATO preserve world peace? Probably not, because it has not acted as a unified group on many current issues. Organized in 1949, the North Atlantic Treaty Organization was intended to act as a unified resistance to Soviet aggression following World War II. Since that time, however, many of the member countries have become friendly with the Soviets. Where does this leave the United States? Ferrara discusses this question as he traces NATO activities since the founding of the organization.

Ferrell, Nancy Warren. **Passports to Peace: Embassies and the Art of Diplomacy.** Lerner Publications, 1986. 87 p. ISBN 0-8225-0644-0.

Who really keeps the lines of communication open between nations that share mutual distrust? Here is a look at diplomats, foreign embassies, and the art of sharing one's culture abroad and keeping the peace. The book gives an overview of attempts at peacemaking from early times to the present and presents information about a career in foreign service. A glossary of terms and a gallery of diplomats are included.

Goff, Denise. **Early China.** Illustrated by Angus McBride, Karen Johnson, and Terry Dalley. Gloucester Press, 1986. 32 p. ISBN 0-531-17025-X.

Chinese civilization first began to emerge in 1600 B.C. in the valley of the Yellow River. This book discusses the origins of China, the history of its turbulence, life under the imperials, city life and peasantry, early art forms and beliefs, family life, and China's emergence as a strong and distinct culture. Part of the Civilization Library series.

Goor, Ron, and Nancy Goor. **Pompeii: Exploring a Roman Ghost Town.** Thomas Y. Crowell, 1986. 118 p. ISBN 0-690-04515-8 (0-690-04516-6, library binding).

Illustrated with black-and-white photographs, maps, and drawings, this is a thorough account of the discovery of the city of Pompeii. Covered with eighteen feet of ash and stone after Mt. Vesuvius erupted in A.D. 70, the city remained buried for 1500 years.

Archaeologists have excavated the ruins, piecing together what the social, political, cultural, and religious life was like in a town during the Roman Empire.

Hackwell, W. John. **Digging to the Past: Excavations in Ancient Lands.** Illustrated by the author. Charles Scribner's Sons, 1986. 50 p. ISBN 0-684-18692-6.

Now you can learn what it's like to take part in a typical archaeological dig. Included is the daily routine of the participants, the steps involved in the dig, and the long time it takes to uncover the homes, artifacts, and tombs of a lost civilization. The book discusses what ancient civilizations were like, based on archeological digs in the Middle East.

Hauptly, Denis J. **The Journey from the Past: A History of the Western World.** Atheneum, 1983. 238 p. ISBN 0-689-30973-2.

This story begins millions of years ago, when humankind first emerged in the forests of East Africa. Our original ancestors were hunters and gatherers. Then, about nine thousand years ago, later generations learned to plant seeds and raise crops. At this point, civilization as we know it began. Cities were built; empires were created and destroyed. This account of the history of the Western world is continued through the 1960s, including developments in Africa, South America, and Islamic countries.

Hughes, Jill. **Aztecs.** Illustrated by David Godfrey, Gary Hincks, Rob Shone, John Flynn, and Rob McCaig. Gloucester Press, 1986. 32 p. ISBN 0-531-17024-1.

Who were the Aztecs? Where did they live? How were they ruled? Whom did they worship? What was their life like? How did they trade? What were the people like in Tenochtitlán, one of their cities? How did they construct their calendar? How were they defeated and destroyed? These and other questions are answered in this book about the Aztecs of Mexico. Part of the Civilization Library series.

Hughes, Jill. **Imperial Rome.** Illustrated by Ivan Lapper. Gloucester Press, 1985. 32 p. ISBN 0-531-17003-9.

The "power and glory" of Imperial Rome comes to life in this book. The rise of Rome's political and religious power, the strength of the Roman army, the people's love of cruel sports, and the everyday life of the poor and wealthy are all presented. Each page is illustrated, and there is a glossary of terms.

Hyde, Margaret O., and Elizabeth H. Forsyth. **Terrorism: A Special Kind of Violence.** Dodd, Mead, 1987. 113 p. ISBN 0-396-08902-X.

This book provides a detailed look at the forms of terrorism, where it occurs, its historical origins, and its political, religious, and psychological aspects.

James, Simon. **Rome: 750 B.C.–500 A.D.** Illustrated by Rob Shone. Franklin Watts, 1987. 32 p. ISBN 0-531-10399-4.

Here is a vivid introduction to one of the great civilizations of the world. The book presents an overview of the history, politics, culture, economics, and social life of the Roman Empire and explores its influence on today's world.

Jones, John Ellis. **Ancient Greece.** Illustrated by David Salariya and Shirley Willis. Warwick Press, 1983. 37 p. ISBN 0-531-09220-8.

The influence of the Greeks is still with us — in our literature, our government, and our games. But just how did the Greek culture begin, and what changes occurred to develop the prehistoric Mycenae into a civilization that initiated the Western way of life? Part of the History as Evidence series.

Langley, Andrew. **Cleopatra and the Egyptians.** Illustrated by Gerry Wood. Bookwright Press, 1986. 58 p. ISBN 0-531-18079-4.

Cleopatra, the last queen of Egypt, was an ambitious and determined woman. She used her beauty to win the love of two Roman statesmen. The story of her life introduces the reader to the fascinating world of ancient Egypt — its development from a nation of tribes to one unified country under the rule of the Pharaohs, its submission to Alexander the Great, the many religions, and the customs and daily lives of the people.

Lauber, Patricia. **Tales Mummies Tell.** Thomas Y. Crowell, 1985. 118 p. ISBN 0-690-04388-0 (0-690-04389-9, library binding).

Using such tools as the X-ray to help them study mummies, scientists are now learning about how the ancient people of Egypt, Peru, and Denmark lived. Medical scientists use X-rays to help reveal the shape of faces; they examine the bones to reveal the age at death, diseases, and if there were broken bones; and they study the teeth to gain information about diet and health. Many photos, some gruesome, illustrate the book.

Lyttle, Richard B. **The Golden Path.** Atheneum, 1983. 153 p. ISBN 0-689-31006-4.

Gold is not the most valuable metal — platinum and uranium are worth more. But gold has had a greater impact on human history than any other metal. The ancient Egyptians, Greeks, and Romans all valued gold for its abilities to resist corrosion and to be worked into many different shapes. This book gives a clear account of the techniques used to mine gold and to apply it in many different ways, from jewelry to computers.

Lyttle, Richard B. **Land beyond the River: Europe in the Age of Migration.** Illustrated by the author. Atheneum, 1986. 175 p. ISBN 0-689-31199-0.

In the years after the fall of Rome, Europe and Asia were shaped by migrations of tribes with such names as the Huns, the Goths, the Vandals, the Anglo-Saxons, the Muslims, the Vikings, and the Mongols. This book tells the history of these ancient tribes, of their movements through Europe and Asia, and of their importance to our modern world.

McPhillips, Martin. **Hiroshima.** Silver Burdett, 1985. 62 p. ISBN 0-382-06976-5 (0-382-06829-7, library binding).

On August 6, 1945, the United States dropped an atomic bomb on Hiroshima, crippling Japan and leading to the end of the war in the Pacific. This book traces the development of the atomic bomb, relates how the decision was made to drop the bomb on Japan, focuses on the world leaders of that time, and explores the aftermath of the bomb and implications of this event for the future of the world. Part of the Turning Points in American History series.

Markl, Julia. **The Battle of Britain.** Franklin Watts, 1984. 106 p. ISBN 0-531-04861-6.

In May of 1940, Adolf Hitler controlled all of Western Europe except England. His strategy to conquer that island was to use air warfare to bomb it into submission. He assigned Hermann Goering to lead the strikes. On the other side, the English leader, Winston Churchill, assigned Sir Hugh Dowding. The struggle between these men, their forces, and their machines is carefully related in these pages. Each level of the contest, from the human side of commander and pilot to the mechanical side of radar, plane, and gun, is clearly analyzed. Part of the Turning Points of World War II series.

Marrin, Albert. **Aztecs and Spaniards: Cortés and the Conquest of Mexico.** Atheneum, 1986. 212 p. ISBN 0-689-31176-1.

The Aztecs arrived in central Mexico toward the end of the twelfth century and were a powerful political and cultural group by the time that Hernán Cortés, the Spanish conquistador, arrived in 1519. Cortés conquered this wealthy and powerful nation, thus bringing riches and fame to Spain, but his reward was not exactly what he had expected.

Marrin, Albert. **The Sea Rovers: Pirates, Privateers, and Buccaneers.** Atheneum, 1984. 173 p. ISBN 0-689-31029-3.

Drake, Morgan, Captain Kidd, and Blackbeard all were swashbucklers in the 1500s to the 1800s, when pirates, privateers, and buccaneers roamed the seas. Read about their colorful lives in this book. Also included are stories about women sailing under the Jolly Roger pirate flag and the Barbary Pirates.

Martell, Hazel. **The Vikings.** Illustrated by David Salariya and Shirley Willis. Warwick Press, 1986. ISBN 0-531-19008-0.

The Vikings have a reputation for being a warlike, conquering people as they explored the British Isles, Europe, Greenland, and North America. But many of their voyages to other lands were quests in search of new homes. Read about their lives as farmers, shipbuilders, and explorers. Learn also of the enduring influence these early voyagers had on the countries they inhabited. Part of the History as Evidence series.

Maynard, Christopher, and David Jefferis. **The Aces: Pilots and Planes of World War I.** Illustrated by Ron Jobson and Michael Roffe. Franklin Watts, 1987. 32 p. ISBN 0-531-10367-6.

When the Wright brothers made their celebrated airplane flight in 1903, little did they know that planes would be used in combat just ten years later. Here is a brief introduction to the pilots and planes of World War I. The book discusses airborne dogfights between planes, the use of machine guns on planes, the development of bomber planes, flying and fighting over water, the legendary Red Baron, and essential data about World War I aircraft. Part of the Wings: The Conquest of the Air series.

Maynard, Christopher, and David Jefferis. **Air Battles: Air Combat in World War II.** Illustrated by Terry Hadler, Ron Jobson, and Michael Roffe. Franklin Watts, 1987. 32 p. ISBN 0-531-10368-4.

Aircraft combat in World War II is the topic of this book. Included in the discussion are fighting planes, the German blitzkrieg over Poland, the Battle of Britain, the attack on Taranto, the attack on Pearl Harbor, the Pacific air war and the Japanese Kamikazes, aircraft carriers, the Battle of the Atlantic, night fighting and daylight raiding, as well as the development of jets and the atomic bomb.

Meyer, Carolyn. **Voices of South Africa: Growing Up in a Troubled Land.** Harcourt Brace Jovanovich/Gulliver Books, 1986. 244 p. ISBN 0-15-200637-0.

In kaleidoscopic fashion, the author has woven together stories from young South Africans who tell from different viewpoints what it is like to live in this highly segregated country. The rich, the poor, the black, and the white all love their country, but in vastly different ways. Included are a bibliography and glossary.

Meyer, Carolyn, and Charles Gallenkamp. **The Mystery of the Ancient Maya.** Atheneum/Margaret K. McElderry Books, 1985. 159 p. ISBN 0-689-50319-9.

Disappearing after six centuries, the Maya left unparalleled achievements as a mysterious legacy — traces of a complex culture and vast carved-stone temples and buildings found in the forbidding jungles of Central and South America. Since the Spanish conquered that region in the 1500s, people have struggled to answer these perplexing questions: Who were these people? How did they build without modern technology? What happened to them? Discover this lost civilization for yourself.

Moolman, Valerie. **The Future World of Transportation.** Franklin Watts/ Walt Disney World, EPCOT Center Books, 1984. 112 p. ISBN 0-531-04882-9.

Based on the World of Motion exhibit at Walt Disney's EPCOT Center, this book discusses the history of transportation, traces the development of travel on land, on sea, and in air, and looks ahead at future vehicles and modes of transportation. Included are photographs, diagrams, and a glossary of terms.

Morrison, Marion. **Atahuallpa and the Incas.** Illustrated by Gerry Wood. Bookwright Press, 1986. 58 p. ISBN 0-531-18080-8.

Atahuallpa was the last of the great Inca rulers. He was captured in the mid-sixteenth century by the Spanish invaders, who were greedy for the riches of the Inca Empire. The story of Atahuallpa's life introduces the reader to the world of this South American civilization — the legends surrounding its history, the warrior Incas, their magnificent cities, the lives of the ordinary people, and the final destruction of their empire by the Spanish. Part of the Life and Times series.

Nahm, Andrew C. **A Panorama of 5000 Years: Korean History.** Hollym International, 1983. 121 p. ISBN 0-930878-23-X.

The country of Korea has a unique culture and a strong national heritage, even though it is surrounded by larger and stronger countries: China, the Soviet Union, and Japan. Despite centuries of foreign invasion and its division into two republics, Korea is rich in history, art, architecture, and artifacts. This book includes historic highlights and many photographs.

North, James. **Freedom Rising.** New American Library/Plume Books, 1986. 347 p. ISBN 0-452-25805-7.

How is it possible for the South African government to impose the policy of apartheid — strict racial segregation and discrimination — on its native peoples? These and countless other questions are answered through the eyes of a young American white author who spent four and a half years in southern Africa.

Perl, Lila. **Mummies, Tombs, and Treasure: Secrets of Ancient Egypt.** Illustrated by Erika Weihs. Clarion Books, 1987. 120 p. ISBN 0-89919-407-9.

Here is an account of the ancient Egyptian way of death. The book begins with the first Egyptian mummies, which were the result of the natural effects of the sun, and then looks at why the Egyptians made mummies, how a mummy was made, what the tomb was like, and what the Egyptians believed about the afterlife. It also discusses the mummy's treasure, the resulting tomb robbers, and why the Egyptians stopped making mummies.

Pimlott, John. **The Cold War.** Franklin Watts, 1987. 62 p. ISBN 0-531-10320-X.

The *cold war* is the term used to describe the struggle for power and prestige that existed between the Western nations and the Communist bloc. This struggle manifested itself after the end of World War II and continued until 1962, when U.S. intelligence discovered Soviet missile installations in Cuba. U.S. vessels were sent to intercept Soviet ships carrying rockets to Cuba, but the Soviets decided to halt the shipments. The confrontation demonstrated that neither side would risk nuclear war, and tensions between the two factions decreased. This book traces the history of the cold war from 1945 to 1962, examines shifting allegiances within each superpower group, and looks at the role played by NATO and the Warsaw Pact. Appendixes focus on personalities, East-West flashpoints, East-West balance of forces, spies and spying, the space race, and a chronology of events. Part of the Conflict in the Twentieth Century series.

Pimlott, John. **The First World War.** Illustrated by Ron Hayward Associates and Peter Bull. Franklin Watts, 1986. 62 p. ISBN 0-531-10234-3.

From the assassination of Archduke Francis Ferdinand of Austria-Hungary in 1914 to the armistice between Germany and the Allied powers in 1918, the events of World War I are detailed in this book. It profiles important figures on both sides and describes warfare on land, on sea, in the air, and in the trenches. Part of the Conflict in the Twentieth Century series.

Powell, Anton. **Greece: 1600–30 B.C.** Illustrated by Rob Shone. Franklin Watts, 1987. 32 p. ISBN 0-531-10398-6.

The ancient Greek civilizations contributed much to the modern world. Drama and democracy, politics and philosophy — all were inventions of the ancient Greeks. This book documents the highlights of the Greek civilization and provides date charts and colorful, accurate artwork. The Greek civilization is divided into four eras: the Mycenaeans (1600–1150 B.C.), the age of expansion (1000–479 B.C.), the golden age (478–405 B.C.), and the Hellenistic age (336–30 B.C.).

Rahn, Joan Elma. **More Plants That Changed History.** Illustrated by the author. Atheneum, 1985. 126 p. ISBN 0-689-31099-4.

While we might not initially think of plants as affecting our history, some plants have had a great impact on humankind. This book looks at the importance of several plants: papyrus, one source of paper; the rubber tree, from which tires and other rubber products are made; tea, the source of a popular drink; and the opium poppy, used in producing morphine, codeine, and other medicines. All have had an effect on individuals as well as on the relationships between nations.

Raynor, Thomas P. **Terrorism: Past, Present, Future.** Rev. ed. Franklin Watts, 1987. 176 p. ISBN 0-531-10344-7.

Terrorism emerged as a concept during the Reign of Terror in eighteenth-century France, when Marie Antoinette was executed. Since that time terror has been used increasingly to achieve particular ends. This book focuses on the rise of terrorists, their objectives, their activities, the groups that they involve, and how they are financed, trained, and equipped.

Rowland-Entwistle, Theodore. **Confucius and Ancient China.** Illustrated by Gerry Wood. Bookwright Press, 1987. 62 p. ISBN 0-531-18101-4.

Relatively unknown during his own lifetime (mid-500 to mid-400 B.C.), Confucius has had a great influence upon the values, principles, and customs of the Chinese people. In this book you will be introduced to the land of ancient China and its development from a collection of tribes to a unified state under the "First Emperor," Shih-Huang-ti. It provides an entertaining and informative insight into the origins of Chinese culture and civilization. Part of the Life and Time series.

Saunders, Alan. **The Invasion of Poland.** Franklin Watts, 1984. 103 p. ISBN 0-531-04864-0.

World War II began in Poland. But the struggle between Poland and Germany began long before September 1, 1939. To understand why Germany invaded Poland at that time, one must go back to the year 1000 and work through the nine hundred years of major conflicts between these two nations. This book gives the reader a brief history of Europe, emphasizing events related to the invasion of Poland. Part of the Turning Points of World War II series.

Sauvain, Philip. **Do You Know about Castles and Crusaders?** Illustrated by Jim Robins. Warwick Press, 1986. 32 p. ISBN 0-531-19015-3.

Have you ever wondered what life was like in the days of knights and castles? This book examines the period of history called the

Middle Ages, which lasted from roughly 500 to 1500. Topics range from the long and violent wars that were waged between kingdoms to the everyday lives of people living in towns and country villages. Part of the Do You Know? series.

Sender, Ruth Minsky. **The Cage.** Macmillan, 1986. 245 p. ISBN 0-02-781830-6.

At age sixteen, Riva became guardian of her family in the Lodz ghetto, a barbed wire cage in Poland. One brother became ill, and all efforts were directed to saving him. Riva's indomitable spirit and fortitude take her from 1942 to 1945, when her family was deported from Poland and sent to the concentration camp at Auschwitz.

Spencer, William. **Islamic States in Conflict.** Franklin Watts/Impact Books, 1983. 90 p. ISBN 0-531-04544-7.

Here is a wide-ranging analysis of the relationships between the Islamic states. The book shows how a common faith in Islam unites the Arab states and Iran in spite of their real divisions and concludes that these states are trying to maintain their independence from outside influences.

Stead, Miriam. **Ancient Egypt.** Illustrated by Angus McBride, Eric Thomas, and John Brettoner. Gloucester Press, 1985. 32 p. ISBN 0-531-17002-0.

This book provides an easy-to-read, easy-to-follow history of the growth and power of ancient Egypt. Its religion, pharaohs, gods, military adventures, trade, and life on the land are all presented with accompanying illustrations. A glossary of terms is included.

Ventura, Piero. **There Once Was a Time.** G. P. Putnam's Sons, 1987. 159 p. ISBN 0-399-21356-2.

In this account, the history of western civilization is divided into eight periods. Nine aspects of everyday life are examined in each era: society, homes, agriculture, crafts, trade, dress, transportation, inventions, and warfare. Important people, major events, and the reasons for these events taking place are noted.

Ventura, Piero, and Gian Paolo Ceserani. **In Search of Ancient Crete.** Silver Burdett, 1985. 47 p. ISBN 0-382-09120-5 (0-382-09117-5, library binding).

Archaeological excavations on the Mediterranean island of Crete revealed the remains of the legendary Minoan civilization that flourished between 3000 and 1450 B.C. A volcanic eruption destroyed the civilization, but the molten lava also preserved a record of daily life for future generations to see.

Ventura, Piero, and Gian Paolo Ceserani. **In Search of Troy.** Silver Burdett, 1985. 47 p. ISBN 0-382-09121-3 (0-382-09118-3, library binding).

Did the city of Troy really exist? Where was it? This book traces Heinrich Schliemann's nineteenth-century search for and discovery of the site of ancient Troy. It discusses the mythology of the Trojan horse and possible historical facts surrounding the siege. Much controversy still exists about Schliemann's findings — judge for yourself whether he located the ancient city of Troy.

Ventura, Piero, and Gian Paolo Ceserani. **In Search of Tutankhamun.** Silver Burdett, 1985. 47 p. ISBN 0-382-09122-1 (0-382-09119-1, library binding).

The modern world was enthralled when the treasures of Tutankhamun's tomb were revealed in the 1920s. This book traces the search for and eventual discovery of the hidden tomb of Tutankhamun in Egypt and discusses life in Egypt during the pharaoh's reign over three thousand years ago.

Windrow, Martin. **The British Redcoat of the Napoleonic Wars.** Illustrated by Angus McBride. Franklin Watts, 1985. 32 p. ISBN 0-531-10082-0.

A *redcoat* was a name for a British soldier during the American Revolutionary War and the Napoleonic wars of the early nineteenth century. This book discusses recruiting soldiers to fight against Napoleon's forces, the drills to prepare for battle, barrack life, equipment of the era, and topics related to being a soldier during this time period. Part of the Soldier through the Ages series.

Windrow, Martin. **The World War I Tommy.** Illustrated by Richard Hook. Franklin Watts, 1986. 32 p. ISBN 0-531-10083-9.

British soldiers during World War I were called *Tommies.* The nickname came from Thomas Adkins, the name used as a sample on official army forms. After a few months of inadequate training, Tommies were shipped across the English Channel to France, or to wherever else British forces were stationed. This book describes the Tommies' uniforms, the equipment they carried or operated, and the life they encountered during the war. Also included are a glossary of terms and a time chart.

Woods, Harold, and Geraldine Woods. **The United Nations.** Franklin Watts/First Books, 1985. 65 p. ISBN 0-531-10048-0.

The United Nations is a country within itself. This book describes the history leading to the founding of the U.N. in 1945, how it is organized, and the role it plays in the governing of the world. The U.N. deals with crises between nations and judges offenses between countries. It also researches illnesses and diseases and sponsors emergency services.

Worth, Richard. **Israel and the Arab States.** Franklin Watts/Impact Books, 1983. 90 p. ISBN 0-531-04545-5.

Great conflicts exist between Israel and the Arab states, making this region one of the most explosive in the world today. This book supplies the background information necessary to place the Middle East in its proper historical and political context. Major conflicts are examined, and efforts at attaining peace are described. Equal consideration of both sides is presented.

Hobbies and Crafts

Abrams, Lawrence F. **Throw It out of Sight! Building and Flying a Hand-Launched Glider.** Dillon Press, 1984. 93 p. ISBN 0-87518-247-X.

Instructions for building and flying a balsa-wood glider are given in this book. The directions include a pattern and range from wood selection and tools to how to enter flying competitions. Suggestions are given on how to handle such problems as breakage and finding lost planes. A glossary of terms is included.

Anderson, Gretchen, compiler. **The Louisa May Alcott Cookbook.** Illustrated by Karen Milone. Little, Brown, 1985. 81 p. ISBN 0-316-03951-9.

Nine-year-old Gretchen Anderson compiled this book of authentic nineteenth-century recipes inspired by two classics by Louisa May Alcott, *Little Men* and *Little Women.* The author-tested recipes are coded as to levels of difficulty and follow excerpts from Alcott's novels mentioning the foods.

Burchard, Peter. **Venturing: An Introduction to Sailing.** Photographs by the author. Little, Brown, 1986. 138 p. ISBN 0-316-11613-0.

Seafaring adventurers of all ages can benefit from this book. Written by an experienced sailor, it offers practical advice and specific information on how to sail small boats. A glossary of terms is included.

Caket, Colin. **Model a Monster: Making Dinosaurs from Everyday Materials.** Illustrated by the author. Blanford Press, 1986. 160 p. ISBN 0-7137-1671-1 (0-7137-1672-X, paperback).

With this book and a little practice, the reader will be able to make interesting and lifelike models of prehistoric animals. How to make each model is explained in easy stages. A list of tools and materials needed, all inexpensive and easy to find, is at the start of each section. Readers will learn how to make the most of the materials they use, and also something about the way of life of the monsters being modeled.

Cone, Ferne Geller. **Classy Knitting: A Guide to Creative Sweatering for Beginners.** Photographs by J. Morton Cone and the author; illustrated by Joann Evans. Atheneum, 1984. 127 p. ISBN 0-689-31062-5.

Who knits? Rock stars, politicians, ballet dancers, television performers, teenagers, anyone who really wants to. It's easy! It's fun! Even the most fumble-fingered knitter will discover that making a sweater can be enjoyable. Please join us in unraveling the "mystery" of knitting.

Coombs, Charles. **Ultralights: The Flying Featherweights.** William Morrow, 1984. 149 p. ISBN 0-688-02775-X.

Here's an introduction to ultralights — the new, small, engine-powered recreational aircraft. The book summarizes the development of ultralights and explains the basic parts and controls of these aircraft. Safety rules as well as aerodynamics and navigation are discussed.

Dean, Anabel. **Going Underground: All about Caves and Caving.** Dillon Press, 1984. 155 p. ISBN 0-87518-255-0.

Spelunking, or exploring caves, is the topic of this book. It describes the various types of caves and how they have been used through the years. Safety rules and precautions, necessary equipment, and the basic techniques of spelunking are discussed. Included are a list of caving organizations, a glossary of terms, and a selected bibliography.

Dunnahoo, Terry. **Break Dancing.** Photographs by Robert Sefcik. Franklin Watts/First Books, 1985. 64 p. ISBN 0-531-04883-7.

If you've ever wanted to learn break dancing, this is the book for you. After a short history of how this type of dancing originated, the book takes the reader step-by-step through the intricacies of each movement and then shows how to put the moves together into a routine. Also included is information on rapping and on forming a break-dancing club at school.

Faggella, Kathy, and Janet Horowitz. **Make It Special: Gift Creations for All Occasions.** New American Library/Plume Books, 1986. 214 p. ISBN 0-452-25746-8.

Giving the right gift brings you a good feeling. This book matches hundreds of wonderfully unique gift ideas to appropriate occasions and shows how even the novice craftsperson can create delightful, inexpensive presents with a personal touch.

Fowler, Virginie. **Christmas Crafts and Customs around the World.** Illustrated by the author. Prentice-Hall, 1984. 171 p. ISBN 0-13-133661-4.

Christmas celebrations occur between December 6, Saint Nicholas Day, and January 6, Epiphany (also known as Twelfth Night or Three Kings' Day). This book describes the Christmas celebrations in twelve countries. Thirty-eight projects are included — some edible, some decorative. The book provides general instructions for baking, for working with clay, wood, and fabric, for enlarging and reducing designs, and for locating sources of supplies.

Hautzig, Esther. **Make It Special: Cards, Decorations, and Party Favors for Holidays and Other Special Occasions.** Illustrated by Martha Weston. Macmillan, 1986. 86 p. ISBN 0-02-743370-6.

More than fifty easy-to-make home and table decorations, party favors, and cards are described to help celebrate a variety of occasions. There are clear, simply written directions for projects that are fun to do, different, and inexpensive, and the book includes many illustrations and diagrams and plenty of helpful hints.

Henschel, Georgie. **Horses and Riding.** Warwick Press/Gateway Fact Books, 1986. 93 p. ISBN 0-531-19021-8.

Everything you might want to know about horses is included in this book. There is information on the kinds of horses, how to take care of them, learning to ride, showing horses, and special events.

Hunt, Linda, Marianne Frase, and Doris Liebert. **Celebrate the Seasons: A "Love Your Neighbor" Gardening Book.** Herald Press, 1983. 163 p. ISBN 0-8361-33371-14.

This is a complete guide to gardening written in an easy-to-read style. There are sections on gardening terms, where, what, and when to plant, and how to plan an individual or community garden. Clear instructions are given for preparing the soil, for planting and caring for various vegetables and herbs, and for harvesting the crops. Many recipes are suggested, and there are ideas for flower gardens and for using flowers and other by-products of a garden for crafts.

Janeczko, Paul B. **Loads of Codes and Secret Ciphers.** Illustrated by Kathie Kelleher. Macmillan, 1984. 108 p. ISBN 0-02-747810-6.

Spies have always used codes and ciphers; so have hoboes, cowboys, and Indians. Now you too can use them. This book provides practice in making and breaking codes and ciphers and in building simple coding devices to transmit secret messages. You'll want to read this book with paper and pencil in hand, and be sure to YBTXOB LC QOBXZEBOV. (You'll learn to decipher this code on page 42 of the book.)

McGill, Ormond. **Balancing Magic and Other Tricks.** Illustrated by Anne Canevari Green. Franklin Watts/First Books, 1986. 91 p. ISBN 0-531-10208-4.

This book describes how to do a variety of magic tricks and balancing tricks. Fifty-plus tricks are included in the following categories: balancing tricks, ball tricks, coin tricks, egg tricks, tricks with glasses, conjuring tricks, juggling, and an assortment of other tricks. Explanations are clear and thorough, so readers should be successful in learning the tricks.

McGowen, Tom. **War Gaming.** Franklin Watts/First Books, 1985. 64 p. ISBN 0-531-04918-3.

This book introduces the hobby of war games. It explains the different kinds of war games, describes how to build, paint, and organize miniatures and battlefields, and suggests how to develop your own war games.

Orleans, Selma, and Jack Orleans. **The Best Book of Pencil Puzzles.** Putnam/Perigee Books, 1985. 160 p. ISBN 0-399-51135-0.

Grab your pencils — and an eraser. Here is a book filled with puzzles to amuse you for hours. Crosswords, logic games, pictograms, word games, and even math puzzles abound in this book to entertain you and your friends.

Purdy, Susan. **Christmas Cooking around the World.** Illustrated by the author. Franklin Watts, 1983. 96 p. ISBN 0-531-03578-6 (0-531-04654-0, paperback).

This book features Christmas cooking and customs from around the world. Countries featured are the British Isles, France, Italy, the Scandinavian countries, Germany, various middle and eastern European nations, and Mexico. The book includes an introduction to basic cooking skills, a table of metric conversions, and step-by-step illustrations. Part of the Holiday Cookbook series.

Roberts, Charles P., and George F. Roberts. **Fishing for Fun: A Freshwater Guide.** Illustrated by Virgil Beck. Dillon Press, 1984. 155 p. ISBN 0-87518-252-6.

For the beginning fisherman, this book discusses equipment, bait, lures, tying knots, where to fish, when to fish, and how to clean the catch. The emphasis is on simple and inexpensive approaches to angling. A glossary of terms is included.

Roessler, Carl. **Mastering Underwater Photography.** Photographs by the author. William Morrow, 1984. 102 p. ISBN 0-688-03881-6 (0-688-03882-4, paperback).

This very readable photography handbook gives the kind of practical information you will need to improve basic photographic skills and to take successful underwater photographs. The author, a professional underwater photographer, details his methods, techniques, equipment, and secrets for handling the underwater medium and its inhabitants. All of the major difficulties encountered in underwater photography are addressed in clear, nontechnical language.

Streb, Judith. **Holiday Parties.** Illustrated by Anne Canevari Green. Franklin Watts, 1985. 64 p. ISBN 0-531-10041-3.

Let's celebrate! The origins and symbols for Valentine's Day, Halloween, Thanksgiving, Christmas, and Hanukkah are described in this book. Suggested decorations and activities for parties that celebrate each of these holidays are given.

White, Laurence B., Jr., and Ray Broekel. **Optical Illusions.** Franklin Watts/First Books, 1986. 93 p. ISBN 0-531-10220-3.

This book explains how optical illusions trick the eye and fool perception. Several examples and explanations of various optical illusions are included. The book describes how color plays tricks on our eyes, and discusses optical illusions that are with us in our everyday lives. A bibliography is included.

How-To Books

Brandt, Sue R. **How to Write a Report.** Rev. ed. Illustrated by Anne Canevari Green. Franklin Watts/First Books, 1986. 90 p. ISBN 0-531-10216-5.

Report writing is a frequent assignment. This book gives step-by-step instructions for writing a report, including choosing and understanding your subject, building a bibliography, taking notes, outlining, and writing the final draft.

Carey, Helen H., and Judith E. Greenberg. **How to Read a Newspaper.** Franklin Watts/Social Studies Skills Books, 1983. 95 p. ISBN 0-531-04672-9.

The purpose of this book is to increase your understanding of how a newspaper is put together and to make reading the newspaper more efficient. Topics discussed include what makes an event newsworthy, who reports the news, how stories are written, why objectivity is important, where to find the newspaper's opinion on an issue, and what are feature stories and photojournalism.

Carey, Helen H., and Judith E. Greenberg. **How to Use Primary Sources.** Franklin Watts/Social Studies Skills Books, 1983. 95 p. ISBN 0-531-04674-5.

Using primary sources can improve your papers and reports. This book discusses such possible primary sources as people, photographs, paintings and other works of art, artifacts, legal documents, letters, diaries, and journals. The reader is told where to find the sources, how to obtain the information needed, and how to present the information.

Carey, Helen H., and Deborah R. Hanka. **How to Use Your Community as a Resource.** Franklin Watts/Social Studies Skills Books, 1983. 95 p. ISBN 0-531-04675-3.

Your community can be a valuable source of information. This book gives information on how to set up a community resource file, how to structure a community project, and how to retrieve information quickly. Directions are given for conducting an interview, conducting a poll or survey, and presenting the information gathered. A list of topics that can be researched is included.

Diem, Richard A. **How to Use Computers as a Resource.** Franklin Watts/Social Studies Skills Books, 1983. 95 p. ISBN 0-531-04676-1.

This book focuses on using computers for social studies projects. It traces the use of computers from the abacus to the microcomputer. Computer terminology and vocabulary are explained, and the book discusses solving problems with computers and the future of computers.

Dunbar, Robert E. **How to Debate.** Franklin Watts/Language Power Books, 1987. 102 p. ISBN 0-531-10335-8.

Making your point effectively is a valuable skill. This book discusses what debating is, how to prepare for it, methods of argument, taking the affirmative stand, how the negative side attacks, listening and responding effectively, how judges make their decisions, and procedures for formal debates. A glossary of terms is included, plus debate topics and sources and a listing of annual national debate competitions.

Greenberg, Judith E., and Helen H. Carey. **How to Participate in a Group.** Franklin Watts/Social Studies Skills Books, 1983. 95 p. ISBN 0-531-04671-0.

In your many years in school, you'll probably belong to at least one student club or group. Here is a book that will help that organization run more smoothly. It contains tips on finding a club or group that interests you, becoming a responsible member, choosing club officers, and resolving conflicts within the group. The book also includes directions on how to write a constitution and bylaws, how to use parliamentary procedure, and other group participation skills. Case studies of several student-run organizations provide examples.

Nida, Patricia Cooney, and Wendy M. Heller. **The Teenager's Survival Guide to Moving.** Atheneum, 1985. 136 p. ISBN 0-689-31077-3.

Moving can be a pretty stress-filled experience, whether it is to a new neighborhood, a new town, another state, or another country. This book tells you about leaving old friends, making new ones, fitting in at a new school, and packing your things. It also helps you understand your emotions during a move and how to feel your best and adjust to a new situation.

Provost, Gary. **100 Ways to Improve Your Writing.** New American Library/Mentor Books, 1985. 158 p. ISBN 0-451-62425-4.

Throughout life, there will be many occasions when you'll want your writing to be clear and precise. This book will teach you to write better love letters, stories, magazine articles, sermons, parole requests, poems, graffiti, essays, and shopping lists, to name just a few. Some of the section titles are Nine Ways to Improve Your Writing When You're Not Writing, Five Ways to Write a Strong Beginning, Ten Ways to Develop Style, Eleven Ways to Make People Like What You Wrote, and Seven Ways to Edit Yourself.

Ryan, Margaret. **So You Have to Give a Speech!** Franklin Watts/Language Power Books, 1987. 122 p. ISBN 0-531-10337-4.

Being assigned to give a speech can produce butterflies in the stomach, but here's a book that might help ease your nerves. It covers choosing a topic, gathering information, preparing a draft, practicing, and delivering the speech.

Stein, Harry. **How to Interpret Visual Resources.** Franklin Watts/Social Studies Skills Books, 1983. 95 p. ISBN 0-531-04670-2.

Visual resources are all around us — printed materials such as graphs and charts, electronic images such as television, and artistic expressions such as paintings and photographs. This book will help you obtain and interpret the most information possible from these visual resources.

Information, Please

Apfel, Necia H. **Calendars.** Franklin Watts/First Books, 1985. 85 p. ISBN 0-531-10034-0.

Did you ever wonder how the calculation of time evolved? Or perhaps you've puzzled over the formation of rocks in England known as Stonehenge. Factual and well illustrated, this book explains how early humans and various cultures created calendars to organize their lives and reflect their beliefs.

Arnold, Eric H., and Jeffrey Loeb, editors. **Lights Out! Kids Talk about Summer Camp.** Illustrated by True Kelley. Little, Brown/Hole in the Sock Books, 1986. 74 p. ISBN 0-316-05184-5 (0-316-05183-7, paperback).

For all campers, this book presents kids' own experiences and their comments and observations on life at summer camp. Camp food, adjusting to life in a bunkhouse, homesickness — all aspects of camping are addressed frankly. Space is provided for recording personal experiences and autographs. The book would make a good camping companion, especially for prospective campers.

Arnow, Jan. **Hay from Seed to Feed.** Photographs by the author. Alfred A. Knopf/Borzoi Books, 1986. 39 p. ISBN 0-394-96508-6.

Text and photographs depict the growing of alfalfa hay on a farm in Kentucky. The book explains how the ground is prepared and the seeds are sown — at a rate of more than four million seeds per acre. When the alfalfa reaches 20 to 30 inches, it is ready for the first cutting, providing valuable nutrients for the animals that eat it.

Aylesworth, Thomas G., and Virginia L. Aylesworth. **The Mount St. Helens Disaster: What We've Learned.** Franklin Watts/Impact Books, 1983. 86 p. ISBN 0-531-04488-2.

On May 18, 1980, Mount St. Helens erupted in Washington, sending volcanic ash into the air and molten lava into the valleys below. This book is an account of the buildup, the blowup, and the aftermath of the volcano. It provides information on the damage done by volcanoes, on the different kinds of volcanoes, and on our ability to predict volcanic eruptions.

Baldwin, Dorothy, and Claire Lister. **Your Senses.** Bookwright Press, 1984. 32 p. ISBN 0-531-04798-9.

We use our five senses constantly — seeing, hearing, tasting, touching, and smelling the world around us. Here is a look at how our senses work, such as how our eyes move, and how and why we feel pain. Colorful photographs and illustrations accompany the text. Part of the You and Your Body series.

Berger, Gilda. **Aviation.** Franklin Watts/Reference First Books, 1983. 92 p. ISBN 0-531-04645-1.

Although we might think of aircraft as a fairly recent invention, back in 1650 Francisco de Lana of Italy published the first design for an airship. This book offers information on aircrafts ranging from the Wright brothers' *Flyer,* to World War II fighter planes, to today's supersonic Concorde. It provides definitions for aviation terms, describes the physical principles of air flight, and identifies people and organizations involved with aviation.

Blumberg, Rhoda. **Monsters.** Franklin Watts/Reference First Books, 1983. 89 p. ISBN 0-531-04648-6.

Frankenstein: was he a monster or monster maker? Actually, the first Frankenstein was a medical student in the 1817 novel *Frankenstein* by Mary Wollstonecraft Shelley. The soulless monster created by this student from various corpses became the source for countless imitations in monster lore. Read about Frankenstein and other creatures of horror from mythology and legend in this humorous dictionary.

Branley, Franklyn M. **Mysteries of Life on Earth and Beyond.** Illustrated by Sally J. Bensusen. E. P. Dutton/Lodestar Books, 1987. 57 p. ISBN 0-525-67195-1.

Imagine bat-people eating melons by the edge of a lake, surrounded by small buffalos and bears walking on their hind legs — all on the moon! This is what an English astronomer claimed to have seen through his telescope in 1835, and thousands of people believed him. This book discusses the possibilities of life on the moon and other planets and ways of communicating with extraterrestrials, from optical supertelescopes to huge, eye-catching triangles blazing in the Sahara Desert.

Cheney, Glenn Alan. **Mineral Resources.** Franklin Watts/First Books, 1985. 62 p. ISBN 0-531-04915-9.

Over 2,000 mineral resources have been identified, and they are classified as metallic, nonmetallic, and strategic. Here is an examination of the composition of these minerals, where they are found, how they are mined, and how they are used. A glossary of terms is included.

Cobb, Vicki. **More Power to You.** Illustrated by Bill Ogden. Little, Brown, 1986. 50 p. ISBN 0-316-14899-7.

We take it for granted that we can flip the switch and then have lights, music, heat, air-conditioning — all the electric appliances that make our modern world work. This book explains just how electricity and other forms of power work, and includes experiments and tricks. Part of the How the World Works series.

Cobb, Vicki. **The Scoop on Ice Cream.** Illustrated by G. Brian Karas. Little, Brown, 1985. 53 p. ISBN 0-316-14895-4.

Who doesn't love ice cream? This book will tempt your taste buds with its complete, easy-to-read description of the making of ice cream. It describes the ingredients, where they come from, and how the ice cream is processed, frozen, and tested. There is also a recipe for homemade ice cream. Part of the How the World Works series.

Cobb, Vicki. **Sneakers Meet Your Feet.** Illustrated by Theo Cobb. Little, Brown, 1985. 48 p. ISBN 0-316-14896-2.

The feel and smell of new sneakers — there's nothing like it! But these marvels of engineering and manufacturing don't just happen. Many people, machines, and industries work to make rubber, cotton, nylon, and leather into the shoes we love to wear. Part of the How the World Works series.

Cobb, Vicki. **The Trip of a Drip.** Illustrated by Elliot Kreloff. Little, Brown, 1986. 50 p. ISBN 0-316-14900-4.

Did you ever wonder how the water gets into your faucet? Or where it goes when it disappears down the drain? This book traces our water supply from its source to its final destination. Part of the How the World Works series.

Corrick, James A. **Recent Revolutions in Chemistry.** Franklin Watts/Science Impact Books, 1986. 128 p. ISBN 0-531-10241-6.

Recent developments in chemistry have affected all aspects of our life, giving us everything from plastic products to computers. Several important events, including the discovery of atoms and the theories of atomic and molecular combination, have led twentieth-century chemists to a number of inventions. This book looks at the different branches of chemistry and discusses some recent discoveries and their practical uses. A glossary of terms and bibliography are included.

Detz, Joan. **You Mean I Have to Stand Up and Say Something?** Illustrated by David Marshall. Atheneum, 1986. 86 p. ISBN 0-689-31221-0.

This is a humorous, step-by-step explanation of how to prepare and give a speech. It suggests references to use and discusses the role of audiovisual aids. Speaking situations range from oral book reports in English class to encouraging participation in a club fund-raising drive.

Dubrovin, Vivian. **Running a School Newspaper.** Franklin Watts/First Books, 1985. 84 p. ISBN 0-531-10046-4.

This book covers all the basics of a school newspaper, from how to get started to how to plan future issues. It describes writing news stories, features, and editorials, interviewing news sources, writing headlines, planning the design, obtaining and planning ads, determining the layout, and preparing the final pasteup of the paper. A sample style sheet and proofreaders' marks are included.

English, Betty Lou. **Behind the Headlines at a Big City Paper.** Photographs by the author. Lothrop, Lee and Shepard Books, 1985. 128 p. ISBN 0-688-03936-7.

Have you ever wanted to see how a big-city newspaper is put together? This book does just that, by discussing the different tasks that are involved: gathering and writing foreign, national, metropolitan, cultural, sports, business, and science news; editing the copy; design and layout; printing; and the business side of newspapers. Jobs of real newspaper people are featured.

Epstein, Sam, and Beryl Epstein. **Tunnels.** Little, Brown, 1985. 105 p. ISBN 0-316-24573-9.

If you can't go over or around a mountain, what do you do? Go through it, of course. Learn about the fascinating history, purpose, and construction of tunnels ranging from the small underground ganaats used to carry water in the desert, to the subways of today. A glossary of terms and photographs are included.

Fairley, John, and Simon Welfare. **Arthur C. Clarke's World of Strange Powers.** G. P. Putnam's Sons, 1984. 248 p. ISBN 0-399-13066-7.

Here are eyewitness accounts of some of the strangest phenomena ever told — tales of ghosts and poltergeists, dowsers who find oilwells, men who can walk on fire, mediums who conjure up the dead, and children who say they have lived before. Here is the evidence; now you be the judge!

Gallant, Roy A. **Our Restless Earth.** Illustrated by Anne Canevari Green. Franklin Watts/First Books, 1986. 96 p. ISBN 0-531-10205-X.

Do you ever wonder just how the Earth was made? This book presents a step-by-step progression through billions of years — from huge dust clouds called nebulae, which scientists think contained materials from which stars and planets emerged, to the Earth's present but still-changing form. Photographs, graphs, and a glossary of terms make reading easy.

Giblin, James Cross. **From Hand to Mouth; or, How We Invented Knives, Forks, Spoons, and Chopsticks and the Table Manners to Go with Them.** Thomas Y. Crowell, 1987. 86 p. ISBN 0-690-04660-X (0-690-04662-6, library binding).

When we sit down to our favorite dinner, we give little thought to the utensils we use in eating the meal. This book provides a history of the eating utensils and table manners of various cultures from the Stone Age to the present day. It is thoroughly illustrated with pictures of eating utensils from the past through the present and includes an extensive bibliography.

Giblin, James Cross. **Walls: Defenses throughout History.** Little, Brown, 1984. 113 p. ISBN 0-316-30954-0.

Walls are as old as civilization. Once built to protect and defend, many walls now stand in ruins as reminders of the people and civilizations who built them. But from the Ice Age to the present, walls have often failed in their purpose. Discover why in this book. Black-and-white photographs and a glossary of terms are included.

Grey, Michael. **Ships and Submarines.** Illustrated by Rob Shone and Cooper-West. Franklin Watts, 1986. 32 p. ISBN 0-531-10201-7.

Ships perform hundreds of functions in the modern world, often seeming like mini-cities at sea for months at a time. Read about these amazing vessels and find out about navigation, communication, and ports, as well as construction and special features of some ships and submarines. Included are a date chart, a glossary of terms, and color photographs and graphics. Part of the Modern Technology series.

Gunning, Thomas G. **Strange Mysteries.** Dodd, Mead, 1987. 96 p. ISBN 0-396-09038-9.

Here are ten strange tales — all mysteries and all true stories. Some are so puzzling that you may wonder if they really did happen. A few of the mysteries have been solved, but some may never be solved. Can you figure them out?

Hawkes, Nigel. **Nuclear Arms Race.** Illustrated by Ron Hayward Associates. Gloucester Press, 1986. 32 p. ISBN 0-531-17029-2.

Just what is the nuclear arms race all about and how large a threat does it pose? Since nuclear warheads are no longer limited to the United States and the Soviet Union, the problem seems to be ballooning. Are talks and treaties the answer, or is mutual distrust too great? Discover the extent of this situation and possible outcomes. Part of the Issues series.

Herbst, Judith. **Bio Amazing: A Casebook of Unsolved Human Mysteries.** Atheneum, 1985. 142 p. ISBN 0-689-31151-6.

Do you ever wonder about ESP, the world of your dreams, or miracle cures? If so, this book is for you. Ten "bio amazing" unsolved mysteries are explored. Can you determine the solution?

Hughes, Jill. **Deserts.** Illustrated by Roy Coombs and Maurice Wilson. Gloucester Press, 1987. 32 p. ISBN 0-531-17037-3.

Is a desert just a hot, empty place filled with sand and cacti? Not at all! For one thing, there are different kinds of deserts, even cold ones, and they all have fascinating life forms, both animal and plant, that have adapted to the extreme conditions. This book includes color photographs, graphics, and a glossary of terms. Part of the Closer Look series.

Janulewicz, Mike. **Plants.** Gloucester Press, 1984. 38 p. ISBN 0-531-03477-1.

All kinds of plants are described in this book. It explains the basic differences between plants, how plants grow and reproduce, and the best atmospheric conditions for growing them. Colorful pictures and diagrams illustrate the text. Part of the Insight series.

Kaye, Cathryn Berger. **Word Works: Why the Alphabet Is a Kid's Best Friend.** Illustrated by Martha Weston. Little, Brown/Brown Paper School Books, 1985. 128 p. ISBN 0-316-48376-1 (0-316-48375-3, paperback).

The world of words and the ways they are used in everyday life are explored in this book. It discusses how words are used in talking, writing, and thinking, as well as in creating stories and poems, printing books, playing games, and programming computers. Activities, word games, and many examples and exercises are included.

Kohler, Pierre (translated by Albert V. Carozzi and Marguerite Carozzi). **Volcanoes and Earthquakes.** Photographs by Katia Krafft. Barron's Educational, 1987. 79 p. ISBN 0-8120-3832-0.

Volcanoes and earthquakes demonstrate the awesome power of nature. This book explains the causes of volcanoes and earthquakes and also discusses the continents, continental drift, and fire in the earth.

Lambert, Mark. **Transportation in the Future.** Bookwright Press, 1986. 48 p. ISBN 0-531-18076-X.

How will we travel in the future? Possible ways include people-movers, computer-controlled autotaxis, and electric trains flying through underground vacuum tunnels. Descriptions of these and other vehicles of tomorrow are contained in this book. Part of the Tomorrow's World series.

LeBlanc, Wayne J., and Alden R. Carter. **Modern Electronics.** Franklin Watts/First Books, 1986. 95 p. ISBN 0-531-10218-1.

If you are interested in electronic devices, this is the book for you. The world of electronics is explained, ranging from the electron to the optical chip (using light instead of electricity), which may soon revolutionize the field. Included are diagrams, photographs, a glossary of terms, and suggestions for experiments to do at home.

Meltzer, Milton. **A Book about Names.** Illustrated by Mischa Richter. Thomas Y. Crowell, 1984. 128 p. ISBN 0-690-04380-5 (0-690-04381-3, library binding).

Where do names come from? Names are symbols and have special meanings and special rules in every culture. Drawing on the scholarly study of names — onomastics — Meltzer gives an amusing and informative sampling of the information that scholars have discovered about names.

Miller, Christina G., and Louise A. Berry. **Wastes.** Franklin Watts/First Books, 1986. 64 p. ISBN 0-531-10130-4.

Did you ever wonder what happened to the refuse you toss into the trash can? "Thrown away" doesn't really mean "gone" because nothing is ever truly destroyed. The disposal of mountains of waste materials poses major decisions for communities everywhere and sometimes creates crises. Modern disposal methods for solid wastes and sewage are explained, as are the potential dilemmas posed by our throw-away society.

Newman, Susan. **Never Say Yes to a Stranger: What Your Child Must Know to Stay Safe.** Photographs by George Tiboni. Putnam/Perigee Books, 1985. 127 p. ISBN 0-399-51114-8.

This book is a preventive aid to help keep children safe. Different situations in which children are approached by strangers are described and illustrated, and the importance of understanding the danger of such situations is explained. The book stresses awareness, not fear.

Percefull, Aaron W. **Balloons, Zeppelins, and Dirigibles.** Franklin Watts/First Books, 1983. 64 p. ISBN 0-531-04535-8.

Flight by balloon began in 1780 when the Montgolfier brothers soared above the French countryside. Later, in an effort to make the balloon steerable, the dirigible was invented and then perfected by the German Zeppelin family. The author presents the history and development of these kinds of airships and discusses their contribution to wartime efforts and to Arctic exploration. A list of balloon clubs and associations and a bibliography are included.

Perl, Lila. **Blue Monday and Friday the Thirteenth.** Illustrated by Erika Weihs. Clarion Books, 1986. 96 p. ISBN 0-89919-327-7.

Why is Monday called *blue*? Why is Friday the Thirteenth an unlucky day to some people? Where do the names of the week come from? Why do we have seven days in a week instead of five or ten? These questions and many more are answered in this book. The author uses myths, legends, folklore, and recent social history to discover the stories behind the days of the week.

Robinson, Stella. **Textiles.** Illustrated by Derek Lucas. Bookwright Press, 1984. 48 p. ISBN 0-531-04784-9.

Textiles have played an important part in the history of the last 7,000 years. This book discusses the reasons for their importance and explains how the first textiles were made and how they have been improved. Part of the Endeavor Books series.

Ronan, Colin A. **The Skywatcher's Handbook.** Crown, 1985. 224 p. ISBN 0-517-55703-7.

For centuries, people have observed the sky and relied on it for knowledge. Here is a handbook to help you gather and interpret information from the sky. Besides discussing constellations in the night sky, the book explains sources of information in the daylight sky, including colors, cloud formations, wind patterns, storms, and the sun.

Rossbacher, Lisa A. **Recent Revolutions in Geology.** Franklin Watts/ Science Impact Books, 1986. 127 p. ISBN 0-531-10242-4.

Beginning with an examination of the plate tectonics theory, the author examines how humans have looked at the Earth and how new discoveries have changed this view. Several chapters are devoted to lunar and planetary geology. A glossary of terms and a bibliography are included.

Sandak, Cass R. **Explorers and Discovery.** Illustrated by Anne Canevari Green. Franklin Watts/Reference First Books, 1983. 92 p. ISBN 0-531-04537-4.

Are you fascinated by those courageous persons who set out to discover new worlds? This book provides information on explorers, the geographical regions they explored, and the impact of their discoveries. Settlements in North America are traced to Asiatics who crossed the Bering Strait and to Lewis and Clark, who explored the West.

Scott, Elaine. **Oil! Getting It, Shipping It, Selling It.** Frederick Warne, 1984. 86 p. ISBN 0-7232-6260-8.

For early people, oil was a sticky mess that seeped out of the ground. But then ways were found to use it, especially after it was heated, to produce lamp oil, electricity, fuel for automobiles, and plastics for dishes, football helmets, combs, and even drugs. This book tells how we find oil, remove it from the earth and from under the sea, move oil, and store it, and the impact of oil gluts and shortages in the United States.

Silverstein, Alvin, and Virginia Silverstein. **World of the Brain.** Illustrated by Warren Budd. William Morrow, 1986. 195 p. ISBN 0-688-05777-2.

The brain is an amazing organ. This book discusses the anatomy and function of the brain, memory, intelligence, emotions, sleep, brain disorders, and the effects of drugs on the brain.

Sullivan, George. **Treasure Hunt: The Sixteen-Year Search for the Lost Treasure Ship *Atocha*.** Henry Holt, 1987. 150 p. ISBN 0-8050-0569-2.

Treasure hunter Mel Fisher spent sixteen years searching for the remains of the *Atocha,* a seventeenth-century Spanish galleon that sank just off the Florida Keys. The last voyage of the ship is traced, the $200 million in silver, gold, and emeralds are described, and the archaeological methods used to retrieve the ship and preserve it are explained.

Taylor, L. B., Jr., and C. L. Taylor. **Chemical and Biological Warfare.** Franklin Watts/Impact Books, 1985. 104 p. ISBN 0-531-04925-6.

Chemical and biological weapons have been used since ancient times, but these weapons have become more widely used and more deadly. This book focuses on the continuing debate over their danger to human survival and their usefulness as a deterrent to war. Included are the issue of whether the United States should continue its twenty-year moratorium on such weapons and a look at major incidents in which chemical or biological warfare has been used.

The Unit at Fayerweather Street School (edited by Eric E. Rofes). **The Kids' Book about Death and Dying.** Little, Brown, 1985. 119 p. ISBN 0-316-75390-4.

How does a kid handle death? Fourteen kids, from eleven to fourteen years old, give you their ideas about death. With the guidance of their teacher, they discuss the meaning of death and life after death. They talk about how they feel following the death of a pet, a parent, and a friend. They learn what happens to the body after death and visit a funeral home to find out about making funeral arrangements. They also suggest books on these topics for other kids to read.

Whipple, Jane B. **Forest Resources.** Franklin Watts/First Books, 1985. 64 p. ISBN 0-531-04909-4.

Our country is rich in forests, and over the years we have used and often abused them. This book describes the history of forest use and protection, our national forests, fire and other major threats, and the resources provided by forests. It points out that even though many buildings are constructed of other materials, the influence of forests can still be seen in the interior woodwork, furniture, paper, books, and pencils found within the buildings.

Williams, Gene B. **Nuclear War, Nuclear Winter.** Franklin Watts/ Impact Books, 1987. 128 p. ISBN 0-531-10416-8.

What is nuclear winter? Can it be survived? This book discusses the history of the arms race, the weapons that have been developed, the probable effects of a nuclear war, steps toward disarmament, and the Star Wars program.

Law and the Legal System

Batchelor, John E. **States' Rights.** Franklin Watts/First Books, 1986. 64 p. ISBN 0-531-10112-6.

Which has more power, the states or the federal government? This troublesome question is as old as our country itself, and the framers of the Constitution tried to achieve a balance of power between the two sides. By reading this book, you will learn of many interesting dilemmas that arose because there is no real answer to this question.

Cantwell, Lois. **Freedom.** Franklin Watts/First Books, 1985. 64 p. ISBN 0-531-10040-5.

This book explores the concept of freedom. It focuses on the First Amendment to the Constitution, which guarantees freedom of religion, speech, press, petition, and assembly. Each of these rights is described in detail, including how the Supreme Court has tested and refined the rights throughout history. Part of the American Values series.

Corbin, Carole Lynn. **The Right to Vote.** Franklin Watts, 1985. 97 p. ISBN 0-531-04932-9.

The Mayflower Compact brought democracy to the New World in 1620, and the Declaration of Independence gave equal rights to the new Americans in 1776. Yet neither of these documents gave us the right to vote. This book explains the steps taken to secure the right to vote for all Americans. Special sections discuss black voters, women voters, and voters under age twenty-one. Part of the Issues in American History series.

Dolan, Edward F., Jr. **Animal Rights.** Franklin Watts, 1986. 144 p. ISBN 0-531-10247-5.

Do animals have rights? And if they do, how might their rights limit the uses human beings have historically made of animals? Promoting humane treatment in lab testing, farming, hunting, and butchering, this book demands that we consider the other creatures who share our planet and whose lives are often spent for our food, comfort, and sport. Included are photographs and graphic descriptions.

Dolan, Edward F., Jr. **The Insanity Plea.** Franklin Watts/Impact Books, 1984. 102 p. ISBN 0-531-04756-3.

On March 30, 1981, John Hinckley shot President Reagan. On June 21, 1982, a jury found Hinckley not guilty by reason of insanity. This verdict raises many questions: What is the history of the insanity plea? What is wrong with this plea? What is right about it? What can be done to improve it? This book provides solid unbiased information on all of these questions and enables readers to take intelligent stands on this controversial issue.

Goode, Stephen. **The Right to Privacy.** Franklin Watts, 1983. 139 p. ISBN 0-531-04585-4.

The right to privacy, although not specifically protected by the Constitution, has evolved through many judicial decisions based on such constitutional principles as freedom from unreasonable searches and protection against self-incrimination. At the same time, advances in computer technology have increased the data-gathering abilities of government agencies, law enforcement agencies, credit bureaus, insurance companies, and other investigators. This book looks at the threat to personal privacy that technology can pose.

Holder, Angela Roddey. **The Meaning of the Constitution.** 2d ed. Barron's Educational Series, 1987. 130 p. ISBN 0-8120-3847-9.

This very informative text explains the history behind each section of the Constitution and explains how the particular section has been or might be interpreted in lifelike situations.

Hyde, Margaret O. **Juvenile Justice and Injustice.** Rev. ed. Franklin Watts, 1983. 114 p. ISBN 0-531-04594-3.

The juvenile court system is under attack for the work it does and does not do. The author presents a brief history of the treatment of juvenile offenders and then uses case histories to illustrate that the system does not always provide justice for those involved in serious and nonserious crime. She discusses legislation designed to alleviate the problem and gives a list of resource agencies for additional information.

Hyde, Margaret O. **The Rights of the Victim.** Franklin Watts, 1983. 92 p. ISBN 0-531-04596-X.

When a person is the victim of a crime, it may take him or her weeks, months, or even years to recover. Victims may exhibit long-lasting fear, grief, or emotional upset. This book tells how to understand victims, how to help them, and how to reduce the possibility that you may become a victim. Included are a list of further readings, sources of additional information, and a glossary of terms.

Johnson, Joan. **Justice.** Franklin Watts/First Books, 1985. 64 p. ISBN 0-531-10043-X.

This book describes our justice system, including how it was developed, its strengths and weaknesses, and what kind of justice we are guaranteed by the Constitution. It goes into detail regarding the Miranda warnings, search warrants, and wiretapping and explains how these can be interpreted by the courts. Also included is information on determining bail, plea bargaining, and jury selection. Part of the American Values series.

Kronenwetter, Michael. **Free Press v. Fair Trial: Television and Other Media in the Courtroom.** Franklin Watts/Impact Books, 1986. 104 p. ISBN 0-531-10153-3.

This book explores whether a fair trial is possible if the press is involved in the trial. It discusses actual cases whose outcomes were affected by the press. Conduct of court proceedings, television news broadcasting, and videotapes in the courtroom are also covered.

McPhillips, Martin. **The Constitutional Convention.** Silver Burdett, 1985. 62 p. ISBN 0-382-06827-0.

Through documents ranging from the Magna Charta to the Constitution, this book traces the history of the American struggle for independence. It describes how the delegates from the thirteen original states came together in 1787 to draft the Constitution and highlights such important figures as James Madison, John Adams, and Thomas Jefferson. The book is illustrated with several full-page portraits and reproductions of various documents. Part of the Turning Points in American History series.

Mannetti, Lisa. **Equality.** Franklin Watts/First Books, 1985. 64 p. ISBN 0-531-10039-1.

Equality has played a major role in American history, as evidenced by the Civil War, the Reconstruction period, the movement for women's rights, and the advancement of blacks. This book discusses equality and why it is cherished as an American ideal. Special emphasis is given to the struggle for equality among blacks and other minority groups. Part of the American Values series.

Whitney, Sharon. **The Equal Rights Amendment: The History and the Movement.** Franklin Watts, 1984. 93 p. ISBN 0-531-04768-7.

The Equal Rights Amendment is dead. It failed to be ratified by the required thirty-eight states. Would this amendment do away with separate male and female restrooms? Would it put women into combat? Would it solve the problem of unequal pay for men and women? This book gives a full account of the ERA: how the amendment came about, what changes it would bring, who supported it and who opposed it, and what the prospects are for another amendment.

Woods, Geraldine, and Harold Woods. **The Right to Bear Arms.** Franklin Watts/First Books, 1986. 72 p. ISBN 0-531-10109-6.

The right to bear arms is staunchly defended by some and strongly opposed by others. This book reviews the history of violent crime in the United States, highlighting attempted and successful presidential assassinations. It presents arguments for and against gun control and the opposing interpretations of the Second Amendment right to bear arms.

Zerman, Melvyn Bernard. **Taking On the Press: Constitutional Rights in Conflict.** Thomas Y. Crowell, 1986. 212 p. ISBN 0-690-04301-5 (0-690-04302-3, library binding).

The conflict between the First Amendment rights of the press and the rights of individuals and the government is explored through actual, well-known cases. This is a readable, thought-provoking, and important book on a subject that is especially timely now, when the press seems a constant target of criticism and outrage. It will help readers make up their own minds, not only about the conflicts of the past but also about those that are sure to erupt tomorrow.

Mass Media

Aldous, Donald. **Sound Systems.** Warwick Press, 1983. 37 p. ISBN 0-531-09224-0.

This general introduction to hi-fi and radio explains how turntables, tape decks, tuners, amplifiers, loudspeakers, and headphones work. It also looks at recording at home, broadcasting, how disks and cassettes are made, radio communications, and portable hi-fi. A glossary of terms is included. Part of the Science in Action series.

Cheney, Glenn Alan. **Television in American Society.** Franklin Watts/Impact Books, 1983. 83 p. ISBN 0-531-04402-5.

The latest research is used to answer important questions about television's influence on our lives. Who decides what we see? Why are commercials important? How do ratings influence advertisers and networks? The credibility of TV news, the power of special-interest groups, and the effect of TV on politics and on children are discussed, along with what changes may be brought about for TV in the computer age.

Cohen, Daniel, and Susan Cohen. **How to Get Started in Video.** Franklin Watts, 1986. 108 p. ISBN 0-531-10250-5.

This is a practical guide to getting started in video. How much training you should receive, how to get your foot in the door and secure interviews, and what to expect as you start out are all discussed in this volume. A listing of colleges specializing in video training is included.

Ferrell, Nancy Warren. **The New World of Amateur Radio.** Franklin Watts/First Books, 1986. 63 p. ISBN 0-531-10219-X.

This text reviews the development of radio and looks at its impact on those who aspire to be ham operators. There are chapters on the varieties and services of amateur radio and a section on where to find more information. A glossary of terms is included.

Irvine, Mat. **TV and Video.** Illustrated by Paul Cooper, Elsa Godfrey, Nick May, and Rob Shone. Franklin Watts, 1983. 29 p. ISBN 0-531-04726-1.

Video is all around us — music videos, advertising videos in stores, movie videos, video games, video arcades, and self-filmed videos. This book looks at video today and makes some predictions about tomorrow's videos. A glossary of terms is included. Part of the Electronic Revolution series.

Klein, David, and Marymae E. Klein. **How Do You Know It's True?** Charles Scribner's Sons, 1984. 164 p. ISBN 0-684-18225-4.

Each of us receives many messages every day from family, friends, teachers, television, billboards, radios, and all kinds of print material. But not all the messages agree. How can we reason through those conflicting messages and find the one that's true? This book gives instructions for evaluating information from the media, statistics and survey results, and experts.

Kronenwetter, Michael. **Politics and the Press.** Franklin Watts, 1987. 139 p. ISBN 0-531-10333-1.

How did the American press become so powerful? Is it too powerful? This book looks at the relationship that exists between politics and the press. It covers such issues as freedom of the press, editorial fairness, and press endorsement of political candidates. In particular, the book discusses the power of the press during the Revolutionary War, the abolitionist movement, the Civil War, and the Iranian hostage crisis of 1980. Part of the Issues in American History series.

Manchel, Frank. **An Album of Modern Horror Films.** Franklin Watts, 1983. 90 p. ISBN 0-531-04661-3.

Horror movies are as old as the movie business itself. This book discusses a number of horror films and the trends that have been set during the last thirty years. Over eighty photographs from well-known films made in the late 1950s to 1980s add to the enjoyment of the book.

Meigs, James B., and Jennifer Stern. **Make Your Own Music Video.** Illustrated by Anne Canevari Green. Franklin Watts/First Books, 1986. 82 p. ISBN 0-531-10215-7.

What is music video? How do the pros do it? What equipment will you need and how does it work? These questions plus many more are answered in this book. A glossary and suggestions for further reading are included.

Mintern, Helen. **Television and Video.** Warwick Press, 1983. 37 p. ISBN 0-531-09225-9.

This is an account of how television programs are made, transmitted, and received. It also looks at how television and video influence our lives. There are sections on home video recorders and videodiscs, and hints on using video cameras. A glossary of terms is included. Part of the Science in Action series.

Renowden, Gareth. **Video.** Gloucester Press, 1983. 37 p. ISBN 0-531-04584-6.

Terms like *shadow mask, quadrascan,* and *raster scan* will be mysteries no more. This book, illustrated in color and containing clear diagrams, covers the basics of the video world. Learn how video techniques are applied at home and in the work world, how pictures are created and transmitted, how videotapes and videodiscs work, and how television programs are made, including those with spectacular visual effects. Even the newest application of video, video archaeology, is explored. Part of the Inside Story series.

Staples, Terry. **Film and Video.** Warwick Press/Gateway Fact Books, 1986. 93 p. ISBN 0-531-19020-X.

Here is a look at the changing technology of film and video. The book provides instructions for making your own movies and videos, explains how animation and special effects are created, and discusses future developments in film and video. Diagrams and a glossary of terms are included.

Nature

Arnosky, Jim. **Flies in the Water, Fish in the Air.** Illustrated by the author. Lothrop, Lee and Shepard Books, 1986. 96 p. ISBN 0-688-05834-5.

Jim Arnosky enjoys being outdoors and seeing nature up close, and he enjoys fly fishing. In this book for both fishermen and naturalists, he'll tell you all about choosing the proper fishing equipment, identifying the insects that fish feed on, wading in streams, and using both dry and wet flies.

Blair, Carvel Hall. **Exploring the Sea: Oceanography Today.** Illustrated by Harry McNaught. Random House/Library of Knowledge, 1986. 96 p. ISBN 0-394-85927-8 (0-394-95927-2, library binding).

This is an in-depth look at the ocean world and how it was formed. Large color photographs illustrate coastal terrain, plant and animal life, and ways of discovering ocean treasures.

Bright, Michael. **Saving the Whale.** Gloucester Press, 1987. 32 p. ISBN 0-531-17061-6.

Whales have been around for millions of years, but they now face extinction due to centuries of intense whaling. This short book graphically portrays why people kill whales. It discusses how whales are overfished, the industry of whaling, the concern for protecting whales, facts about whales, how dolphins are being killed by fishing, and whales and dolphins in captivity.

Buckley, Virginia. **State Birds.** Illustrated by Arthur Singer and Alan Singer. E. P. Dutton/Lodestar Books, 1986. 63 p. ISBN 0-525-67177-3.

From the yellowhammer of Alabama to the meadow lark of Wyoming, this is a beautifully illustrated book about our state birds. Each bird is shown in its natural surroundings, and brief articles explain how and when each bird was selected to represent its state.

Coldrey, Jennifer. **Discovering Worms.** Bookwright Press, 1986. 47 p. ISBN 0-531-18046-8.

Here is an introduction to the thousands of different kinds of worms in the world. We are most familiar with smooth, slimy earthworms, but there are many worms that live underwater. Some worms are covered with scales or bristles, while others have tentacles or suckers. A glossary of terms is included. Part of the Discovering Nature series.

Curtis, Neil. **Discovering Snakes and Lizards.** Bookwright Press, 1986. 47 p. ISBN 0-531-18048-4.

Snakes and lizards are reptiles. This book explains that there are about 6,000 different kinds of reptiles in the world. They vary in length from ten meters to a few centimeters. Some are poisonous, but most are harmless. A glossary of terms is included. Part of the Discovering Nature series.

Dixon, Dougal. **A Closer Look at Prehistoric Reptiles.** Illustrated by Richard Orr. Gloucester Press, 1984. 32 p. ISBN 0-531-03480-1.

An easy-to-read book, this traces the animals of ages past to the reptiles of today. The various reptiles of earlier times — flying reptiles, sea reptiles, the terrible lizards, dinosaurs, sea serpents, the first birds, flying dragons — are described and discussed. A glossary of terms is included. Part of the Closer Look series.

Gallant, Roy A. **From Living Cells to Dinosaurs.** Illustrated by Anne Canevari Green. Franklin Watts/First Books, 1986. 96 p. ISBN 0-531-10207-6.

If you are intrigued by the evolution of early life forms, this is your chance to explore scientific discoveries and theories that attempt to explain steps essential in establishing the progression of life preceding and including the dinosaurs. Photographs and a glossary of terms are included.

Gallant, Roy A. **The Rise of Mammals.** Illustrated by Anne Canevari Green. Franklin Watts/First Books, 1986. 93 p. ISBN 0-531-10206-8.

Rats as large as calves and elephants that could eat two-story-tall plants are examples of mammals that lived during the last two million years. This book discusses the evolution of continents, weather, plants, and other animals during this period of time.

Hasegawa, Yō. **The Cricket.** Photographs by Hidekazu Kubo. Raintree, 1986. 32 p. ISBN 0-8172-2557-9 (0-8172-2532-3, library binding).

Here's a look at the insect whose chirping is heard most summer evenings. This book describes the cricket's life cycle, behavior, and habitat. A glossary of terms is included. Part of the Nature Close-ups series.

Hughes, Jill. **A Closer Look at Lions and Tigers.** Illustrated by Peter Barrett, Richard Orr, and Maurice Wilson. Gloucester Press, 1985. 32 p. ISBN 0-531-17000-4.

This book introduces the natural world of the big cats, looking at their weapons, disguises, habits, and activities. The different kinds of cats are described and compared — including tigers, spotted cats, leopards, panthers, and jaguars. A glossary of terms is included. Part of the Closer Look series.

Kerby, Mona. **Friendly Bees, Ferocious Bees.** Illustrated by Anne Canevari Green. Franklin Watts/First Books, 1987. 96 p. ISBN 0-531-10303-X.

If you want to learn all about honeybees, this is a great place to begin. From a description of the anatomy of the honeybee, to life in the hive, to a beekeeping guide, to great honey recipes, this book covers it all. A glossary of terms, a bibliography, and black-and-white photographs are included.

Lerner, Carol. **A Forest Year.** William Morrow, 1987. 48 p. ISBN 0-688-06413-2 (0-688-06414-0, library binding).

Organized by seasons, this book explores the lives of the mammals, birds, reptiles, amphibians, insects, and plants commonly found in deciduous forests. How each species responds to the changes in each season is depicted in lucid prose and full-color, scientifically accurate paintings.

McClung, Robert M. **Gorilla.** Illustrated by Irene Brady. William Morrow, 1984. 92 p. ISBN 0-688-03876-X.

A writer highly skilled in writing about animals in their natural setting, McClung presents a sensitive life-cycle story. He highlights the habits and life experiences of the African mountain gorilla, an endangered species. McClung follows a band of gorillas through the exotic African setting, showing the reader that gorillas are actually shy vegetarians and not at all like they are pictured in film and story.

Oda, Hidetomo. **Animals of the Seashore.** Photographs by Hidekazu Kubo. Raintree, 1986. 32 p. ISBN 0-8172-2568-4 (0-8172-2543-9, library binding).

This book discusses the life cycle, behavior patterns, and sea dwellings of several seashore creatures, including crabs, sea anemones, and sea snails. A glossary of terms is included. Other books by this author focus on butterflies, dragonflies, and bees and wasps. Part of the Nature Close-ups series.

Ogawa, Hiroshi. **The Potter Wasp.** Photographs by the author. Raintree, 1986. 32 p. ISBN 0-8172-2566-8 (0-8172-2541-2, library binding).

Here is a look at the life cycle, behavior and habitats of various kinds of potter wasps found in Europe and North America. These wasps get their name from the little pots of mud in which the female lays her eggs and deposits small caterpillars for the developing young wasps to eat. A glossary of terms is included. Part of the Nature Close-ups series.

O'Toole, Christopher. **Discovering Bees and Wasps.** Bookwright Press, 1986. 47 p. ISBN 0-531-18047-6.

Bees and wasps are described in this book — where they live, what they eat, how they reproduce, and what you can do to learn more about the 10,000 different kinds of bees and wasps in the world. A glossary of terms is included. Part of the Discovering Nature series.

Patent, Dorothy Hinshaw. **Mosquitoes.** Holiday House, 1986. 40 p. ISBN 0-8234-0627-X.

What makes a mosquito bite itch? This book explains the itch and discusses the mosquito's life cycle, habits, body parts, and the diseases it carries.

Penny, Malcolm. **Discovering Spiders.** Bookwright Press, 1986. 47 p. ISBN 0-531-18045-X.

While many people don't care for spiders, most spiders are harmless to humans. But some — like the funnel-web and the black widow — are deadly poisonous. This book looks at the habits and behavior of spiders and explains that not all spiders spin webs — some dig tunnels, and others live underwater. A glossary of terms is included. Part of the Discovering Nature series.

Petty, Kate. **Birds of Prey.** Illustrated by Louise Nevett and Tessa Barwick. Gloucester Press, 1987. 32 p. ISBN 0-531-17050-0.

This is a book that will encourage you to become interested in the world around you and that promotes participation in the conservation of wildlife. It looks at various birds of prey — how they live, how to recognize them, and how they survive in today's changing world. It indicates the species that are in danger of extinction. An identification chart and a related project will involve you even further in the study of birds of prey. Part of the First Sight series.

Ryden, Hope. **America's Bald Eagle.** Photographs by the author. G. P. Putnam's Sons, 1985. 63 p. ISBN 0-399-21181-0.

This book explains the mating, parenting, nesting, and hunting habits of this endangered species. Few Americans understand how exacting an environment the bald eagle must have in order to reproduce. As our forests disappeared and our waterways became polluted, the eagle's chance for survival diminished. Today efforts are well under way to give this grand bird a fighting chance.

Sanger, Marjory Bartlett. **Forest in the Sand.** Illustrated by D. D. Tyler. Atheneum/Margaret K. McElderry Books, 1983. 145 p. ISBN 0-689-50248-6.

This is a season-by-season account of the animals and plants of the Ocala National Forest in Florida. The author focuses on a family of bluejays (scrub jays), while describing the formation of the forest on a limestone foundation over a period of five thousand years and the necessity for preserving the forest.

Sattler, Helen Roney. **Sharks, the Super Fish.** Illustrated by Jean Zallinger. Lothrop, Lee and Shepard Books, 1986. 96 p. ISBN 0-688-03993-6.

Sharks can be a frightening sight for a swimmer in the water. This book explains how sharks hunt for their food, their predator instinct, and other aspects of their behavior. It includes a dictionary of shark types and tips for swimmers for avoiding sharks.

Selsam, Millicent E. **Mushrooms.** Photographs by Jerome Wexler. William Morrow, 1986. 48 p. ISBN 0-688-06248-2 (0-688-06249-0, library binding).

The story of the mushroom is described in this book. It looks at the history, structure, growing procedures, and types of mushrooms.

Selsam, Millicent E. **Tree Flowers.** Illustrated by Carol Lerner. William Morrow, 1984. 32 p. ISBN 0-688-02768-7 (0-688-02769-5, library binding).

After the cold winter months, the colorful blossoms on spring flowering trees are a welcome sight. Here is an examination of the growth and reproduction of twelve common flowering trees, including the sugar maple, horse chestnut, flowering dogwood, and tulip tree. Tips are given for identifying each tree.

Settle, Mary Lee. **Water World.** E. P. Dutton/Lodestar Books, 1984. 120 p. ISBN 0-525-66777-6.

The world beneath the water has fascinated humans from the beginning of time. From Mediterranean mythology to exploring underwater in a JIM suit, the book explores the mysteries of the creatures and currents of oceans and looks at the scientific methods used by modern undersea biologists, geologists, and archaeologists. A bibliography is included.

Stolz, Mary. **Night of Ghosts and Hermits: Nocturnal Life on the Seashore.** Illustrated by Susan Gallagher. Harcourt Brace Jovanovich, 1985. 47 p. ISBN 0-15-257333-X.

It's quiet and still on the Florida beach. It's night time, and there is no one to disturb our silence — or is there? This book describes the night-time activities of such creatures as the hermit crab, horse conch, heron, and loggerhead turtle.

Strachan, Elizabeth. **A Closer Look at Prehistoric Mammals.** Illustrated by Peter Barrett, Giovanni Caselli, and Richard Orr. Gloucester Press, 1985. 32 p. ISBN 0-531-17001-2.

This book describes the basic characteristics of mammals and how they differ from other animals. The development of mammals is traced through the age of dinosaurs. Recognizable ancestors of present-day mammals are discussed, leading to the most highly developed mammal — the human being. A glossary of terms is included. Part of the Closer Look series.

Sugarman, Joan. **Snowflakes.** Illustrated by Jennifer Dewey. Little, Brown, 1985. 53 p. ISBN 0-316-82112-8.

The fleeting beauty of snowflakes is captured in this illustrated and informative book. The shapes from the microscopic world of snowflakes are brought to the reader in detailed pen-and-ink drawings. The book describes the weather conditions that produce the seemingly infinite varieties of snow crystals. Included are a review of how snowflakes have been studied in history, instructions for catching a snowflake, and a glossary of terms.

Occupations and Careers

Allman, Paul. **Exploring Careers in Video.** Rosen Publishing Group, 1985. 114 p. ISBN 0-8239-0623-X.

This book offers information on specific careers in video, including where the available jobs are, where and how to train for them, and the rewards — both financial and personal — to be expected. Related books and magazines are listed, as well as training programs and schools.

Anderson, Lynne. **Exploring Careers in Library Science.** Rosen Publishing Group, 1985. 135 p. ISBN 0-8239-0642-6.

Today's librarians do more than stamp and shelve books. Here is an overview of the jobs open to media experts and the characteristics necessary to be successful in this changing field. The appendix gives specific resources for more information, including other books, periodicals, educational programs, associations, and representative tables of placement and salaries.

Berger, Gilda. **Women, Work and Wages.** Franklin Watts, 1986. 122 p. ISBN 0-531-10074-X.

The role of working women is becoming more significant every day. Yet widespread discrimination still exists in salaries, benefits, and educational opportunities. This book offers documented cases and statistics that will make you aware of the problems and the choices women face.

Berlyn, David W. **Exploring Careers in Cable TV.** Rosen Publishing Group, 1985. 127 p. ISBN 0-8239-0666-3.

Beginning with an explanation of the dimensions of television, this book looks at TV journalism, station management, sales, engineering, and much more. It provides information that the reader needs to consider in preparation for specific careers in cable television.

Brockman, Dorothy. **Exploring Careers in Computer Software.** Rosen Publishing Group, 1985. 160 p. ISBN 0-8239-0653-1.

As computers become more widespread in the office, classroom, and home, opportunities for employment in the computer field have soared. This book offers specific information on careers in computer software, including necessary aptitudes for software designers and marketers, required education and training, and range of employers. Using a compact format, outlines, graphs, and tables, the book gives a step-by-step presentation of information concerning all aspects of careers in the computer field.

Cantwell, Lois. **Modeling.** Franklin Watts/First Books, 1986. 71 p. ISBN 0-531-10123-1.

There are many kinds of models: photograph, runway, illustrator's, hand and foot, ethnic, and larger sizes. If you've ever considered a career in modeling, you'll appreciate the information presented on modeling history, agencies and schools, guidelines for success, and tips for getting started in modeling.

Dautrich, Jack, and Vivian Huff. **Big City Detective.** Photographs by Vivian Huff. E. P. Dutton/Lodestar Books, 1986. 117 p. ISBN 0-525-67183-8.

Travel to Philadelphia and learn the day-to-day activities of a city police detective. Using actual cases Dautrich worked on, the authors take the reader along on investigations of homicide, arson, robbery, and rape cases. You'll learn about the training needed for detective work and the techniques used in solving a case. A glossary of terms is included.

Fields, Carl L. **Exploring Careers in the Tool and Die Industry.** Rosen Publishing Group, 1985. 136 p. ISBN 0-8239-0633-7.

Careers in the skilled trades are not easy to learn about. This book presents information on the industries requiring skilled laborers in tool and die making, in sheet-metal work, and in plastic mold, extrusion, and shell casting. Included are specific ways to get into these trades, practical information on the tools required, and tips on retaining a job in the skilled trades.

Fitzgerald, Merni Ingrassia. **The Peace Corps Today.** Dodd, Mead, 1986. 125 p. ISBN 0-396-08511-3.

The Peace Corps was founded in 1961. Since then, thousands of Americans have volunteered to go to other countries and to help the local people help themselves. This book provides information about what Peace Corps workers do and how you can become a volunteer. Many photographs and quotations from people who have worked in the Peace Corps are included.

Greene, Laura. **Careers in the Computer Industry.** Franklin Watts/First Books, 1983. 66 p. ISBN 0-531-04636-2.

Looking for an exciting career? The computer industry is the fastest-growing industry in the world. Well-trained people are needed at all levels. What will the next breakthrough be and the one after that? Perhaps *you* will be the one to make it! Read about all the opportunities for engineering and technical careers, systems analysis and programming, data processing, computer-service jobs, and computer-related jobs in business. Part of the Computer-Awareness series.

Hackwell, W. John. **Digging to the Past: Excavations in Ancient Lands.** Charles Scribner's Sons, 1986. 50 p. ISBN 0-684-18692-6.

Excavations in ancient lands are carefully planned and managed to be certain that no small piece of information escapes notice. At one time ancient settlements were plundered for their treasures. Now these settlements are painstakingly examined for any clues about ancient life. For example, archaeologists study settlement, land use, and diet to better understand the food system used by ancient peoples. This book might get you thinking about a career in archeology.

Jones, Ilene. **Jobs for Teenagers.** Ballantine Books, 1983. 133 p. ISBN 0-345-30905-7.

Advice on how to find and secure a job is given. The author takes you through the process step-by-step, including appearance, attitude, references, résumés, places likely to hire, learning the job, and keeping the job. Tips are given for serving the needs of people and business in your neighborhood through self-employment. Included is a listing of camp jobs, helpful books, and state and federal job centers.

Jones, Marilyn. **Exploring Careers as a Carpenter.** Rosen Publishing Group, 1985. 139 p. ISBN 0-8239-0624-8.

Short sketches about real people in the carpenter trade offer insights into what it's really like to be a carpenter. Learn about the tools, training, and skills necessary for this career. Apprenticeship, union membership, and the advantages and disadvantages of this occupation are also described. A list of suggested reading and periodicals of interest to woodworkers is included.

Lang, Denise V. **Footsteps in the Ocean: Careers in Diving.** E. P. Dutton/ Lodestar Books, 1987. 142 p. ISBN 0-525-67193-5.

If you enjoy diving, it can be more than just a recreational activity. This book carefully examines careers in diving by dividing them into four main categories: sport diving, commercial diving, underwater science and research, and additional specialties. Included are a directory of training schools, a list of associations and publications, a glossary of terms, and a bibliography.

Laurance, Robert. **Electronic Service Careers.** Franklin Watts/High-Tech Careers, 1987. 111 p. ISBN 0-531-10423-0.

Career opportunities abound in electronics. This book describes the necessary education and training for becoming an electronic service technician and discusses careers servicing business computers and office equipment, in consumer electronic services, in industrial electronics, in service management, and in the military. Special mention is made of women in electronic service careers. A list of further readings is included.

Mabery, D. L. **Tell Me about Yourself: How to Interview Anyone from Your Friends to Famous People.** Lerner Publications, 1985. 69 p. ISBN 0-8225-1604-7.

Proper preparation is essential to a successful interview, whether you're talking to your friends or famous people. This book discusses arranging an interview, preparing for the interview, conducting the interview, and transcribing your notes. Suggestions are given for interview opportunities in school and for careers involving interviewing. A glossary of terms is included.

Manning, Robert N. **Exploring Careers in Filmmaking.** Rosen Publishing Group, 1985. 128 p. ISBN 0-8239-0641-8.

There are many jobs in filmmaking: director, cinematographer, editor, writer, and actor, to name a few. There are also numerous types of films, including documentaries, commercials, teaching films, and films for industrial use. This book gives an overview of the film industry as well as specific information on grants, unions and guilds, periodicals, festivals and awards, and schools and other training.

Southworth, Scott. **Exploring Computer Careers at Home.** Rosen Publishing Group, 1986. 131 p. ISBN 0-8239-0651-5.

A possible alternative to the nine-to-five office job is offered here for the computer expert. Specific types of computer work that can be done at home, courses needed for preparation, and buying and using a computer are discussed. Read helpful hints for getting organized and started in your own computer service, and take a look at the promising future in telecommuting. A glossary of terms and a list of resources are included.

Spencer, Jean W. **Exploring Careers as a Computer Technician.** Rosen Publishing Group, 1985. 112 p. ISBN 0-8239-0626-4.

The giant boom in the computer industry has created countless job opportunities, and this book can guide the young computer buff toward the best sources of information about a career in the field. From job descriptions to job prospects to training to equipment, all facets are addressed. Included are a glossary of terms and information on colleges and schools, organizations, and publications.

Spencer, Jean W. **Exploring Careers in the Electronic Office.** Rosen Publishing Group, 1986. 124 p. ISBN 0-8239-0657-4.

Office workers of the future will no longer type and take shorthand. The paperless office will soon become real. This book introduces the reader to the new wave in office work and management. It presents information on telecommunications and computers and gives practical suggestions for dealing with stress in tomorrow's office.

Sullivan, George. **Baseball Backstage.** Holt, Rinehart and Winston, 1986. 114 p. ISBN 0-03-000758-5.

Here's a look at behind-the-scenes jobs in baseball. The author interviews twelve members of the invisible team of general managers, clubhouse attendants, groundskeepers, and others who keep a low profile. He explores their contributions toward the team and the responsibilities of their jobs.

Thro, Ellen. **Robotics Careers.** Franklin Watts/High-Tech Careers, 1987. 111 p. ISBN 0-531-10425-7.

If you have a strong interest in robots, you might be interested in a career in robotics. This book covers such possible careers as designing new robots, hiring robots for factories, planning the use of robots, programming, servicing, and selling robots, inventing robots of the future, running your own robotics business, and using robots in oceanography. The book discusses opportunities, duties, salaries, and training required for these careers. Also included is a list of sources for further information.

Vahl, Rod. **Exploring Careers in Broadcast Journalism.** Rosen Publishing Group, 1983. 122 p. ISBN 0-8239-0595-0.

Whether you aspire to be the anchor on a network news program or are interested in reporting the news for a local station, you'll find useful information in this book about careers in newscasting. Eleven well-known personalities, including Jane Pauley, offer their opinions on and experiences in broadcast journalism careers. Included are information on college and university programs in broadcast journalism and sources to consult for further information.

Wolf, Bernard. **Amazing Grace: Smith Island and the Chesapeake Watermen.** Photographs by the author. Macmillan, 1986. 76 p. ISBN 0-02-793330-X.

In the midst of Chesapeake Bay lies a series of strands called Smith Island. The lives of about 550 residents revolve around making a living ("makin' a lick") from the sea, hauling up 150 pounds of mud, eel, grass, and crabs each day. The work, the joy, and the pride of these islanders are captured in photographs.

People and Places

American

Arnold, Caroline. **The Golden Gate Bridge.** Franklin Watts/First Books, 1986. 68 p. ISBN 0-531-10213-0.

The Golden Gate Bridge, the well-known suspension bridge connecting San Francisco with Sausalito to the north, was built in the 1930s. This book takes you through the steps of building this magnificent bridge, from the dream to the completion and opening. It discusses Joseph Strauss, the builder, and the triumphs and dangers experienced during the building. A list of facts and statistics about the bridge is included.

Bain, Geri. **New Jersey.** Franklin Watts/First Books, 1987. 95 p. ISBN 0-531-10389-7.

Here's a close look at New Jersey, from the time of Indian settlement, to the arrival of the Europeans, to statehood, to the present. The book describes New Jersey's geographical features, natural resources, agriculture, industry, cities, daily life, and importance as a center for innovation. Vital statistics, important dates, and a list of things invented in New Jersey are also included.

Berger, Gilda. **The Southeast States.** Franklin Watts/First Books, 1984. 83 p. ISBN 0-531-04738-5.

The geography, climate, industries, agriculture, history, and population of our southeastern states are described in this book. The eleven states discussed are Alabama, Florida, Georgia, Kentucky, Maryland, Mississippi, North Carolina, South Carolina, Tennessee, Virginia, and West Virginia.

Carter, Alden R. **Illinois.** Franklin Watts/First Books, 1987. 95 p. ISBN 0-531-10387-0.

If you're interested in learning about the history, government, economy, natural resources, and culture of Illinois, you might want to consult this book. It discusses the Indians, fur traders and early settlers, the great Chicago fire, the rise of the Chicago political machine, and the prairie state's rich agricultural resources. A list of further readings is included.

Coil, Suzanne M. **Florida.** Franklin Watts/First Books, 1987. 95 p. ISBN 0-531-10384-6.

Florida, our sunshine state, is the focus of this book. It describes the history, economy, industry, government, and educational opportunities in Florida. Also discussed are the principal cities, the people, Florida's contributions to science and art, pirates, hurricanes, sports and recreation, wildlife and conservation, and Florida's future.

Dunnahoo, Terry. **Alaska.** Franklin Watts/First Books, 1987. 95 p. ISBN 0-531-10375-7.

This book discusses the history of Alaska, from its discovery by Russian explorers, to its sale to the United States in 1867, to its statehood in 1959; its waterways and mountains; its park lands, wildlife refuges, and wildlife; its resources, such as gold, oil, and timber, and the role they play in its economy; and what life is like in Alaska.

Editors of Time-Life Books. **The United States.** Photographs by Winnie Denker. Time-Life Books, 1984. 160 p. ISBN 0-8094-5303-7.

Here is a tribute to all the United States. In text and photographs, this book describes the history, natural resources, economy, government, and people of our country. Cultural roles, art and religious diversity, and the changing lives of women are also included. Part of the Library of Nations series.

Fox, Mary Virginia. **Ohio.** Franklin Watts/First Books, 1987. 95 p. ISBN 0-531-10392-7.

Ohio's history, politics, industries, natural resources, economy, and people are featured in this book. It discusses the land itself, the settling of Ohio as people moved westward, early means of transportation, Ohio's role in the Civil War, and the cities of Columbus, Cleveland, Cincinnati, and Akron.

Gilfond, Henry. **The Northeast States.** Franklin Watts/First Books, 1984. 85 p. ISBN 0-531-04732-6.

The northeast states were settled in the seventeenth and eighteenth centuries and were instrumental in winning our country's freedom from England in the Revolutionary War. Here is an overview of the region's history, geography, climate, rise of industry, and growth of population. Accounts of the individual states list such facts as the state capital, nickname, motto, and flower.

Harlan, Judith. **American Indians Today: Issues and Conflicts.** Franklin Watts/Impact Books, 1987. 128 p. ISBN 0-531-10325-0.

Today's Native Americans face economic, legal, health, and civil rights problems. This book explores these problems and the history of conflict between American Indians and the U.S. government.

Hintz, Martin. **Michigan.** Franklin Watts/First Books, 1987. 95 p. ISBN 0-531-10362-5.

Michigan is the only state that is made up of two separate parts, which are joined by the Straits of Mackinac. Here is a look at this state's history, economy, cities, natural resources, and people. A list of suggested readings about this state is included.

Hughes, Jill. **Plains Indians.** Illustrated by Maurice Wilson and George Thomson. Gloucester Press, 1984. 32 p. ISBN 0-531-03479-8.

Three hundred years ago the Plains Indians dominated the Great Plains, until increasing numbers of white settlers defeated the Indians and took control of their land. This book focuses on the Plains Indians' culture — their hunting of buffalo, other sources of food, their homes, their nomadic lifestyle, their games and pastimes, their weapons, and, finally, their adjustment to a new world, the Indian reservation.

Jacobson, Daniel. **Indians of North America.** Franklin Watts/Reference First Books, 1983. 88 p. ISBN 0-531-04647-8.

Just how much of the television image of the American Indian is based on fact? Learn about Native Americans from A to Z: AIM (American Indian Movement) to the Zuni in New Mexico. This book offers comprehensive information about different Indian nations and their customs, beliefs, and leaders.

Jacobson, Daniel. **The North Central States.** Franklin Watts/First Books, 1984. 87 p. ISBN 0-531-04731-8.

This book looks at the American heartland: its history, geography, climate, industries, agriculture, cities and rural areas, and future. Information about the individual north central states is also included.

Lawson, Don. **The Pacific States.** Franklin Watts/First Books, 1984. 89 p. ISBN 0-531-04733-4.

The Pacific states of California, Oregon, Washington, Alaska, and Hawaii are featured in this book. It discusses their history, geography, climate, people, resources, industries, and future.

Levert, Suzanne. **New York.** Franklin Watts/First Books, 1987. 95 p. ISBN 0-531-10390-0.

Here's a look at the history of New York, the empire state. Chapters are included on New York City, upstate New York, and present-day aspects of the state as a whole. Suggestions for further reading are included.

Pack, Janet. **California.** Franklin Watts/First Books, 1987. 95 p. ISBN 0-531-10379-X.

This book presents the history of California from the 1500s through the 1960s, with discussions of the gold rush, immigration, and resulting racial difficulties. It also looks at California's industries, cities, government, and modern problems. Lists of important dates, governors, and famous residents are included.

Phillips, Betty Lou, and Bryce Phillips. **Texas.** Franklin Watts/First Books, 1987. 95 p. ISBN 0-531-10395-1.

The history of Texas is long and varied. This book looks at the Indian nations and Spanish settlements in Texas and traces how Texas gained its independence from Mexico in 1836, became part of the United States in 1845, and then seceded from the Union during the Civil War. Texan agriculture, industries, cities, and lifestyles are also discussed. Suggestions for further reading about Texas are included.

Shebar, Sharon Sigmond, and Susan E. Shebar. **Pennsylvania.** Franklin Watts/First Books, 1987. 95 p. ISBN 0-531-10393-5.

Pennsylvania's land, climate, natural resources, history, government, people, cities, economy, education, and communication facilities are described in this book. A list of important dates in Pennsylvanian history is also included.

Taylor, L. B., Jr., and C. L. Taylor. **The Rocky Mountain States.** Franklin Watts/First Books, 1984. 61 p. ISBN 0-531-04735-0.

Our Rocky Mountain states — Idaho, Arizona, Colorado, New Mexico, Utah, Wyoming, Nevada, and Montana — are featured in this book. It describes their history, geography, resources, cities, park lands, economic development, and future. Facts about the individual Rocky Mountain states are also included.

Woods, Harold, and Geraldine Woods. **The South Central States.** Franklin Watts/First Books, 1984. 62 p. ISBN 0-531-04737-7.

The four south central states — Texas, Oklahoma, Louisiana, and Arkansas — are considered a separate region in this book. It discusses their history, geography, agriculture, industries, cities, and places of special interest. Specific information about the four states is also included.

World

Adams, Faith. **El Salvador: Beauty among the Ashes.** Dillon Press, 1986. 135 p. ISBN 0-87518-309-3.

Amid the beauty of ancient volcanoes lie the ashes brought by war. The Salvadorans live in constant fear of death or imprisonment from government forces. Many try to escape to other countries until life in the Central American country of El Salvador is safer. This book tells about the people of El Salvador and their struggle for survival in this land of poverty and war.

Adler, Ann. **Passport to West Germany.** Illustrated by the Hayward Art Group. Franklin Watts, 1986. 48 p. ISBN 0-531-10017-0.

What is West Germany really like? This book answers that question by telling you about the land, the food, the main industries, and much more. Discover West Germany's uniqueness and its dazzle as you view the color photographs of its landmarks and its citizens.

Ashabranner, Brent. **Children of the Maya: A Guatemalan Indian Odyssey.** Photographs by Paul Conklin. Dodd, Mead, 1986. 93 p. ISBN 0-396-08786-8.

From highland Guatemala to Mexico to Florida, these Maya have fled, seeking freedom from the warring government troups and guerrillas in their homeland. Meet real-life refugee families who now live in the midst of controversy over the U.S. government's responsibility for their welfare.

Balerdi, Susan. **France: The Crossroads of Europe.** Dillon Press, 1984. 138 p. ISBN 0-87518-248-8.

France blends the new and the old. Ancient architecture and nuclear power plants sit side by side in this second largest European country, which gave us April Fools' Day, the Christmas tree, tennis, and the Statue of Liberty. French history, government, folklore, traditions, and lifestyles are discussed. Part of the Discovering Our Heritage series.

Ball, John. **We Live in New Zealand.** Photographs by Chris Fairclough. Bookwright Press/Living Here Books, 1984. 64 p. ISBN 0-531-04781-4.

The photographs in this book will make you feel that you are really traveling through New Zealand as you journey through the pages. Twenty-eight residents will tell you about their jobs and the islands that make up their country. A colorful map will help you locate New Zealand in the South Pacific, and a fact sheet will provide you with detailed information about the country and its people.

Biucchi, Edwina. **Italian Food and Drink.** Bookwright Press, 1987. 48 p. ISBN 0-531-18120-0.

The food and drink of Italy are described in relation to its people, culture, and geography. Simple recipes are included so that you can experience "a taste of Italy." A look at Italian history, agriculture, stores and markets, eating habits, national and regional specialties, and festive foods will give you insight into life in Italy.

Brickenden, Jack. **We Live in Canada.** Bookwright Press/Living Here Books, 1985. 60 p. ISBN 0-531-03818-1.

In this book you will meet several of our neighbors who work in the natural resources areas: a tour guide, a trapper, a prairie farmer, a lobster fisherman, a park naturalist, an oil geologist, a miner, and a seven-time world champion lumber jack. You will also learn about life in Canada from the comments of a pro football player, the captain of a boat that takes tourists to the base of Niagara Falls, and other interesting Canadian workers.

Bristow, Richard. **We Live in Spain.** Bookwright Press/Living Here Books, 1984. 64 p. ISBN 0-531-04780-6.

"Last year no one was killed, and the year before only one bullfighter died," brags Enrique Molina of his profession. He is just one of the people who will tell you about life in Spain. You will also hear from a flamenco dancer, an olive grower, and a horse trainer.

Cameron, Fiona, and Preben Kristensen. **We Live in Belgium and Luxembourg.** Bookwright Press/Living Here Books, 1986. 60 p. ISBN 0-531-18069-7.

Many interesting people live in the two small European countries of Belgium and Luxembourg. Twenty-six of them describe their lives, including a marionettist, a crystal-glass master, a chocolate maker, and a professional bicycle racer.

Carpenter, Mark L. **Brazil: An Awakening Giant.** Dillon Press, 1987. 125 p. ISBN 0-87518-366-2.

Here's an introduction to Brazil, a Portuguese-speaking country in South America. The book describes the people, traditions, folkways, holidays, family life, foods, schools, sports, recreation, and history of Brazil. Also included are general facts about Brazil, a glossary of terms, and a selected bibliography.

Cheney, Theodore A. Rees. **Living in Polar Regions.** Franklin Watts, 1987. 87 p. ISBN 0-531-10150-9.

The Eskimos, Yakaghir, and Cree inhabit some of the coldest climates in the world. How do they survive? This book will explain as it takes you on visits to Alaska, the Soviet Union, and Canada. Part of the Cultural Geography series.

Clayton-Felt, Josh. **To Be Seventeen in Israel: Through the Eyes of an American Teenager.** Franklin Watts, 1987. 96 p. ISBN 0-531-10249-1.

Take a trip to Israel to see how Israeli teenagers live, and let your guide be a seventeen-year-old American boy who has made three trips to Israel in recent years. He describes Israeli family life, schools, participation in the army, and friends.

Currimbhoy, Nayana. **Living in Deserts.** Franklin Watts, 1987. 91 p. ISBN 0-531-10145-2.

Walking fifteen miles a day in temperatures over one hundred degrees is just one event in the daily life of the desert people in Africa's Sahel. This book also takes you to Australia's Western Desert and Chile's Norte Grande to show you how the inhabitants adapt to the desert conditions and their harsh environment. Part of the Cultural Geography series.

Davidson, Judith. **Japan: Where East Meets West.** Dillon Press, 1983. 139 p. ISBN 0-87518-230-5.

The population of Japan is half as large as that of the United States, although the country is only as large as California. In such crowded conditions, the people must learn to be polite and to get along with one another. This book looks at the Japanese history and culture and discusses how Japan has influenced the West and how, in turn, the West has affected Japan. Part of the Discovering Our Heritage series.

de Zulueta, Tana. **We Live in Italy.** Bookwright Press/Living Here Books, 1983. 64 p. ISBN 0-531-0469-7.

Here is a collection of interviews with some of the people who live, study, and work in Italy. Included are a clown in a traveling circus, a waiter who serves over a thousand cups of coffee a day, and a famous sportswoman. Join them for a tour of their country, the home of the Fiat and pizza.

DiFranco, Anthony. **Italy: Balanced on the Edge of Time.** Dillon Press, 1983. 124 p. ISBN 0-87518-229-1.

The Italians gave us ice cream, opera, the first cookbook, and physicist Enrico Fermi. They finance their Olympic team through a national lottery. They house the Pope in a separate country within the city of Rome. These and many other interesting facts about the Italian people and their country await you in this book. Part of the Discovering Our Heritage series.

Dixon, Dougal. **A Closer Look at Jungles.** Illustrated by Richard Orr. Gloucester Press, 1984. 32 p. ISBN 0-531-03478-X.

Plants, animals, and people of the jungle and their interaction are discussed in this book. It also looks at jungles of the future since the increasing numbers of people living in jungle regions and cultivating the land have great impact on the jungles. Part of the Closer Look series.

Dolan, Edward F., Jr., and Shan Finney. **The New Japan.** Franklin Watts, 1983. 113 p. ISBN 0-531-04665-6.

This book presents a comprehensive view of Japan, with an emphasis on the blend of tradition and change that marks every aspect of Japanese life. These changes stem from its democratic system of government designed after World War II and affect Japan's miraculous industrial development, schools, homes, religions, and recreation. Of particular interest are the changes for women, young people, and family life.

Donica, Ewa, and Tim Sharman. **We Live in Poland.** Bookwright Press/ Living Here Books, 1985. 60 p. ISBN 0-531-03819-X.

A museum founder, a TV sports journalist, an international truck driver, and a woman who spent part of World War II in a concentration camp talk about what it's like to live in Poland today. A map will help you locate the Polish cities mentioned, and the book includes a fact page about the country and its people and a helpful glossary of Polish terms.

Editors of Time-Life Books. **Arabian Peninsula.** Photographs by Pascal and Maria Maréchaux. Time-Life Books, 1985. 160 p. ISBN 0-8094-5312-6.

This book presents a comprehensive overview of the people and places of the Arabian Peninsula. Described are their culture, history, and people and the political and economic role that oil has played. Part of the Library of Nations series.

Editors of Time-Life Books. **Mexico.** Time-Life Books, 1985. 160 p. ISBN 0-8094-5307-X.

The author describes Mexico as an old land of young people. Included are past histories and accomplishments, in addition to future developments and dreams. Mexico's geography and climate have shaped its history and development. It is a semi-arid region of mountain ranges and plateaus. It is also an old land of new people. Before Spanish conquistadors arrived in the early sixteenth century, several highly developed Indian settlements flourished. This book discusses Mexico's past and present and looks ahead to the future. Part of the Library of Nations series.

Editors of Time-Life Books. **The Soviet Union.** Time-Life Books, 1984. 160 p. ISBN 0-8094-5302-9.

The Soviet Union is the largest country in the world, and its citizens represent numerous ethnic backgrounds. This book presents a comprehensive overview of the Soviet Union: its geography, history, economy, government, and diverse population and cultural traditions. Included are a bibliography and charts of demographic and climatic data. Part of the Library of Nations series.

Einhorn, Barbara. **Living in Berlin.** Silver Burdett, 1986. 45 p. ISBN 0-382-09114-0.

The German city of Berlin developed from two separate thirteenth-century cities and became a divided city after World War II. This book discusses Berlin's history, government, and daily life; explains why Berlin is divided by a concrete wall; and tells how the division alters life for those living there. Part of the City Life series.

Elliott, Drossoula Vassiliou, and Sloane Elliott. **We Live in Greece.** Photographs by Eugene Vanderpool. Bookwright Press/Living Here Books, 1984. 60 p. ISBN 0-531-93795-9.

Do you remember the stories of gods and goddesses, of centaurs and minotaurs, of heroic Olympians? Vanderpool's photographs will lead you on a personal tour through Greece, the home of all of these characters. As well as viewing the beautiful countryside and cities, you will meet with twenty-six residents of Greece who will tell you about life in their country.

Ellis, Rennie. **We Live in Australia.** Bookwright Press/Living Here Books, 1983. 64 p. ISBN 0-531-04687-7.

Do you like to do cutbacks, re-entries, and tubes? Eleven-year-old Nicky Pope of Sydney does. He does these tricks every day when he goes surfing. He even has a wet suit so he can surf in the winter and stay warm. Nicky and many other interesting people will tell you about their favorite activities in Australia.

Fairclough, Chris. **We Live in Britain.** Bookwright Press/Living Here Books, 1984. 64 p. ISBN 0-531-04783-0.

This book will take you on a short visit to the British Isles. Colorful photographs provide both country and city scenes, and twenty-eight residents talk about their lives in Britain. A detailed map will help you locate major cities and landmarks, and a fact page will give you major information about the country.

Fairclough, Chris. **We Live in Hong Kong.** Bookwright Press/Living Here Books, 1986. 60 p. ISBN 0-531-18027-1.

Despite the problems caused by overpopulation, Hong Kong is becoming a center of modern industry. It is the world's largest producer of transistors and the largest exporter of toys. This book will introduce you to Hong Kong and to some of the people who live there.

Fairclough, Chris. **We Live in Indonesia.** Bookwright Press/Living Here Books, 1986. 60 p. ISBN 0-531-18025-5.

Over two hundred fifty languages are spoken on the many islands of Indonesia, which has the world's fifth largest population. Here you will find the largest single source of copper in the world. Indonesia's nearly impenetrable forests contain some of the world's last cave dwellers and tribes that have only been recently discovered. You will meet about two dozen Indonesians in this book, and they'll tell you what it's like to live in this island nation.

Fairclough, Chris. **We Live in Ireland.** Bookwright Press/Living Here Books, 1986. 60 p. ISBN 0-531-18070-0.

When you travel to Ireland, you will want to kiss the Blarney Stone, shop for some Waterford crystal, and play a few holes of golf. Be well prepared for your trip by reading this book. Twenty-six residents will discuss their lives and occupations in Ireland and will tell you what to see and do when you visit.

Farley, Carol. **Korea: A Land Divided.** Dillon Press, 1983. 140 p. ISBN 0-87518-244-5.

Korea is a land divided with each half considered a separate country. What led to this division? Learn the answer to this question as you read about the history, language, holidays, homes, education, and sports of the Korean people. Part of the Discovering Our Heritage series.

Fernando, Gilda Cordero. **We Live in the Philippines.** Bookwright Press/Living Here Books, 1986. 60 p. ISBN 0-531-18024-7.

The Philippines is a country of 7,107 islands. In this book, some of the people who inhabit these islands will tell you about their lives and their jobs. You will learn about a jeepney driver, a pinipig maker, and a fish fry catcher, to name just a few. Colorful pictures show where these people live and work.

Filstrup, Chris, and Janie Filstrup. **China: From Emperors to Communes.** Dillon Press, 1983. 156 p. ISBN 0-87518-227-5.

Almost one-fourth of the Earth's people live in China. Learn about their history, language, arts, holidays, sports, and lifestyles and about contributions Chinese have made to life in the United States. Part of the Discovering Our Heritage series.

Gillies, John. **The Soviet Union: The World's Largest Country.** Dillon Press, 1985. 155 p. ISBN 0-87518-290-9.

The Soviet Union, the world's largest country, occupies one-half of Europe and one-third of Asia. Its inhabitants represent a variety of ethnic backgrounds, and the government is trying to mold them into one unified population. This book explains present government policy and explores the history, holidays, foods, sports, and education of the Soviet people. Part of the Discovering Our Heritage series.

Griffiths, John. **We Live in the Caribbean.** Bookwright Press/Living Here Books, 1985. 60 p. ISBN 0-531-03832-7.

Would you pay to go to school? Most students on the islands of the Caribbean have to pay, so they work very hard to earn the money. They realize that getting a good education is the only chance to find success. Some of these students share their dreams with you. You will also meet workers with very unusual kinds of jobs, including a sugarcane cutter, a cocoa grower, a rum blender, a cigar roller, and a pineapple plantation worker.

Hanmer, Trudy J. **Nicaragua.** Franklin Watts/First Books, 1986. 66 p. ISBN 0-531-10125-8.

The largest Central American country, Nicaragua, is often in the news. In 1979, rebel forces called the Sandinistas overthrew the government, and since that time they have constantly fought against the Contra troops trying to regain control of the government. Despite the battles going on, life for many people is improving. There are nationwide efforts to teach the people to read and to vaccinate them against polio and measles. You will learn about Nicaraguan history, culture, customs, and people as you read this book.

Holbrook, Sabra. **Canada's Kids.** Atheneum, 1983. 161 p. ISBN 0-689-31002-1.

The author spent seven months in rural, urban, and suburban areas of Canada and in Eskimo and Indian villages. She got to know a wide cross-section of Canadian youth and recorded their impressions of what it's like to live in Canada, the second largest country in the world.

Horton, Casey. **Grasslands.** Illustrated by Cooper-West and Rob Shone. Franklin Watts/Picture Atlas, 1985. 38 p. ISBN 0-531-04922-1.

This book is one in a series of titles that highlights the physical geography of our world. Grasslands are identified on maps of each continent, and text and photographs describe the plants and animals found in these regions. Emphasis is given to the way in which people both depend on and affect these grassy environments.

Huber, Alex. **We Live in Argentina.** Bookwright Press/Living Here Books, 1984. 60 p. ISBN 0-531-03793-2.

Short interviews and action photographs will introduce you to twenty-six people who work or study in Argentina. Colorful pictures of different cities and points of interest will give you a closer look at the country itself, which is the second largest nation in South America. Also included in this book are a map and a fact page.

Huber, Alex. **We Live in Chile.** Bookwright Press/Living Here Books, 1986. 60 p. ISBN 0-531-18023-9.

This visit to Chile will lead you to the Atacama Desert, the driest place on Earth, and to Lake Chungara, the highest lake in the world. It will introduce you to such notables as a world champion BMX racer and a world champion underwater hunter, as well as to an oil worker and a woodcutter. Learn their impressions of life in Chile.

Hughes, Jill. **A Closer Look at Arctic Lands.** Gloucester Press, 1987. 32 p. ISBN 0-531-17036-5.

The frigid area known as the Arctic is revealed in numerous illustrations and information about what lives there. The hardy arctic plants and animals are discussed, and the book describes the seasons and the people of this North Pole region. Part of the Closer Look series.

Irizarry, Carmen. **Passport to Mexico.** Illustrated by the Hayward Art Group. Franklin Watts, 1987. 47 p. ISBN 0-531-10271-8.

This book provides information about the land, people, major cities, homelife and leisure, economy and trade, government, and world role of Mexico. Included are colorful photographs and several fact files about our neighbor to the south.

Kanitkar, V. P. (Hemant). **Indian Food and Drink.** Bookwright Press, 1987. 48 p. ISBN 0-531-18119-7.

The Asian country of India is explored in this book: its people, climate, agriculture, and the processing, distribution, and selling of food. Regional foods of the north and south, midday and evening meals, and special foods are described. Simple recipes are included so that you can experience a taste of India. Part of the Food and Drink series.

Kawamata, Kazuhide. **We Live in Japan.** Bookwright Press/Living Here Books, 1984. 60 p. ISBN 0-531-03796-7.

Interviews with two dozen Japanese people provide information about Japanese education, trades, ancient customs, and daily life. Color photographs, a map of this island nation, and a fact page are included in the book.

Keeler, Stephen, and Chris Fairclough. **We Live in Sweden.** Bookwright Press/Living Here Books, 1985. 60 p. ISBN 0-531-03833-5.

Swedish craftspeople are famous all over the world, and you will get a close-up look at several in this book. A toymaker, a glassblower, and a potter will tell you about their work. You will also meet a reindeer herdsman, a singer, and many other people who work and study in Sweden.

Khalfan, Zulf M., and Mohamed Amin. **We Live in Kenya.** Bookwright Press/Living Here Books, 1984. 60 p. ISBN 0-531-03797-5.

Kenya became independent from the British Empire in 1963. Since that time, the many different people in this East African country have been working together to form a strong new nation. In this book, men and women from Kenya's new educational, medical, and commercial areas will tell you about their lives. You will also meet workers with more traditional jobs.

Kleeberg, Irene Cumming. **Ethiopia.** Franklin Watts/First Books, 1986. 63 p. ISBN 0-531-10115-0.

Starvation, drought, civil war, and cholera affect everyone in this sunburned country, where over seventy languages are spoken and only 10 percent of the people can read and write. For years, Ethiopia's own government kept news of these events from the rest of the world, but now other nations are sending food, medical supplies, and money to help. This book describes the geography, history, culture, and current political, economic, and social problems of this African nation.

Kristensen, Preben, and Fiona Cameron. **We Live in South Africa.** Bookwright Press/Living Here Books, 1985. 60 p. ISBN 0-531-18005-0.

Travel to South Africa, the world's largest producer of gem diamonds and the producer of over half of the world's gold. In addition to these resources, you will find wildlife reserves, ostrich farms, and famous wineries. You will meet Zulu dancers, modern witch doctors, and archaeologists in this collection of interviews with twenty-six people who live, work, and study in South Africa.

Kristensen, Preben, and Fiona Cameron. **We Live in the Netherlands.** Illustrated by Preben Kristensen. Bookwright Press/Living Here Books, 1985. 60 p. ISBN 0-531-18004-2.

Twenty-six residents of the Netherlands will describe what life is like in their country. A circus artist, a professional soccer player, a tulip grower, and a shrimp fisherman are among those who discuss their jobs and studies and the Dutch way of life.

Lafargue, Françoise. **French Food and Drink.** Bookwright Press, 1987. 44 p. ISBN 0-531-18130-8.

French chefs are renowned for their cooking expertise. This book describes national and regional specialties, dishes for festive occasions, and the influence French cuisine has had on the preparation of food in other countries. Included are a glossary of French words and phrases and a list of titles for further reading. Part of the Food and Drink series.

Langley, Andrew. **Passport to Great Britain.** Illustrated by the Hayward Art Group. Franklin Watts, 1986. 48 p. ISBN 0-531-10015-4.

This colorful, fact-filled book describes the geography, people, home life and leisure, economy and trade, government, and world role of Great Britain. Complete maps are included.

Lawson, Don. **South Africa.** Franklin Watts/First Books, 1986. 88 p. ISBN 0-531-10128-2.

South Africa is smaller in land size than Alaska, but its racial and economic problems keep it forefront in the news. This book discusses the history of South Africa and its development of the policy of apartheid, examines relations between the United States and South Africa, and introduces South Africa's modern leaders.

Levine, Gemma. **We Live in Israel.** Bookwright Press/Living Here Books, 1983. 64 p. ISBN 0-531-04689-3.

Do you want to join the army? In Israel, you would not be asked. Every woman must serve two years, and every man must serve three. Even high school students learn how to defend their country. In this book, some of these soldiers will join with other Israeli workers to tell you about life in their country.

Lye, Keith. **Africa.** Illustrated by Ron Hayward Associates. Gloucester Press, 1987. 36 p. ISBN 0-531-17065-9.

The vast continent of Africa is featured in this brief book. It surveys the current political, economic, and social conditions and the interaction of African countries with other nations in the world. Photographs, diagrams, and maps help describe this continent. Other volumes in the Today's World series feature the Americas, Asia and Australasia, and Europe.

McCarthy, Kevin. **Saudi Arabia: A Desert Kingdom.** Dillon Press, 1986. 125 p. ISBN 0-87518-295-X.

The Red Sea is not really red but is a blue-green that becomes discolored when algae plants die in it. This is one of many interesting things that you will discover about Saudi Arabia in this book. You will read about the world's largest desert, water that is more expensive than gasoline, and women who are not allowed to drive cars. You will learn about famous people and traditions that we have borrowed from the Saudi people. Part of the Discovering Our Heritage series.

McDowall, David. **The Palestinians.** Illustrated by Ron Hayward Associates. Gloucester Press, 1986. 32 p. ISBN 0-531-17031-4.

The struggle by Jews for a Jewish state in Palestine began in the late nineteenth century and became a reality in 1948. From the outset, militant Arabs opposed dividing Palestine into a Jewish state and an Arab state, and armies from Lebanon, Syria, Jordan, Egypt, and Iraq invaded the newly established Israel in 1948. The conflict continues today. This book examines the causes and the effects of the fighting. Part of the Issues series.

Mannetti, Lisa. **Iran and Iraq: Nations at War.** Franklin Watts/Impact Books, 1986. 87 p. ISBN 0-531-10155-X.

Have Iran and Iraq always been at war? What is the source of the conflict between them? What worldwide effects may result from their mutual hatred? Based upon careful research, this book offers possible answers to these questions as it reviews the history of the conflict, considers the resulting political and economic impacts, and examines religious and political beliefs of both cultures.

Mariella, Cinzia. **Passport to Italy.** Illustrated by the Hayward Art Group. Franklin Watts, 1986. 48 p. ISBN 0-531-10016-2.

This book will help you understand the culture, traditions, and lifestyle of the Italians. Discover their favorite sports, pastimes, and entertainment, as well as important industries.

Markl, Julia. **Living on Islands.** Franklin Watts, 1987. 89 p. ISBN 0-531-10147-9.

Have you ever fantasized about living on an island? If so, you might find your island on this geographical tour of New Zealand's South Island, Crete, and all of the Hawaiian Islands. The book describes the land and customs of the people in these island communities and discusses some of the work of a cultural geographer. Part of the Cultural Geography series.

Meyer, Kathleen Allan. **Ireland: Land of Mist and Magic.** Dillon Press, 1983. 140 p. ISBN 0-87518-228-3.

Ireland, the Emerald Isle, is a land of beauty and a land of conflict between Protestants and Catholics. This book focuses on the social life and cultural traditions of Ireland. Read about Jonathan Swift, W. B. Yeats, James Joyce, and other famous Irish authors, and try a recipe for Irish soda bread. Learn about St. Patrick's Day traditions and how the holiday began. Included are maps and a page of fast facts about Ireland.

Norbrook, Dominique. **Passport to France.** Illustrated by the Hayward Art Group. Franklin Watts, 1986. 48 p. ISBN 0-531-10014-6.

This colorful, fact-filled book presents information on the geography, people, home life and leisure, economy and trade, government, and world role of France. Included are maps and photographs.

Olsson, Kari. **Sweden: A Good Life for All.** Dillon Press, 1983. 140 p. ISBN 0-87518-231-3.

A national law forbids parents to spank their children. A university education is free to students with good grades. Artists and writers are supported by the government, and there is one lake for each eighty-seven people. These are just a few of the interesting facts in this book about the country and people of Sweden. Part of the Discovering Our Heritage series.

Pepper, Susan. **Passport to Australia.** Illustrated by the Hayward Art Group. Franklin Watts, 1987. 47 p. ISBN 0-531-10270-X.

Take a close look at Australia. This book is full of facts about the land, people, major cities, home life and leisure, economy and trade, government, and world role of Australia. Colorful photographs and several fact files are included.

Pfeiffer, Christine. **Poland: Land of Freedom Fighters.** Dillon Press, 1984. 171 p. ISBN 0-87518-254-2.

The United States has more people of Polish descent than any other country except Poland, and Chicago has more Poles than any other city in the world except Warsaw. This book tells what contributions these Polish descendants have made to life in the United States and describes the history, traditions, and daily lives of the Polish people. Part of the Discovering Our Heritage series.

Rau, Margaret. **Holding Up the Sky: Young People in China.** E. P. Dutton/Lodestar Books, 1983. 129 p. ISBN 0-525-656718-0.

Twelve young Chinese describe living in China. Some live and work in the cities, others in the countryside. Some are members of the Han nationality, who are the majority people in China, while others represent some of China's fifty-seven minority peoples. Through these descriptions, you'll learn what it's like to grow up Chinese and you'll learn about the political, cultural, and economic conditions that affect their lives.

Regan, Geoffrey. **Israel and the Arabs.** Lerner Publications and Cambridge University Press/Cambridge Topic Books, 1986. 51 p. ISBN 0-8225-1234-3.

Just what lies at the heart of the conflict in the Middle East? Has European and American involvement heightened the tense situation? Will the continual fighting explode into a worldwide conflict? Factual and frank, this book traces the British rule of

Palestine, the founding of the Jewish state of Israel, the growth of Arab nationalism, and the fighting between the Israelis and the Arabs.

Roberson, John R. **Japan: From Shogun to Sony, 1543–1984.** Atheneum, 1985. 198 p. ISBN 0-689-31076-5.

Japan has a fascinating history, from the imperial power of the shoguns and their samurai to the economic power of companies like Sony. Japan has played a major role in shaping world history. This book details such events as the arrival of the first Europeans in Japan in the sixteenth century, the Japanese empire during World War II, and Japan as a modern world power.

Ryabko, E. **We Live in the Asian U.S.S.R.** Bookwright Press/Living Here Books, 1985. 60 p. ISBN 0-531-03831-9.

In this introduction to the people of the Asian portion of the U.S.S.R., you will meet a professional hunter who rides a reindeer when she goes hunting, a woman who has won national honors for her work in agriculture, and a woman who became captain of her own ship at age twenty-six. This is certainly a land of equal opportunity. Other people who work and study the Soviet Union talk about what their lives are like.

Sandal, Veenu. **We Live in India.** Photographs by Brahm Dev. Bookwright Press/Living Here Books, 1984. 64 p. ISBN 0-531-04784-9.

Wouldn't it be strange to turn on the TV set and find just one channel and no color? That is what you would find if you turned on the TV in India. But chances are great that you would not even have a television because most people there can not afford one. In this book you'll meet a sampling of people who describe living in India: a sidewalk vendor, a camel-riding postman, a prince, a wrestling coach, and a woman blacksmith.

Sarin, Amita Vohra. **India: An Ancient Land, a New Nation.** Dillon Press, 1985. 170 p. ISBN 0-87518-273-9.

India has more children than the United States has people, yet the country is only half as large. Great efforts are being made to accommodate this many people and to upgrade the quality of education and life in this country that gave us algebra, polo, badminton, chess, and Parcheesi. This book describes the history and cultural traditions of India and looks at how life in India is changing. Part of the Discovering Our Heritage series.

Shapiro, William E. **Lebanon.** Franklin Watts/Impact Books, 1984. 88 p. ISBN 0-531-04854-3.

Here is a look at the current internal battle in Lebanon between Christian and Moslem forces. This struggle is set against the backdrop of the larger conflict between Syria and Israel, who are fighting one another on Lebanese soil. The book traces the history of Lebanon and its people, politics, and ethnic problems.

Sharman, Tim. **We Live in East Germany.** Bookwright Press/Living Here Books, 1986. 60 p. ISBN 0-531-18026-3.

A toymaker, a porcelain designer, and a schoolgirl are some of the people who talk about life in East Germany. They explain what their daily lives are like and how the Germans continue to work to modernize their country following its destruction in World War II.

Shui, Amy, and Stuart Thompson. **Chinese Food and Drink.** Bookwright Press, 1987. 43 p. ISBN 0-531-18129-4.

A rich tradition of Chinese food and drink is described in this book: family meals, regional cuisine, typical ingredients, cooking equipment, and food for festive occasions. The book concentrates on the cuisine of the majority Han Chinese, but points out that the more than fifty minorities have their own styles of cooking and eating. A pronunciation guide, a glossary of terms, and suggestions for further reading are included. Part of the Food and Drink series.

Smith, Eileen Latell. **Mexico: Giant of the South.** Dillon Press, 1983. 156 p. ISBN 0-87518-242-9.

Mexican schools, work opportunities, sports, recreation, and food are described in this book. You will learn about rich Mexican traditions and changes in Mexican lifestyles. Part of the Discovering Our Heritage series.

Somonte, Carlos. **We Live in Mexico.** Bookwright Press/Living Here Books, 1985. 60 p. ISBN 0-531-03820-3.

Many people hope that increasing Mexico's tourist trade will help solve their economic problems. You will meet some of these people in this book: a weaver, a bow-and-arrow maker, a dolphin trainer, a cactus-plantation worker, a professional street performer, and a major league baseball player. They describe their jobs and their daily routines and express their hopes for Mexico's future.

Soule, Gardner. **Antarctica.** Franklin Watts/First Books, 1985. 72 p. ISBN 0-531-10033-2.

If you went to the South Pole, you could circle the world in just a few seconds. You could visit an active volcano and see the largest floating ice mass in the world. You would stay healthy because there are no germs. But the terrible ice and cold will probably keep you from visiting. So why not travel to this remote land in the comfort of your own home as you read this book?

Stadtler, Christa. **We Live in West Germany.** Bookwright Press/Living Here Books, 1984. 60 p. ISBN 0-531-03798-3.

Twenty-six people who live, work, and study in West Germany discuss their jobs, schools, and customs. Colorful photographs depict events from their daily lives. Also included are a map and a fact page of West Germany.

Stark, Al. **Australia: A Lucky Land.** Dillon Press, 1987. 151 p. ISBN 0-87518-365-4.

Aborigines are thought to have migrated to Australia 20,000 years ago. In 1788 the British established the first European settlement, a penal colony, which led to extensive development and change within the country. This is a study of the people, culture, geography, history, and customs of "the land down under." Included are fast facts about Australia, a map, a list of Australian expressions and their meanings, a list of consulates and embassies, and a selected bibliography.

Stark, Al. **Zimbabwe: A Treasure of Africa.** Dillon Press, 1985. 160 p. ISBN 0-87518-308-5.

Zimbabwe, the former British colony of Rhodesia, lies directly north of South Africa. It became an independent nation in 1980, with a government elected by majority rule. This book provides a detailed description of life in Zimbabwe. Topics include the history, people, traditions, religions, geography, and wildlife of Zimbabwe. The book looks at the way of life in Zimbabwe and how it relates to ours. Part of the Discovering Our Heritage series.

Strange, Ian J. **The Falklands: South Atlantic Islands.** Photographs by the author. Dodd, Mead, 1985. 157 p. ISBN 0-396-08616-0.

Until the Falkland Islands War in 1982, this South Atlantic group of islands was known for its unique wildlife and beauty. In this brief history, naturalist Ian J. Strange provides a look at the island's traditions, including the inhabitants' desire for a simple way of life. The photographs and text will help you understand how important it is for the people of the Falklands to keep their natural surroundings and wildlife preserved.

Taitz, Emily, and Sondra Henry. **Israel: A Sacred Land.** Dillon Press, 1987. 159 p. ISBN 0-87518-364-6.

This book describes the land and people of Israel today and explains the history of the Jews, Arabs, and Christians who have lived in this portion of Palestine in the past. Also included are facts about Israel, a map, a list of consulates, a glossary of terms, and a selected bibliography.

Tomlins, James. **We Live in France.** Bookwright Press/Living Here Books, 1983. 64 p. ISBN 0-531-04688-5.

In France, there is no school on Wednesdays, explains thirteen-year-old Arianne Douchand, who then goes on to tell about her life as a teenager in France. Arianne is just one of the French people you will meet in this book. Some of the others are a chef, a priest, a taxi driver, a cobbler, and a perfumery owner.

We Live in China. Bookwright Press/Living Here Books, 1984. 64 p. ISBN 0-531-04779-2.

This book contains interviews with twenty-eight residents of China. You will learn about their daily lives and occupations. Colorful photographs depict various parts of the country, and a map and fact page will help you locate these places and learn more about China and its people.

Wee, Jessie. **We Live in Malaysia and Singapore.** Bookwright Press/ Living Here Books, 1985. 60 p. ISBN 0-531-18007-7.

Visit the Asian countries of Malaysia and Singapore as you read this book. Meet twenty-six people who live and work there and who talk about their daily lives. Tour mines that produce twenty-five percent of the world's tin and farms that make Malaysia the world's leading exporter of pepper. You'll learn about another part of the world and the people who live there.

Personal Improvement

Arnold, Caroline. **Too Fat? Too Thin? Do You Have a Choice?** William Morrow, 1984. 92 p. ISBN 0-688-02779-2 (0-688-02780-6, library binding).

Physical appearance is important to teenagers, especially being the ideal weight. This book looks at the problem of weight control and why it is so difficult to achieve. The author feels that if you are aware of the many elements that affect your body weight, you can concentrate on altering those that can be changed. Some, like heredity, are unchangeable.

Arnold, Eric H., and Jeffrey Loeb, editors. **I'm Telling! Kids Talk about Brothers and Sisters.** Illustrated by G. Brian Karas. Little, Brown/ Hole in the Sock Books, 1987. 137 p. ISBN 0-316-05185-3 (0-316-05186-1, paperback).

A sibling can be a pain in the neck one minute and a best friend the next. Good times and bad times and the wide range of feelings kids have for their brothers and sisters are captured in this book. It also offers advice on how to get along better with brothers and sisters in the most trying circumstances.

Brown, Fern G. **Etiquette.** Illustrated by Anne Canevari Green. Franklin Watts/First Books, 1985. 84 p. ISBN 0-531-04908-6.

Have you ever wondered how to introduce your grandparents to your friends, to write a thank-you letter for a gift you don't like, or whether you may eat asparagus with your fingers? This book answers these questions and many more about contemporary good manners at home, at school, at parties, and while visiting as a houseguest.

Carlson, Dale, and Dan Fitzgibbon. **Manners That Matter: For People under 21.** E. P. Dutton, 1983. 134 p. ISBN 0-525-44008-9.

This handbook suggests proper etiquette in situations ranging from dances and dinners to dating and conversations. It even tells you how to say no and how to accept no for an answer.

Davis, Bertha. **How to Write a Composition.** Illustrated by Anne Canevari Green. Franklin Watts/First Books, 1985. 85 p. ISBN 0-531-10042-1.

Does writing a composition scare you? Do book reports make you shiver and shake? Here is a step-by-step plan for developing writing skills that can help you now while you're in school and later when you have a career.

Gale, Jay. **A Young Man's Guide to Sex.** Illustrated by Scott E. Carroll. Holt, Rinehart and Winston, 1984. 214 p. ISBN 0-03-069396-9.

This book recognizes sex as a complicated subject and helps you try to make sense of it. It contains practical, complete, and accurate information about young men's sexuality and covers such subjects as sexual truths and lies, the emotional side of sex, sexually transmitted diseases, contraception, abortion, adoption, masturbation, and homosexuality. It also contains a complete glossary of sexual vocabulary and more than a dozen illustrations. Some readers may find the frankness objectionable.

Gelinas, Paul J. **Coping with Weight Problems.** Rosen Publishing Group, 1983. 131 p. ISBN 0-8239-0598-5.

To be successful at nearly anything, our society almost dictates that one must be thin. But not all people are. This book discusses many reasons why people turn to food as a way to solve their problems, and suggests how one can conquer obesity by dealing with the issues that cause it.

Kelly, Gary F. **Learning about Sex: The Contemporary Guide for Young Adults.** 3d. ed. Barron's Educational Series, 1986. 188 p. ISBN 0-8120-2432-X.

This book can help the reader understand his or her sexuality plus the feelings of confusion, fear, guilt, and anxiety that frequently accompany sexual concerns. The book does not tell you "right" or "wrong" sexual behavior; instead, it focuses on thinking, feeling, sorting, and deciding the answers to sexual questions at specific times in your life.

Klein, David, and Marymae E. Klein. **Your Parents and Your Self: Alike, Unlike; Agreeing, Disagreeing.** Charles Scribner's Sons, 1986. 166 p. ISBN 0-684-18684-5.

Genetics and environment both play a part in your development, and both involve your parents. This book examines the role of parents in the development of intelligence, behavior, personality, education, and careers.

Levine, Saul, and Kathleen Wilcox. **Dear Doctor: Sensitive, Sensible Answers to Teenagers' Most Troubling Questions.** Lothrop, Lee and Shepard Books, 1986. 265 p. ISBN 0-688-07094-9 (0-688-07095-7, library binding).

Do you have a problem that you're sure no one else ever had? Is there no one for you to confide in? You may find the answer to your problem or one similar to it in this open discussion of many teens' actual personal questions. The book provides wise and sensitive answers for most every teenager.

Lukes, Bonnie L. **How to Be a Reasonably Thin Teenage Girl: Without Starving, Losing Your Friends or Running Away from Home.** Illustrated by Carol Nicklaus. Atheneum, 1986. 86 p. ISBN 0-689-31269-5.

Written by a self-proclaimed ex-fatty, this book is a humorous explanation of how to lose and keep off weight. Its emphasis is on good nutrition and calorie counting, not on dieting. The author recommends rewards instead of punishments and suggests ten things to do when you're starving and it's still two hours until dinner.

Matthews, Dee, Allan Zullo, and Bruce Nash. **The You Can Do It! Kids Diet.** Holt, Rinehart and Winston, 1985. 256 p. ISBN 0-03-069653-4.

If you are one of the twenty million young people in the United States who are overweight, this book may be of help to you. It tells of a diet plan that was developed by Dee Matthews with the assistance of doctors and nutritionists who have an 84 percent success rate in helping kids lose weight and stay thin. The book is loaded with comments from kids who have lost weight, and it shows how to plan menus, prepare meals, and cope with temptations.

Olney, Ross R., and Patricia J. Olney. **Imaging: Thinking Your Way to Success in Sports and Classroom.** Atheneum, 1985. 94 p. ISBN 0-689-31121-4.

Imaging is a technique for developing a positive attitude and for visualizing success. It might be used by the Olympic contender who visualizes the winning jump or skating routine, or by the tennis player who sees in his mind the perfect serve. These same techniques can be used in the classroom to concentrate on passing a difficult test rather than worrying about failing it, or to avoid the stress of public speaking or some social situations.

Parks-McKay, Jane. **The Make-Over: A Teen's Guide to Looking and Feeling Beautiful.** Illustrated by Betty de Araujo. William Morrow, 1985. 170 p. ISBN 0-688-04155-8 (0-688-04156-6, paperback).

Did you ever feel like you wanted to change everything about yourself — to just start over? Well, here's your chance — a book filled with advice on grooming, diet, makeup, exercise, wardrobe planning, nutrition, and behavior.

Sanchez, Gail Jones, and Mary Gerbino. **Overeating: Let's Talk about It.** Illustrated by Lucy Miskiewicz. Dillon Press, 1986. 119 p. ISBN 0-87518-319-0.

Being fat — at any age — is no fun. The authors first discuss reasons why people overeat, and then address the many solutions for obesity, including setting goals, choosing food wisely, and exercising. There is information to help you learn to shop for food and to learn about vitamins. A glossary of terms is included.

Shaw, Diana. **Make the Most of a Good Thing: You!** Little, Brown/Joy Street Books, 1987. 204 p. ISBN 0-316-78340-4 (0-316-78342-0, paperback).

Especially for girls, this book discusses nutrition, exercise, sexuality, smoking, drinking, drugs, and stress. The focus is on growing healthier and staying healthier.

Sternberg, Patricia. **Speak to Me: How to Put Confidence in Your Conversation.** Lothrop, Lee and Shepard Books, 1984. 160 p. ISBN 0-688-02722-9 (0-688-02694-X, library binding).

Talking to other people, perhaps to those we don't know very well, can make us nervous. This book provides a simple, yet successful, strategy for curing conversation jitters. Different tactics are suggested for leading into a conversation and for listening carefully to questions and remarks. The tips might be helpful in preparing for an interview or when trying to make a good first impression.

Sweetgall, Robert, James Rippe, and Frank Katch. **Fitness Walking.** Illustrated by Frederick Bush. Putnam Publishing Group/Perigee Books, 1985. 176 p. ISBN 0-399-51149-0.

Having traveled the equivalent of seven times across the North American continent in a span of three years, Robert Sweetgall is capable of offering a substantial amount of information on the benefits of walking, how to get started, individualizing your fitness program, the importance of diet, and cardiovascular rehabilitation.

Tchudi, Susan, and Stephen Tchudi. **The Young Writer's Handbook.** Charles Scribner's Sons, 1984. 156 p. ISBN 0-684-18090-1.

This handbook describes procedures and approaches to writing that might be of help for the beginning young writer. Guidance is given on such topics as journal writing, report writing, letter writing, and creative writing. Also discussed are such other topics as what to write about, editing, and publishing.

Ward, Brian R. **Body Maintenance.** Franklin Watts, 1983. 48 p. ISBN 0-531-04457-2.

Homeostasis is the process of keeping the internal systems of your body in a constant state. Your hormones, pituitary gland, thyroid, and kidneys are just a few of the body components that keep your internal clock in balance. The readable language and artwork will help you understand how your body maintains itself. Part of the Human Body series.

Ward, Brian R. **Diet and Nutrition.** Illustrated by Dick Bonson, Penny Dann, and Howard Dyke. Franklin Watts, 1987. 48 p. ISBN 0-531-10259-9.

We are what we eat! Find out all about foods, from their nutritional value and functions in the body to the proportions needed in a healthy diet. Short sections, simple wording, and color photographs make this a highly readable source of information. Part of the Life Guides series.

Ward, Brian R. **First Aid.** Franklin Watts, 1987. 48 p. ISBN 0-531-10260-2.

Do you ever wonder what you would do if someone were hurt or became suddenly ill and it was up to you to help? This book will give you practical knowledge for many emergency situations that might arise at home, in the classroom, or when you're out with friends. It includes a glossary of terms and helpful illustrations.

Ward, Hiley H. **Feeling Good about Myself.** Westminster Press, 1983. 163 p. ISBN 0-644-32704-4.

Adolescence can be the best of times and the worst of times. This book captures the highs and lows that face today's teenagers. Teenagers talk about how they deal with such problems as anger, boredom, clothes, cults, embarrassment, friends, money, single parents, and stress.

Reference

Biology Encyclopedia. Rand McNally, 1985. 141 p. ISBN 0-528-82167-9.

As an aid to understanding some of the complex biological terms and concepts, this encyclopedia discusses such topics as life on Earth, animals and plants, survival in nature, evolution, and genetics. Colorful illustrations and a glossary of terms are included.

Concise World Atlas. Rand McNally, 1987. 224 p. ISBN 0-528-83285-9.

This atlas begins with a section on how to use an atlas and an explanation of map symbols. There are 128 pages of easy-to-use, easy-to-read reference maps of the world, followed by almost one hundred pages of indexes to the world reference maps.

Espenshade, Edward B., Jr., editor. **Goode's World Atlas.** 17th ed. Rand McNally, 1986. 367 p. ISBN 0-528-83127-5.

Dozens of full-color physical, political, thematic, historical, and city maps are included in this atlas. It also has a pronunciation index with more than 30,000 entries. Introductory materials explain map scales, map projections, remotely sensed imagery, Landsat, and high-altitude imagery. This atlas includes maps of major world cities, as well as continent-by-continent sections with regional thematic maps, environment maps, and physical-political maps.

The Franklin Watts Atlas of North America and the World. Franklin Watts, 1984. 128 p. ISBN 0-531-09830-3.

This colorful and useful atlas provides a chart of the stars, maps of the continents and oceans, flags of the world, Landsat images of major American land features, a world political map, a map of the polar regions, detailed mapping of the North American continent, individual state maps, and detailed maps of the major countries and subcontinents of the world.

Frome, Michael. **America's Favorite National Parks.** Rand McNally, 1986. 72 p. ISBN 0-528-84689-2.

This guidebook describes the fifteen most popular national parks in the United States, including information on photography, accommodations, campgrounds, nearby attractions, and recommended readings.

History Encyclopedia. Rand McNally, 1985. 141 p. ISBN 0-528-82166-0.

Covering world history in so short a book is, of course, difficult. This book presents short explanations of different people in history, different time periods, and different events that took place. Included are color photographs and charts.

New Century World Atlas. Rand McNally, 1986. 496 p. ISBN 0-528-83213-1.

This atlas is a combination of atlas, almanac, and encyclopedia. It contains a pronunciation index, a glossary of foreign geographical terms, and a listing of abbreviations. Major sections include a discussion of the solar system and the ecology of the Earth, maps of major international cities, topic maps of each continent, a world political information table with basic statistics about each country in the world, and a world gazetteer.

Quick Reference World Atlas. Rand McNally, 1986. 64 p. ISBN 0-528-83226-3.

All maps in this world atlas have been updated with the latest cartographic information, including recent name changes. Political information tables for countries and dependencies include the form of government and ruling power, capital and largest city, predominant languages, estimated population, area, and population per square mile.

Reader's Digest Atlas of the World. Reader's Digest, 1987. 240 p. ISBN 0-89577-264-7.

The first part of this atlas, called "A World of Wonders," provides an overview of the world, ranging from the possible beginnings of the universe to managing the planet's future. An introduction to mapmaking and a complete list of maps appear next, followed by the legend, which explains how to use the maps, and the locator, which shows the areas covered. Following the maps are charts, statistics, and an index to place-names.

The Viking Student World Atlas. Viking Penguin/Viking Kestrel, 1986. 64 p. ISBN 0-670-81122-X.

This book attempts to bridge the gap between pictorial atlases, intended for young children, and the more complicated atlases for adults. It features a logical arrangement of information and such added attractions as a "did you know" section, charts, and illustrations.

Religions

Arbuckle, Gwendolyne (revised by Carolyn Wolcott). **Paul: Adventurer for Christ.** Abingdon Press, 1984. 89 p. ISBN 0-687-30487-3.

This journal follows the life of the apostle Paul, from A.D. 32 to about 61. It begins with Saul, Boy of Tarsus, who became Paul, Persecutor of Jesus' followers, to Saul the Persecuted after his conversion on the road to Damascus. Then it chronicles his travels, preachings, letters, and, finally, imprisonment. Included are a section especially for parents and teachers and a glossary of terms.

Batchelor, Mary. **Our Family Christmas Book.** Abingdon Press, 1984. 92 p. ISBN 0-687-29587-4.

You can plan your Christmas preparations with this book. It features foods, carols, stories, and gifts from around the world that are connected with Christmas. The book is filled with colorful illustrations and photographs that bring the heart of Christmas home to the family.

Berger, Gilda. **Easter and Other Spring Holidays.** Illustrated by Anne Canevari Green. Franklin Watts/First Books, 1983. 66 p. ISBN 0-531-04547-1.

This book discusses the origins and ways of celebrating the spring holidays in various religions. It describes the Jewish spring festivals and emphasizes Easter, including the days before and after. The book includes holiday customs, projects, and recipes.

Bull, Norman J., reteller. **100 New Testament Stories.** Illustrated by Val Biro. Abingdon Press, 1984. 156 p. ISBN 0-687-29073-2.

In simplified language, the author retells New Testament stories, which are divided into four categories: stories of Jesus, stories Jesus told, stories of Peter, and stories of Paul. The book includes maps of the Holy Land and Paul's journeys. There are full color illustrations on each page.

Domnitz, Myer. **Judaism.** Bookwright Press, 1986. 45 p. ISBN 0-531-18066-2.

This book outlines the basic beliefs and origins of Judaism. It describes the way of life, rites and festivals, and particular hardships pertinent to the Jewish religion. Paintings, photographs, a glossary of terms, and suggested further readings are included. Part of the Religions of the World series.

Greenberg, Judith E., and Helen H. Carey. **Jewish Holidays.** Franklin Watts/First Books, 1984. 66 p. ISBN 0-531-04913-2.

Everywhere they live, people celebrate holidays that are special to them. This book describes the yearly cycle of Jewish holidays, including high holy days, harvest holidays, festivals, and modern holidays. All Jewish holidays occur at specific times of the year, according to the Jewish calendar. The holidays help the Jewish people understand their past, which helps them build their future. Recipes and instructions for Jewish holiday foods and crafts are included.

Haywood, Carolyn. **Make a Joyful Noise! Bible Verses for Children.** Illustrated by Lane Yerkes. Westminster Press, 1984. 96 p. ISBN 0-644-32711-7.

Words from the Bible can help us see beauty in everything and can give us guidance. This author has gathered verses especially for her friends, the children, and has arranged them according to twelve topics, such as love, fear, hunger, and prayer.

Herda, D. J. **Christmas.** Illustrated by Anne Canevari Green. Franklin Watts/First Books, 1983. 64 p. ISBN 0-531-04524-2.

Here are brief descriptions of Christmas traditions from various parts of the world and how they came into being. The book includes instructions for making gifts, food, and decorations, all well illustrated with black-and-white drawings and photographs.

Herman, Erwin, and Agnes Herman. **The Yanov Torah.** Illustrated by Katherine Janus Kahn. Kar-Ben Copies, 1985. 47 p. ISBN 0-930494-45-8 (0-930494-46-6, paperback).

In 1941, the Jews of L'vov, Poland, were gathered together and forced into a work camp in Yanov by Hitler's Nazi army. But the men in the work camp still tried to gather strength and hope from their Jewish religion. They created a plan by which they could smuggle in, piece by piece, a copy of the Torah, the Jewish holy scroll. After World War II was over, the Yanov Torah was taken from Poland to the United States and the story of this special Torah continued.

Kanitkar, V. P. (Hemant). **Hinduism.** Bookwright Press, 1986. 45 p. ISBN 0-531-18068-9.

This book outlines the basic beliefs and origins of Hinduism, the dominant religion of India. It describes the way of life, rites and festivals, and particular hardships pertinent to the Hindu religion. Paintings, photographs, a glossary of terms, and suggested further readings are included. Part of the Religions of the World series.

Martin, Nancy. **Christianity.** Bookwright Press, 1986. 45 p. ISBN 0-531-18064-6.

Christianity is the dominant religion in the Americas and Europe, where it has been a powerful historical force and cultural influence. In addition, there are followers of Christianity in nearly every country of the world. The basic beliefs and origins of Christianity are explained in this book. The Christian way of life, rites and festivals, and particular hardships of the Christian religion are explained. Paintings, photographs, a glossary of terms, and suggested further readings are included. Part of the Religions of the World series.

Miller, Luree. **The Black Hat Dances: Two Buddhist Boys in the Himalayas.** Photographs by Marilyn Silverstone. Dodd, Mead, 1987. 86 p. ISBN 0-396-08835-X.

Tashi and Samdup are two Buddhist boys who live in a small village in Sikkim, a state in the northeast corner of India. They spend their days much as children everywhere do — attending school, doing chores, playing — but the religion of Buddhism plays a major role in their lives. The boys study their religion and prepare for the ultimate ritual — the Black Hat Dances — which drives out evil. This peek into monastery life in the Himalayan Mountains explains much about the history and basic principles of Buddhism.

Norwood, Frederick A. (with Jo Carr). **Young Reader's Book of Church History.** Illustrated by Tom Armstrong. Abingdon Press, 1982. 175 p. ISBN 0-687-46827-2.

After Pam crashes her skateboard into a statue of St. Francis of Assisi, she and her friends persuade Dr. Jackson to tell them about the saint. As their interest grows, they hear other stories of people, traditions, and events important in the history of Christianity.

Snelling, John. **Buddhism.** Bookwright Press, 1986. 45 p. ISBN 0-531-18065-4.

Buddhism is a religion of eastern and central Asia based on the teaching that suffering is inherent in life and that mental and moral self-purification will alleviate this suffering. This book outlines the basic beliefs and origins of Buddhism. It describes the way of life, rites and festivals, and the particular hardships pertinent to Buddhism. Paintings, photographs, a glossary of terms, and suggested further readings are included.

Tillem, Ivan L., compiler and editor. **The 1986 Jewish Directory and Almanac.** Pacific Press, 1985. 748 p. ISBN 0-915399-01-6 (0-915399-02-4, paperback).

This hefty reference work is a comprehensive guide to the history, beliefs, and practices of Judaism. It should answer any question you might have on this major religion.

Waskow, Arthur, David Waskow, and Shoshana Waskow. **Before There Was a Before.** Illustrated by Amnon Danziger. Adama Books, 1984. 85 p. ISBN 0-915361-08-6.

What was it like before the seven days of creation — before there were heaven and earth, dark and light, water and land? These writers imagine God talking to Himself as He creates each special part of the universe.

Werblowsky, R. J. Zwi, and Geoffrey Wigoder, editors. **The Encyclopedia of the Jewish Religion.** Adama Books, 1986. 415 p. ISBN 0-915361-53-1.

This cross-referenced reference work provides the layperson with clear, concise definitions and explanations of terms associated with the beliefs and practices of the Jewish religion. Helpful inclusions are a list of abbreviations, a transliteration key, and a Hebrew-English index.

Science and Medicine

Ardley, Neil. **Making Metric Measurements.** Illustrated by Janos Marffy, Hayward Art Group, and Arthur Tims. Franklin Watts, 1983. 32 p. ISBN 0-531-04615-X.

The basics of the metric system of measurement are explained through text and activities. The experiments are fun, require no special equipment, and can be done alone or in groups. These activities include projects for constructing simple measuring instruments, for making measurements, and for understanding how to use metric units.

Arnold, Caroline. **Genetics: From Mendel to Gene Splicing.** Franklin Watts, 1986. 72 p. ISBN 0-531-10223-8.

This book traces the history of genetics from its discovery in 1865 by Johann Gregor Mendel to the research of today. It explains the basics of heredity and gene splicing. Genetic research of today and in the future may hold the answers for many of humankind's problems. Part of the History of Science series.

Arnold, Caroline. **Trapped in Tar: Fossils from the Ice Age.** Photographs by Richard Hewett. Clarion Books, 1987. 57 p. ISBN 0-89919-415-X.

This photo essay describes the fossils of ancient animals, insects, and plants found in the Rancho La Brea tar pits in California. Saber-toothed tigers, mammoths, American lions, birds, frogs, spiders, and even plant pollen have been recovered. Most of the fossils are between 14,000 and 16,000 years old, although one is 38,000 years old. By finding out more about plants and animals that were in North America 10,000 to 40,000 years ago, scientists hope to discover why some species survived and some became extinct.

Bain, Iain. **Mountains and Earth Movements.** Bookwright Press, 1984. 48 p. ISBN 0-531-03802-5.

This book describes the Earth's surface, the movement of continents, how mountains were formed, erosion and sinking, faults and folds, earthquakes, and volcanoes. It includes facts and figures, a glossary of terms, and a list of further readings. Part of the Planet Earth series.

Bain, Iain. **Water on the Land.** Bookwright Press, 1984. 48 p. ISBN 0-531-04790-3.

Here is a look at the importance of water, rain, river channels, landforms made by rivers, underground rivers, changing rivers, and human-made rivers. It also contains facts and figures, a glossary of terms, and a list of further readings. Part of the Planet Earth series.

Berger, Melvin. **The Artificial Heart.** Illustrated by Anne Canevari Green. Franklin Watts/Impact Books, 1987. 128 p. ISBN 0-531-10409-5.

It's hard to believe that doctors have developed artificial hearts and have implanted them into human beings. This book looks at the function of the human heart, heart transplants, the heart-lung machine, artificial heart implants, the Baby Fae case, and the ethical, psychological, and legal issues surrounding the use of artificial hearts.

Berger, Melvin. **Energy.** Illustrated by Anne Canevari Green. Franklin Watts/Reference First Books, 1983. 92 p. ISBN 0-531-04536-6.

There is concern today about the availability and extent of energy sources. This book addresses such concerns and provides a wide spectrum of data on types of energy, means of discovery and development, and those persons who have played important roles in our quest for better, more efficient sources of energy. Information is presented in alphabetical order, from active solar energy system, air conditioning, and Alaska pipeline, to wind turbine, windmill, and work.

Bramwell, Martyn. **Mountains.** Illustrated by Chris Forsey and Colin Newman/Linden Artists. Franklin Watts, 1986. 29 p. ISBN 0-531-10261-0.

This book describes the origin of a mountain range, folding and faulting, wearing away of mountains, mountains on the move, mountains and weather, mountain specialists, and people of the mountains. A glossary of terms is included, as are many photographs and drawings. Part of the Earth Science Library series.

Bramwell, Martyn. **The Oceans.** Illustrations by Chris Forsey, Hayward Art Group, and Colin Newman/Linden Artists. Franklin Watts, 1987. 32 p. ISBN 0-531-10356-0.

The world of the ocean is examined in detail in this book. It begins with information about the beginning of "the blue planet," which is how Earth looks from space since oceans cover more than 70 percent of its surface. Also discussed are currents, tides, wind waves and tsunamis, and materials provided by the oceans — minerals and foods. A glossary of terms related to the ocean is included. Part of the Earth Science Library series.

Bramwell, Martyn. **Rivers and Lakes.** Illustrated by Chris Forsey and Colin Newman/Linden Artists. Franklin Watts, 1986. 29 p. ISBN 0-531-10262-9.

Here is a look at the Earth's rivers and lakes. It describes the origin of a river, sizes of different rivers, rapids and waterfalls, underground rivers, droughts and floods, trading on the rivers, and the lives of the lake and river people. Included are photographs and a glossary of terms related to rivers and lakes. Part of the Earth Science Library series.

Branley, Franklyn M. **Mysteries of the Universe.** Illustrated by Sally J. Bensusen. E. P. Dutton/Lodestar Books, 1984. 71 p. ISBN 0-525-66914-0.

Written in simple terms, this book deals with the different theories concerning the creation, expansion, and possible end of the universe. Such mysteries as black holes, pulsars, and red shifts are explored. The reader is taken on an exciting journey through this puzzling space world to search for explanations. Can they be found? Part of the Mysteries of the Universe series.

Brenner, Martha. **Fireworks Tonight!** Hastings House, 1983. 120 p. ISBN 0-8038-2400-9.

For many, the vivid colored lights in the night sky provide the perfect ending to the Fourth of July celebrations. This book traces the history of fireworks from primitive times to the computer-controlled special effects of today. It describes the step-by-step development of a modern fireworks show, from the drawing board to the lighting of the fireworks. Also discussed are how fireworks are made, safety with fireworks, and the current laws regulating the sale and use of fireworks in all the states.

Brown, A. S. **Fuel Resources.** Franklin Watts/First Books, 1985. 66 p. ISBN 0-531-04911-6.

Coal, petroleum, and uranium are the main fuel products used for energy. This book explores their origins and practical uses and the problems associated with using these fuels. It also describes the location and refining of these fuels.

Corrick, James A. **Recent Revolutions in Biology.** Franklin Watts/ Science Impact Books, 1987. 127 p. ISBN 0-531-10341-2.

Here is a look at new theories and discoveries in the field of biology. The book discusses evolution, gene therapy, genetic engineering, life on other planets, and other current topics. Included are a glossary of terms and a selected reading list.

Daegling, Mary. **Monster Seaweeds: The Story of the Giant Kelps.** Dillon Press, 1986. 119 p. ISBN 0-87518-350-6.

Giant kelps are the largest and fastest growing plant in the ocean. They serve as a home for countless sea creatures, are a source of many chemicals, and serve as a valuable food for human beings. This book provides a look at these giant seaweeds. Part of the Ocean World Library series.

Dixon, Dougal. **Geography.** Illustrated by Chris Forsey, Hayward Art Group, and Jim Robins. Franklin Watts, 1984. 38 p. ISBN 0-531-04744-X.

Geography is the study of the Earth's surface. This book covers the changing surface of the Earth, the oceans, the atmosphere, the seasons, weather, and the kinds of places in which people choose to settle. Part of the Science World series.

Douglas, John H. **The Future World of Energy.** Franklin Watts/Walt Disney World EPCOT Center Books, 1984. 112 p. ISBN 0-531-04881-0.

Energy, from prehistoric times to the future, is explained in this book. Vivid pictures and examples are taken from the Universe of Energy exhibit at the EPCOT Center.

Evans, Ifor. **Biology.** Illustrated by Chris Forsey, Hayward Art Group, and Jim Robins. Franklin Watts, 1984. 38 p. ISBN 0-531-04743-1.

Many aspects of biology are addressed in this book. It looks at the cell as a building block, the chemistry of life, reproduction and growth, heredity, evolution, plants and animals, microorganisms, and living communities. Part of the Science World series.

Fichter, George S. **Cells.** Illustrated by Anne Canevari Green. Franklin Watts/First Books, 1986. 72 p. ISBN 0-531-10210-6.

The cell is the basic unit of structure and function in plants and animals. This introductory book discusses the discovery of cells, typical cells, our bodies' special cells, how cells survive and do work, how cells reproduce, how cells make you unique, and new experiments in DNA research.

Gallant, Roy A. **Fossils.** Illustrated by Vantage Art. Franklin Watts/First Books, 1985. 63 p. ISBN 0-531-04910-8.

Fossils provide a record in stone of plant and animal life from prehistoric times. This book discusses how fossils are formed and how they can tell us about our past and the changes that the Earth has gone through. Black-and-white photographs accompany the text.

Gardner, Robert. **Energy Projects for Young Scientists.** Franklin Watts/Projects for Young Scientists, 1987. 119 p. ISBN 0-531-10338-2.

The concepts of energy, work, and power can lead to a variety of science projects. This book features sixty projects that focus on heat and thermal energy, electrical energy, solar energy, kinetic energy, and saving energy. The projects are appropriate for science classrooms or science fairs.

Gardner, Robert. **Ideas for Science Projects.** Illustrated by Vantage Art. Franklin Watts/Experimental Science Series Books, 1986. 144 p. ISBN 0-531-10246-7.

How big are raindrops? This book tells you how to find out. It also suggests interesting science projects in the areas of astronomy, light, chemistry, physics, heat, electricity, human physiology, psychology, plants, and animals. Projects range from the simple to the very complex. There is something to challenge everyone.

Giblin, James Cross. **Milk: The Fight for Purity.** Thomas Y. Crowell, 1986. 106 p. ISBN 0-690-04572-7 (0-690-04574-3, library binding).

Although pasteurization was developed in the late 1800s, the fight for pure milk continues to the present day. This book traces the history of the centuries-long movement to make milk a safe product. It includes discussion of the 1960s crisis over radioactive contamination and the accidental poisoning of dairy cattle in Michigan in the 1970s.

Gutnik, Martin J. **Electricity: From Faraday to Solar Generators.** Franklin Watts, 1986. 96 p. ISBN 0-531-10222-X.

We credit Benjamin Franklin with proving the existence of electricity by flying a kite in a thunderstorm and with inventing the lightning rod in the mid-1700s. This book traces the interest in electricity to early Greek experiments and discusses the more recent developments in communication and solar generators. It provides information about scientists who made important contributions to the area of electricity and about inventions made possible through the use of electricity.

Heckman, Philip. **The Magic of Holography.** Atheneum, 1986. 251 p. ISBN 0-689-31168-0.

Holography is the process of reproducing a three-dimensional image of an object by recording light-wave patterns on a photographic plate or film. You can see the object because it is visible from all sides and appears to be suspended in space. But if you tried to touch it, you would discover that it's only an image. This book explores the optical laws behind holography. Included are a list of places to see holograms, a glossary of terms, and suggestions for further reading.

Henbest, Nigel, and Heather Couper. **Physics.** Illustrated by Denis Bishop, Chris Forsey, Hayward Art Group, and Jim Robins. Franklin Watts, 1983. 38 p. ISBN 0-531-04652-4.

This book will introduce you to the field of physics. It discusses forces and motion, pointing out that just three basic laws describe the relationship between the two. Also discussed are the nature of matter itself, heat and sound, light, electricity, and magnetism. Part of the Science World series.

Jackson, Gordon. **Medicine.** Illustrated by Chris Forsey, Hayward Art Group, and Jim Robins. Franklin Watts, 1984. 38 p. ISBN 0-531-04837-3.

Here's a look at the structure and function of the human body as a whole, the function of the organs in digestion and nutrition, the brain and nervous system, and the sense organs. The book also contains information on some of the main causes of illnesses, how the body deals with illness, and ways of controlling and eradicating some diseases.

Jacobs, Francine. **Breakthrough: The True Story of Penicillin.** Dodd, Mead, 1985. 128 p. ISBN 0-396-08579-2.

We learn in this book what really happened in the discovery of penicillin, since that story has been hidden beneath myth and misinformation. Why did Alexander Fleming all but discard his germ-killing mold? Learn how scientists struggled with wartime shortages to produce the drug, how a dying woman volunteered to test the drug, and the way many groups helped in this race against death.

Kramer, Stephen P. **How to Think Like a Scientist: Answering Questions by the Scientific Method.** Illustrated by Felicia Bond. Thomas Y. Crowell, 1987. 44 p. ISBN 0-690-04563-8 (0-690-04565-4, library binding).

The scientific method involves collecting facts and using logic and deductive reasoning to reach a conclusion. This book poses questions about hypothetical situations to introduce the process of thinking according to the scientific method. As you become familiar with this approach to problem solving, you can apply it to nonscientific issues.

Lambert, David. **The Oceans.** Bookwright Press, 1984. 48 p. ISBN 0-531-04791-1.

Take a closer look at our oceans. This book discusses tides, currents, the seashore, the ocean floor, the relationship of humans to the ocean, and the changing ocean. It includes facts and figures about oceans, a glossary of terms and a list for further reading. Part of the Planet Earth series.

Lambert, David. **Vegetation.** Bookwright Press, 1984. 48 p. ISBN 0-531-03804-1.

The variety of plant life on our planet is amazing. Here is an examination of prehistoric plants, water plants, plants in cold places, temperate and northern forests, tropical forests, the grasslands, and plants that survive the drought. The book includes facts and figures, a glossary of terms, and a list of further readings. Part of the Planet Earth series.

Lambert, David. **The Work of the Wind.** Bookwright Press, 1984. 48 p. ISBN 0-531-04789-X.

In this book you will learn what wind can do, what prevailing winds and special winds are, how land is attacked by the wind, how desert trash heaps form, and how wind affects plants, animals, and people. Included are facts and figures about the wind, a glossary of terms, and a list of further readings. Part of the Planet Earth series.

Lambert, Mark. **Medicine in the Future.** Bookwright Press, 1986. 48 p. ISBN 0-531-18078-6.

A vaccination against cancer? This may be possible in tomorrow's world of medicine. Other likely advancements are the transplant of whole limbs, greater use of lasers and computers, and the extension of the human life by ten years. Some of today's readers may find themselves involved in medical research in the future. Part of the Tomorrow's World series.

Lampton, Christopher. **Mass Extinctions: One Theory of Why the Dinosaurs Vanished.** Franklin Watts/Impact Books, 1986. 86 p. ISBN 0-531-10238-6.

The dinosaurs disappeared from the Earth's surface millions of years ago. This book suggests that their disappearance is part of a cycle of twenty-six million years that is connected to comet or asteroid showers hitting the Earth. The author's approach is to combine the theories of scientists in the fields of astronomy, geology, and paleontology. Included are a glossary of terms and a list for further reading.

Leinwand, Gerald. **Transplants: Today's Medical Miracles.** Franklin Watts/Impact Books, 1985. 88 p. ISBN 0-531-04930-2.

The ability to replace diseased human organs with healthy organs has saved thousands of lives. But with any medical advancement come legal, moral, ethical, financial, and medical problems. This book explores these problems and provides insight into very difficult questions facing medical practitioners and potential organ recipients.

McGowen, Tom. **Radioactivity: From the Curies to the Atomic Age.** Franklin Watts, 1986. 59 p. ISBN 0-531-10132-0.

What is that mysterious glow? Could it be caused by radiation? This book discusses the discoveries and developments of scientists in the field of radioactivity. It looks at how physics and medicine have been revolutionized, thanks greatly to the breakthrough work on radioactivity done by Marie and Pierre Curie in the late 1800s and early 1900s.

Meltzer, Milton. **The Landscape of Memory.** Viking Penguin/Viking Kestrel, 1987. 133 p. ISBN 0-670-80821-0.

French writer and philosopher Albert Camus once said, "Everything fades, save memory." As we know, though, memory fades also. Here is an explanation of what memory is, how it works, why we remember, and why we forget.

Mercer, Ian. **Gemstones.** Illustrated by Louise Nevett. Gloucester Press, 1987. 32 p. ISBN 0-531-17057-8.

Gemstones have been in high demand for centuries for their beauty and for their value. This book explains how gemstones are formed, how they are processed, and how they are used in industry and in jewelry. The mining, sorting, and shaping of diamonds is described in detail. Real gems are compared to artificial gems. Part of the Resources Today series.

Nixon, Hershell H., and Joan Lowery Nixon. **Land under the Sea.** Dodd, Mead/Skylight Books, 1985. 62 p. ISBN 0-396-08582-2.

Oceanographers have hunted for ways to learn about the unexplored land under the sea as a way of understanding the planet on which we live. Discoveries have been made: canyons deeper than any known on land, volcanoes erupting, huge mountain ranges. Ocean exploration — ranging in topic from the world of the early explorers, to oceanographers' tools, to the future of exploration — is covered in this clear, simple text, along with photographs and undersea maps.

Padget, Sheila. **Coastlines.** Bookwright Press, 1984. 48 p. ISBN 0-531-04792-X.

Coastlines can vary in appearance from smooth, sandy beaches to steep, rocky cliffs. Here is a look at what coastlines are, how the sea erodes the land, how new land is formed by the sea, the changing levels of the sea, and islands. Facts and figures about coastlines, a glossary of terms and a list of further readings are included. Part of the Planet Earth series.

Pettigrew, Mark. **Weather.** Illustrated by Louise Nevett. Gloucester Press, 1987. 32 p. ISBN 0-531-17060-8.

An understanding of weather can be vital to daily life. Sometimes our safety depends on knowing about the weather. Here you will find out about the causes of weather, why different places are mainly hot or cold, wet or dry, and why the weather changes through the year. Instructions are given for doing your own weather forecasting and for making your own weather base station. Part of the Science Today series.

Poynter, Margaret, and Donald Collins. **Under the High Seas: New Frontiers in Oceanography.** Atheneum, 1983. 166 p. ISBN 0-689-30977-5.

Beginning with folklore and legends of the high seas and the history of sailing, this book then discusses the great explorers of the oceans. Also included are diagrams and explanations of the composition of the world's oceans; how they are used for transportation and as a source of food, oil, minerals, and energy; pollution of the oceans; and who controls international waters.

Purvis, George, and Anne Purvis. **Weather and Climate.** Bookwright Press, 1984. 48 p. ISBN 0-531-04788-1.

This book describes the atmosphere, the wind, clouds, rain, weather charts and satellites, climate and atmosphere, and the Earth's orbit. It also includes facts and figures, a glossary of terms, and a list of further readings. Part of the Planet Earth series.

Rahn, Joan Elma. **Ears, Hearing, and Balance.** Illustrated by the author. Atheneum, 1984. 153 p. ISBN 0-689-31055-2.

Most of us would probably consider sight to be our most precious sense. However, in total darkness our eyes are useless. Our ears work just as well in darkness or light. We can't see through walls or around corners, but we can hear through most walls and around corners. This book thoroughly discusses the subjects of ears, hearing, and balance.

Robin, Gordon de Q. **Glaciers and Ice Sheets.** Bookwright Press, 1984. 48 p. ISBN 0-531-03801-7.

Glaciers are confined to the cold and snowy regions of the United States today, but during the ice age these moving masses of ice covered much more of our country, permanently affecting the topography. Here is a look at glaciers and their movement, mountain erosion, icecaps and ice sheets, and ice ages. Included are facts and figures about glaciers, a glossary of terms, and a list of further readings. Part of the Planet Earth series.

Sedge, Michael H. **Commercialization of the Oceans.** Franklin Watts/Impact Books, 1987. 128 p. ISBN 0-531-10326-9.

The oceans occupy 70 percent of the Earth's surface. As the population of the planet increases and the demand for all types of resources rises, the oceans will play a greater role in our lives. This book discusses the commercial food, mineral, and energy resources that are found in the ocean and explores such business ventures as fishing, ocean mining, and ocean farming.

Sharp, Pat. **Brain Power! Secrets of a Winning Team.** Illustrated by Martha Weston. Lothrop, Lee and Shepard Books, 1984. 56 p. ISBN 0-688-02679-6 (0-688-02680-X, library binding).

A lively description of the most amazing team at work — the human brain — fills the pages of this book. It explains the parts of the brain and how they function.

Stafford, Patricia. **Your Two Brains.** Illustrated by Linda Tunney. Atheneum, 1986. 75 p. ISBN 0-689-31142-7.

Did you know that your brain is actually two brains in one? The two sides and their separate functions allow you to perform all sorts of tasks, like singing, talking, writing, drawing, and solving math problems. In this book you can read about how boys' and girls' brains differ, why some people are left-handed, and how you can put your brain to work for you.

Stwertka, Albert. **Recent Revolutions in Physics: The Subatomic World.** Franklin Watts/Science Impact Books, 1985. 86 p. ISBN 0-531-10066-9.

Intended for the advanced student or for anyone who wants to find out about the recent revolutions in particle physics, this book introduces the reader to the material of matter, the theory of relativity, giant atom smashers, strange forms of matter, quarks, and the grand unification theory.

Stwertka, Albert, and Eve Stwertka. **Physics: From Newton to the Big Bang.** Franklin Watts, 1986. 86 p. ISBN 0-531-10224-6.

This book details the contributions of Isaac Newton, the English mathematician and natural philosopher, to mathematics, optics, and gravitation. It includes a review of the knowledge available to Newton and shows how he built his principles. Some of these principles were later overthrown by Einstein's discoveries, but Newton remains an important figure in the field of physics. Part of the History of Science series.

Tocci, Salvatore. **Biology Projects for Young Scientists.** Franklin Watts/ Projects for Young Scientists, 1987. 127 p. ISBN 0-531-10429-X.

Here is an outstanding collection of science projects suitable for independent study, classroom assignments, or science fairs. The projects are designed for beginning students to advanced students and cover a wide range of topics.

Tocci, Salvatore. **How to Do a Science Fair Project.** Illustrated by Vantage Art. Franklin Watts, 1986. 128 p. ISBN 0-531-10245-9.

Many useful ideas are offered for selecting a science fair project, conducting the appropriate research, documenting the results, and presenting the conclusions to the judges. This book outlines the scientific method for research and includes a list of companies that carry special materials and equipment often needed for science projects. Part of the Experimental Science series.

Vogt, Gregory. **Electricity and Magnetism.** Franklin Watts/First Books, 1985. 84 p. ISBN 0-531-10038-3.

What is electricity? How does it work? How is it related to magnetism? How can these two forces help humankind? What are some experiments we can perform to better understand these forces? These questions and more are answered in this book.

Wallace, Diane A., and Philip L. Hershey. **How to Master Science Labs.** Franklin Watts, 1987. 117 p. ISBN 0-531-10323-4.

If you've ever approached a science lab feeling frustrated and confused, this book is for you. It's a book to prevent or cure lab fright by showing you how to succeed. It features specific instruction on organizing time and materials, keeping good records, and practicing safe procedures. Part of the Experimental Science Series books.

Whitfield, Phillip, and Joyce Pope. **Why Do the Seasons Change?** Viking Penguin/Viking Kestrel, 1987. 96 p. ISBN 0-670-81860-7.

Why is it hot in the summer and cold in the winter? Why do the tides rise and fall? These and other such questions on nature's cycles and rhythms are addressed. The book includes full-color photographs, detailed drawings, and diagrams.

Whyman, Kathryn. **Wood.** Illustrated by Louise Nevett. Gloucester Press, 1987. 32 p. ISBN 0-531-17058-6.

Text and illustrations show how wood is harvested and processed into the familiar products we use. The book begins with growing the wood and describes the sawmill and the various sorts of wood processing. Also discussed are recycling, extracting chemicals from wood, destructive distillation, and producing textiles from wood. Part of the Resources Today series.

Young, Frank. **Radio and Radar.** Illustrated by Rob Shone and Elsa Godfrey. Franklin Watts, 1984. 29 p. ISBN 0-531-04724-5.

In this book, radio and radar technology are presented as being among the most important aspects of the electronic revolution. The book shows how and where this technology can be used. A glossary of terms is included. Part of the Electronic Revolution series.

Zubrowski, Bernie. **Wheels at Work: Building and Experimenting with Models of Machines.** Illustrated by Roy Doty. William Morrow/ Boston Children's Museum Activity Books, 1986. 112 p. ISBN 0-688-06349-7 (0-688-06348-9, library binding).

Find out for yourself just how useful and versatile the ordinary wheel is. Step-by-step instructions are given for assembling six simple wheel machines from inexpensive materials. Then fifty experiments, using these models, are described. Scientific principles about force, power, and motion are explained.

Social Issues

Bradley, John. **Human Rights.** Illustrated by Ron Hayward Associates. Gloucester Press, 1987. 32 p. ISBN 0-531-17055-1.

Human rights, equality, and freedom are examined in a democracy and in the Soviet Union. Also explored are such issues as dissidents, poverty, apartheid, and human rights in Africa, Central and South America, Southeast Asia, and the Muslim world. Included is a list of facts about human rights.

Burch, Jennings Michael. **They Cage the Animals at Night.** New American Library/Signet Books, 1985. 293 p. ISBN 0-451-13853-8.

In this true account of his painful childhood, Burch takes the reader along on his stays in a series of foster homes and institutions, which test the youngster's strength and ability to retain his identity and a sense of hope. A tattered, stuffed dog and a few real friends keep Jennings on target as he miraculously learns to cope with a shattering situation. (Literary merit)

Cheney, Glenn Alan. **Responsibility.** Franklin Watts/First Books, 1985. 66 p. ISBN 0-531-10045-6.

In addition to the personal responsibilities we might have, there are social and civic responsibilities, duties, and rights that American citizens have. This book explores those responsibilities. Part of the American Values series.

Claypool, Jane. **Unemployment.** Franklin Watts/Impact Books, 1983. 85 p. ISBN 0-531 04586-2.

Learn who the unemployed in our country are, how the statistics for unemployment are calculated, and how unemployment is related to the economy. Included in this book are a discussion of the causes of unemployment and a description of financial help available for the unemployed. Jobless people tell their stories in first-person accounts, and suggestions for protecting yourself from unemployment are offered.

Craig, Eleanor. **If We Could Hear the Grass Grow.** New American Library/Signet Books, 1985. 285 p. ISBN 0-451-13619-5.

Craig, a family therapist, felt a need to share intimately with twelve troubled children and their parents. This threatened her authority image at her Camp Hopewell, a unique oasis of stability and no-nonsense holistic therapy. Perhaps she cared too much to be objective about her patients, or perhaps her efforts to reunite her own family were getting in the way. Follow this remarkable woman and her camp through their development as a means of emotional salvation for severely disturbed youngsters.

Davis, Bertha. **Instead of Prison.** Franklin Watts/Impact Books, 1986. 111 p. ISBN 0-531-10237-8.

Increasing numbers of criminals are being convicted and sentenced to terms in prison, but existing prisons are already full, and the public is unwilling to pay to build more prisons. This book tells about alternatives to prison for some types of crimes, including probation with mechanical surveillance, community service, and restitution of goods or money to their rightful owners.

Day, Carol Olsen, and Edmund Day. **The New Immigrants.** Franklin Watts/Impact Books, 1985. 120 p. ISBN 0-531-04929-9.

Currently, most immigrants to the United States do not come from Europe; rather, they are leaving their homes in Mexico, Central America, Vietnam, and the Far East. Among the reasons for this change are the severe poverty of third-world nations, the shifting nature of our political alliances, and changes in our immigration laws. This book analyzes the causes for the arrival of new immigrants and describes their lives before and after their arrival.

Gardner, Sandra. **Street Gangs.** Photographs by Rebecca Lepkoff. Franklin Watts, 1983. 77 p. ISBN 0-531-04666-4.

Street gangs are a part of life in many urban areas. This book discusses why young people, mostly boys, join gangs, what gang life is like, and the gang codes of conduct and loyalty. The relationship between adult criminal organizations and street gangs is explored. Included is a chapter on the House of Umoja, a special group home in Philadelphia that focuses on reducing gang violence and improving job skills for urban youth.

Gay, Kathlyn. **The Rainbow Effect: Interracial Families.** Franklin Watts, 1987. 141 p. ISBN 0-531-10343-9.

To be part of an interracial or interethnic family in America is to be set apart, sometimes by ignorance, sometimes by fear. The author shares stories from many biracial families about what it's like to be part of an interracial community and the problems these children of mixed backgrounds encounter in school, dating, and adoption. Their stories are moving and present a unique view of family life.

Holbrook, Sabra. **Fighting Back: The Struggle for Gay Rights.** E. P. Dutton/Lodestar Books, 1987. 89 p. ISBN 0-525-67187-0.

Ten percent of all Americans may find guarantees of freedom under the U.S. Constitution deprived because of their homosexuality. The trend continues in spite of new research that may place cause for homosexuality in the body's chemical composition. This book includes a historical look at attitudes toward homosexuality and progress in civil rights for all Americans.

Hyde, Margaret O. **Sexual Abuse: Let's Talk about It.** Westminster Press, 1984. 90 p. ISBN 0-664-32713-3.

This book tells about sexual abuse and how children can protect themselves and can prevent abuse from happening to them. Included are stories about other youngsters who have been abused. The book includes addresses of places to go for more information and help.

Hyde, Margaret O., and Lawrence E. Hyde. **Missing Children.** Franklin Watts, 1985. 104 p. ISBN 0-531-10073-1.

Over one million children leave their homes each year. Half of them are runaways; the others are victims of abduction. This book addresses family problems that sometimes cause children to run away and what can happen once the runaway is on the street. Abductions both by parents and by strangers, methods of parental record keeping, and groups devoted to finding missing children are also discussed. A resource section on hotlines and helpful agencies and a bibliography are included.

Jones, Charlotte Foltz. **Only Child — Clues for Coping.** Westminster Press, 1984. 103 p. ISBN 0-664-32718-4.

Are you an only child who has been accused of being selfish, lonely, or spoiled? This book will free you from these myths and show you how to be socially outgoing, independent, and self-confident. It also provides helpful ideas and sound information on the advantages and problems of being an only child.

Kaplan, Leslie S. **Coping with Stepfamilies.** Rosen Publishing Group, 1986. 162 p. ISBN 0-9239-0654-X.

Today, more and more families are blended families or stepfamilies, composed of new parents and, sometimes, of stepbrothers and stepsisters. This book provides good background reading on developing new family relationships and roles, and addresses the numerous problems of combined families.

Kleeberg, Irene Cumming. **Latchkey Kid.** Illustrated by Anne Canevari Green. Franklin Watts, 1985. 93 p. ISBN 0-531-10052-9.

Are you alone after school? If so, you are one of several million latchkey kids in the United States. This book describes what to do with the time you're alone, including when to do homework, what snacks to eat, how often to use the telephone, when to visit friends, and what to do in emergencies. The book suggests safe and fun things to do when you're finished with your chores and homework.

Kolehmainen, Janet, and Sandra Handwerk. **Teen Suicide: A Book for Friends, Family, and Classmates.** Lerner Publications, 1986. 70 p. ISBN 0-8225-9514-1 (0-8225-0037-X, library binding).

Five thousand teenagers kill themselves each year. Why do they commit suicide? How can this be prevented? This book contains six stories, based on case histories, that show the reader the options to suicide, typical causes of suicide, and the warning signs. It suggests where and when to go for help and advises how to cope with grief and guilt after a suicide.

Kosof, Anna. **Incest: Families in Crisis.** Franklin Watts, 1985. 98 p. ISBN 0-531-10071-5.

People never used to talk about incest, and it was thought that this problem happened only rarely. But statistics now show that many children and young adults have been victims of incest. This book explores the family situations where incest occurs and the importance of telling the secret. Children who have been victims of incest and child abuse often grow to be troubled adults who repeat these abuses on the next generation. The book includes a list of places to write and call for further information and help.

Kosof, Anna. **Why Me? Coping with Family Illness.** Franklin Watts, 1986. 95 p. ISBN 0-531-10254-8.

This book will take you into a world of pain and courage. It focuses on young people who cope with a chronic or fatal disease or illness, either in themselves or in a family member. How does the illness change their lives? How do they cope?

Langone, John. **Dead End: A Book about Suicide.** Little, Brown, 1986. 176 p. ISBN 0-316-51432-2.

This book presents an overview of the history of suicide and discusses physical and psychological causes, society's view of suicide, warning signs, and ways to prevent suicide.

Leinwand, Gerald. **Hunger and Malnutrition in America.** Franklin Watts/Impact Books, 1985. 90 p. ISBN 0-531-10063-4.

In this nation of wealth, there are people suffering from malnutrition and starvation. After discussing this paradox, the author describes current programs to feed America's hungry. A brief overview of world hunger, its causes, and possible solutions concludes the book. A table of essential nutrients and suggestions for further reading are included.

LeShan, Eda. **What's Going to Happen to Me? When Parents Separate or Divorce.** Macmillan/Aladdin Books, 1986. ISBN 0-689-71093-3.

Here is a look at the problem of divorce and the lives of people affected by it. Currently one out of every six children lives in a one-parent family. This book explains the steps that children must go through when facing the problem of divorce — before it happens, when it happens, and after it happens.

LeShan, Eda. **When a Parent Is Very Sick.** Atlantic Monthly Press, 1986. 129 p. ISBN 0-87113-095-5.

This book takes children of all ages through the typical feelings experienced when a parent is very ill. The author explains where to get helpful information, what to expect from doctors, nurses, and hospitals, how to understand your feelings during the illness, how to keep the family together, and what to expect if the illness results in death or if the parent gets well.

Loeb, Robert H., Jr. (with George F. Cole). **Crime and Capital Punishment.** Rev. ed. Franklin Watts/Impact Books, 1986. 93 p. ISBN 0-531-10209-2.

Capital punishment remains one of the most controversial issues in America today. After a short historical examination of the death penalty, the book discusses criminal behavior and its causes, the deterrent effects of capital punishment, the moral and legal aspects, and the problem of faulty convictions in our judicial system. A bibliography is included.

Meltzer, Milton. **Ain't Gonna Study War No More: The Story of America's Peace Seekers.** Harper and Row, 1985. 282 p. ISBN 0-06-024199-3 (0-06-024200-0, library binding).

Meltzer tells the story of people who risked their reputations, livelihoods, and lives to raise their voices against war and violence. The book discusses the Quakers and those who have opposed the Mexican War, the Civil War, World Wars I and II, the Korean War, and the Vietnam War.

Meltzer, Milton. **Poverty in America.** William Morrow, 1986. 122 p. ISBN 0-688-05911-2.

Poverty in America is everybody's problem: 35 to 50 million people now live below the poverty level in this country. More than inadequate income is involved. For many, poverty is "a condition of life" that they cannot escape. This book disproves the myths and uncovers the facts as it examines the effects of poverty on children, women, the elderly, and racial minorities.

Nelsen, Cheryl Diane. **Unemployment.** Franklin Watts/First Books, 1985. 64 p. ISBN 0-531-04917-5.

For many people, this land of opportunity is also the land of unemployment. This book explains how unemployment is influenced by depressions and recessions in the economy, technology, and discrimination, and it explores what the government and the private sector can do to lessen the problem. Included are a glossary of terms and bibliography.

Sheehan, Susan. **Kate Quinton's Days.** New American Library/Mentor Books, 1985. 189 p. ISBN 0-451-62423-8.

Kate Quinton, eighty-one, was a victim of neglect. Her two children were unable to help her, and she had serious medical problems. The only source of aid was the social agencies where they lived. All were overworked and inefficient, but Kate maintained her most precious trait, her dignity.

Timberlake, Lloyd. **Famine in Africa.** Illustrated by Ron Hayward Associates. Gloucester Press, 1986. 31 p. ISBN 0-531-17017-9.

This book shows the interrelationships among famine, drought, and poor agricultural practices. Africa's best land is being used for cash crops that are exported, and poorer land is used for food for Africa's people. As poor land is farmed, it often erodes, increasing the amount of desert land in Africa. The book includes a historical look at famine and numerous photographs, charts, and graphs.

Worth, Richard. **The American Family.** Photographs by Robert Sefcik. Franklin Watts, 1984. 115 p. ISBN 0-531-04859-4.

The rising divorce rate, the changing roles of men and women, and the increasing need for both parents to work are all factors that seem to be working against the traditional American family. This book provides an overview of the American family's history, problems, and strengths and looks at the future of this institution.

Worth, Richard. **You'll Be Old Someday, Too.** Franklin Watts, 1986. 118 p. ISBN 0-531-10158-4.

Many facets of aging are explored here, among them the saddening effects of poverty among the aged, housing and socialization options open to the elderly, and the possibility for an active life after retirement. The book also describes "the ageless ones" — those remarkable human beings whose contributions to others do not diminish with the years.

Space

Apfel, Necia H. **Space Station.** Franklin Watts, 1987. 72 p. ISBN 0-531-10394-3.

From the dawn of the space age, people have envisioned living in space. This book provides a basic introduction to this idea by discussing how rockets work, the first space probes, manned space flights, the space shuttle, the space station planned for the near future, life aboard a space station, and space colonies.

Bramwell, Martyn. **Planet Earth.** Illustrated by Chris Forsey and Colin Newman/Linden Artists. Franklin Watts, 1987. 32 p. ISBN 0-531-10346-3.

Color photographs, explanatory diagrams, and the text demonstrate how our planet is affected by the sun, moon, seasons, oceans, atmosphere, and the living and nonliving things that inhabit the Earth. Part of the Earth Science Library series.

Branley, Franklyn M. **Mysteries of Outer Space.** Illustrated by Sally J. Bensusen. E. P. Dutton/Lodestar Books, 1985. 69 p. ISBN 0-525-67149-8.

This book demystifies such questions as how is time kept in space, do colors exist there, what is solar wind, and can asteroids be mined? It discusses kinds of space, potential uses of space, survival in space, and the end of space. The text is supplemented by many diagrams and photographs. Part of the Mysteries of the Universe series.

Branley, Franklyn M. **Mysteries of the Satellites.** Illustrated by Sally J. Bensusen. E. P. Dutton/Lodestar Books, 1986. 71 p. ISBN 0-525-67176-5.

At some points in their orbits, Pluto and Neptune trade off being the planet farthest from the sun. How does this happen? This mystery and many others about the planets and the natural satellites that travel around them are explained in this book. Part of the Mysteries of the Universe series.

Cooke, Donald A. **The Life and Death of Stars.** Crown, 1985. 193 p. ISBN 0-517-55268-X.

The story of the sun and the stars is explained in this book. It examines the formation of a star, stellar groupings and variable stars, the space between stars, and stars in the prime of life. Also discussed are the sun, the death of stars, supernovas, black holes, and the future of the universe.

Couper, Heather. **Comets and Meteors.** Franklin Watts, 1985. 32 p. ISBN 0-531-10000-6.

When will Halley's comet return? How are comets formed? This book provides answers to questions you might have about cosmic debris, death of a comet, and asteroid belts. Part of the Space Scientist series.

Couper, Heather. **The Stars.** Franklin Watts, 1985. 32 p. ISBN 0-531-10054-5.

Here is a complete look at the exciting heavens. Your participation is encouraged by information on how to observe the stars and what to look for at various times of the year. Star charts and maps are provided to aid in identification. Included are a glossary of terms and a list of where to go and what to do. Part of the Space Scientist series.

Couper, Heather, and Nigel Henbest. **Astronomy.** Illustrated by Dennis Bishop, Chris Forsey, Hayward Art Group, and Jim Robins. Franklin Watts, 1983. 38 p. ISBN 0-531-04651-6.

Astronomy is the study of all the matter and all the space in the universe, which is so incredibly vast that we can just begin to understand it. Although astronomy has been studied since ancient times, the recent development of equipment has enabled scientists to study the universe in detail. This book reviews the history of astronomy and discusses the sun, our solar system, the stars, and our galaxy. Part of the Science World series.

Couper, Heather, and Nigel Henbest. **Galaxies and Quasars.** Franklin Watts, 1986. 32 p. ISBN 0-531-10265-3.

Are you fascinated by the stars? Do you wonder how our galaxy, the Milky Way, and others began? If so, this book will answer your questions and pose even more thought-provoking ones. Many photographs and graphics and a glossary of terms are included. Part of the Space Scientist series.

Couper, Heather, and Nigel Henbest. **The Moon.** Franklin Watts, 1986. 32 p. ISBN 0-531-10266-1.

It's all here — from the beginning of the moon, to its phases, to human exploration, to even a future base on the moon. The book contains large color photographs and other graphics, a glossary of terms, and a listing of further readings. Part of the Space Scientist series.

Couper, Heather, and Nigel Henbest. **The Sun.** Franklin Watts, 1986. 32 p. ISBN 0-531-10055-3.

Here is a good look at our local star, the sun. The authors encourage participation in studying the sun and space by telling how to observe and what to look for at various times of the year. They caution the reader about never looking directly at the sun, even through dark film or tinted glass. Charts, maps, and a sky-watcher's almanac are included, as are a list of museums and places to visit, names of organizations to join, and a glossary of terms. Part of the Space Scientist series.

Darling, David J. **Comets, Meteors, and Asteroids: Rocks in Space.** Illustrated by Jeanette Swofford. Dillon Press, 1984. 64 p. ISBN 0-87518-264-X.

Rocks in space fall into three categories: comets, meteors, and asteroids. This book explains the source, the nature, and the varying characteristics of these space rocks. Whether they come flaming into our atmosphere or hollow out craters on impact, these space intruders fascinate amateurs and professionals alike. A glossary of terms, a question-and-answer section, and photographs are included. Part of the Discovering Our Universe series.

Darling, David J. **The Moon: A Spaceflight Away.** Illustrated by Jeanette Swofford. Dillon Press, 1984. 64 p. ISBN 0-87518-262-3.

The moon has lost much of its mystery but none of its fascination. Join the spaceflight to the moon and visit Earth's nearest neighbor, learning about "moonquakes," human explorers, and the moon's own resources for further space travel. This book offers facts, tables, a glossary of terms, and appendixes for the amateur lunar explorer. Part of the Discovering Our Universe series.

Darling, David J. **The Planets: The Next Frontier.** Illustrated by Jeanette Swofford. Dillon Press, 1984. 63 p. ISBN 0-87518-263-1.

Many planets and their moons have fascinating characteristics. As scientists study them through new cameras, telescopes, and other instruments, the day of firsthand human exploration draws nearer. This book explains how each of the planets was most likely formed, and what makes each planet unique. It includes information on astronomy groups, a glossary of terms, and photographs taken from spacecraft. Part of the Discovering Our Universe series.

Darling, David J. **The Sun: Our Neighborhood Star.** Illustrated by Jeanette Swofford. Dillon Press, 1984. 63 p. ISBN 0-87518-261-5.

All life in our solar system is dependent on the sun. Its light provides our food and our energy; its warmth maintains our weather and heats our oceans. This book provides information about the history of the sun and its relationship to other bodies in space, and it even offers tips for studying the sun. Included are questions and answers and a glossary of terms. Part of the Discovering Our Universe series.

Darling, David J. **Where Are We Going in Space?** Illustrated by Jeanette Swofford. Dillon Press, 1984. 64 p. ISBN 0-87518-265-8.

This book gives the beginning space explorer a fine overview of human ventures into space. It covers the history of space travel from *Sputnik I* through the Project Daedalus, which may one day permit space travel at high speeds and to destinations rivaling those of the starship *Enterprise.* Part of the Discovering Our Universe series.

Fisher, David E. **The Third Experiment: Is There Life on Mars?** Atheneum, 1985. 192 p. ISBN 0-689-31080-3.

In 1976 two *Viking* spacecraft landed on the surface of Mars to conduct three experiments testing whether there was life on Mars. Data were collected from the *Viking* mission, but the question still remains — is there life on Mars? This book outlines the history of human thoughts and dreams about Mars and Martians and looks at why life on Mars is of particular interest to us.

Hawkes, Nigel. **Space Shuttle.** Gloucester Press, 1983. 37 p. ISBN 0-531-04583-8.

Beginning with a short history of the search for a reusable space vehicle, this book provides an overview of the development of the space shuttle. Illustrated in color, the book shows the reader how the vehicle's shape evolved, how the *Enterprise* was used as a prototype, how tiles protect the vehicle during reentry, and how tests were run to perfect the ship. Readers are taken on a visual journey showing how the *Columbia* behaves in flight and how astronauts live and work in space.

Herda, D. J. **Research Satellites.** Franklin Watts/First Books, 1987. 71 p. ISBN 0-531-10311-0.

A brief history of the space race is touched upon in this book. Credit is given to the dreamers who conceived the ideas about space travel and to the doers who implemented these ideas. The book reviews the development of research satellites and discusses their uses in cartography, meteorology, and climatology.

Lampton, Christopher. **Space Sciences.** Illustrated by Anne Canevari Green. Franklin Watts/Reference First Books, 1983. 93 p. ISBN 0-531-04539-0.

Alphabetically arranged, this book gives the young astronomer factual information about space exploration, space craft, and the people involved in this exciting area of discovery. Many space-related terms are defined and explained, such as *maria,* the dark areas on the surface of the moon, and *epicycle,* an orbit within an orbit.

Lampton, Christopher. **The Space Telescope.** Franklin Watts/First Books, 1987. 72 p. ISBN 0-531-10221-1.

Sometime in 1988 or 1989, a space shuttle will carry a large telescope into orbit around the Earth, where it will begin taking pictures of the sky. It will then transmit those pictures back to Earth as television images. This book describes the history, goals, and functions of the Hubble Space Telescope and explains what makes it different from all other telescopes.

Lampton, Christopher. **Star Wars.** Franklin Watts/First Books, 1987. 70 p. ISBN 0-531-10314-5.

The Strategic Defense Initiative, or Star Wars, is the proposed defense plan that uses satellites and lasers to shoot down missiles. Some feel the defense plan would prevent nuclear war, while others feel it would increase the chance. This book describes how the system would function, and discusses the controversy surrounding space weapons research.

McKay, David W., and Bruce G. Smith. **Space Science Projects for Young Scientists.** Franklin Watts/Projects for Young Scientists, 1986. 108 p. ISBN 0-531-10244-0.

What is it like in space? What are the effects of space on human beings? on plants? on animals? These are the kinds of questions that you might be able to answer after completing some of the projects suggested in this book. Some projects will be actual simulations of conditions in space. Other experiments will be similar to those performed on the space shuttles or satellites. Included are a glossary of terms, a list of appropriate computer programs, and an appendix of sources, references, and organizations to consult for additional information.

O'Connor, Karen. **Sally Ride and the New Astronauts: Scientist in Space.** Franklin Watts, 1983. 83 p. ISBN 0-531-04602-8.

This biography was written before Sally Ride took her historic space flight, but it does discuss her experiences preparing to be the first American woman astronaut in space. The book describes the selection and training of astronauts, the development and modification of equipment, terms specific to space travel, and how it feels to fly in space.

Poynter, Margaret, and Michael J. Klein. **Cosmic Quest: Searching for Intelligent Life among the Stars.** Atheneum, 1984. 124 p. ISBN 0-689-31068-4.

This book is about the SETI (Search for Extraterrestrial Intelligence) Project, which was founded by a group of international scientists committed to finding signs of intelligent life beyond Earth. It discusses such questions as what would extraterrestrials look like, have they visited the Earth, and how can we communicate with beings from another planet? The book also provides an account of the various theories about the origin of the universe and our Earth.

Ride, Sally (with Susan Okie). **To Space and Back.** Lothrop, Lee and Shepard Books, 1986. 96 p. ISBN 0-688-06159-1.

How does it feel to go into space and back? What is the space shuttle like? Here is an account of space flight by one who has been there — Sally Ride. The book includes photographs of Sally Ride's flight and a glossary of terms.

Taylor, L. B., Jr. **Commercialization of Space.** Franklin Watts/Impact Books, 1987. 126 p. ISBN 0-531-10236-X.

At present, the most advanced area of space commercialization is the use of satellites to transmit information. This book discusses the potential and the plans for commercialization of space by private industry. Tourism, research, mining, and surveillance are all possibilities.

Vogt, Gregory. **Space Satellites.** Franklin Watts, 1987. 32 p. ISBN 0-531-10141-X.

Today's frontier is outer space. The Soviets launched their first satellite, *Sputnik I*, in October of 1957, while the first U.S. satellite, *Explorer I*, went into space in January of 1958. Currently there are satellites for space research, communications, meteorological purposes, and navigational purposes. This book traces the history of space satellites and looks ahead to future advances. Part of the Space Library series.

Vogt, Gregory. **Space Walking.** Franklin Watts, 1987. 32 p. ISBN 0-531-10142-8.

Someday maybe *you* will walk in space! Read about early space suits, walking on the moon, and shuttle space walkers — as well as astronaut training, space stations, and things to come as we continue to conquer space. Included are a glossary of terms, a listing of space-walking dates, and color photographs.

Weiss, Malcolm E. **Far Out Factories: Manufacturing in Space.** E. P. Dutton/Lodestar Books, 1984. 84 p. ISBN 0-525-67143-9.

Successful space shuttles will manufacture silicon crystals, lifesaving enzymes, and metals that can't be produced on Earth. These innovative manufacturing ideas have been tested aboard the *Columbia* space shuttle, but plans have been temporarily put on hold because of the uncertainty of boundaries in space. Who will be responsible for the actual running and ownership of these space factories? This book explores the prospects for manufacturing in space.

White, Jack R. **Satellites of Today and Tomorrow.** Dodd, Mead, 1985. 119 p. ISBN 0-396-08514-8.

Here is a book for those interested in satellites and space technology. The book covers what it would be like to blast off into space, designing a spacecraft, the uses of satellites (including weather reports, watching the environment, astronomy, surveillance), and what the future holds for this technology. Included are many black-and-white illustrations and photographs.

Whyman, Kathryn. **Solar System.** Illustrated by Louise Nevett. Gloucester Press, 1987. 32 p. ISBN 0-531-17059-4.

Our solar system consists of the sun, the planets, and their moons. This book reviews past and current knowledge of the solar system and its origins. Patterns and directions are included for making a mobile of the solar system. Part of the Science Today series.

Wright, Pearce. **The Space Race.** Illustrated by Ron Hayward Associates. Gloucester Press, 1987. 32 p. ISBN 0-531-17041-1.

The space age has entered a new phase. The 1986 accident that killed seven crew members of the space shuttle has thrown the U.S. space industry into a crisis of confidence. How the race for space began, what it involves, and where it is going are discussed in this book. Included are color photographs and diagrams. Part of the Issues series.

Sports

Anderson, Dave. **The Story of Football.** William Morrow, 1985. 197 p. ISBN 0-688-05634-2 (0-688-05635-0, paperback).

This book highlights certain time periods in the history of football by focusing on some of football's greats. It not only introduces the reader to famous coaches and players, but it also gives some fundamental information on playing techniques and how the game developed its reputation of today.

Brimner, Larry Dane. **BMX Freestyle.** Franklin Watts/First Books, 1987. 72 p. ISBN 0-531-10301-3.

Freestyle bicycle riding had its beginnings in 1976. This book provides information on bicycle equipment, safety, techniques, and routines and describes how to build your own ramp, how to get into competitions and organizations, and how to freestyle for money. A list of publications about freestyling is included.

Coombs, Charles. **All-Terrain Bicycling.** Henry Holt, 1987. 113 p. ISBN 0-8050-0204-9.

Here is a complete guide for this new sport of on-road and off-road biking. Information is provided for choosing equipment, maintaining it, and riding to obtain the best performance. Included are photographs and a section on how to get in touch with other all-terrain bikers.

Coombs, Charles. **Let's Rodeo!** Holt, Rinehart and Winston, 1986. 112 p. ISBN 0-03-001207-4.

Text and photographs explore the world of rodeos, including the definition, origin, and historical development of the sport. The book also discusses the kinds of people involved, the livestock, and such events as bareback bronc riding and steer wrestling. A glossary of terms is included.

Goffi, Carlos. **Tournament Tough.** Holt, Rinehart and Winston, 1984. 144 p. ISBN 0-03-071598-9.

This book describes basic tennis techniques and includes the comments of superstar John McEnroe. It also expresses the opinion that tennis players are making too much money too soon in life and stresses that players should concentrate their interest in the game itself, not in the money it brings in.

Haas, Robert. **Eat to Win: The Sports Nutrition Bible.** New American Library/Signet Books, 1985. 365 p. ISBN 0-451-13394-3.

A nutrition counselor to many world-class champions shares the advice he has given sports figures to bring their performance to peak levels. He shows what to eat at every stage of competence in sports and fitness programs to achieve top levels of endurance, speed, and power; how to evaluate your body chemistry to determine which of the Peak Performance Program's three levels is best for you; and how to adapt that level to your particular needs.

Jacobs, G., and J. R. McCrory. **Baseball Rules in Pictures.** Rev. ed. Putnam/Perigee Books, 1985. 74 p. ISBN 0-399-51129-6.

Rules. Rules. Rules! As any baseball player knows, you've got to know the rules if you're going to play the game. This book, which features step-by-step illustrations, makes it easy to learn all those rules. The sections follow those outlined in the official baseball rules, which are reprinted in the book.

Lipsyte, Robert. **Assignment: Sports.** Rev. ed. Harper and Row, 1984. 177 p. ISBN 0-06-440138-3 (0-06-023908-5, library binding).

Sportswriter Robert Lipsyte discusses his years as a sportswriter for the *New York Times* and his television assignments for CBS's "Sunday Morning" with Charles Kuralt. He talks about such sports figures as Mickey Mantle, Nancy Lieberman, Muhammad Ali, and Casey Stengel.

Murphy, Joseph E. **Adventure beyond the Clouds: How We Climbed China's Highest Mountain — and Survived!** Dillon Press, 1986. 120 p. ISBN 0-87518-330-1.

Joe Murphy led a six-week expedition in 1982 to climb Gongga Shan, the tallest mountain in China. This American expedition confronted blizzards, avalanches, and below-zero temperatures but was successful in reaching the summit and returning safely.

Ryan, Margaret. **Figure Skating.** Illustrated by Holly Stuart Hughes. Franklin Watts/First Books, 1987. 72 p. ISBN 0-531-10383-8.

Do you admire figure skaters who glide gracefully over the ice? If so, and especially if you're already a skater, you'll enjoy this how-to manual that covers everything from the history of skating to careers and competitions.

Tinkelman, Murray. **Little Britches Rodeo.** Photographs by Ronni and Susan B. Tinkelman. Greenwillow Books, 1985. 56 p. ISBN 0-688-04261-9 (0-688-04262-7, library binding).

The Little Britches Rodeo is a competition for boys and girls from eight to eighteen years old. Events resemble those in an adult rodeo, and the young people have the opportunity to meet others with an interest in rodeos. This book describes the rules and events of this annual rodeo and contains photographs from past rodeos.

Technology and Machines

Gunston, Bill. **Aircraft.** Franklin Watts, 1986. 32 p. ISBN 0-531-10135-5.

Everyone's first flight is exciting — the noise of the jets, the sights of the city far below, the ease of traveling great distances in a short amount of time. It's hard to believe it was just over eighty years ago that the Wright brothers made their famous flight at Kitty Hawk! Here you will find a description of the latest aircraft technology. Part of the Modern Technology series.

Hogg, Ian. **Missiles and Artillery.** Franklin Watts, 1985. 47 p. ISBN 0-531-04934-5.

This book includes a historical overview of missiles and artillery. It explains how guns, howitzers, and missiles fit into today's military strategy and how their launch control and guidance systems work. The book also explains how modern nuclear equipment necessitates that missiles and artillery work together. Part of the Twentieth Century Weapons series.

Jaspersohn, William. **Motorcycle: The Making of a Harley-Davidson.** Little, Brown, 1984. 80 p. ISBN 0-316-45817-1.

This book shows the reader how motorcycles are built, starting with the initial order at the local dealer and ending with the actual design and manufacture at the plant. The Harley-Davidson plant in Milwaukee, Wisconsin, is highlighted.

Lampton, Christopher. **Flying Safe?** Franklin Watts/Impact Books, 1986. 81 p. ISBN 0-531-10169-X.

The first fatal air crash happened in 1907. Now a safe flying year is one in which fewer than one thousand people die in air-traffic accidents. But flying is still ten times safer than riding in a car. This book includes information about federal regulatory agencies that oversee air-traffic safety and explains how you can be prepared to keep yourself safe in the air.

Norman, C. J. **Aircraft Carriers.** Franklin Watts, 1986. 32 p. ISBN 0-531-10088-X.

Aircraft carriers are discussed in detail in this book. It provides information on the types of aircraft carriers, on procedures for takeoff and landing, and on what is above and below the deck. The history of carriers is presented, and the book includes specific facts and figures about aircraft carriers and a glossary of terms. Part of the Picture Library series.

Norman, C. J. **Combat Aircraft.** Franklin Watts, 1986. 32 p. ISBN 0-531-10089-8.

Here are detailed information about and illustrations of warplanes, fighter planes, strike aircraft, weapons, reconnaissance planes, and transport planes. Also included are facts and records on combat aircraft and a review of their history. Part of the Picture Library series.

Norman, C. J. **Military Helicopters.** Franklin Watts, 1986. 32 p. ISBN 0-531-10090-1.

The history of combat helicopters is given in this book. The various helicopters discussed include attack helicopters, utility helicopters, fighting helicopters, transport helicopters, and navy helicopters. Facts and records involving helicopters and a glossary of terms are included. Part of the Picture Library series.

Rossiter, Mike. **Nuclear Submarine.** Illustrated by James G. Robins and Hayward Art Group. Gloucester Press, 1983. 37 p. ISBN 0-531-03463-1.

Nuclear submarines today serve as moving platforms for nuclear weapons. How do they generate this nuclear power? Is this radiation harmful to the sailors? How is global surveillance possible? This book provides uncomplicated descriptions and diagrams that answer these and many other questions about this complicated defense weapon. Part of the Inside Story series.

Ryder, Julian. **Motorcycles.** Illustrated by Rob Shone. Franklin Watts, 1986. 32 p. ISBN 0-531-10200-9.

This book contains a detailed explanation of the parts of a motorcycle and motorcycle engine. Many illustrations show how the parts and engines differ among the various brands of machines. Part of the Modern Technology series.

Silverstein, Alvin, and Virginia B. Silverstein. **Futurelife: The Biotechnology Revolution.** Illustrated by Marjorie Thier. Prentice-Hall, 1982. 98 p. ISBN 0-13-345884-9.

Here is a look at some of the newest equipment for diagnosing human illness — the CAT scanner, the DSR, the PET scanner, and NMR scanner. Recent advancements in artificial organs and body parts are also described. The book discusses new technologies that have the potential for wiping out disease, breeding new species of plants and animals, and improving the quality of life.

Sullivan, George. **Famous Air Force Bombers.** Dodd, Mead, 1985. 64 p. ISBN 0-396-08621-7.

Air Force bombers played a vital role in defeating the Nazis in World War II. They have been an essential part of our military ever since. Read about the growth and development of the bomber in this book, which profiles the American bombers from the early biplanes to today's jets.

Sullivan, George. **Famous Air Force Fighters.** Dodd, Mead, 1985. 64 p. ISBN 0-396-08620-9.

Read about famous Air Force fighters in this photograph-filled book. The *Lightning, Warhawk, Thunderbolt, Mustang, Shooting Star, Phantom, Eagle,* and many more are profiled here with a brief history and essential data about each plane. The book describes the development of fighter planes, from the biplane, to the monoplane, to the jet aircraft of today.

Sullivan, George. **Famous Navy Attack Planes.** Dodd, Mead, 1986. 63 p. ISBN 0-396-08770-1.

Follow the development of the famous Navy attack planes and bombers that have taken off from and landed on aircraft carriers throughout the history of U.S. sea planes, from before World War I to the present. History, statistics, and special features are given for twenty-six models of planes. Black-and-white photographs are included.

Sullivan, George. **Famous Navy Fighter Planes.** Dodd, Mead, 1986. 64 p. ISBN 0-396-08769-8.

Have you ever wondered what the first Navy fighter plane looked like? Or the top speed of a Grumman *F11F Tiger?* If so, then this exciting book is for you. It is packed full of information, statistics, and photographs, ranging from the well-known models before World War I to some of the most powerful modern fighter planes of today.

Sullivan, George. **Famous U.S. Spy Planes.** Dodd, Mead, 1987. 64 p. ISBN 0-396-8844-9.

Here is a look at intelligence-gathering aircraft, from the simple planes used in World War I to today's sophisticated electronic spy systems. Included are statistical information about various spy planes, their history, a description, and photographs.

Sullivan, George. **The Thunderbirds.** Dodd, Mead, 1986. 64 p. ISBN 0-396-08787-6.

The Air Force's demonstration squadron, the Thunderbirds, has performed for millions since its formation in 1953. Read about pilot selection and training, aircraft maneuvers, teams of specialists who keep these dazzling machines going, and the planning and execution of a show.

Wickham, Nicholas. **Medical Technology.** Illustrated by Rob Shone and Cooper-West. Franklin Watts, 1986. 32 p. ISBN 0-531-10199-1.

This book provides an introduction to the modern hospital and its advanced equipment and procedures. Illustrations help describe the highly specialized machinery and its functions. Part of the Modern Technology series.

Trivia

Bertling, Paul. **M*A*S*H: The Official 4077 Quiz Manual.** New American Library/Signet Books, 1986. 172 p. ISBN 0-451-14135-0.

Attention "M*A*S*H" lovers! Here are 1000 questions in a hundred categories about the eleven seasons that "M*A*S*H" was on television. Category titles include special sections on each character as well as on hometowns, the operating room, mail call, Radar's critters, and guest stars. Answers are provided.

Brock, Ted, and Jim Campbell. **The Super Official NFL Trivia Book.** New American Library/Signet Books, 1985. 182 p. ISBN 0-451-13822-8.

Here is a collection of pro football facts and legends from sixty-five years of NFL history. Statistics on players and their exploits are given, as well as information on such little-known teams as the Duluth Eskimos and the Oorang Indians. The book is divided into four main sections: an NFL trivia quiz, "You Make the Call," NFL lists, and answers.

Gottlieb, William P. **Science Facts You Won't Believe.** Photographs by the author. Franklin Watts, 1983. 96 p. ISBN 0-531-02875-5.

Did you know that humans don't breathe with their noses? That elephants don't drink water through their trunks? That the South Pole receives less snowfall than any area equal to its size in the United States? These and the other scientific misconceptions exposed in this book reveal that everything in the world around us is not as it seems.

Hearne, Geri. **The Texas Trivia Quiz Book.** Warner Books, 1985. 177 p. ISBN 0-446-32626-7.

Who shot J.R.? Which Texas town shares the name of a famous Ohio tree? These are only two of the questions answered in this book devoted solely to myths about the big state of Texas. Each question is answered with a detailed discussion.

Kupfer, Allen C., and David L. Sheehan III. **The West: A Trivia Quiz Book.** Warner Books, 1985. 175 p. ISBN 0-446-32525-2.

Prepare to carve notches on your Colt .45 handle to keep score as you attempt to answer these 1000 questions about the Old West and today's New West. This trivia quiz book traces the West through fictional accounts, television cowboys, the Indian wars, and Clint Eastwood.

McCombs, Don, and Fred L. Worth. **World War II Super Facts.** Warner Books, 1983. 646 p. ISBN 0-446-32238-5.

This book presents a wide array of historical facts about World War II, going far beyond standard history textbook accounts of the war. World War II buffs will find a storehouse of information here. It covers everything from the soldiers and their machines and equipment to military campaigns and honors.

Murphy, Jim. **Guess Again: More Weird and Wacky Inventions.** Bradbury Press, 1986. 91 p. ISBN 0-02-767720-6.

In this funny and thought-provoking book, forty-five weird and wacky inventions are described in the form of a guessing game. Simple, clear explanations are provided on how the inventions worked or failed to work. Some of the inventions made perfect sense, while others were considered silly.

Pyke, Magnus. **Weird and Wonderful Science Facts.** Illustrated by Terry Burton. Sterling Publishers, 1985. 124 p. ISBN 0-8069-6254-2 (0-8069-4689-X, library binding).

Did you know that if you cut a starfish into a number of pieces, each piece will grow into a complete starfish? That a whale's heart beats only nine times a minute, compared to an average human heart rate of seventy times a minute? This collection of startling, amusing, and fascinating science facts ranges in topic from world records to the Earth and its inhabitants.

Reese, Kitty, and Regis Sinclair. **The Mystery Trivia Quiz Book.** Warner Books, 1985. 180 p. ISBN 0-446-32527-9.

For those fans of whodunit books, the 1000 questions and answers about Sir Arthur Conan Doyle, Agatha Christie, Edgar Allan Poe, Ellery Queen, and Dick Francis will cultivate your keen powers of observation and deductive reasoning. Perfecting these skills can improve your reading and mathematical abilities, as well as ensure that even without your deerstalker hat, you can be the hit of Scotland Yard.

St. John, George. **M.A.S.H. Trivia: The Unofficial Quiz Book**. Warner Books, 1983. 160 p. ISBN 0-446-32000-5.

Are you an avid viewer of "M*A*S*H," one of the best-loved shows ever? If so, there are 1000 questions here for you on "M*A*S*H" memories and moments. The book was written by a group of college pals who had fun asking each other "M*A*S*H" trivia questions in their spare time.

Seuling, Barbara. **You Can't Sneeze with Your Eyes Open and Other Freaky Facts about the Human Body.** E. P. Dutton/Lodestar Books, 1986. 67 p. ISBN 0-525-67185-4.

This book is full of informative and fun facts about the amazing human body. As you gain knowledge, you will get a chuckle, for this book reveals strange details about birth, death, growth, and healing and crazy curiosities about the body that have come down through history.

Sobol, Donald J. **Encyclopedia Brown's Book of Wacky Animals.** Illustrated by Ted Enik. William Morrow, 1985. 117 p. ISBN 0-688-04152-3.

In addition to being the most capable crime-solver in Idaville, Encyclopedia Brown is also an avid collector of weird facts and trivia. This is his newest gathering of odds and ends from his scrapbook, featuring over one hundred unusual activities and events from the animal kingdom. He covers everything from shaggy dog stories to animal weddings.

Sobol, Donald J. **Encyclopedia Brown's Book of Wacky Sports.** Illustrated by Ted Enik. William Morrow, 1984. 112 p. ISBN 0-688-03884-0.

The dauntless detective has taken time out from his work to gather the strangest, funniest, most mind-boggling stories from the world of sports. This book is filled with over a hundred zany stories from baseball, basketball, boxing, and more.

Sobol, Donald J. **Encyclopedia Brown's 3rd Record Book of Weird and Wonderful Facts.** Illustrated by Sal Murdocca. William Morrow, 1985. 134 p. ISBN 0-688-05705-5.

This is a collection of weird facts, silly facts, startling facts, and almost unbelievable facts. Encyclopedia Brown shares his notebook with fans to reveal information about the world's fastest typing contest, left-handed bears, and a computer that won a $25 gift certificate, among many other facts.

Terdoslavich, William. **The Civil War Trivia Quiz Book.** Warner Books, 1984. 182 p. ISBN 0-446-32523-6.

This nation's bloodiest war has become a part of popular culture and literature. Historians and Civil War buffs will be fascinated by the details within these covers, and the general reader can challenge any trivia expert by becoming familiar with thousands of facts related to the Civil War.

Tison, Annette, and Talus Taylor. **The Big Book of Animal Records.** Grosset and Dunlap, 1985. 93 p. ISBN 0-448-18968-2.

You can develop your own Trivial Pursuit game with such amazing animal facts as the following: What animal has an eye that measures 16 inches across? (giant squid) What type of chicken has a 35-foot tail? (Phoenix fowl) What is the largest recorded litter of pigs? (35) These and many other facts are found in this book about animal facts and figures.

Directory of Publishers

Abingdon Press, 201 Eighth Avenue South, Nashville, TN 37202.

Ace Books. Division of Berkley Publishing Group. Distributed by Warner Publishing Services, 75 Rockefeller Plaza, New York, NY 10019.

Adama Books. Distributed by Franklin Watts. Orders to: Sherman Turnpike, Danbury, CT 06816.

Atheneum Publishers. Distributed by Macmillan Publishing Company. Orders to: Riverside Distribution Center, Front and Brown Streets, Riverside, NJ 08075.

Atlantic Monthly Press, 19 Union Square West, 11th Floor, New York, NY 10003.

Avon Books. Division of the Hearst Corporation. Orders to: P. O. Box 767, Dresden, TN 38225.

Ballantine Books. Division of Random House. Orders to: 400 Hahn Road, Westminster, MD 21157.

Bantam Books. Division of Bantam Doubleday Dell Publishing Group. Orders to: 414 E. Golf, Des Plaines, IL 60016.

Barron's Educational Series, 250 Wireless Boulevard, Hauppauge, NY 11788.

Berkley Books. Imprint of the Berkley Publishing Group. Orders to: Berkley Order Department, P. O. Box 506, East Rutherford, NJ 07073.

John F. Blair, Publisher, 1406 Plaza Drive, Winston-Salem, NC 27103.

Blanford Press. Distributed by Sterling Publishing Company, 2 Park Avenue, New York, NY 10016.

Bradbury Press. Affiliate of Macmillan Publishing Company. Orders to: Riverside Distribution Center, Front and Brown Streets, Riverside, NJ 08075.

Bookwright Press. Distributed by Franklin Watts. Orders to: Sherman Turnpike, Danbury, CT 06816.

Clarion Books. Division of Tickner and Fields. Distributed by Houghton Mifflin. Orders to: Wayside Road, Burlington, MA 01803.

David C. Cook, 850 North Grove Avenue, Elgin, IL 60120.

Crestwood House, P. O. Box 3427, Mankato, MN 56002.

Thomas Y. Crowell. Distributed by Harper and Row. Orders to: Keystone Industrial Park, Scranton, PA 18512.

Delacorte Press. Imprint of Dell Publishing Company, One Dag Hammarskjold Plaza, 245 East 47th Street, New York, NY 10017.

Dell Publishing Company, One Dag Hammarskjold Plaza, 245 East 47th Street, New York, NY 10017.

Dial Books. Division of NAL Penguin. Orders to: New American Library, 120 Woodbine Street, Bergenfield, NJ 07621.

Dial Books for Young Readers. Division of NAL Penguin. Orders to: New American Library, 120 Woodbine Street, Bergenfield, NJ 07621.

Dillon Press, 242 Portland Avenue South, Minneapolis, MN 55415.

Dodd, Mead and Company. Orders to: 6 Ram Ridge Road, Spring Valley, NY 10977.

E. P. Dutton. Division of NAL Penguin. Orders to: New American Library, 120 Woodbine Street, Bergenfield, NJ 07621.

M. Evans and Company. Distributed by Henry Holt and Company, 115 West 118th Street, New York, NY 10011.

Faber and Faber. Distributed by Harper and Row. Orders to: Keystone Industrial Park, Scranton, PA 18512.

Farrar, Straus and Giroux. Distributed by Harper and Row. Orders to: Keystone Industrial Park, Scranton, PA 18512.

Fawcett Books. Division of Ballantine Books/Random House. Orders to: 400 Hahn Road, Westminster, MD 21157.

Four Winds Press. Imprint of Macmillan Publishing Company. Orders to: Riverside Distribution Center, Front and Brown Streets, Riverside, NJ 08370.

Gloucester Press. Division of Franklin Watts. Orders to: Sherman Turnpike, Danbury, CT 06816.

Greenwillow Books. Division of William Morrow and Company. Orders to: 39 Plymouth Street, P. O. Box 1219, Fairfield, NJ 07007.

Harcourt Brace Jovanovich. Orders to: 465 South Lincoln Drive, Troy, MO 63379.

Harmony Books. Imprint of Crown Publishers, 225 Park Avenue South, New York, NY 10003.

Harper and Row. Orders to: Keystone Industrial Park, Scranton, PA 18512.

Hastings House, c/o Kampmann and Company, 9 East 40th Street, New York, NY 10016.

Herald Press. Division of Mennonite Publishing House, 616 Walnut Avenue, Scottsdale, PA 15683.

Hill and Wang. Division of Farrar, Straus and Giroux. Orders to: Harper and Row, Keystone Industrial Park, Scranton, PA 18512.

Holiday House, 18 East 53rd Street, New York, NY 10022.

Hollym International Corporation, 18 Donald Place, Elizabeth, NJ 07208.

Henry Holt and Company, 115 West 18th Street, New York, NY 10011.

Holt, Rinehart and Winston, Order Fulfillment Department, 4th Floor, 6277 Sea Harbor Drive, Orlando, FL 32887.

Houghton Mifflin Company. Orders to: Wayside Road, Burlington, MA 01803.

Kar-Ben Copies, 6800 Tildenwood Lane, Rockville, MD 20852.

Alfred A. Knopf. Subsidiary of Random House. Orders to: 400 Hahn Road, Westminster, MD 21157.

Lerner Publications Company, 241 First Avenue North, Minneapolis, MN 55401.

Little, Brown and Company. Division of Time. Orders to: 200 West Street, Waltham, MA 02254.

Lothrop, Lee and Shepard Books. Orders to: William Morrow, 29 Plymouth Street, P. O. Box 1219, Fairfield, NJ 07007.

Macmillan Publishing Company. Orders to: Riverside Distribution Center, Front and Brown Streets, Riverside, NJ 08370.

Julia MacRae Books. Imprint of Franklin Watts. Orders to: Sherman Turnpike, Danbury, CT 06816.

William Morrow and Company. Subsidiary of the Hearst Corporation. Orders to: Wilmor Warehouse, 39 Plymouth Street, Fairfield, NJ 07006.

Metropolitan Museum of Art. Orders to: Special Services Office, Middle Village, NY 11381.

New American Library. Orders to: 120 Woodbine Street, Bergenfield, NJ 07621.

Orchard Books. Division of Franklin Watts. Orders to: Sherman Turnpike, Danbury, CT 06816.

Overlook Press. Orders to: R.R. 1 Box 496, Woodstock, NY 12498.

Pacer Books. Member of the Putnam Publishing Group. Orders to: P. O. Box 506, Department B, East Rutherford, NJ 07073.

PAJ Publications. Division of *Performing Arts Journal,* 325 Spring Street, Suite 318, New York, NY 10013.

Penguin Books. Imprint of Viking Penguin. Orders to: 299 Murray Hill Parkway, East Rutherford, NJ 07073.

Philomel Books. Imprint of the Putnam Publishing Group. Orders to: P. O. Box 506, Department B, East Rutherford, NJ 07073.

Plays, Inc., 120 Boylston Street, Boston, MA 02116.

Clarkson N. Potter Books. Imprint of Crown Publishers, 225 Park Avenue South, New York, NY 10003.

Prentice-Hall. Division of Simon and Schuster. Orders to: 200 Old Tappan Road, Old Tappan, NJ 07675.

Putnam Publishing Group. Orders to: P. O. Box 506, Department B, East Rutherford, NJ 07073.

G. P. Putnam's Sons. Imprint of the Putnam Publishing Group. Orders to: P. O. Box 506, Department B, East Rutherford, NJ 07073.

Raintree Publishers. Subsidiary of Somerset House. Orders to: 310 West Wisconsin Avenue, Mezzanine Level, Milwaukee, WI 53203.

Rand McNally and Company, P. O. Box 7600, Chicago, IL 60680.

Random House. Orders to: 400 Hahn Road, Westminster, MD 21157.

Rosen Publishing Group, 29 East 21st Street, New York, NY 10010.

Scholastic. Orders to: P. O. Box 7502, 2931 East McCarty Street, Jefferson City, MO 65102.

Charles Scribner's Sons. Division of Macmillan Publishing Group. Orders to: Riverside Distribution Center, Front and Brown Streets, Riverside, NJ 08075.

Silver Burdett and Ginn. Division of Simon and Schuster. Orders to: Simon and Schuster, 4343 Equity Drive, P. O. Box 2649, Columbus, OH 43216.

Stemmer House, 2627 Caves Road, Owings Mills, MD 21117.

Sterling Publishing Company, 2 Park Avenue, New York, NY 10016.

Tidal Press, P. O. Box 150, Portsmouth, NH 03801.

Tundra Books of Northern New York. Affiliate of Tundra Books (Canada). Distributed by the University of Toronto Press, 340 Nagel Drive, Cheektowaga, NY 14225.

Viking Penguin. Orders to: 299 Murray Hill Parkway, East Rutherford, NJ 07073.

Viking Press. Imprint of Viking Penguin. Orders to: 299 Murray Hill Parkway, East Rutherford, NJ 07073.

Frederick Warne and Company. Division of Viking Penguin. Orders to: 299 Murray Hill Parkway, East Rutherford, NJ 07073.

Warner Books. Distributed by Ballantine Books, 201 East 50th Street, New York, NY 10022.

Warwick Press. Distributed by Franklin Watts. Orders to: Sherman Turnpike, Danbury, CT 06816.

Franklin Watts. Subsidiary of Grolier. Orders to: Sherman Turnpike, Danbury, CT 06816.

Westminster Press. Orders to: P. O. Box 718, William Penn Annex, Philadelphia, PA 19105.

Author Index

Title Index